THE NEW RETIREMENT

THE NEW RETIREMENT

The Ultimate Guide to
THE REST OF YOUR LIFE

Claudia & Dave —
To new beginnings!

J— Cull—

JAN CULLINANE AND **CATHY FITZGERALD**

RODALE

Printed in the United States of America

Rodale Inc. makes every effort to use acid-free ♾, recycled paper ♺.

Book design by Tara Long

Library of Congress Cataloging-in-Publication Data

Cullinane, Jan.
    The new retirement : the ultimate guide to the rest of your life / Jan Cullinane and Cathy Fitzgerald.
        p.   cm.
    Includes bibliographical references and index.
    ISBN-13 978–1–57954–796–7 paperback
    ISBN-10 1–57954–796–6 paperback
    1. Retirement—United States—Planning.   I. Fitzgerald, Cathy.
II. Title.
HQ1063.2.U6C85   2004
646.7'9—dc22   2004005600

Distributed to the trade by Holtzbrinck Publishers

    6   8   10   9   7   paperback

We inspire and enable people to improve their lives and the world around them

For more of our products visit **rodalestore.com** or call 800-848-4735

ACKNOWLEDGMENTS

We would like to thank our brothers, sisters, children, and especially our spouses for all of their assistance and support. We'd also like to thank our agent, Rosalie Siegel; our editors, Jennifer Kushnier and Chris Potash; and our publicist, Meghan Phillips.

And, to the CPAs, Certified Financial Planners, and other experts who generously shared their technical knowledge, we are very grateful. Finally, we'd like to express our appreciation to those who have retired or are planning to retire for sharing their stories, concerns, and experiences with us.

TABLE OF CONTENTS

INTRODUCTION

Every 7.5 seconds, someone turns 50. *The New Retirement: The Ultimate Guide to the Rest of Your Life* provides a one-stop resource for the 78 million baby boomers approaching this important transition. While most retirement books deal only with the financial issues or the location aspect of retirement, *The New Retirement* offers a comprehensive, balanced view of the subject for those who are planning to relocate or those who plan to age in place. This book is easy-to-read, concrete, practical, full of illustrative anecdotes, and hands-on. The end of the book provides additional references.

The New Retirement serves as a guide for individuals such as:

✱ Jayne—53 years old, CPA, single. She retired as Chief Financial Officer of a biotech company in Gaithersburg, Maryland, as a multimillionaire after exercising her stock options. She's financially savvy, and she'd like to live in a city that's both amenable to singles and has a warmer climate, yet with four distinct seasons.

✱ Carl and Betty—late 50s. Carl retired from an assembly plant at Ford Motor Company, and he and Betty want to sell their home, buy an RV, and travel around the country during their retirement years.

✱ Mike and Carol—60 and 56 years old, respectively. He was a self-confessed workaholic partner in a prestigious law firm. She's a golf fanatic, regular exerciser, and does a lot of volunteer work. Retired for two years, and financially stable, they are having some difficulties with their roles in retirement. Carol is used to her routine; Mike feels he doesn't have any hobbies or interests because of his all-consuming career and misses his status and the structure of work. They'd like to keep their primary home in St. Louis, near most of their four grown children, yet they love the ocean and warm weather.

✳ Ed—a high school Spanish teacher, planning to retire in four years with his partner, Kevin, who works in retail. They are interested in moving to a gay-friendly community and are concerned about whether they will have enough money to retire.

✳ Rosalyn and Phil—a two-career couple with a major manufacturing company. She is a marketing manager; Phil works in human resources. They have been transferred six times, and, as a result, feel they have no real "home." Rosalyn is several years younger than Phil and would like to continue working, although they are concerned about the impact this might have on the personal dynamics of their relationship. They would like a low-cost, safe retirement area, and, having remained childless by choice, would like to live in an adult community.

How can *The New Retirement* assist this diverse group of people? It is the first book to approach retirement from these multiple perspectives:

✳ The "Who" of retirement: examines the scientific research concerning those who have or are planning to retire, then analyzes and summarizes the studies to see what can be learned from them.

✳ The "What" of retirement: explains how to reprogram your time, explores work issues, describes life-long learning opportunities, and suggests leisure and volunteer activities.

✳ The "Where" of retirement: explores whether readers should move at all. It describes specific places to retire, including recommended communities. In addition, it covers the process of choosing a place, housing possibilities, and issues such as universal design.

✳ The "How" of retirement: clearly lays out a blueprint for planning your retirement. Additional simple, clear worksheets help to ensure a secure financial future.

The authors, Jan Cullinane and Cathy Fitzgerald, have given seminars about retirement and have researched and traveled extensively, investigating places to retire, having interviewed those planning to retire and those who have already taken the leap. They have also consulted experts in various fields, utilizing their skills and knowledge, to bring together the most current, the most sound, the most accurate advice available. *The New Retirement: The Ultimate Guide to the Rest of Your Life* is the only book you'll ever need on this subject.

PART I

WHAT SHALL I DO
WITH MY RETIREMENT?

WHAT MAKES RETIREMENT SUCCESSFUL?

"Everybody says you've got to get ready financially. No, no, you've got to get ready psychologically."
—*Lee Iacocca*

This isn't your father's (or mother's) retirement!

Longer life spans, better health, more opportunities, greater geographical mobility, a new generation's attitude . . . the paraphrasing of General Motors' 1980s ad campaign for Oldsmobile seems particularly relevant today.

Retirement is a fairly recent phenomenon; at the beginning of the 19th century, few people retired, because they simply could not afford to do so. As white-collar jobs replaced a predominantly agricultural economy, however, incomes rose, and people had more money with which to retire. They lived longer and had more leisure activities from which to choose. The advent of Social Security and pensions also contributed to the ability to retire.

Today, however, the conventional definition of retirement itself needs to be retired! Before the baby boomers, retirement was seen primarily as a male's onetime passage from the workforce, and research concerning retirement dealt almost exclusively with men. Retirement was viewed more in isolation, as a solitary passage, though the reality is that most retirees are married. Retirement is now recognized as a *process*, involving perhaps several forays into and out of alternative projects, pastimes, and jobs. Newly retired persons may have different experiences than those who have been retired for longer periods. And with almost half the workforce female, retirement is no longer a male phenomenon; it's also recognized as more of a couples' issue.

We frequently hear predictions by pundits and the press about how the future of retirement will resemble the past of retirement. That is, in the future as in the past, we will work until we die. The news contains innumerable anecdotes about middle-aged workers losing their nest eggs with the bursting of the dot-com bubble of the early 2000s. Surely each of us could add tales from our own acquaintances, if not ourselves, to the list. The anecdotes make interesting news, but the facts point in a different direction: We are spending more of our lives in retirement than at any time in history, a trend that's projected to continue into the foreseeable future.

According to Robert William Fogel, Nobel Laureate economist, the average length of retirement for those age 65 is 15 years longer than it was in 1880. Fifty percent of today's 60- to 64- year-olds are retired, while a century ago, 92 percent of them were still working. Today, six out of every seven men age 65 are retired, while only one in five was retired a century ago. As Americans have grown wealthier, and the real (inflation-adjusted) cost of meeting our material needs has steadily decreased, we have demanded more leisure. Some of that leisure comes in the form of a reduced workday, but much of that leisure is consumed in a lump sum called retirement—the proverbial "golden years."

REAL RETIREMENT

Let's take a look at three couples to see how the concept of retirement has changed.

John and Mary (born 1900; retired 1965): Lucky to be alive! The very idea of retirement must have seemed peculiar to John and Mary. Certainly none of their forebears were likely to have lived long enough to provide an example of retirement. With a life expectancy of about

---

FDR signed the Social Security Act into law on August 14, 1935. In January 1940, Ida May Fuller became the first recipient of Social Security benefits. And did she ever benefit! Ida lived 35 more years, and collected more than $22,000 before finally giving out at the age of 100.

47 years, neither John nor Mary should have anticipated living long enough to retire, but they defied the odds and lived well past their working years. In fact, John and Mary would live through our collective awakening to the idea of "life after work."

Retiring in 1965, John and Mary would have felt lucky to be alive. Moreover, their admittedly modest (possibly nonexistent) expectations about retirement surely would have been exceeded. During their working years, it would have been unfathomable to them that, at age 65, they would be able to stop working, yet continue to receive a check, and have something enjoyable to do in their leisure years.

Kenneth and Doreen (born 1920; retired 1982): A well-deserved respite. Kenneth and Doreen came of age during the Great Depression, when a quarter of all workers were unemployed. Their defining life experience was undoubtedly World War II, when Kenneth was shipped overseas to fight the Nazis as an officer in the venerable Eighth Air Force, while Doreen stayed at home to work as a typist at the local aircraft assembly plant. After the war, Kenneth began his civilian career as a mechanical engineer at The Company, and Doreen left the formal workforce to pursue the business of raising her children and keeping house. Kenneth toiled loyally for The Company over the next 38 years, earning his steady pay raises and sharing in the economic success of both The Company and the country during the expansionary years of the 1950s and 1960s.

Kenneth and Doreen no doubt possessed a strong work ethic born of their experiences both in weathering the Great Depression and in fighting the war. But, Kenneth and Doreen were also human, and they wanted to retire at a reasonable age in order to pursue the life of leisure. Gladly for them, retirement was swiftly becoming an institution in the United States. And, when the couple did retire in 1982, they could have reasonably expected to live in leisure for 18 or so years. Moreover, they would be able to afford a comfortable retirement. During the 1950s, Social Security benefits increased by nearly 80 percent, truly helping to make retirement an entitlement. Additionally, in the sixties, The Company introduced a pension plan to provide postretirement income to its employees. Medicare became a reality in the sixties as well, providing health care benefits to older people. Kenneth and Doreen had cause to feel financially secure about retirement, as did many of their contemporaries. In fact, during the 1960s, about 50 percent of all Americans were covered by a private pension plan in addition to Social Security. That must have been nice, but then again, their respite was hard earned and well-deserved.

Bob and Linda (born 1950; retiring circa 2010): The retirement "boom." The baby boomers are only now beginning to retire, and yet, we are reminded of this demographic phenomenon at every turn. No single topic, save perhaps the dying sport of shuffleboard, is more commonly identified with retirement than is the demographic fact of the baby boom. Most commonly we hear the dire predictions of a bankrupt Social Security system or of intergenerational strife caused by the increased financial burden on future workers required to subsidize the retirement of the boomers.

Though these concerns are real, Bob and Linda are likely to enjoy a long and prosperous retirement, relative to that of prior generations. Because of the steady increase in life expectancy, Bob and Linda should enjoy 20-plus retirement years, longer than any group of retirees in history. Moreover, Bob and Linda's material needs in retirement will be met through a combination of Social Security payments, pension income, and personal savings.

Though the terms "leisure" and "retirement" call to mind images of relaxation, Bob and Linda are not likely to spend the second half of their lives idling. The most important questions about their retirement relate to *how* and *where* they will spend their time. Whereas previous generations were lucky to see retirement at all, the current generation of retirees can safely expect to spend a significant portion of their lives retired, but probably not merely relaxing—perhaps working, and certainly not bored.

Because both the duration and nature of retirement have changed, Bob and Linda need the resources to plan adequately for an active, emotionally satisfying, and financially secure retirement.

Imagine *you* have reached this milestone. Envision your typical day. Is it spent walking on the beach, playing tennis, golfing? Are you volunteering? Pursuing an advanced degree? Working, like 80 percent of boomers ages 45 and older expect to do (based on a survey by AARP)? Doing absolutely nothing?

The good news is that approximately three-quarters of retirees report being generally happy, according to Phyllis Moen, codirector of the Cornell Applied Gerontology

---

Retirement: The first two years after leaving one's primary career.

Research Institute. So, is there a perfect time to retire? Is there a secret to a successful retirement? Recent scientific studies involving the psychology of retirement deal with our current realities of this important time and can provide practical suggestions for achieving a successful and satisfying retirement.

TIMING IS EVERYTHING

To work, or not to work? Ignoring financial considerations for the moment (we'll address them in chapter 9), the psychological research is a bit inconclusive about work after retirement and its effect on well-being. In a nutshell, it just depends!

There are two competing outlooks. The first, continuity theory, is the perspective that our levels of self-esteem and life satisfaction stay the same, independent of work. Under this theory, it wouldn't matter whether a person worked—he or she would maintain the same feelings of well-being. The second perspective, role theory, has two sides. Although role theory considers working to be paramount to a person's identity, retirement can *improve* feelings of well-being if the career being left was considered very difficult or stressful; or, retirement can *cause* distress if people feel they have lost a valuable role by not being employed. It turns out that the effect of leaving the primary career is more a function of how you perceived that career—that is, whether working played a crucial role in your life, was something to give up with relief, or was immaterial to how you thought about yourself. Consider the following studies.

Reasons to Retire

In a survey of more than 700 soon-to-retire, newly retired, and retired men and women, participants in the *Cornell Retirement and Well-Being Study* were asked their reasons for retiring. Their responses are below.

Women
- To Do Other Things (69%)
- Financial Incentives (40%)
- Have Enough Income (38%)
- Spouse Retired (33%)
- Older Worker Policy (24%)

According to the *Life Events Scale*, which ranks 42 life events from most stressful (death of a spouse) to least stressful (minor law violations, such as a parking ticket), retirement ranks 10th!

- Poor Health (24%)
- Didn't Like Work (24%)
- Didn't Get Along With Boss (22%)
- Family Health (21%)
- Not Appreciated (19%)
- Job Ended (7%)

Men
- To Do Other Things (70%)
- Financial Incentives (62%)
- Have Enough Income (45%)
- Didn't Like Work (33%)
- Older Worker Policy (22%)
- Poor Health (21%)
- Didn't Get Along With Boss (19%)
- Not Appreciated (17%)
- Family Health (16%)
- Job Ended (13%)
- Spouse Retired (9%)

This ranking gives some insight into the *when* of retirement. The desire to do something else, and the *perception* among both the men and the women that they were financially able to retire were paramount. Note that for women, however, the fact that their spouses retired was a much more motivating force to retire than it was for men. While virtually all those surveyed had done *some* planning for their retirement, more than half felt they had not planned *enough*. So, a word to the wise: Plan ahead.

Working can provide rewards and satisfaction such as status, intellectual engagement, social interaction, purpose, feelings of pride and accomplishment, structure, and, of course, a paycheck and health coverage. Regardless of your reason for retiring, whether you stop working entirely, cut back on hours, or pursue other endeavors such as volunteering, enjoying a hobby, or cultivating a skill, you will still want to experience these rewards in your everyday life.

In another study, 17 employed and 54 retired professors, ages 70 to 74, were interviewed to determine the reasons some retired and some continued working.

Suicide rates for women decline after retirement but increase for men. One hypothesis is that women have or develop more outside interests, so they don't need to depend on employment in order to feel fulfilled.

Whether deciding to retire or remain employed, both groups reported high levels of satisfaction with life, although the employed faculty ratings were higher (97 versus 90 on a scale of 100).

For those who remained employed, the primary reason was because they enjoyed their work (77 percent). Other factors included work being important to them (35 percent), financial issues (12 percent), and inertia (6 percent). For those who retired, the primary reasons were a desire to do other things (35 percent) and because it was time (35 percent). Other factors included changes in the work environment (24 percent), tired of work (20 percent), health issues (17 percent), and could afford to retire (13 percent).

Interestingly, there were more married couples among the retired group than the working group, and the retired group also had more children and grandchildren than those who were employed.

This study is noteworthy because it removes the entire issue of *having* to leave the workplace (there was no mandatory retirement age). There's no one right answer to the question "When should I retire?" The answer can partially be determined by the role work plays in a person's life, as well as the satisfaction that working provides. The reasons to work or not work were primarily psychological, and unlike in the Cornell survey mentioned earlier, financial aspects played a minor role in deciding whether to retire.

Gender and Roles

Research has shown some common threads about the effects of retirement and working on couples. One study looked at transitions in retirement involving 534 married couples in their fifties, sixties, or seventies who were retired or about to retire from several large businesses in upstate New York. The findings might not be all that surprising.

Husbands and wives reported greater marital satisfaction if they retired at the same time. While men with nonworking spouses had greater marital satisfaction than those with working wives, regardless of whether the men themselves worked, those men who didn't work but had

---

"No! I have never and would never consider retiring. For one thing, I would be unable to deduct all my business and travel expenses from my taxes."
—Julia Child (in her nineties) from "An Interview with Julia Child" by Phillip Silverstone

a working spouse reported the most marital conflict. Women experienced the highest marital satisfaction if they entered new jobs after retiring and their husbands were also working, but men who worked after retiring from their primary job experienced more marital discord than those men who didn't work.

The first 2 years of retirement are comparable to the first 2 years of marriage—it's a time to negotiate (or renegotiate) roles and share ideas and dreams. As when getting married, it's important to discuss and plan for the future *before* retiring, from an emotional as well as a financial standpoint. Realize that the transition to retirement is a period of marital difficulty for *both* sexes. Take heart—although there are lots of adjustments to be made, the divorce rate among retired couples is only in the single digits. In fact, 60 percent of couples report that there is (ultimately) an improvement in their marriage after retirement.

If the role of work is important to you but is causing stress in the relationship, take a look at alternative forms of work. Work doesn't necessarily mean only paid and full-time work. It could include volunteering, community service, working fewer hours, doing projects, starting a new, scaled-down career—all of these could fit the definition of productive work. In the United States, success tends to be defined in monetary terms, but separating success and productivity from paid employment will create many more options for making retirement a time of new and meaningful roles.

John B. retired early. Here is his story.

true **LIFE** So you want to retire from a job that consumed most of your life, a job where you spent more time with the people at the office than you did with your wife. It's not that easy to just stop working and enjoy the easy life, tee time at 9 A.M., lunch at the club, a short afternoon nap, cocktails at 5 P.M., not even knowing what day of the week it is. It probably sounds pretty good to a "working stiff," and retirement can be great—if you approach it with the right attitude and mindset.

In 1998, when I was 50, we sold our medical software company at the beginning of the dot.com bubble. To complicate things even more, we moved from Cincinnati to Marsh Landing in Ponte Vedra Beach, Florida, prior to the sale. Being Midwestern people, we quickly realized that the weather in northeast Florida was like being on vacation 12 months of the year. On March 15, 2000, I officially retired with earnout in hand and 725,000 frequent flyer miles in the bank.

Golf, lunch, cocktails, and knowing it was Sunday only because the newspaper was thicker seemed like I had died and gone to heaven. Shorts and T-shirts became the dress code for just about everything you did in Ponte Vedra Beach. Life was so good that I got a hole in one only three days after I retired; haven't even come close since then. The routine got to be monotonous, and then the stock market started to collapse. After about 8 months of retirement, I needed more than golf to satisfy me mentally.

At that time, our house in Ponte Vedra had appreciated about 60 percent, so I thought real estate looked like a good place to park some money. We made an offer on a house on the beach, about 100 feet from the ocean. It was a wreck and was in dire need of repair, but we got the property at a good price and began the project. I was always building things, so this was going to be a job that would allow me to get back to doing something full time.

Over the next several months, I made about 75 trips to Home Depot, buying things for the house. Because I was doing much of the work myself, I justified buying all the tools (only contractor grade). My wife said that I would never go shopping with her, but she never shopped at Home Depot until she had to pick out carpet, pa[..] pliances, etc., for the beach house. Now, [..] shopping with her—but only at Home Dep[..] worked 7 days a week for the first 100 days and enjoyed every minute of it. I worked along with the subcontractors and learned how to do some of the things that I didn't already know how to do and how much time it actually took to do a specific project. I was the general contractor and learned so much during this process, which took about 11 months. In the last 2 years the house has appreciated about 45 percent. We also invested in more oceanfront real estate over the next 6 months.

Things are working out very well with our retirement in Florida. Two of our children have moved here, and we are in the process of opening three Pan-Asian restaurants in the Jacksonville area, a project that should keep us busy for the next few years. As you can see, my life after retirement has been fulfilling, exciting, and fun—a new career that is only demanding when I want it to be. Don't expect to retire and immediately turn off that work ethic you have developed over the last 30 years. You need fulfillment, change, and a dose of fun in retirement, and all golf all the time does not make a happy man. ⓛ

EASE THE TRANSITION
TO RETIREMENT

Obviously, retirement brings about a shift in roles and activity. Those who can adjust and adapt to these changes will have a more successful transition to retirement. But what personality traits facilitate the easiest transition? Research indicates there are two chief ways of looking at the world that increase the chances for smooth sailing through this choppy time: an internal locus of control (the belief that outcomes are under one's control) and retirement self-efficacy (the belief or self-confidence that one can cope with the changes retirement brings). Here are some tips to help ease the transition, no matter which outlook on life you adopt.

Consider moving to "neutral" ground. Shortly before retiring, Brian and Joanne K. sold their home and moved to an active adult community in their same town. This had the unintended but positive effect of creating a new environment that was free of their previous territorial patterns (*her* kitchen, *his* garage).

Take action. Demonstrate that you believe outcomes are under your control (even if you don't) and that you are confident you can cope with retirement changes (even if you aren't). For example, if you're married, be willing to go beyond conventional gender-based roles. Renegotiate! Consider housework or yard work. Take, for example, Cindy and Bob P. Bob was the primary breadwinner, putting Cindy in charge of all homemaking activities. On a celebratory retirement trip to Hawaii, Cindy discussed with Bob how their roles had changed, and that now it was time for Bob to pick up some of the household jobs. Cindy wanted to retire, too! She presented Bob with a list of 10 chores, from which she suggested he choose 5 to take on as his own. Cindy agreed that Bob could handle these in his own way, without interference or suggestions from her. After a year, so far, so good.

Develop resilience. Resilience, the ability to bounce back after adversity, is an important ingredient in the recipe for successful retirement. It is possible to cultivate this quality. Accept that change is part of life; concentrate on changing adverse circumstances that can be altered; act decisively rather than wishing problems would just disappear; maintain perspective; take big problems and break them into smaller, manageable challenges; foster positive relationships; and take good care of yourself.

Consult others. Discuss how your friends and relatives in the same situation adjusted (and compromised and renegotiated) during this transition period. Consulting with a counselor or couples' therapist, a life coach, a trusted religious leader, and/or attending seminars on retirement (if they include more than just financial issues) may help if there is difficulty transitioning.

Saddle up! Right after retirement, retirees report an increased energy level. Use this "honeymoon period" to your advantage and plan, plan, plan.

On Being Single

You may have been single all your life or ended up single as a result of divorce or death. According to Elizabeth Holtzman at the University of Massachusetts in Amherst, there are some psychological aspects that relate specifically to being a single retiree.

"Being single both simplifies and complicates the problems of retirement," she says. "It simplifies them because you have only yourself to look after; you can make your own choices. On the other hand, you don't have a partner to share things with or lean on emotionally or financially. Being a single retiree may lead to isolation and loneliness."

Luckily, there are tangible ways to combat these psychological considerations. For one, you can choose to live in a location that is single friendly. Some specific places include Sarasota and Naples, Florida, Las Vegas, and Asheville, North Carolina, and there are other suggestions discussed in chapters 5 and 6.

Another way to combat loneliness is to join a social support group, which is equally as important for singles as it is for couples. If you've stopped working, or you relocate to a new area, isolation could become an issue. Consider moving into an active adult community that has built-in social activities or a community with a clubhouse or center that offers planned get-togethers and outings. Other options include returning to paid employment, volunteering, starting or working on a hobby that involves people—in other words, joining in! See chapter 2 for more specific suggestions.

As a single, since there is no financial backup, it's especially important to begin your retirement planning early. If you're a woman, this is particularly true, since women generally are paid less than men, may have been out of the workforce for years to raise children, and/or may not have the funds to support the retirement lifestyle they would like. It's a good idea to seek professional advice now from a certified financial planner or a CPA to begin the planning process.

Believe That You Have Enough Money

The *perception* that you have enough money to retire has a bearing on your feelings of satisfaction concerning retirement. In one study, more than 1,000 people aged 55 and over were surveyed about their satisfaction in retirement. The study found that satisfaction increased with the number of years a person saved for retirement. Of those who saved for 25 years or more, 60 percent said they were "extremely satisfied" with retirement, as did half of those who saved for 15 to 24 years. Less than half of those who saved for fewer than 15 years could report the same feeling.

Note that the correlation is between *feeling* financially prepared and feeling satisfied in retirement, regardless of actual net worth or wealth. So, save, save, save!

Studies also show those who place a high priority on the pursuit of money and the accumulation of material things are more depressed and suffer from lower self-esteem than those who make relationships their top priority. Trite but true: Money really can't buy happiness!

Have a Support System

How important is it to be connected to others? According to the research, very!

One 13-year study, involving 2,812 men and women in New Haven, Connecticut, 65 years of age and older, investigated the relationship between social activity and longevity. It found that men and women who were socially active lived an average of 2½ years longer than those who were not socially active.

This study is important because it links a longer life span to activities such as playing cards, eating out, or going to movies with others, without regard to physical exercise. It had been widely thought that activity prolonged life because of the physical aspect; now we know that social engagement alone can increase the life span. (That doesn't mean you can retire to the couch, though!)

Other studies have found that social interactions have a significant effect in maintaining mental health, regardless of whether retirees live alone, live with someone not their spouse, or are childless.

Women might have an easier time reaping these benefits, though, because they tend to cast their nets wider than men when choosing friends. Men tend to find their friends at work. So, what's a guy to do? Give these a whirl: group activities such as watching or participating in sporting events, attending spiritual retreats, joining organizations such as model railroad clubs, eating out with others, and volunteering.

DON'T WORRY, BE HAPPY!

Recently, psychologists have taken to identifying people who consider themselves happy and examining what traits they share. This focus on a wellness model, rather than a disease model, has resulted in some interesting findings.

Factors such as education level, income, marital status, religious affiliation, and socioeconomic status appear to have very little effect upon happiness. In fact, even under extreme conditions, such as becoming physically disabled or winning the lottery, people tend to return to their happiness "set-point" or baseline after about 6 months. These findings suggest, according to researchers, that "it may be that trying to be happier is as futile as trying to be taller and therefore is counterproductive."

But, practically speaking, these findings are pretty depressing! There are, however, ways of reaching the highest levels of our "set-point" for happiness, says University of Pennsylvania psychologist Martin Seligman, Ph.D. He's been studying happiness and optimism for more than 25 years and claims he's used his own techniques to change his outlook on life to a much sunnier one. He suggests we go beyond seeking pleasure and look, instead, for gratification. What's the difference?

Pleasure is not necessarily meaningful and does not always result in a greater good (for example, eating a hot fudge sundae may feed your stomach, but not your soul). Gratification involves cultivating and nurturing your strengths and putting them to positive use. Consider Darla and Jim W., whose first child died just prior to childbirth. Although devastated by the loss, they set up a foundation at a local hospital to provide indigent women the financial resources to bury children who died under similar circumstances. Darla and Jim took their strengths of compassion, generosity, and financial savvy and parlayed them into a gratifying experience in the midst of their sorrow. Likewise, we can cultivate happiness by incorporating strengths such as kindness, humor, optimism, and courage into everyday life.

In a 1993 interview with *Omni* magazine, Dr. Seligman gave more advice for becoming a happier person. For starters, find your calling. A *job* provides a paycheck; a *career* provides power, prestige, a paycheck, and a personal commitment; but a *calling* is a passion where the activity itself is its own reward regardless of any status or income it may provide. Those with callings reach the upper ends of their "set-point" of happiness much more frequently. A calling can be any line of "work," be it caregiver, artist, spouse, or engineer. It's a matter of finding an activity that provides challenges that mesh with your unique strengths.

Another way to become happy is by learning to see the glass as half full. "Pessimists tend to have hopeless thoughts . . . or worse, they stamp themselves with a negative label—'jerk,'" says Dr. Seligman. If this sounds like you, he suggests speaking to yourself as a close friend would. Tell yourself that you learned from the experience and will do better the next time. And, rather than name-calling, try something like, "Sometimes I'm not as considerate as I'd like to be, but overall, I'm a kind person." Dr. Seligman coined the term "learned helplessness"—giving up because you feel you can't change outcomes—and says we can escape this belief with "learned optimism."

He advises "not to ruminate about bad events that happen to you . . . I recommend fun distractions because studies show, if you think about problems in a negative frame of mind, you come up with fewer solutions." And, you're more likely to become depressed. Pessimists can overcome this cycle, though, and train themselves to think more optimistically—once they boost their mood. "It takes most people a few weeks to get the knack, but once the technique is learned, the less likely they are to relapse," says Dr. Seligman.

So put a stop to distorted ways of thinking. When you think something negative, note it, evaluate it, and replace the thought with something more realistic. It takes practice, but it's an effective tool for increasing happiness. Here are some examples of the common negative thinking patterns, according to Stanford University psychiatrist David D. Burns, M.D.

All-or-nothing thinking. Theresa C. has been trying to eat more fruits and vegetables and fewer processed foods, but overindulges at a lunch buffet. She berates herself, thinking, "I'm a total failure. I can't do anything right. I can't even pass up the cheesecake!" She then proceeds to take seconds on everything, and overindulges the next several days, figuring if she can't be perfect, she might as well eat everything in sight! Theresa could replace these thoughts with, "Well, I ate more than I planned today. Tomorrow, I'll exercise a little more and get back on track. I know I feel better when I eat better, and I've been eating well for the past few weeks."

Overgeneralizing. Kevin W. had always wanted to write and, after retiring, submitted an article to the *New Yorker* magazine. His submission was rejected. Kevin thought, "No one will ever publish my article. I guess I have nothing to offer after all." Alternatively, Kevin could think, "OK, I met with rejection, but hey, Stephen King was rejected many, many times by publishers before *Carrie* was published. I'll need to investigate and submit to more magazines that would be interested in my type of article." Don't conclude that one negative outcome will be endlessly repeated.

Dwelling on the negative/filtering out the positive. Tom A. had always been interested in community theater and, upon retiring, joined a local troupe. He was thrilled to land a role in a musical and rehearsed his lines and practiced his songs diligently. On opening night, all went well, except that he didn't quite reach one high note in a solo. On subsequent evenings, his performance was flawless. In spite of the kudos he received, he obsessed on the one bad note, vowing he would never try out for a part again. Tom needs to respond to his overly critical thought process, and substitute rational thinking in its stead. He could say to himself, "I know I made one small mistake, but the rest of my performance was praiseworthy. Even the most famous actors make a mistake now and then."

Shoulds, musts, and oughts. Whether "should haves" and "musts" and "ought tos" are directed at yourself or others, they can cause anger, frustration, and bitterness. Rachael Y. was trying to help her daughter navigate through a divorce. Her daughter was distraught, and Rachel tried to comfort her, but to no avail. Rachael castigated herself, knowing that she "should" be able to console her daughter. She also felt her daughter "must" pull herself together, because tears would get her nowhere. One simple but effective remedy is to substitute words for should, must, and ought, such as "I wish" or "it would be nice." For example, Rachael could think, "It would be nice if I could comfort my daughter because she is so sad," and "I wish my daughter would think about what actions she needs to take, instead of crying in her room all day."

I think (negatively), therefore I am. This thought distortion is based on the premise that if you feel something, it must be so. Diane W. felt guilty because she

---

"Happiness makes up in height for what it lacks in length."
—**Robert Frost**

turned down a request, from her church, to tutor children in an underperforming school district. As a result, she felt she must be a selfish, worthless person. Instead, Diane could realize that she participates in many worthwhile volunteer activities, but this one just didn't appeal to her. She does not have to accept every offer just because she is available.

Accentuate the Positive

To paraphrase the Cowardly Lion: "What's she got that I ain't got? Attitude!" How else to explain Edna Lockwood, 91 years old and a pilot to boot. Edna is a member of United Flying Octogenarians, a group of pilots aged 80 and older, which boasts more than 250 members. Indeed, it's attitude—not altitude—that may help to ratchet the happiness set-point to a higher level and lengthen your life.

One 23-year study surveyed 338 men and 332 women age 50 and over regarding their attitudes toward aging, which were then matched to mortality data to determine attitude's effect on life span. As evidenced by Edna, men and women with more positive views of aging had an increased life span of 7.5 years.

An additional 7.5 years of life because of a positive attitude? That's astounding! Surround yourself with positive people today—a healthy attitude is contagious. Here are some other ways you can boost your mood.

* Accept yourself as you are, and accept that you deserve to be happy.
* Live joyfully in the moment. Do today what you would do if you found out you had only months left to live.
* Help others, and ask for help when you need it. Be able to answer the question: "What did I do for someone else and for myself today?"
* Plan pleasurable activities in advance—looking forward to something is a mood-brightener.
* Just do it! Though most of us believe that we must change our attitude before we change our behavior, the reverse is also true. Behaving in a desirable way can actually change your brain's chemistry and thus affect your way of thinking.
* Be aware of stereotypes. Negative attitudes about aging are believed to begin in childhood, so many people grow up with erroneous beliefs about get-

---

Consider this Zen saying: "The barn burned down. Now I can see the moon."

ting older. If you have a jaundiced view of aging, knowing the origin of your feelings may help to change them.

* View the world optimistically.

* Foster an internal locus of control for your successes and an external locus of control for your failures. Locus of control, a concept developed by Julian Rotter in 1966, refers to how you perceive the outcomes of certain events. People with an internal locus of control generally believe that personal actions are responsible for outcomes, while those with an external locus of control attribute outcomes to forces beyond their control (fate, luck, society, etc.). We have to be realistic, however, and recognize when failure is due to lack of effort or our own limitations. And, of course, sometimes things may truly be beyond our control!

* Laugh often, smile frequently, and look for the humor in daily life. Work at being curious, realistic, and flexible. Remember, you cannot always control what happens to you, but you *can* control your response.

* Cultivate a sense of wonder about the world.

* Think of five things each day for which you are grateful—and write them down.

Healthiness Equals Happiness

Sure, you feel better when you're well, but it's the physical act of exercise that brings about a shift in mood. A psychological bonanza of more pleasurable feelings results from just a short investment of time. In one study, men and women, average age 53, completed surveys before, during, and after a 15-minute walk. Everyone reported a more positive affect (feelings or emotions) and greater energy, both during and after the walk, and felt greater calmness and relaxation 15 minutes after completing the walk.

Healthwise, marriage really is for better or for worse! If one spouse has high blood pressure, high cholesterol, depression, asthma, ulcers, or arthritis, the spouse is much more likely to suffer from the same disease. Couples tend to share many lifestyle choices, such as nu-

---

Attitude: Two shoe salesmen were sent to a faraway island to sell shoes. After the first day, both men sent back telegrams. One read: "This place is a disaster. No one wears shoes." The other telegram said: "This place is a gold mine. No one wears shoes."

trition, exercise, smoking, drinking, and work habits. They also tend to share such factors as emotional stressors (financial problems or dealing with children), allergens, and other environmental risk factors. People tend to marry people like themselves—similar backgrounds, education levels, and economic status. It turns out that this holds true for health status as well. One study, of more than 4,700 married men and women between the ages of 51 and 61, investigated the relationship between spouses and health status. The researchers found that men aged 51 to 55 who are in excellent health have barely a 5 percent chance of being married to women in fair health and just a 2 percent chance of being married to women in poor health. Bottom line: We choose a spouse that we can not only grow old with, but that we can grow old *well* with.

Health is not just an individual matter. As Sven Wilson, the study's author, points out, "household matters!" Taking stock of your present health situation as a couple may provide a window to your future health. Since each of you shares the same environmental conditions, psychological stresses, and behavioral patterns, the concept of spouses tending to mirror one another's health level is something to consider as you plan your retirement. For example, knowing that your spouse is in poor health in his or her fifties could be the impetus to purchase long-term care insurance or perhaps help determine where you live—staying near family or choosing a location near excellent medical facilities.

 Some of the psychological issues of retirement are brought home in this anecdote from Patricia K., who lives with her husband, Richard, in Jacksonville, Florida.
Retirement was a bit of a shock for me.

I knew it was coming but could not reconcile it with my present age. I seemed to forget my

---

"Walking is inexpensive, familiar, and safe. That's why many have argued that
the most effective piece of exercise equipment is a dog."
—Dr. Penteleimon Ekkekakis (Reuters Health)

husband is more than 6 years older than I. Well, the day came and I thought, "This really isn't too bad"—and it wasn't bad—but it was definitely different. As a corporate wife I was used to long periods alone. When my husband traveled, went to meetings, was transferred, I stayed home and held down the fort, drove the carpools, and sold the house. When he had another transfer and promotion, I tried to resettle children, decorate another house, and find my place in a new community. Richard had a slot waiting for him and an instant sense of belonging. I usually spent three months selling a house with crying children and seeing him on the weekends or every other. One year he was gone every Monday to Friday. That was the year I put 22,000 miles on the car driving the carpool. Frankly, I felt it was my job and I did it without complaint . . . and enjoyed some wonderful benefits from his hard work.

The point of all of this is that the life I have described creates a great sense of independence and self-reliance, not to mention the freedom I had after the children grew up and left home. I created my own life wherever we went without his help, and I did that again when we moved to our retirement home. WHAM! I now had to deal with someone asking, "Who was on the phone?" "What did they want?" "What's for breakfast? lunch (horrors)? dinner?"; the computer being turned off if I left it for a minute; friends not as freely dropping in because my husband was home; guilt feelings if I left him alone all day . . . and I did, in a way, resent it. I had my life just as I wanted it and he changed it *again*. I suddenly realized that this is the rest of our lives. After a year of retirement, we worked out a lot of the problems and misunderstandings that arose.

One day he came home and said that he could not just play golf for the rest of his life. He needed more. He had run companies and was now bored. So he went back to school to become a high school teacher. Not surprisingly, he was hired immediately—by an inner-city school to teach the slow and nonreaders English literature. He is a man used to logic and discipline—a man with ambition and motivation. He has had difficulty understanding the attitudes he has to deal with every day. He hates the lack of control and of personal responsibility that permeates the class. But what he does not hate is the feeling he is doing something important—giving back a little when we have had so much. He also enjoys the other teachers and is amazed by their work and dedication! It has been revitalizing and exhausting and rewarding.

The final irony: I miss him at home. ⓣⓛ

Life's a Test—And You're Graded on a Curve

At age 4, success is . . . tying your shoes.

At age 12, success is . . . having friends.

At age 16, success is . . . having a driver's license.

At age 20, success is . . . having sex.

At age 35, success is . . . having money.

At age 50, success is . . . having money.

At age 60, success is . . . having sex.

At age 70, success is . . . having a driver's license.

At age 75, success is . . . having friends.

At age 80, success is . . . tying your shoes.

HOW DO YOU REPROGRAM YOUR TIME?

"Never be afraid to try something new. Remember: Amateurs built the Ark; professionals built the *Titanic*."
—Anonymous

Now is the time to think about the next phase of your life. The average retirement age in the United States has dropped from 67 in 1950 to 62 today. Retirees are generally more affluent, younger, and healthier and can expect to live as many as three decades in their "golden years." In fact, terms such as "zoomers" (coined by Tim Smart, *U.S. News & World Report*), and the concepts of redirecting, re-firing, or reinventing your life after leaving your primary career have all appeared in the media, reflecting the reality that retirement doesn't mean sitting on the sidelines of life.

As noted in chapter 1, activities that are challenging and provide a sense of self-worth are one of the keys to a happy retirement. Yes, you can play golf and watch television, but what other options exist? What types of volunteer and lifelong learning opportunities are there? What are some interesting hobbies? Should you start a second (or third or fourth) career?

If you were to do the math, you'd realize there are 168 hours a week to fill—which you can do mindlessly or mindfully. Assuming you have the financial wherewithal, ask yourself if there are things you'd like to try, or if you want more time to pursue certain interests. (To give you some insight on this, complete the worksheet, "Should You Stop Working?" on page 450.) If the answer is no, and your spouse is amenable, keep working. It may be the best thing for you. If the answer is yes, however, the big question then is, how do you reprogram your time?

PERSONALITY AND GOAL-SETTING

Are you a planner? One of the authors (Jan) has her next 4 years' vacations planned out, knows the next 5 books she is going to read, and looks at *TV Guide* for the coming week to see if there are any programs she'll need to tape because of conflicting commitments. Cathy, on the other hand, lives mainly in the moment, picks up and goes on a trip (without hotel reservations) at the drop of a hat, signs up for a cooking class or tennis round-robin at the last minute, and jumps in to volunteer for a worthy cause without any hesitation. Although they have different personalities and vastly different methods, Cathy and Jan have one thing in common: They both have goals they want to accomplish.

In order to have a successful retirement, you'll want to set goals. Otherwise, rather than enjoying leisure activi-ties, you'll really just be experiencing idleness, and the research shows that people who aren't engaged in purposeful activities are generally not as happy as those who are. Whether you're talking about starting a new business, taking up birding, becoming a mentor, or trying out for a community theater production, it's best to be flexible, try out new things, have a natural curiosity about life, and have some kind of plan for your future. So, regardless of your individual personality traits, how do you go about setting goals?

First, take the time to decide what you'd like to ac-complish, and make lists. If you are part of a couple, set down both individual and joint ideas relating to work, leisure activities, health, lifelong learning, relationships, or any other area. Recognize that each person in the re-lationship has valid needs and wants. Decide which are interests you share, and realize having time apart for sep-arate interests is also important. Brainstorm all possibil-ities, then evaluate and prune the unworkable ones.

Now comes the fun part. Take your list, pick three items on it, and turn them into goals. Here's how:

SMART. This easy-to-remember acronym describes the characteristics of goal-setting: Specific, Measurable, Attainable, Realistic, and Time sensitive.

✳ Turn each item into a specific, positive statement. For example, "I don't want to be intellectually stagnant" doesn't cut it. "I want to take a European history course at the local community college during the fall semester" does.

✳ Make your goals achievable within a defined time period. If you know you're scheduled for hernia surgery on October 1, you may want to rethink whether you can complete a fall semester history course. You want to dream, yet still be realistic.

✳ Remind yourself of your goals. Writing them out and placing them in a visible spot will help reinforce them.

Some people already know the goals they wish to attain, while others may want to consider some possibilities in the areas of education, hobbies, volunteering, the world of work, and travel (which is such a big area, we've given it a chapter by itself). And still others, well, they could use a little help deciding. If this sounds like you, keep reading.

LIFELONG LEARNING

Remember "the three R's"? There are more opportunities than ever for the mature learner to complete a degree, go back to school for professional reasons, or pursue classes for enrichment, to increase social contacts, or just for the fun of it. In some cases, you don't even have to "go back"—if you have a computer and a modem, you can curl up with a cup of coffee in your favorite robe and slippers and take a course online!

Degree Programs

The majority of adult students (about 70 percent) enroll in higher education to attain a degree. Most are seeking a bachelor's degree, some are working on a master's or doctorate, and others are after an associate's. The reasons vary: finishing a degree that was interrupted years ago by family or work constraints, working on professional development, achieving a goal for which they now have the time and financial resources, or training for a new career.

If pursuing a degree is a path you want to consider, keep in mind that many colleges and universities will exempt you from entrance exams such as the SAT and ACT if you're over a certain age. If you're thinking of advanced degrees in medicine or law, however, you will need to take the MCAT or LSAT. When applying to a college, you'll have to provide any previous transcripts you have, which will be assessed by the college counselor to determine which credits you already possess may be applied toward your degree. You may also be able to receive credit by taking the CLEP (College Level

Examination Program) test, a credit-by-exam program that tests your knowledge of undergraduate subjects (www.collegeboard.com/clep).

If finances are a concern, there are several avenues to explore. Many colleges and universities offer classes at free or reduced tuition rates to mature learners. Community colleges often offer particularly attractive incentives. For example, at Holyoke Community College in Massachusetts, students 60 and over can take credit courses on a space-available basis for $50 a semester. Check out the deals at the college or university near you. You may also be eligible for tax breaks, such as the Hope Tax Credit or a Lifetime Learning Credit (call the IRS Help Desk at 800-876-1715 or visit www.irs.gov and read Tax Topic 605: Education Credits or IRS Publication 970: Tax Benefits for Higher Education). Consider tapping into your IRA (without a tax penalty) for approved educational needs. College, federal, and state loans and grants are available, as well as scholarships. Meet with a financial aid officer at the colleges you are considering, and check out the Free Application for Federal Student Aid (FAFSA) at www.fafsa.ed.gov, Sallie Mae (www.salliemae.com), Free Scholarship Search (www.freschinfo.com), and Fast Web (www.fastweb.com). If you're female, The Business and Professional Women's Foundation offers scholarships if you meet certain criteria (www.bpwusa.org or 202-293-1200, ext.169); the American Association of University Women Education Foundation offers fellowships, grants, and awards (www.aauw.org or 800-326-2269).

The phrase "college senior" can have a whole new meaning.

Distance Learning

If you've always wanted to conquer calculus, but fear you'll be in a class of young adults desperately competing to get into medical school—or if taking a class while sipping coffee in your robe and slippers appeals to you—distance learning is the way to go.

Distance learning, also called distance education, is found in a variety of formats—there are classes offered in

According to the National Center for Educational Statistics, the mature learner is the fastest growing contingent on campus, a trend that will continue, with nontraditional students predicted to outnumber traditional students by four to one.

"real time," classes that you can take on your own schedule, classes where you never meet in person, and classes in which some actual face-to-face interactions are required. Entire degrees (from a bachelor's to a doctorate), certificate courses, credit and noncredit classes, continuing education courses, and courses for professional development are all possibilities with distance learning. Delivery of class materials can be via the Internet, videoconferencing, satellite, cable TV, and so on.

If you're looking to take classes toward a degree, or transfer credit classes to another institution, it's imperative that you choose your distance learning classes from an accredited institution; and if you want your credits to transfer, check to see whether the receiving college will accept your distance education credits. To be honest, the perception of "diploma mills" dies hard. Surveys show about one out of three employers looks somewhat askance at a distance education degree. So, before signing up for credit courses, do your homework. Visit www.distancelearn.about.com for a wealth of information on distance learning, accredited institutions, free online courses, financial information, and the like. Another site, www.classesusa.com, also contains information related to distance education. Even Yahoo has a site (click on "Education," then on "Distance Learning").

Those who do best with this type of instruction are self-starters, like to work independently, have good time management skills, are goal oriented, and feel comfortable using technology as a teaching tool. If you know you'd miss the interaction of spirited discussions and immediate feedback from professors and fellow students, distance learning wouldn't be the right choice for you. In fact, distance learning courses have a dropout rate about 20 percent higher than do brick and mortar courses.

Cost varies widely. For example, at the University of Phoenix, a major accredited player in distance education, about 40,000 students "attend" undergraduate, graduate, and doctoral programs. In 2003, the cost per credit for an undergraduate course was about $400; for a graduate

---

According to www.distancelearning.about.com, there are over 20 million students enrolled in distance education courses; 15 percent of students enrolled in higher education are taking a distance learning course.

course, about $500; and for a doctoral course, about $600. Canyon College in Idaho, on the other hand, offers a three-credit Organizational Psychology course for $400 and a Brief Couples Counseling course for $30. Or you could take a noncredit, one-hour Managing Stress class through QuickKnowledge (www.quicknowledge.com or 877-491-6868) for $15. If you don't want to pay at all, ThirdAge (www.thirdage.com) offers free online courses, such as Get Ready to Invest or Workout Tips for Maximum Effectiveness. SeniorNet (www.seniornet.org) offers free tutorials, guides, and discussion-based courses as well.

The world of education is literally at your fingertips.

Adult Education

Although adult education courses can be taken in the distance format, let's turn our attention to taking courses in an actual classroom setting, but without worrying about credits, degrees, or transferability.

As mentioned before, many institutions of higher learning give breaks to mature learners. At Florida's 10 state universities, for example, tuition is waived for adults 60 and older, if there is space available, and classes are not taken for credit. State colleges and universities in Texas allow seniors (65 and older) to take up to 6 free hours of credit or noncredit courses per semester, if space allows. Of course, credit-free also means exam-free, homework-free, and term paper-free! Great deals are out there—contact the local colleges to see about their individual tuition policies.

If you're more interested in a residential program (but not a dorm!), look into Senior Summer School (www.seniorsummerschool.com or 800-847-2466). You can take a 2-week class offered by Appalachian State University in Boone, North Carolina, for an all-inclusive (sans transportation) price of $1,900. Elderhostel (www.elderhostel.org) combines education and travel. How about the 19-day "Essence of the Greek Islands" offering for about $4,000? Sign us up!

If you'd rather stay closer to home and are interested in learning for its own sake, many noncredit adult education classes, community classes, and enrichment classes exist. A member-driven organization of adult learners, Learning in Retirement Institute (LRI), also

---

According to the National Center for Education Statistics, more than one in three Americans 45 years or older are participating in some form of adult education.

called the Lifelong Learning Institute (LLI) or Institute for Learning in Retirement (ILR), is available on approximately 400 college and university campuses in the United States and Canada. Over 100,000 students are enrolled in classes that are frequently developed and taught by an LRI volunteer; membership is required for attendance, and there is usually a nominal annual fee to enroll in classes that range from the arts to zoology. For example, listings from the Duke Institute for Learning in Retirement include Women in Antiquity, Financial Statements, T'ai Chi, and Gulliver's Travels. Duke charges a $25 annual membership fee, and either $135 for multiple classes or $75 for a single course.

With all the options available, lifelong learning can easily become a reality.

HOBBIES

Winston Churchill once said, "Broadly speaking, human beings can be divided into three classes: those who are toiled to death, those who are worried to death, and those who are bored to death." To be sure you don't fall into the third category, consider some hobbies as you reprogram your time. A hobby enriches your life by increasing your knowledge, sharpening your skills, and/or bringing you inner peace.

You may already be an avid golfer, tennis player, reader, oenophile (wine lover), or philatelist (stamp collector). There is an endless variety of hobbies out there; the second stage of your life its a perfect opportunity to hone old hobbies and explore new ones, such as:

Genealogy. If you want to find out more about your ancestors, there are dozens of books written on the subject, courses you can take, and the treasure trove that is the Internet. (Check out the resources listing for this chapter for a few suggestions.)

Dance. Exotic, salsa, line, ballroom, square, swing . . . you get the idea. Some of these don't even require a partner—just show up.

Photography. With digital cameras, you can now zip your creations to far-flung relatives with the press of a button.

Grandma Moses (Anna Mary Robertson Moses) began painting in her late seventies, and continued painting for more than 20 years.

Reading. After relocating to Bellingham, Washington, Melanie F. began a book club that meets every 6 weeks. Members alternate picking a book and hosting the meeting in their homes. She not only met more people and expanded her social support group, but she's reading a heck of a lot of good literature. Many books now contain discussion guides because of the booming popularity of reading clubs. Your local library or bookstore can give you information about setting up book clubs, as well as recommend lists (the bookstore where Melanie's club members purchase their books gives them a 10 percent discount). Or you can access a site such as www.book-browse.com. If you don't want to leave your home, you can join an online book club; for a list of possibilities, browse www.his.com/~allegria/clubs.html.

Exercise/sports. Improving your body as well as your mind is certainly a noble endeavor. Your local health club, YMCA/YWCA or Jewish community center, and many medical centers offer fitness programs or facilities, from aerobics and swimming to weights and yoga. Sign up with a personal trainer for a few classes to get you started on the right track, or lace up those sneakers and start walking. So many baby boomers have taken up snowboarding that they've been called "grays on trays."

Acting. If you've been longing to perform under the bright lights, consider joining an acting troupe. Joseph L. recently moved to Leisure World in Silver Spring, Maryland, and snagged a role in the Neil Simon play *Rumours* through Leisure World's Fun and Fancy Theatre Group. If you don't want to be onstage, consider a behind-the-scenes role such as helping with makeup, lighting, costumes, scenery, or publicity. If you are uncertain where to look, call the theater department of your local college or university and ask for suggestions, look under "theaters" in the Yellow Pages, or go online to www.seniortheatre.com. This Web site lists some of the senior theatre groups in the United States and Canada (there are more than 400 of them). You can contact them for advice, or purchase their book, *Senior Theatre Connections*, by Bonnie L. Vorenberg.

true LIFE **Eleanor and Al A. own and operate the Bluemont Bed & Breakfast in Luray, Virginia. Here is Eleanor's story of their new career path.**

The year was 1985. We were vacationing in Bar Harbor, Maine. It was our first B&B experience. The innkeepers were marvelous and set a standard by which we would compare all of our B&B stays over the next 18 years.

As we stayed at different B&Bs, my comments were something similar to "We certainly could do this better than they are!" A friend of mine at the University in Economic Development was responsible for many of the B&B start-ups in Ohio. I too became interested and went to several of his classes. I did lots of reading and research and then began co-teaching some aspiring-innkeeper workshops. I discussed with my husband the idea of starting our own B&B after retiring from university teaching. We both felt it was a good goal to pursue, so we mapped out a strategy in our minds as to how we could accumulate savings to make it happen.

It took us almost 15 years, but we never forgot our dream. Somewhere in the back of our minds, our plans were brewing. I wrote down ideas, collected information, kept the pros and cons of each B&B stay, made a checklist of all our wants and needs, and then, as retirement approached, we set out on many searches for our own property. It didn't happen overnight. It took almost 2 years of searching the Internet, reading ads, contacting Realtors, and visiting many prospective inns. We were getting depressed because we could not find what we wanted and were assured many times, "You will know it when you find it!" Then one day we saw an ad for this property in the Shenandoah Valley. An area with mountains and tourism was at the top of our list. When we visited the property, we immediately knew—*this was it!*

The previous owners were so wonderful, and we clicked right away. We are now the best of friends and continue a great relationship, as they live very close to us. Quite unusual for a B&B sale, I think.

The B&B we purchased met almost all of our requirements. We did not enter into the decision lightly and did all of our homework before we signed on the dotted line. To this day, we have no regrets about our decision. We love our home because it is *our* home first, then a B&B. So far we have had nothing but positive comments from our guests, who enjoy our home and our location overlooking the Shenandoah Valley and the Blue Ridge Mountains. We have the advantage of being only 2 hours or less from several major metropolitan areas, so we can take advantage of the cultural events and shopping in those areas, which keeps me satisfied.

I have tried to become as involved in the community as I possibly can and still run the B&B. I see a great future for our town in regards to tourism, and I hope I can help be a part of that. Our plan is to do this for at least 10 years. But if we like it, who knows?

Running a bed and breakfast seems like a great job to many people, and it is! But it must be entered into realistically and with a plan so that one will not "burn out" on the job. Prospective innkeepers must be financially prepared because running a small B&B will not produce enough income on which to live. It is a lot of hard work in peak season, but the rewards are very tangible when you get compliments from your guests. It makes all the hard work worthwhile, and it makes us very proud. ⓉⓁ

Birding. The U.S. Forest Service reports that the quickest growing outdoor activity in the United States is birding. With 10,000 bird species, enjoyment of nature, and the social aspect of being in a group, this is a great hobby. A few good sites: www.birding.com, www.birder.com, www.audubon.org, www.birdwatching.com. As this last Web site states, enjoy "your lifetime ticket to the theater of nature."

Games. "Use it or lose it" is an adage frequently invoked in relation to keeping our brains energized. Research has shown those who stay cerebrally challenged tend to lead richer, fuller lives, and may even stave off diseases such as Alzheimer's. Jason R. and his wife, Beverly, arrange a monthly "game night" with four other couples. They usually alternate among Pictionary, Trivial Pursuit, Outburst, charades, and card games and enjoy the social interaction as much as the intellectual stimulation. On a more solitary note, you can enjoy crossword puzzles, anagrams, acrostics, and jigsaw puzzles. Try www.upuzzles.com for a good selection.

Of course, the above examples just scratch the surface of possibilities. You could try painting, woodworking, music, cooking, astronomy, gardening, fishing, boating, cars, aquaria, arts and crafts, collecting, electronic gaming, journaling—the only limit is your imagination.

VOLUNTEERING

If you find that classes, working, hobbies, and/or travel aren't enough to give you a feeling of satisfaction and fulfillment, consider Winston Churchill's words: "We make a living by what we get, we make a life by what we give."

More than one in four Americans volunteered in 2003, averaging about 50 hours per year, according to the Labor Department. The study found that women donate their time more than men, and men and women between the ages of 35 and 54 had the highest volunteer rate. Although by no means all-inclusive, here's an A to Z list of volunteer opportunities:

Adult literacy. One in four adults in America struggles with literacy issues. To address this crisis, Proliteracy Worldwide (www.proliteracy.org or 888-528-2224) is attempting to recruit 100,000 volunteers.

Big Brothers/Big Sisters. "The only requirement is a willingness to make a new friend and a desire to share some fun with a young person." Contact www.bbbs.org or check the Yellow Pages for an agency near you.

Community policing/patrols. Contact your local police department, or contact the Retired and Senior Volunteer Program at www.seniorcorps.org or 800-424-8867.

Disaster response. The workforce of the American Red Cross is 97 percent volunteers! This organization provides training, if necessary. Go online to www.redcross.org (click "Volunteer") or call your local Red Cross unit or the National Headquarters at 202-303-4498.

Elimination of substandard housing. Habitat for Humanity is working in more than 80 countries to build affordable housing for those in need. Visit www.habitat.org, call the affiliate nearest you, or contact their Partner Service Center at 229-924-6935.

Food for the homebound. Bring food to those who are disabled or homebound through Meals on Wheels. More than one million nutritious meals are served every day through churches, charities, and citizen and community groups. Find a provider in your area, or contact the National Meals on Wheels Foundation at www.nationalmealsonwheels.org or 319-358-9362.

Guardian ad litem work. Represent neglected and abused children during judicial proceedings. Training is offered through the Retired and Senior Volunteer Program (www.seniorcorps.org or 800-424-8867).

Hospice care. Bring dignity and comfort to the terminally ill and their families. Over 80 percent of those involved in hospice care in the United States are volunteers. One contact is the Volunteer Hospice Network at www.growthhouse.org (click on "Hospice and Home Care," then on "Volunteer Hospice Network") or call 630-232-2233. This is an umbrella organization for more than 150 organizations that provide free service for those needing care for the dying.

Income tax preparation. Be one of more than 30,000 volunteer tax aides through the AARP Foundation. Training is provided, and out-of-pocket expenses are reimbursed. Contact www.aarp.org/taxaide or call 888-227-7669.

Job assistance. Dress for Success helps low-income women enter the workforce through the donation of work and interview-appropriate clothing. Or, donate your time as a personal shopper, office helper, or clothes sorter to the more than 75 cities where this organization operates. Contact them at www.dressforsuccess.org or click on the closest affiliate for more information.

K.E.E N. (Kids Enjoy Exercise Now). Pair up with a mentally or physically challenged child or young adult and participate in recreational activities. Check out www.keenusa.org or call 301-770-3200.

Library work. Be a greeter, give tours, assist in clerical work, help introduce patrons to electronic resources, shelve books, prepare children's programs, index newspapers, and so on. Call your local library for available positions.

Mentoring. Help a young person improve his or her life by "being there" and providing a good example. Many companies, churches, and civic groups sponsor mentoring programs. Or, contact the National Mentoring Partnership at www.mentoring.org or 703-224-2200, where you can enter your zip code and find a list of local organizations that provide mentoring.

Nurturing. Join the Foster Grandparent Program and help children and teens with special or exceptional needs. There are several requirements to be one of the more than 30,000 foster grandparents, relating to your age, time commitment, and income level. Foster Grandparents earn an hourly stipend and are reimbursed for out-of-pocket expenses. For more information, contact www.seniorcorps.org or call 800-424-8867.

Offering assistance to the elderly and homebound. Join the Senior Companion Program and help those in need with transportation to appointments, shopping, and other helpful chores. Senior companions receive a small hourly stipend, reimbursement for some costs, and service-related accident and liability insurance. The Senior Companion Program can be accessed through www.seniorcorps.org or 800-424-8867.

Providing help for the homeless. Two million people are homeless for at least part of every year, and three-quarters of a million people are homeless on any given night, according to the National Alliance to End Homelessness. Churches, companies, and many civic organizations aid the homeless, or you can contact the National Law Center for Homelessness & Poverty, whose goal is to help prevent and end homelessness. They can be reached at www.nlchp.org or 202-638-2535.

Quilting. If you like to sew, you can provide new, homemade blankets or quilts to ill or traumatized children from birth to 18 years of age through the Linus Project (www.projectlinus.org or 309-664-7814), or make a quilt/sleeping bag for the homeless (www.reese.org/sharon/uglyqult.htm or 717-289-4335).

Reading. Read to children in clinic waiting rooms through Reach Out and Read (www.reachoutandread.org or 617-629-8042), or contact the American Council of the Blind at 800-424-8666 for volunteer opportunities.

Special Olympics work. Join over half a million Special Olympics volunteers at the local, state, national, or international level. Contact www.specialolympics.org or call 202-628-3630.

Tutoring. Go through a community or faith-based organization to tutor children or adults. Contact the Retired and Senior Volunteer Program at www.seniorcorps.org or 202-606-5000 to be linked to a local service organization.

Ushering. If you want to enjoy operas or plays as well as contribute to the art world, consider volunteering to be an usher. Generally, theaters prefer a commitment on a regular basis, and of course you'll need to arrive early, be helpful and courteous, dress the part, and be able to assist those who need it. Contact your local theaters.

Voter registration. The voter turnout since 1945 has averaged about 49 percent, according to the *Christian Science Monitor*. Help get the vote out! Contact your Board of Elections to become a voter registration volunteer.

Walking a shelter dog. Contact your local Humane Society, Animal Shelter League, or ASPCA. Get exercise while you do a good deed!

Xenophon Therapeutic Riding Center. Sign up to help with therapeutic riding lessons for disabled children and adults. You may groom the horses, provide lessons, or work on landscaping or repairs. For a list of some therapeutic riding centers, go to www.narha.org and click on "Find a Center."

Your chance to make a difference. Here's the catchall category. Think of what you can do to give back. For example, the fourth Saturday of every October has been designated "Make a Difference Day" by *USA Weekend* magazine. To get involved with this initiative, go to www.usaweekend.com and click on "Make a Difference Day." The site has an idea generator to help you formulate a project, as well as register a project. Or, think locally. Which of your friends, neighbors, or relatives could use a hand with his or her household or yard chores, grocery shopping, babysitting, or yard work? Offer your services; people often feel uncomfortable asking for help.

Zoo work. What's doing at the zoo for volunteers? Interpret exhibits, help maintain the grounds, care for baby animals, assist with promotional events, be a docent, help the keepers feed the animals, or clean and maintain animal exhibits.

If that list isn't enough, here are some additional organizations that list numerous opportunities to volunteer.

More than 35 million Americans over 50 belong to AARP, an organization that seeks "to enhance the quality of life for all by promoting independence, dignity, and purpose." Click "volunteer" on www.aarp.org or call 800-424-3410. Sign up for a newsletter about volunteering, or access the many links to national and local organizations.

Network for Good (www.networkforgood.org) was founded by the AOL Time Warner Foundation, Cisco Systems, and Yahoo. This site allows you to speak out on issues that interest you, volunteer, and/or donate money.

Points of Light Foundation, founded by President George H. W. Bush in 1990, works with the Volunteer Center National Network to help bring solutions to community problems through its approximately 500 volunteer centers. Contact the foundation at www.pointsoflight.org or 800-VOLUNTEER.

United Nations Volunteers offers opportunities to volunteer abroad, in your own country, or online. They also provide links to other international organizations that recruit volunteers. Contact www.unv.org or their office in Bonn, Germany, at 49-228-815-2000.

Volunteer Match helps you to search for volunteer opportunities by zip code or type of organization. Contact them at www.volunteermatch.org or 415-241-6868. They also have a "virtual volunteer" section so you can volunteer your talents (perhaps design a Web site, answer questions on the phone, or critique press releases) without leaving the comforts of home.

Volunteers of America has programs that work to rehabilitate people, not just treat their symptoms. Their outreach includes correction facilities, schools, churches, and social service and law enforcement agencies. Offices are community based, so find one near you, or go to www.volunteersofamerica.org or call the national office at 800-899-0089.

STAYING IN THE GAME

According to an AARP survey, 80 percent of boomers plan to work full or part time after retirement. Sounds like an oxymoron, doesn't it? Finances are the biggest reason, but over one-third of those surveyed cited enjoyment of work as a factor, and 5 percent are enticed by the idea of doing something different.

Let's take a look at the financial aspects of work first. The nonprofit Employee Benefit Research Institute found that in 2003, about 67 percent of workers thought they'd have enough money to live on when they retired, down from 70 percent in 2002; also, 24 percent were anticipating postponing retirement, compared to 15 percent in 2002. So, though still generally optimistic, people are becoming increasingly cautious about the financial side of retirement. The typical American, at age 44, has saved $40,000 toward retirement; the median stock holdings for baby boomers in 2001 were $39,000. About 70 percent of boomers were homeowners, with a median home value of $130,000. Annika Sunden, associate director of Boston College's Center for Retirement Research, predicts that when all the number crunching is done, most people will have to work until they are somewhere between 68 and 70 in order for their money to last as long as they live.

Assume that you don't *have* to work for financial reasons. Should you still work? The nonfinancial rewards of work can be just as compelling. As described in chapter 1, these include a sense of identity, status, intellectual engagement, social interaction, structure, and feelings of pride and accomplishment. Recall that in the *Cornell Retirement and Well-Being Study*, referred to in chapter 1, the major reason for retiring for both men and women was "to do other things." If there aren't other things you'd rather be doing, by all means, keep working as long as you can (if you have a significant other who's okay with it).

Of course, work options don't have to be all or nothing—full time or no time. You can work part time or part of the year, consult on a freelance basis, transition to a new career, or start your own business.

For example, we call Charlie B. "the man who won't retire." A former neighbor of one of the authors, Charlie was the principal of a public elementary school for 21 years in Prince George's County, Maryland. He retired at 56, and then became the principal of a private elementary school until 60, when he retired again. Bored, desiring some additional income, and wanting flexibility for his interests (water skiing, motorcycling, gardening, and building model railroads), Charlie painted houses and was a substitute teacher for 8 years (if you're keeping track, that's till 68). From 69 to 70, he taught fifth grade in the public school system, under the Retire-Rehire program. Now, at

---

Ironically, it's the more affluent retirees, socked by the recent stock market decline and now unable to survive on their investments, who are returning to work in the greatest numbers. People at the lowest income levels don't have as many investments and tend to live primarily off Social Security.

71, Charlie is back painting houses and substitute teaching!

Let's say you want to work, for whatever reason, but also wish to change gears. What are some of the realities and options of staying in the workforce or reentering it after leaving a primary career?

Ageism

Does age discrimination exist? Not legally. The federal Age Discrimination in Employment Act (ADEA), passed in 1967, states, "It shall be unlawful for an employer to fail or refuse to hire or to discharge any individual or otherwise discriminate against any individual with respect to his compensation, terms, conditions, or privileges of employment, because of such individual's age."

There can be a big gap between legality and reality, however. In 2001, the Department of Labor compared age and length of time to get a new job, and found an average of 13 weeks for all workers, but an average of 18 weeks for workers older than 55, and more than 18 weeks for workers over 65. In less desirable economic times, of course, those spans lengthen. The Equal Employment Opportunity Commission (EEOC) received 19,921 age discrimination complaints in 2002, compared to almost 16,000 complaints in 2000.

Unfortunately, some employers feel that older workers are more set in their ways, have less energy and more health problems, aren't as technologically savvy, require higher salaries, and won't work as hard as younger workers. Historically, the implicit agreement was that an employee would stay with one company throughout his or her work career, starting out at lower wages, but progressing to higher wages as he or she became older. This paradigm is no longer true; with people routinely changing jobs every 5 to 10 years, and younger workers wanting higher wages when they come on board, the old way is no longer the model.

Most experts are upbeat about the future of older workers, however. With baby boomers retiring, and fewer younger workers to replace them, labor shortages will force companies to retain, retrain (if necessary), and value the older employee. For many employers, the bottom line will be whether the employee meets their

---

The distinction of oldest employee goes to Robert "Robbie" Eisenberg, who at 103 was still working for Zabin Industries in California, overseeing zipper production.

company's needs; the experience, work ethic, and maturity boomers have will become valuable commodities.

Job-Hunting Suggestions

First, consider what's important to you. Is the amount of money crucial, or is flexibility, novelty, helping others, or using your strengths just as high a priority? Will you need additional formal education? Are you willing to make trade-offs? A career counselor can help crystallize and focus your priorities and narrow your job search. For assistance from one, contact the National Board for Certified Counselors and Affiliates (www.nbcc.org or 336-547-0607), join a group such as the Five O'Clock Club (www.fiveoclockclub.com or 800-538-6645), which assists in job searches, or get help from Experience Works (www.experienceworks.org or 866-397-9757), which helps train mature workers.

You can also take self-tests to help you determine where your interests lie. Free self-assessments are available at www.careergames.com. This site also gives tips on interviewing, negotiating, and answering difficult inter-

view questions. For a fee, there are scientifically based tests, such as the Self-Directed Search, or the Strong Interest Inventory. You can take these assessments online and receive personalized results.

Let friends, former colleagues, members of groups or professional associations you belong to, and acquaintances know you are looking for work—and what type of work you desire. Volunteer in an area you are interested in, or work at a temporary staffing service to "try out" different work paths (Adecco, www.usadecco.com, is one such company). Not only will you find out if you're interested in the field, but you'll be ready and willing if the company decides to hire. Use newspapers or online search engines such as Monster.com and HotJobs.com (although only about 5 percent of job seekers are hired through these Internet sites). You can also go online to sites geared toward workers 50 and older, such as www.seniors4hire.org or www.SeniorJobBank.org.

If you have a particular area of expertise, look for Web sites that reflect your background and have job postings. For example, Mary S. relocated to New Jersey after a di-

---

To file an age discrimination complaint with the EEOC at either the state or federal level, call 800-669-4000.

BEST EMPLOYERS FOR THOSE OVER 50

Here's a look at AARP's 2003 rankings of the best employers for workers over 50. If you live in one of these areas, check these companies out.

✻ Adecco Employment Services (Melville, NY)

✻ The Aerospace Corporation (El Segundo, CA)

✻ Augusta Health Care (Fishersville, VA)

✻ Baptist Health South Florida (Coral Gables, FL)

✻ Bon Secours Richmond Health Systems (Richmond, VA)

✻ Brethren Village (Lancaster, PA)

✻ Children's Health System (Birmingham, AL)

✻ Deere & Company (Moline, IL)

✻ Farmer's Insurance Group of Companies (Los Angeles, CA)

✻ First Tennessee National Corporation (Memphis, TN)

✻ Freeport Health Network (Freeport, IL)

✻ Lincoln Financial Group (Philadelphia, PA)

✻ Massachusetts Institute of Technology (Cambridge, MA)

✻ The MITRE Corporation (Bedford, MA/McLean, VA)

✻ The Ohio State University Medical Center (Columbus, Ohio)

✻ Pinnacle West Capital Corporation (Phoenix, AZ)

✻ Principal Financial Group (Des Moines, IA)

✻ Roche (Nutley, NJ)

✻ Scottsdale Healthcare (Scottsdale, AZ)

✻ SSM Health Care—St. Louis (St. Louis, MO)

✻ St. Mary's Medical Center (Huntington, WV)

✻ Ultratech, Inc. (San Jose, CA)

✻ Volkswagen of America (Auburn Hills, MI)

✻ West (Eagan, MN)

✻ Whirlpool Corporation (Benton Harbor, MI)

vorce and wanted to continue in her profession as a media specialist in an elementary school. She went to Rutger's University Web site and found media specialist positions that required her specific credentials, as well as openings in the area where she was relocating. Also, don't overlook small companies!

To find out where the jobs are (and hence, where the demand is), check out the U.S. Department of Labor's *Occupational Outlook Handbook*, which is revised every other year; it contains a treasure trove of information about growth projections, wages, education, and working conditions for specific careers. Click on www.bls.gov/oco to access the newest edition of the handbook online.

You'll also have to update (or dust off) your résumé. Make it a "functional" résumé; that is, structure it around your abilities and skill. Omit the dates of your educational background, and don't feel obligated to list every job you've ever had; concentrate on those positions that are pertinent to the employment you are seeking. If you're looking to change careers, or if you're reentering the workforce after a hiatus, concentrate on the transferable skills applicable to the new position, and downplay job titles.

Emphasize your accomplishments, results, and outstanding qualifications in a succinct paragraph at the top of your résumé. Include any computer expertise, coursework, or professional development to accentuate your openness to learning, as well as your e-mail address. When e-mailing a résumé, don't send it as an attachment in case it can't (or won't) be opened, and e-mail a copy to yourself prior to sending it to a potential employer to make sure it looks like you want it to look. In your cover letter, emphasize that you are a proven entity (don't say you've worked for 30 years), and that you are flexible, adaptable, willing to learn, and have transferable skills.

Once your foot is in the door—you have the interview—again emphasize your flexibility, motivation, interpersonal skills, and willingness to learn. Let them know you want to contribute to the company, and that you're not looking for a job because you're broke! Use your age to your advantage, stressing your experience with problem solving, a proven track record, and strong work ethic. If you're happy to work part time, let the prospective em-

---

By 2010, the Bureau of Labor Statistics estimates that approximately 33 percent of the labor force will be comprised of "mature" workers (those over 45).

FROM CPA TO AP-ECON

Stephen L. worked for many years as a CPA, first in an international accounting firm, then as a controller of a telecommunications firm. After almost 30 years, Stephen decided to change gears and become a high school teacher, something he had always wanted to do, but felt he couldn't afford with a nonworking spouse and three young children. He knew his credentials, including salary and years of service, would be intimidating to a private high school, so he fashioned his résumé to illustrate the strengths that pertained to his teaching business classes, including his instructing continuing education classes for his colleagues, his computer proficiency, and his organizational abilities. He downplayed the elements of his jobs that were not as relevant, such as familiarity with depreciation methods for financial reporting. Today, Stephen is happily teaching AP economics, personal finance, marketing, and accounting (of course!) in a Catholic coeducational school in Virginia.

ployer know you are a bargain; you have tons of experience, but don't have to be paid what they might pay a younger, full-time employee. Slip in (assuming it's true) how you're still playing tennis or love to downhill ski, hike, or swim to convey that you are a vital, energetic person. Address any questions (insidious or obvious) about your age forthrightly by reassuring the interviewer you can handle the job as well as bring experience, enthusiasm, and wisdom to the position. If asked how you feel about working for someone younger than you, AARP suggests you respond, "When I get to the point where I can't learn from someone younger or older than I, I will stop working." Be sure you're knowledgeable about the company, and follow up with a handwritten thank-you note.

New Careers

Don't sell yourself short! There are jobs to consider besides the usual greeter, retailer, cashier, and food preparer and server positions. Here are just a few possibilities to ponder if you'd like to embark on a new direction.

Health care worker. For careers in demand, look to the health care industry and consider diploma courses to become a home health aide, medical assistant, pharmacy technologist, nurse aide, EKG technologist, or physical therapy aide. These are relatively short courses (weeks or months), relatively low cost (usually under $1,000), and many employers will reimburse your tuition costs if you work for them. There are 2-year associate of arts or associate of science degrees in such areas as medical transcription or respiratory therapy. Look to your local community college or technical school for more information. If you have the time, energy, and money, look into pharmacy school—there is a huge demand for pharmacists, and the pay is excellent.

Captioner. According to the training company Train for the Future, a captioner is a person who uses computerized voice-recognition software to produce text in real time on television or computer monitors. Hearing-impaired students, television broadcasts, conventions, stockholder meetings, and hearings may all use the services of a captioner. There is an increased need for captioners due to the growing use of captioned television shows. In fact, by 2006, the FCC is requiring all stations to caption all new programming. It's estimated that 3,000 captioners will be needed; at this time there are only about 300 in the United States. Training can be on-site or from home and takes about 6 months. Salaries range from $15 to $100 per hour, the work can be part or full time, and it can be performed on-site or from home. For a list of schools, contact the National Court Reporters Association at www.ncraonline.org (click on "Education and Certification," then on "Schools and Programs") or call 800-272-6272.

National parks staffer. If you love the great outdoors, consider working at a national park. For a (usually) 3-month commitment, you can receive lodging, meals, and a paycheck. It won't be the Ritz and you won't make a fortune, but it may be the right thing if you're open to new experiences and like to work hard. For more information, contact the National Park Service (www.sep.nps.gov or 877-554-4550) or Xanterra Parks & Resorts (www.xanterra.com or 303-338-6000) if you're interested in managing the concessions (lodging, food, gift shops, etc.) at several of the premiere national parks.

Bank teller. If you like detail, you may want to pursue this position, which handles the routine operations of a

---

For more suggestions on answering difficult interview questions, go to www.aarp.org; click on "Career," then "Tips and Tools."

bank. About 25 percent of bank tellers work part time.

Customer service representative. These employees serve as the liaison between the public and their company. Most are employed by financial, communication, and insurance institutions. The U.S. Department of Labor predicts that employment of customer service representatives will increase faster than the average through 2010. Maybe by then we won't always get a recording when we call a company!

Nursing home feeding assistant. A new federal regulation will allow people to be feeding assistants in nursing homes after an 8-hour training course. Previously, you had to be a nursing assistant, with at least 75 hours of training. The rule pertains to nursing homes that accept Medicare or Medicaid.

Tour guide. Escort groups or individuals through museums, important buildings, parks, and the like. For example, Tourmobile Sightseeing in Washington, D.C., provides narrated shuttle tours to the historic sites in Washington and Virginia. Contact the attractions you are interested in and see if they hire tour guides.

Mystery shopper. According to Service Intelligence, a mystery shopping company, secret shoppers "anonymously observe and document the quality of service at a store or business on a given day. Clients can then evaluate a sample of service delivery, product knowledge, and facility maintenance at corporate stores or franchises." Retail, health care, banking, finance, and fast-food restaurants are examples of where you could be a mystery shopper. Pay is about $10 to $25 per hour. Contact Service Intelligence at www.secretshopnet.com or 403-261-5000.

Focus group member or survey subject. Who doesn't like to give their opinion? And what's better than giving it *and* being paid for it? Participating in surveys or focus groups can result in gifts or extra cash and is a fun way to spend a few hours. One of the authors served in a focus group after being approached by an employee of a consumer research group in a fast-food restaurant. Two weeks later, for about 2 hours, 10 of us met in a conference room in an office building and were questioned on our eating habits, amounts we spent on meals, how often we ate out,

---

Wonder what kind of reference a former employer is giving you?
You can hire a reference company to check for between $50 and $100.
An example of a company that performs such a service is www.jobreference.com.

and our favorite kinds of food, while researchers behind one-way mirrors were taking notes (they informed us of this). When the pleasant discussion, accompanied by snacks, was over, we were each handed $60 in cash. To find a research company near you, access the New York American Marketing Association Greenbook (www.greenbook.org) and search their national directory by desired location, or look for ads in local or college newspapers. Paid surveys over the Internet include www.buzzback.com and www.gozing.com. Whether you are asked to participate in a survey is a function of the demographics a company needs.

Bed and breakfast owner. What about using your home or purchasing a place for a B&B? Some retirees go this route, but be sure to consider some of the issues involved: The location must be desirable, the place you plan to use must be zoned for a B&B, and you'll need to obtain insurance. To see if you have the personality for it, complete the worksheet "Bed and Breakfast: Do You Have the Right Skills?" by Eleanor Ames, a professional innkeeper, on page 451. Gross annual income for an average-size bed and breakfast is around $50,000. If interested, visit some B&Bs, and take a seminar about owning and operating one. You can take on-line courses with Juliette Swenson at www.seminars-online.com, which run from $39 to $99 depending on content.

Job-sharer. Consider taking a full-time position and sharing it with a coworker. Robert T., for example, taught high school biology for many years but wanted to scale back and have his afternoons free for golf and volunteer work. He was able to work out a deal with a new mother who also wanted to return to teaching science, but on a part-time basis. So, they shared the full-time science position, prorating their benefits (sometimes one person is covered by a spouse or has other arrangements and may be able to forgo all or some of the benefits). If you're interested in this type of position, and you have a willing coworker, submit a proposal to your employer outlining the concept of job-sharing, how the position would be structured, and what the benefits are to the employer.

Teacher of English as a second or foreign language (ESL/EFL). If you'd like to combine work and travel, consider teaching English in a foreign country, or at one of many locations within the United States. Many posi-

---

"Jobs for the older and bolder" is how www.coolworks.com advertises seasonal opportunities for work at national and state parks, outdoor centers, and resorts.

tions require a college degree; some require a TEFL (Teaching English as a Foreign Language) certificate, which can be obtained in the United States (www. tesol.org. gives locations of courses). Get an idea of what's available and what it's like at www.eslworldwide. com. Monster.com also lists positions and descriptions for ESL teachers. For example, a 1-year contract teaching in South Korea (no experience is required, but a bachelor's degree is) includes a furnished apartment, insurance, airfare, and paid vacation/holidays/sick leave at a salary of about $1,500/month.

Club Med staffer. No, you don't have to be a hardbody to apply for a position with Club Med, but you do have to be able to relocate for at least 6 months and lift 30 pounds. Positions include child care, food service, sports, housekeeping, guest services, and entertainment. See www.clubmedjobs.com for more specifics.

Realtor. Real estate attracts those who are people oriented, are flexible, realize that there won't be a steady paycheck, and don't wish to have a 9-to-5 job. You'll need to take the appropriate real estate course, pass the licensing exam, and be sponsored by a broker or real estate company in the state in which you wish to be licensed. Contact the Board of Realtors in the location where you wish to be licensed to find out the specifics.

Starting Your Own Business

The dream of some retirees is to take a passion or hobby and turn it into a money-making venture, whether it's painting, writing, opening a restaurant or boutique, or having a consulting business. Although two million Americans 55 and older are self-employed, the cold reality is that most businesses fail within the first 3 to 5 years. Here are a few things to think about if you're contemplating starting your own business.

Money. Cash flow problems are the biggest contributor to small business failures. Look into sources of outside money, rather than funding your business with personal savings. A business plan that includes all the financial information should be reviewed by an accountant or financial planner and should also define your niche market.

Personality. You need perseverance, since the time to plan and turn a profit can take a few years; the ability to cope with rejection, since you are likely to experience some; the stamina to start a new venture; and the desire and energy to solicit business. Think about why you are pursuing the goal of having your own business: Are you bored? Looking for a new life experience? Using it as an escape from dealing with other issues? Do you want to make money? Or is it a combination of factors?

Sole proprietorship, joint enterprise, or franchise.

Consider whether you'd like a partner to share the work as well as the profits, or decide if a franchise is a possibility for you. Investments in franchises can range from under $15,000 to $400,000 or more. Check out www.franchisedirect.com or www.franchise.com for more information.

Will it be "everyone back in the (labor) pool"? Some will be pushed in, some will tentatively test the water, some will jump in wholeheartedly, and some will avoid the (labor) pool like hydrophobes.

In summary, instead of retirement being about what you're *not* doing (working, raising a family, rushing from one commitment to another), make it about what you *are* doing (letting your creative juices flow, learning new things, rediscovering yourself and those you love, giving back, and "smelling the roses"). As George Lorimer, editor of the *Saturday Evening Post*, said, "You've got to get up every morning with determination if you're going to go to bed with satisfaction." It's really never too late to start something new—Golda Meir was first elected prime minister of Israel at 71!

true LIFE **Greg B., a CPA and a partner in an international accounting firm, had the financial savvy to put away enough money for himself and his wife, Janie, in planning for his retirement.**

On Greg's 55th birthday, he sat down and made a list of the nonfinancial goals he wanted to accomplish in the second half of his life. Greg listed 17 items, including learning to play tennis left-handed (tennis elbow now precludes him from playing right-handed), making a CD (he has a good singing voice, but has never attempted anything professionally), teaching a class, traveling (there are four specific places he and Janie would like to visit), coaching a team, and writing a book. Greg's list is specific and positive, includes a timetable, and is doable, and he keeps a copy of his goals at his desk as a visual reminder. Approaching his "wish list" in this way makes it much more likely to become a reality. ⓣⓛ

A retired friend, when asked why he seemed so busy, said: "All I can tell you is that when I wake up in the morning, I have absolutely nothing to do, and when I go to bed at night, I am only half finished."

3

WHAT ARE THE OPPORTUNITIES FOR TRAVEL?

"The world is a book, and those who do not travel read only a page."
—Saint Augustine

Dreaming about that once-in-a-lifetime South Seas vacation? Considering comforting children in an orphanage in Yaroslavl, Russia? Single and interested in travel? Disabled but wish to take a trip? Longing to meet emperor penguins in Antarctica nose to beak? Want an educational vacation, or looking for a place to take the grandkids?

Where can you find the best options for a last-minute getaway? How do you feel confident you're getting a bargain? Let's take a look at some specific aspects of travel. It can be an exciting and rewarding way to spend some of those 168 hours per week as you reprogram your time in the second half of your life.

WHERE TO START

The first thing to think about is your destination. If you have the desire to travel, are not in the mood for a repeat trip to your favorite spot, and are feeling adventurous, these Web sites will be the encouragement you need to branch out and take a leap.

www.about.com/travel will make you feel more confident in choosing a novel location. Here you'll find information about what visitors need to know when traveling in Europe, the United States, or Asia. Find out about the latest budget travel tips, the best

B&Bs, or maybe the latest SCUBA diving information.

www.ricksteves.com/tours has been conducting all-inclusive budget tours since the 1970s. Rick Steves also publishes a series of guidebooks that concentrates on Europe and has had a travel show on PBS since 1991.

www.officialtravelinfo.com helps with destination information, vacation planning, and tourism information and provides virtual tours. Click on a map to choose your desired location. It can be fun to take a virtual tour in Africa, even if you have no plans to travel there.

www.go-today.com offers city and country packages, cruises, and unique tours at budget prices.

www.towd.com. As the Web site states, "The directory lists only official government tourism offices, convention and visitors bureaus, chambers of commerce, and similar agencies which provide free, accurate, and unbiased information to the public. No travel agents, no tour operators, no hotels."

www.atlasnavigator.com links to virtually every airline, airport, hotel chain, and car-rental agency in the world.

www.infohub.com lists 11,000 guided or self-guided vacation options. Some categories to consider: trips geared to active or soft adventure, families, hobbies, romance, spirituality, culture and history, sports, and nature and wildlife. You can also read travel stories and learn about these trips and the guides who lead them.

www.shawguides.com. *Forbes* and the *Wall Street Journal* pick this as a top site to give you literally thousands of choices for learning and creative career programs worldwide. Just a few: cultural travel, cooking schools, golf and tennis schools, photography workshops, language vacations, and writers conferences and workshops.

www.tripadvisor.com provides "unbiased reviews of hotels, resorts, and vacations." If you're trying to decide what kind of vacation you would like to take—island, Europe, Las Vegas, adventure, etc.—Trip Advisor has good articles and reviews to help you decide.

www.resortquest.com has more than 20,000 vacation rental condominiums, villas, and homes in 16 states as well as in Canada.

According to Cruise America, the top 10 vacations for 2003 were time with family, the beach, outdoor trips, amusement parks, cultural trips, adventure travel, cruises, historical experiences, fishing expeditions, and escorted tours.

www.applevacations.com, www.tntvacations.com, www.funjet.com, and www.vacationexpress.com allow you to peruse different packages, then either book online or through a travel agent (Apple Vacations can be booked only through a travel agent).

 Planning can be vital.

Debbie, a retired community college professor, and Steve W., a retired executive from AT&T, wanted to hike, along with their three grown children, to the bottom of the Grand Canyon and spend the night there at Phantom Ranch, then hike up the next morning.

Since Phantom Ranch has such limited space, they called exactly 2 years prior to their trip, the longest advance reservations that the national park will allow. They were lucky and reserved five spots—within minutes, everything at the bottom was booked. They are looking forward to their trip over Memorial Day weekend 2005! ⑴

According to the Travel Industry Association of America, adults 55 and over account for one-third of all trips taken within the United States.

BE AN AIR COURIER

With overtones of Mata Hari or Agent 007, air couriers might seem to exist in a murky area of semilegitimate travel. Nothing could be further from the truth. Air couriers transport packages on overseas flights in exchange for reduced airfare—or sometimes even for free. Courier travel is overseen by the Federal Aviation Administration and has been around for 30 years. The concept behind courier travel is this: If time is of the essence in getting such things as legal or financial documents or computer-related parts from point A to point B, having a courier accompany them will get parcels through customs more quickly than if they are sent as cargo.

As an air courier, one needs to be flexible. Since you usually are not allowed to touch what you are ferrying, the package(s) go as part of your checked baggage, often permitting only one carry-on bag for yourself. You can generally make arrangements 1 to 3 months ahead of time. Last-minute opportunities with even larger savings over the usual 20-85 percent savings on airfare are also possible. You need a passport, and you are responsible for obtaining any necessary visas.

Of course, *where* you go will be dictated by the company's need. Popular destinations include Europe, the Far East, Mexico, and South America. Departures tend to be from major cities (New York, Miami, Chicago), and it's the courier's responsibility to get to these cities. You arrive at the airport, and someone from the company meets you there to assist you while you check in. When you deplane, you are again met by another agent from the company, to whom you hand over your baggage claim and shipping papers, and you're done. Unless you're also functioning as a courier on your return flight, you can go back according to your prearrangement with the company (usually from a few days to several months later). Note that being a courier is most often a one-person deal. If you have a travel companion, that person would be on his or her own for airfare. Keep in mind that being a courier is a function of supply and demand. Courier companies charge the couriers higher airfares when there are more people willing to travel. During the "off" traveling times (winter and fall), your round-trip air prices will be much more attractive than during prime tourist season.

Okay, but how do you actually *do* it? Courier associations act as the intermediary between you and the courier companies. There is an annual membership fee ranging from $25 to $50 for access to the information. Contact these companies, which have been in existence for several years: Air Courier Association (www.aircourier.org or 800-282-1202); International Association of Air Travel Couriers (www.courier.org or 308-632-3273); or Courier Travel (www.couriertravel.org or 866-470-3061). Another route is to approach courier companies directly, but there is a lot of turnover among these organizations. One to try: Global Delivery Systems (www.globaldelsys.com or 800-995-2210).

DISCOUNT TRAVEL

Chances are, the person sitting next to you on the airplane did not pay the same price for his or her ticket that you did. Two staterooms on a cruise liner boasting the same amenities can also have very different price tags.

What kind of shopper are you? Are you a full-price purchaser, ready to buy what you want when you want it? Are you willing to put up with the hassle of bargain shopping? Does price matter to you? If it does, and you look at getting a good deal as a challenge, keep reading and you'll find no end to the bargains available for travel. These budget tips work especially well for retirees, since many are last-minute opportunities, and retirees tend to be more spontaneous because time is not the ruling factor in their lives.

The best tool to use in bargain shopping for travel is the Internet—it will become your best travel agent. When choosing a Web site, find one that is easy for you to navigate since the market's flooded with sites, and you have many from which to choose. Check multiple sites carefully before trusting that one's rates are indeed the lowest. Use your own experiences from past travel as a comparison, and make a few phone calls directly to a hotel or airline, the old-fashioned way, just to be sure. There are also Web sites that post comments from fellow travelers revealing the positive and the negative aspects of their budget travel experience. One way to look at bargain shopping for travel is that your savings can fund your next trip! So, if words like "discount," "budget," "bargain," "good deal," and "cut-rate" are music to your ears, let your fingers do the walking through the Internet, and start packing!

Where to Stay

Where to rest your weary head? Many budget options exist, including renting a villa, condo, or home for short-

Check your e-mail for free at a public library while you're vacationing.

term or lengthy stays, or finding the ideal bed & breakfast or hotel. There are some outstanding places to stay that do not fit into the usual categories: many active-adult communities offer an inexpensive package for a 2- to 4-day visit in exchange for a few hours of your time, universities offer rooms at reasonable prices in vibrant locations during their summer sessions, and even 4- or 5-star hotels offer lower prices if you know when to go. As with any agreement you enter into, however, *caveat emptor* (let the buyer beware). There can be restrictions, fees, penalties, etc., when booking travel, so read everything carefully!

www.globalfreeloaders.com is a free service that has more than 6,000 people in 100 countries willing to let you stay at their home for free (you need to be willing to do the same).

www.roomsaver.com allows you to print coupons from your computer for motels, hotels, and resorts.

www.welcome.cottages.co.uk (44-0-1756-799999) enables you to view, inside and out, more than 3,000 vacation cottages in England, Scotland, Wales, Ireland, and France. A quarter million people have booked using this site in a year's time. Customers report back on their experiences through a questionnaire, which allows any problems to be promptly caught and addressed.

www.thistlehotels.com (0870-333-9292) offers "4-star hotels in 5-star locations" including more than 55 properties in London and countryside locations throughout Britain. Find bargain-priced London hotels or super weekend specials.

www.evergreenclub.com (815-456-3111) is the "champion of the cost-conscious vacationer," according to *Frommer's Budget Travel Magazine* (September 2000). Joining the Evergreen Club ($60 for one person, $75 for two), allows people over 50 to access private homes and stay for rates of less than $25 per day for two people. Hosts provide clean, comfortable accommodations, hearty breakfasts, and acquaint you with their area. Most accommodations are located in North America.

www.lasvegas.com (800-642-8158) is a guide to bargains in Las Vegas (including shows, tours, and golf), as well as an opportunity to browse all the available hotels using a rating system that allows you to compare amenities and price.

www.vacationrentals.com is a service for rental owners and renters. If you wish to rent, just click on the desired vacation location (both U.S. and international) and contact the property owner directly. You may also list, for free, a property you would like to rent out.

www.travelaxe.com (fax 512-857-0895) is a free program you can download (presently available only to Microsoft Windows users) that compares prices from 20 Web sites for hotel rates in almost 900 cities in 50 different countries. Book your room right online.

www.ase.net searches more than 200,000 accommodations throughout the world and permits you to select the type of lodging, amenities, and price range you desire. This search engine can also show the results in different languages and display prices in various currencies.

www.hotels.com (800-246-8357 in the United States and Canada; 00800-1066-1066 in Europe; 1-469-335-5825 elsewhere) claims to "have the best prices at the best places. Guaranteed." With more than 7,000 locations in 300 major destinations worldwide, this Web site has an extensive list of offerings.

www.quikbook.com (800-789-9887) has received kudos from *Conde Nast Traveler*, *Forbes Best of the Web*, and *Frommers.com*. Quikbook promises no ads or pop-ups, just great values on upscale hotels without charging for cancellations or changes to your reservation. Choose from premier collections, seaside favorites, hip hotels, historic hotels, spa retreats, and many more.

www.bbonline.com (615-868-1946) allows you to choose from 4,500 bed and breakfasts in the United States, Canada, Mexico, and the Caribbean with the help of 15,000 color pictures. The site even entices you with more than 2,000 "Innkeeper Tested and Guest Approved" recipes!

www.innsite.com provides information, by location or activity, on bed and breakfasts, country inns, and small luxury hotels in more than 50 countries.

www.hiayh.org (301-495-1240) proves that hostels aren't just for young people! This Web site will lead you to affordable accommodations in its 110 U.S. locations priced from $10 to $30 and more than 4,000 locations in 60 other countries.

Timeshares

You can create a mini-vacation by signing up for a promotional stay offered by the timeshare industry. Even if you have no intention of buying, you can enjoy these resort areas and learn what they have to offer. If you spend a few hours listening to their pitch, you can take advantage of a short stay in a nice area at a greatly reduced price. Or, check to see if a timeshare resort is close to where you are planning to vacation and stay a few extra days, or perhaps receive a gift certificate to an area restaurant for your time. Only about 10 percent of the visitors are actually persuaded to purchase a timeshare. Look into offers from the Marriott Vacation Club International (www.vacationclub.

com or 800-259-1104), the Hyatt Vacation Club (www.hyatt.com or 800-926-4447), or the Ritz Carlton Club (www.ritzcarltonclub.com or 800-221-5780).

Developing Communities

Along the lines of a timeshare vacation, you might enjoy staying in or near a developing community, with an orientation and a tour of the neighborhood as part of the package. Rates vary but usually include use of the facilities, breakfast and/or dinner, and perhaps a round of golf. For example, you can visit Del Webb's Sun City Hilton Head (you actually stay at the Hampton Inn & Suites) for $69 per night. Contact www.suncity.com or 800-808-8088. Similar offers can be enjoyed at many developing communities, such as the Robson Communities in Arizona or Texas (www.robson.com or 800-732-9949), or WCI Communities, which offer preferred guest getaways in 33 locations in Florida. Check it out at www.wcicommunities.com (click on the "WCI Story" then "WCI Magazine,"

then "Preferred Guest Getaway" or call 800-924-2290). This is also a strategy for choosing a place to relocate, since you have an opportunity to interact with residents and really get a feel for the community.

Universities

Do you remember dormitory life way back when? Many universities, both stateside and internationally, will give you the chance to relive that experience when the students are away for the summer. Trinity College, Dublin (www.tcd.ie/conferences/visitor.htm or 353-1-608-1177), has been renting rooms for 20 years through Summer Hotel from mid-June to late September. Interested in Vienna, Salzburg, or Graz, Austria? Try www.academia-hotels.co.at or 43-1-40176, ext. 55 or 77. Rates with a bath and breakfast begin at 37 euros per day. For more than 100 sites in Britain and Ireland, explore www.venuemasters.com. In the States, contact the college or university directly for availability and rates. As an example, Catholic University of

How about staying in a monastery? Prices are extremely reasonable, though there may be curfews, the settings can be a bit isolated, and language may be a challenge if you choose a "silent" monastery or one that's outside the United States. For specifics, see www.bandb.about.com and enter "monastery" in the search bar. Your visit will be heavenly!

America in Washington, D.C., charges $30 per night (pretax, double occupancy) with a minimum seven-night stay for an air-conditioned room with a kitchen and bath.

Bid Your Price

If you're one who enjoys leaving it up to chance, you might like to try "blindfold bookers." These Web sites ask you to bid on lodging, flights, rental cars, or vacation packages. You usually have a short time to decide and sometimes do not know exactly which hotel or airline you're getting, but once you bid (and it's accepted), it's yours! The hotels are rated, the airlines usually guarantee no more than one stop, and the prices are great.

The downside? Your credit card is immediately charged, and you may not be able to make any changes once your offer is accepted. If plans change, you're stuck. In addition, some sites add on a processing fee to each transaction. Better think about trip insurance if you go this route and if there's any chance you'd have to change plans (although keep in mind trip insurance doesn't cover everything, either!).

Some to look into: www.priceline.com (name your price, and find out the details after you pay); www.skyauction.com (start the bidding at $1); and www.ebay.com/travel (where you can sell as well as buy all things travel related).

Last-Minute Deals

These Web sites are great for the spontaneous traveler who is looking for adventure and is ready to go at the drop of a hat. These opportunities can come and go very quickly, so if you see something perfect, grab it, but keep in mind that you probably won't be able to make changes or cancel your trip after you book it.

- www.site59.com (packages only, with special prices from airlines and hotels. "Choose your flights, hotel, and car," they boast. "Earn miles on flights. Buy from 3 hours to 14 days prior to departure. Fifty-six departure cities, and more on the way!")
- www.11thhourvacations.com (cruises, flights, hotels, and vacation packages)
- www.lastminutetravel.com (cruises, cars, hotels, and flights)

More than 60 percent of pleasure travelers in the United States plan a vacation within 2 weeks of their departure, according to the Travel Industry Association of America. No wonder the last-minute travel sites are booming!

- www.moments-notice.com (annual membership fee of $25 required)
- www.hotwire.com (more last-minute deals)

true LIFE **Kathy B. and her husband, John, live in Ponte Vedra Beach, Florida, after relocating from the Midwest. Here is Kathy's description of using a discount travel site.**

My husband and I have been "cruising" for 20 years. Our protocol is always the same. We sit down with a travel consultant at a cruise shop, plan our trip, they send us the documents, and off we go.

This year I decided to take my mom on a cruise. She is 81, still in great shape, and has wanted to take a cruise her entire life. One of my friends told me about a Web site called vacations-to-go.com, so I tried it. The site lists its top 10 cruises each week at greatly reduced prices, plus discusses the status of the travel industry in general. I called their 800 number and spoke to a very knowledgeable and professional travel consultant. He explained the various offerings as we looked at them together on the Web site. I booked the cruise at a 67 percent discount from the published brochure rate.

The travel consultant gave me his cell phone number and his e-mail address. Anytime I had a question or concern, I would e-mail him in the evening and the next morning I would have his answer. I had told him I was a little concerned about my mom having to walk down those long halls, so our room was very close to the elevator, in the middle of the ship.

We were on Holland America's *Zaandam*. Our room was a luxurious mini-suite with a balcony, sitting room, fresh flowers, our own personal engraved stationery, and a fabulous bathroom with a Jacuzzi. Vacations-to-go.com . . . the only way to travel! tL

HOME/HOSPITALITY EXCHANGE

Want to live like the locals? Stay in a neighborhood, shop where they shop, maybe drive their car, almost literally walk a mile in their shoes? If this type of travel appeals to you, consider a home exchange or hospitality exchange. Home exchanges allow you to use someone else's home while they are using yours. Or, you could go the route of a hospitality exchange. In this type of arrangement, you alternate hosting one another in your homes. There are about three quarters of a million people per year swapping

PLANES, TRAINS, AND AUTOMOBILES

Some of these sites are specific to transportation; others allow searches for hotels or vacation packages as well.

* www.expedia.com (allows you to preview some destinations through a slide show)
* www.johnnyjet.com (deals in all categories)
* www.travelocity.com (deals in all categories)
* www.qixo.com (includes Southwest among its airfare sites, which is unusual)
* www.southwest.com (if Southwest flies from an airport near you, it's worth checking out their travel center)
* www.digitalcity.com/travel (lets you check out visitor information for the chosen city)
* www.smarterliving.com (lets you sign up to be notified of last-minute travel deals)
* www.airtreks.com ("We make around-the-world travel easy and affordable.")
* www.ryanair.com (low-cost European airline)
* www.orbitz.com (offers flexible stays, weekends, and bonus days options that you can use to search for cheaper travel times)
* www.raileurope.com (offers special savings if you're over 60)
* www.amtrak.com (click on "Savings and Promotions" for some attractive deals)
* www.sidestep.com (allows you to check out dozens of sites at the same time)

homes, and this number is increasing all the time. If you're considering a particular location for retirement, a home exchange might be the perfect way to "try out" a place.

There are obvious financial benefits to home or hospitality exchanges. The cost of hotel rooms is inching upward, and depending on the size of your group, you may need more than one hotel room. With a home exchange you have access to a full kitchen and all the comforts of home (or apartment, yacht, condo, RV, etc.). In addition, you can be immersed in the area and live where "real" people live. If you go the hospitality exchange route, you'll also have built-in tour guides for your visit and may end up making lifelong friends.

The downside? Well, of course, it's all a matter of trust. Several months prior to your trip, it's a good idea to engage in conversations via e-mail, phone, or letters to get a sense of your swappers and the particulars about the residence. Also, there could be a question of parity. Switching a 1,000-square-foot apartment in Washington, D.C., for a veritable chateau in France may not seem equal, but this should not be the point in home exchanges. Housekeeping standards can be an issue as well, if your cleanliness habits differ appreciably. The abilities to be flexible in your scheduling, to compromise, and to plan in advance are important qualities for this type of travel.

When choosing a company to list or search properties, there are several things worth noting. When listing your home, provide a photo and be honest about its amenities. If you are exchanging cars, it's probably a good idea to get a contract (Global Home Exchange offers a sample on their Web site). Obtain insurance in case the trip is cancelled by either party. Make room in your closets for your visitors. Secure or remove any items you don't want used. Inform your neighbors there will be visitors so they can welcome them (and not call the police!). Come to a prior agreement on such things as phone and electric bills. Leave a guide containing information about your home's appliances, your area's attractions, contacts for repairs, etc. In general, being up-front and taking time to plan go a long way.

CRUISIN' THE USA

Since 9/11, more people have elected to vacation closer to home, traveling to places they can drive to themselves. So, though piling the kids in the van or station wagon every summer may be a thing of the past for you, this mode of travel is now at an all-time high.

And it's not just travel by car. Purchases of motorcycles and recreation vehicles have increased, notably among baby boomers. People who have never bought a motorcycle in their lives are now "easy riders"—in fact, about 33 percent of Harley customers are first-time purchasers, and the surge in buyers over 40 has increased the average age of new Harley owners to 45 years old. Recreational vehicle acquisition has also seen a significant increase, with almost 1 in 12 Americans owning an RV. A 2001 University of Michigan study found that among those who are 55 years and older, nearly 10 percent own an RV.

If you go the route of driving yourself when you travel, there are several options to ease your journey on the long and winding road. Almost everyone is familiar with the American Automobile Association (AAA). This organization has been in existence for over a century, and boasts more than 40 million members in the United States and Canada. Perks of membership include road service, maps, towing, TripTiks (which can be printed from your computer), tour books, books listing RV sites and campgrounds, recommended driving trips, insurance, discounts, and other services. Membership fees are approximately $55 annually but can vary if you add additional members of the family to your plan or wish to extend your coverage options. With various AAA discounts, the membership fee more than pays for itself.

There are also several clubs specifically for RVers, such as the Good Sam Club, Coast to Coast, and Good Neighbor Club (access all through www.rv.net) and Escapees RV Club (www.escapees.com). If you're single,

---

According to a 2001 HomeExchange.com survey, 75 percent of home exchangers are 45 years or older, and about 33 percent have annual incomes of more than $100,000.

HOME/HOSPITALITY EXCHANGE INFORMATION

A sizable number of organizations are in the business of home/hospitality exchanges.

- HomeExchange.com
  (www.HomeExchange.com or 800-877-8723).
  You can access the available homes for free, but
  in order to list your home, you pay a $49.95
  annual membership fee. This site also provides
  a guide called "Trading Places" that includes
  sample contact letters and agreements. You can
  also click on the "seniors" link. Some feel better
  dealing with people closer to the same age or
  figure they could exchange for longer periods
  of time if children's schedules aren't an issue.

- Diggsville.com (www.digsville.com or 800-856-
  9059) charges $49.95 per year to list your
  property, with free access for posted listings.

- Intervac Home Exchange (www.intervacUS.com
  or 800-756-4663) has been around the longest
  (50 years) and boasts the largest percentage
  of international listings, about 80 percent.
  Depending on type of membership (Web or
  Web and printed material), fees range from
  $50 to $149 per year.

- Global Home Exchange (www.4homex.com or
  250-756-6177) is a Canadian company that
  charges approximately $29.95 per year (U.S.)
  for membership.

- Accessible Vacation Home Exchange (www.in-
  dependentliving.org, then click on "Vacation
  Home Exchange") is an exchange organization
  that specializes in homes that are accessible to
  the physically disabled.

that doesn't mean you have to go it alone. Several clubs include Loners on Wheels (www.lonersonwheels.com), Retired Singles (www.retiredsingles.com), and RVing Women (www.RvingWomen.com or 888-55-RVING), which, as the name implies, is for females who either own an RV or would like to become part of the RV lifestyle.

You can also become part of a pack if you choose to travel by cycle. The American Motorcyclist Association (AMA) was founded in 1924 and has more than 250,000 members. It provides services similar to those of AAA, with an annual fee of $39. Great American Motorcycle Touring (www.greatamericantouring.com or 800-727-3390) offers 7-day trips of approximately 1,000 miles to various scenic places in the United States. No bike? No problem! You can rent one through GAMT if you don't own one or don't wish to ship or drive yours to the departure city. Retreads Motorcycle Club International (www.retreads.org) has two requirements to join: a love of biking and an age of at least 40.

true LIFE **Jeanne M., a semiretired actress residing in New York City, shares some thoughts about her home exchange experience.**

Do I like to travel? Is the Pope Catholic? I went to the library to do a little research and settled on an outfit called Homelink. Along with a membership fee of $70, I filled out an application stating what my living space has to offer, and listing three preferred destinations, lengths of stay, etc. Mine were Italy, Ireland, and small European towns—a bit of a change from New York City.

I was thrilled with the many calls for exchanges and was trying to decide among Italy, France, and Germany, when I got a call from Athlone, Ireland, from a nice young couple with a baby girl. It had been my dream to get to Ireland, specifically Cork, the ancestral town of my maternal grandmother. The woman sounded ever so delightful. So many things make up a decision—each of us has our own priorities in rating where we might go—but all things fit together for me with this central site in the heartland of Ireland.

One can propose her own terms, of course. I needed a car if I was going to get around the Emerald Isle, despite the fact I had no car to offer in return—but who needs a car in Manhattan?! I felt the trade was fair and so did they, so we agreed over the phone. We exchanged a few photos of our

---

You can purchase CDs or cassettes that discuss the history, stories, side trips, and landmarks of an area through a company called Ride with Me (www.rwmaudio.com or 800-752-3195). These audio companions are synchronized with the milepost markers. Selections can be by route number, state, national park, or favorite place. There are about 100 domestic audio tours available, as well as a few international tours.

places and persons, including some friends' addresses and numbers, etc.

In any case, for extended stays and getting a true taste of the culture and customs, home exchange is an excellent habitat, not to mention the money saved and the making of new friends. I think it's the only way to go—and you don't need the exact equivalency. For instance, when the mayor of Rome called me, he wanted an apartment in mid-Manhattan and that's what I have. OK, not big enough, so he offered me his beach house instead! Everyone has to do what they're comfortable with at heart. Happy trails! Ⓛ

SOLO TRAVEL

The single traveler is anything but alone! The Travel Industry Association notes that this segment of the travel business accounted for 27 percent of all U.S. travel in 2001—a staggering 47 million middle-aged singles (average age 45) took a solo trip. Although some of these were business trips, leisure travel accounted for almost 70 percent. Older working singles (average age 64) and older retired singles (average age 72) had a combined 58 million trips in 2001. The increase in the number of single people, coupled with the affluence of these age groups, has contributed to this fast-growing trend.

Many people feel comfortable traveling alone, responsible only for themselves in choosing an itinerary, selecting restaurants, arranging their schedule, etc. The once-upon-a-time perceived stigma of a woman traveling alone has largely disappeared, although common sense should be exercised whether you are male or female.

If you're contemplating traveling solo, but are a little uncomfortable with the concept, travel guru Arthur Frommer recommends considering volunteer or learning vacations. A trip that has an outer-directed goal with like-minded participants often works well. Earthwatch, the Sierra Club,

---

Sick of country music as you drive through the middle of nowhere? Crave a national news report? Hate being bombarded by commercials? Consider satellite radio. Purchase a receiver for under $200, pay a monthly fee of about $15, and you can have access to around 100 streams of commercial-free music, news, sports, and/or entertainment. As an example, check out the possibilities at www.sirius.com.

Elderhostel, the Omega Institute, and Habitat for Humanity all sponsor these types of trips. For more specifics on this kind of travel, see the section on "Volunteer Vacations" in this chapter and the suggested reading.

If you're looking for trips that cater to mature singles, several companies fit the bill. Club Med (www.clubmed.com or 888-932-2582) touts Paradise Island in the Bahamas and La Caravelle in Guadeloupe as the preferred locations for mature singles. Windjammer Barefoot Cruises (www.windjammerbarefoot.com or 877-578-1301) has sailings designated specifically for singles. Celebrity, Cunard, Crystal, Seabourn, Silversea, Radisson, and Holland America are other cruise lines to investigate and often provide "gentleman hosts" for dancing and dining. Of course, if you're a man looking to socialize, choosing one of these cruise lines would be good planning as well. Adventure travel also attracts large numbers of mature singles—try Overseas Adventure Travel (www.oattravel.com or 800-955-1925) or Backroads (www.backroads.com, and enter "solo" into the search bar, or call 800-462-2848).

If you are happy traveling alone but don't want to underwrite the cost of a room/cabin by yourself, you also have several options. Often, the cruise line or company (such as Club Med) will arrange a roommate to avoid the single supplement charge for singles staying in a double room. Occasionally, single supplement charges will be waived—it never hurts to ask! There are several organizations that will set you up with a roommate as well. O Solo Mio (www.osolomio.com or 800-959-8568) has been around for more than 10 years and arranges singles' tours both nationally and internationally. O Solo Mio will match you with a person of similar age, smoking preferences, and sleeping habits (i.e., night owl or early bird). Travel Companion Exchange (www.travelcompanions.com or 631-454-0880) has been in business more than 20 years and matches travelers (same and opposite sex) through a list of "profile pages" that are shared among members. There is a membership fee of $199 for 6 months or $298 per year. All Singles Travel (www.allsinglestravel.com or 800-717-3231) will also match you with a roommate to avoid the single supplement.

How about touring Europe or Mexico by RV? For more information, contact Rolling Home Press (www.rollinghomes.com or 425-822-7846) or check out books by Mike and Terri Church: *Traveler's Guide to European Camping* **and** *Traveler's Guide to Mexican Camping.*

More daring is the free classified ad service you can access through Aim-Higher Travel (www.aim-higher.com/singlestravel or 877-752-1858). This organization has been in business since 1998 and also deals in singles' cruises and tours. Other possibilities for finding traveling companions include the free message boards on www.Frommers.com (check out "share a trip" in the message board section) and www.TravelChums.com, where you can fill out a questionnaire online. Both of these services are free, but the demographics of TravelChums reflect a younger group; more than 80 percent of its members are under the age of 55. Mature Tours (www.hometown.aol.com/soloflights or 800-266-1566) is a division of Solo Flights that caters to the 50-and-over group. Another service includes Connecting: Solo Travel Network (www.cstn.org or 800-557-1757), which has its headquarters in Canada. This company provides information on sharing trips and provides suggestions for travel, lodgings, etc., for those taking a trip without a partner. Fees are $25 per year for Internet membership and $35 per year for regular mail subscriptions.

Finally, clubs exist for the solo traveler. One possibility is Going Solo Travel Club, a division of Premiere Travel Centre (www.goingsolotravel.com or 888-446-7656). It doesn't require a membership fee.

If you're female, there are travel groups designed specifically for you. Women Traveling Together (www.women-traveling.com or 410-956-5250) is located in Edgewater, Maryland. Its Web site makes it clear that you do not have to be single (just traveling solo) and that it is not a lesbian group. Participants generally range from their thirties to their sixties. A more recent addition to all-women travel is Gutsy Women Travel, an offshoot of Maupin Tour, a half-century-old company specializing in escorted vacations that utilize

If you're a single man between the ages of 45 and 72 and would like to be a "gentleman host," apply to the cruise lines directly or to a site such as the Working Vacation (www.theworkingvacation.com or 708-301-7535) or Sixth Star Entertainment and Marketing (www.sixthstar.com or 954-462-6760). In most cases, gentlemen hosts pay the cruise line between $28 and $38 a day. Their hosting services are considered voluntary. In exchange, they receive cabin accommodations, dining privileges, complimentary shore excursions, and sometimes airfare.

the services of a knowledgeable guide. Gutsy Women Travel can be contacted at www.gutsywomentravel.com or 866-464-8879. More people than ever are traveling solo, but if you're hoping for a roommate to share expenses, searching for like-minded people, or looking to join a group composed of others traveling without partners, there is help out there!

GROUP TRAVEL

More than a quarter of the U.S. population is over 50, and by 2020 the number is expected to increase by one-third. This may be news to you, but it's not news to tour companies! Travel companies are cropping up to cater exclusively to the mature traveler (50 to 55 and older), and companies that have been in existence for many years recognize the power of the baby boomer market. Senior travelers are more often than not interested in the ease and comfort that a tour affords. Travel companies that court seniors offer soft adventure, luxury cruises, educational opportunities, and tours that combine all three!

Making the decision to travel with a group instead of traveling on your own seems to be a path many boomers are taking. Tour companies eliminate the planning details, and for the budget conscious, tours are often the better bargain. When airfares, hotels, and food are purchased in great quantities, the price goes down (of course, you do sacrifice spontaneity). Tours that are designed for the mature traveler give more attention to health and mobility issues, with slower-paced days and comfortable nights. Some even promise that you won't need to have your suitcase ready by 6 A.M. everyday!

A good place to start looking if you are interested in booking a tour would be the companies that have been in existence for many years. These companies specialize in tours that vary greatly in cost, from budget to luxury. Most travel companies will customize a tour for you if you provide your own group consisting of 15 people or more. Dozens of good companies exist.

Collette (www.collettevacations.com or 800-340-

Keep in mind that there is no guarantee of compatibility or safety when joining a pay service or accessing free match-up sites. In general, organizations where you pay a fee for services tend to attract fewer "undesirables."

5158). Collette offers deluxe travel to over 50 countries and has been in business since 1918. Their tours are priced from $100 to $350 per person, per day, not including airfare.

Grand Circle Tours (www.grandcircletravel.com or 800-959-0405). In existence since 1958, GCT agrees with John Steinbeck that "people don't take trips, trips take people." Prices vary greatly, as do the locations.

Travcoa (www.travcoa.com or 800-992-2003). Travcoa is "blazing new trails in 90 countries around the world with visiting lecturers giving special insights into the history, politics, or art of the region. You need not worry about your accommodations; everything will be first class." Luxury tours begin at $400 a day, per person, airfare not included.

Globus and Cosmos Tours (www.globusandcosmos. com or 866-755-8581/800-276-1241). These two huge travel companies offer great group travel. Prices range from $60 to $300 per day, per person, including airfare.

Tauck Tours (www.tauck.com or 800-788-7885). A family business with almost 80 years of experience, and more than half of its travelers repeat customers, Tauck has won many awards and is known for its all-inclusive, upscale travel.

Trafalgar Tours (www.trafalgar-tours.net) has been in existence for over 55 years. Take escorted motorcoach tours to a variety of destinations worldwide. One of the authors accompanied her elderly mother, along with two sisters, on a nine-day tour of Italy. Although some excursions were extra, and the hotels were mediocre, prices were reasonable, and they enjoyed the services of a terrific tour guide.

"Soft" Adventure Travel

If the same old trip to the beach doesn't sound like enough this year, give some thought to learning new skills and trying them out in a fresh place. Many mature travelers are ready and willing to try a new venture, especially with a group of their peers and the promise of creature comforts at the end of the day. There is no end to the opportunities if you are ready to take the plunge. An adventure cruise with Elderhostel will take you sailing on the Dingle Peninsula of Ireland, or maybe you would like to explore the Galapagos Islands. Perhaps you'd like to start out easy and ride a bike from Cumberland, Maryland, to the nation's capital and stay at upscale bed and breakfasts along the way. Whatever you choose to do, and wherever you choose to do your adventure, there is a trip for you.

Abercrombie and Kent. This tour company has been in business for 40 years and offers upscale adventure tours on all seven continents. Expect the very best in ac-

CYBERSPACE AWAITS!

Ready for more? Take a stab at these additional Internet sites and explore the many options you have. There is a lot of overlap among sites, so get comfortable, and start exploring from the coziness of your computer chair.

✳ SmarTours (www.smartours.net or 800-337-7773) has one goal: "top-quality, exciting tours at the lowest possible price." Highlights include airfare on major scheduled airlines, deluxe and first-class hotels, and professional English-speaking tour guides.

✳ If you're traveling on a budget or looking for that luxurious, once-in-a-lifetime trip or something in between, www.tourvacationstogo.com (800-338-4962) will provide itineraries from the world's leading tour companies, giving you options and prices in an instant. To choose a vacation, search this site by region, tour company, or specialty, or pick from specially priced tour packages.

✳ University of New Hampshire Continuing Education (www.learn.unh.edu/interhostel or 800-733-9753) sponsors worldwide learning vacations for the mature traveler in cooperation with colleges and universities and similar institutions. Most programs are about two weeks in length. They believe that "life begins at 50 for those of you who love to travel and learn about the cultures of different countries."

✳ Elderhostel (www.elderhostel.org or 877-426-8056) is a nonprofit organization, "the nation's first and the world's largest educational travel organization for older adults." Their literature boasts, "Learn to paint on Nantucket.

commodations. Luxury tours begin at $400 per day, per person, not including air. Contact www.abercrombiekent.com or 800-323-7308.

Country Walkers. Explore new environs on foot with an experienced guide, choosing from 66 worldwide tours. Stroll through a village in Greece or kayak down a river in New Zealand. Country Walkers has more than 23 years of experience, and they promise to deliver an exhilarating adventure. Contact www.countrywalkers.com or 800-464-9255.

New England Hiking Holidays. "Footpaths by day and country inns by night!" Enjoy the expertise of 19

Investigate hot air ballooning with your grandchildren. Join a student orchestra. Study literature in London. Bike the rim of the Grand Canyon. Conduct research to help protect endangered species. If you can imagine it, we probably have a program that does it."

✳ For independent travel to Europe, check out www.go-today.com (425-487-9632). Choose a package trip to Florence, Italy, including airfare, hotel, and rental car or have go-today.com organize a group of 15 or more of your family and friends and enjoy group rates and a planned itinerary.

✳ For escorted, independent, group, and custom-designed tours to international and exotic destinations, try www.gate1travel.com (800-682-3333).

✳ If you are interested in tours to Hawaii, Mexico, the Azores, or Costa Rica, check out Sun Trips (www.suntrips.com or 800-786-8747), in business for over a quarter of a century.

✳ Find cruises, bargain packages, and seasonal specials at www.vacmart.com (800-288-1435).

✳ Love to fly Southwest Airlines? Customize your vacation, beginning with round-trip airfare on Southwest (www.swavacations.com or 800-243-8372), including great prices on hotels (luxury to budget), car rental, area attractions, and more.

✳ If you practice a vegetarian lifestyle, you can travel without concern about food via www.vegetarianusa.com.

years of successful trips and the comfort of knowing that two guides accompany each trip—one for the fast walkers and one for the slightly slower group! Take a walking trip within the United States, Canada, or Europe, or sign up for a multiadventure, which combines walking with kayaking, snorkeling, or biking.

Contact www.nehikingholidays.com or 800-869-0949.

Elder Treks. With a 17-year history, Elder Treks offer adventures on five continents for the 50-plus group. Plow your way through the ice pack to the North Pole on an icebreaker, or explore Mongolia by camel. Contact www.eldertreks.com or 800-741-7956.

Senior Cycling. No one is concerned with how far or how fast you go; you can choose your own level of difficulty. These "old folks on spokes" offer 2- to 10-day bicycle trips throughout the United States. Contact www.seniorcycling.com or 540-668-6307.

Walking the World. Experience the world as an active participant. "You'll get to know an area not by how it looks through the window of a bus, but by its true flavor!" In its 17th season, Walking the World's trips "for people 50 and better" include such places as Costa Rica, New Zealand, Portugal, and the wine regions of California. Contact www.walkingtheworld.com or 800-340-9255.

Elderhostel. With more than 200,000 participants enjoying over 10,000 varied trips in 100 different countries, choosing an adventure will be your greatest problem! Contact www.elderhostel.org or 877-426-8056.

Specialty Travel. Founded in 1980, Specialty Travel features travel and adventure travel information from more than 500 tour operators worldwide. Bungee-jumping in New Zealand, anyone? Contact www.specialtytravel.com or 800-624-4030.

World Wildlife Fund. Travel the world and see spectacular wildlife in its natural habitat. WWF trips are for young adults and active seniors. Contact www.worldwildlife.org/travel or 888-993-8687.

50plus Expeditions. Exotic travel for the 50-and-up group. Trips are rated easy, moderate, or demanding, and locations include the Arctic, Antarctica, Asia, East Africa, Latin America, and North America. Contact www.50plusexpeditions.com or 866-318-5050.

Adventure Network International. This group specializes in Antarctica. You can choose a trip from luxury level to extreme endurance level. Prepare to bundle up! Contact www.adventure-network.com or 866-395-6664.

 Martha and Greg H. climbed Mt. Kilimanjaro with two of their adult children. Here is their account.

While flying above the clouds from Mombasa to

In most cases, your driver's license is all that is necessary to rent or drive a vehicle in another country, but some countries require an international driver's license. Contact an organization such as AAA or the rental agency in the country you are planning to visit for details.

WOMEN-ONLY ADVENTURE TRAVEL

These trips combine the best of adventure with single-sex travel.

✳ www.mariahwomen.com (800-462-7424). "Mariah's women-only trips combine river wilderness adventures with exploring the natural and cultural environments of unique international destinations in the safe and secure company of other women!"

✳ www.adventurewomen.com (800-804-8686). You'll want to be an adventure woman! Founded in 1982, Adventure Women is the oldest women-only adventure travel company for women 30 and older. "Our groups are small and nonsmoking, and trips are rated easy, moderate, or high energy—an activity level for every ability," they state. Choose from 23 different vacations, including hiking, sea kayaking, and cultural and ecological journeys, or maybe follow Marco Polo's footsteps.

✳ www.callwild.com (888-378-1978). For over 25 years, this women-only tour group has been providing adventure travel for women from every walk of life: "Our customers find that a hike through a beautiful stretch of wilderness, followed by a gourmet meal, with good companionship, is a memorable experience."

Nairobi, Kenya, in the summer of 1996, we caught our first glimpse of Ernest Hemingway's "Snows of Kilimanjaro." The sight was so spectacular that we determined we would return to see Mt. Kilimanjaro again. The following July, we flew to Tanzania to climb the famous mountain.

Although there are several tour groups that arrange travel to Tanzania and Mt. Kilimanjaro, we selected Abercrombie and Kent. On day 1 of the climb, we started out early and drove to the Marangu Gate, the park entrance to Mt. Kilimanjaro. We picked up our guides and walking sticks, or ski poles, for the ascent.

As a family of 4, we had 3 guides and 4 porters. We had selected a 6-day round-trip itinerary along the Marangu, the easiest route. At the outset of the hike, we were at 6,000 feet in elevation. For our 3,000-foot climb through the rainforest to our destination of Mandara Huts, we found our raingear to be essential. The path started out as a flat, wide, mud trail. It became steeper and narrower as we continued. We arrived at the Mandara Huts around lunchtime. The remainder of the day was spent resting and adjusting to the altitude. The huts were A-frame in construction, solar-powered, and large enough to sleep 4. One bigger cabin had a dining area downstairs and a dormitory upstairs. Rudimentary pit toilets were available at each of the series of huts along the route.

Day 2's destination was Horombo Huts, a 10-mile hike away through forest and open savannah. We climbed at a *poli-poli* (Swahili for "very slow") pace in order to avoid the headaches and nausea that can accompany the high altitude. At Horombo Huts, we reached 12,334 feet in elevation and were high above the clouds. On day 3, we took an acclimatization walk, which included an elevation change of 1,000 feet, before returning to Horombo Huts to sleep for another night.

On day 4, we awoke early and climbed to the saddle at 15,020 feet, between the peaks of Mawenzi (17,000 feet) on the right and Kibo (19,342 feet) on the left. The barren scenery resembled a moonscape. It was a long and difficult hike, and our breathing became labored. We rested at the Kibo Huts from late afternoon until midnight. At this point, we put on our hiking boots, heavy down coats, and mittens. We also grabbed our flashlights and water, but brought little else for the final ascent to Gilman's Point (18,630 feet) on the rim of the crater. The hike up the switchbacks was steep and awkward, as the ground covering was a thick layer of shale. At sunrise, we watched the sun come up on the way to Gilman's Point. Then we continued to Uhuru Point, the tallest peak in Africa at 19,342 feet. While it was an 8-hour hike from Kibo Huts to Uhuru Point, the view from the top made it all worthwhile.

Our family continued the long day 5 by hiking

Want to test-drive an RV or motorcycle to see if this type of travel appeals to you? Try Cruise America (www.cruiseamerica.com or 480-464-7300), which has 150 rental centers in the United States and Canada.

back down to Horombo Huts. On the final day of the hike, we descended to the base of the mountain. The round-trip distance was 55 miles.

Before undertaking the climb, we each met with a physician and were given Diamox, a drug that stimulates the intake of oxygen, Lariam to prevent malaria, and other immunizations. Abercrombie and Kent did a fantastic job of arranging our trip. Our guides and porters were exceptional, and we would not have made it as far as we did without their supervision and healthy cooking. ⓛ

Learning Vacations

Budget traveler Gary Langer once wrote, "Travelers and tourists, the distinction is simple: tourists are those who bring their homes with them wherever they go, and apply them to whatever they see. They are closed to experiences outside of the superficial. Travelers, however, leave home at home, bringing only themselves and a desire to learn." If you feel as he does and want more out of your next vacation, you may be ready for a learning vacation, or the most fabulous field trip you have ever taken! Check out the following.

www.iiepassport.org (877-4040-EDU). This is a search engine for international study programs.

www.closeup.org/lifelong.htm (800-256-7387). Would you like to spend a week in our nation's capital and learn what makes it work? In cooperation with Elderhostel, the Close Up Foundation offers a five-night program combining a vacation with firsthand knowledge of our nation's capital. You might enjoy the six-night program where the "senior citizen interns learn about the people, processes, and issues involved in the making of public policy."

www.travelearn.com (800-235-9114). With 25 years of experience, "TraveLearn provides international learning vacations for adults ages 30 to 80-plus, which are promoted through more than 300 universities, colleges, and associations nationwide." As an example, you can experience the archaeology, ecology, and culture of Peru during a 16-day excursion that includes lectures and seminars.

www.sjcsf.edu (505-984-6104). Spend a few weeks enjoying Santa Fe in July and participate in a summer seminar at St. John's College reading and discussing great classics in literature, science, history, philosophy, and opera. Tuition and fees are $800 per week.

www.smithsonianjourneys.org (877-338-8687). Smithsonian Journeys has been a leader in educational travel for over 30 years. More than 30,000 travelers have enjoyed the network of resources available to the Smithsonian that make this a unique travel and learning experience. The itineraries vary from a guided tour of the Metropolitan Opera to 17 days in Burma.

www.unex.berkeley.edu/travel (415-252-5229). London theater, China's ancient cities, Sicilian mosaics! "We invite you to take more than just a trip. Please join us for a challenging intellectual adventure." The average age of participants is 50 to 60 years old in this "Travel with Scholars" extension of UC-Berkeley.

www.amnh.org, and click on "Discovery Tours" (800-462-8687). The American Museum of Natural History has been offering educational travel for over 50 years. "More than 20,000 travelers have explored the world on a Discovery Tour—from Pole to Pole and everywhere in between—in the company of AMNH scientists." How about a 10-day trip on the Amazon by riverboat for $3,000 (including airfare from Miami)?

www.metmuseum.org (800-221-1944). Click on "Events and Programs," then "Travel Programs." And what programs they have! You will enjoy reading about these trips even if you never go. "Sail aboard the *Sea Cloud* from Sicily to Athens. Explore Greek Islands and antiquities." Thirteen-day land and cruise rates from $6,000.

Elderhostel and Specialty Travel (see their listing on page 70). also offer a wide variety of educational travel, including biblical tours, cooking tours, and tours that focus on birding, antiquing, creative workshops, and adventures afloat. Plan to spend some time on these Web sites—the opportunities are endless!

www.princess.com (800-PRINCESS). The new educational program on Princess Cruise Lines, cleverly titled ScholarShip@Sea, is on the *Coral Princess*. Classes in computer technology, culinary/creative/visual arts, and other special topics will be offered while the *Coral Princess* cruises Alaska and the Panama Canal.

www.africanamericantravel.com; www.soulplanettravel.com; and www.soulofamerica.com are three travel organizations responding to the needs and desires of African-Americans to patronize African-American-owned bed and breakfasts and hotels, and to participate in African-American culture tours, cruises, etc.

www.gaytravel.com; www.outandabout.com; www.damron.com; and www.gayres.com are sites that cater to the gay traveler. The latter lists gay-friendly hotels around the world.

Volunteer Vacations

Vacation: "A time of respite; a scheduled period during which activity is suspended; a period of exemption from work granted to an employee for rest and relaxation." If Merriam-Webster's definition of "vacation" is accurate, then what does volunteering have to do with vacationing? Most people look upon public service as a punishment issued by a judge in lieu of jail time. It may be difficult to believe, but tens of thousands of people the world over are scheduling time away to be of service to others. The idea is to help yourself while helping others. If retirement seems to be lacking in purpose and fulfillment, take a look at the volunteer travel opportunities that might provide adventure for you and help for those who really need it.

Cross-Cultural Solutions (www.crossculturalsolutions.org or 800-380-4777) is a not-for-profit international volunteer organization that operates in Brazil, China, Costa Rica, Ghana, India, Peru, Russia, Tanzania, and Thailand. The *New York Times* refers to Cross-Cultural Solutions as "akin to a mini-stint with the Peace Corps." Work may include caring for infants, teaching teenagers, helping set up a small business for working adults, as well as providing the local people the opportunity to learn about your culture.

Farm Sanctuary (www.farmsanctuary.org or 607-583-2225 in New York; 530-865-4617 in California) cares for injured, abused, or abandoned farm animals and promotes a vegan lifestyle. You can help out with farm chores or office work. If your interest leans more toward pets than farm animals, contact Best Friends Animal Sanctuary (www.bestfriends.org or 435-644-2001). This is the largest pet sanctuary in the United States, is located near Kanab, Utah, and cares for an astounding 1,800 cats, dogs, and other pets.

Global Volunteers (www.globalvolunteers.org or 800-487-1074) offers more than 150 1-, 2-, and 3-week projects year-round. Volunteers are involved in painting and constructing homes, tutoring schoolchildren, improving public health, and teaching English. Global Volunteers are at work in Costa Rica, China, the Cook Islands, Ecuador, Ghana, Greece, India, Indonesia, Ireland, Italy, Jamaica, Mexico, Northern Ireland, Poland, Puerto Rico, Romania, Spain, St. Croix, Tanzania, Turkey, Ukraine, Vietnam, and 25 communities in the United States.

The Flying Doctors (www.flyingdocs.org or 800-585-4568) enables volunteers to provide nonskilled assistance in setting up a clinic and providing medical and dental services. Volunteers fly in small planes from the San Francisco Bay area to the Copper Canyon area of northern Mexico and villages in Baja California. *Los Medicos Voladores* work the second weekend of each month for 4 days.

Wyoming Dinosaur Center (www.wyodino.org or 307-864-2997) lets you dig for dinosaurs for a day or two from late spring to late fall. Kids' digs and teens' digs are offered during the summer.

Habitat for Humanity (www.habitat.org or 229-924-6935) volunteers work in 83 foreign countries as well as throughout the United States. The opportunities are extensive. If you have an RV or have always wanted to rent one, try RV Care-A-Vanners. This group works with Habitat affiliates in the United States and Canada. A Care-A-Van usually lasts 2 weeks and includes 8 to 10 RV units. Participants travel together and work together at the Habitat sites. Bring tools, energy, enthusiasm, and flexibility! You can e-mail RV Care-A-Vanners at RVinfodesk@hfhi.org.

Earthwatch Institute (www.earthwatch.org or 800-776-0188) is involved in ongoing research run by members of the scientific community. Topics include ecology, zoology, archaeology, world health, and more. Earthwatch provides short-term volunteer opportunities lasting about 10 to 14 days. Some weekend opportunities exist.

American Hiking Society (www.Americanhiking.org or 301-565-6104) provides a rewarding experience while visiting picturesque backcountry locations. Meet new people while constructing footpaths or rebuilding existing trails, cabins, and shelters. Enjoy evenings around the campfire and rest up for another great day outdoors.

Similar Web sites to check are www.wildernessvolunteers.org and www.sierraclub.org.

In general, when researching volunteer vacations, you'll need to find out the specifics from the organization in which you're interested, such as age requirements, your expenses (which can vary tremendously depending on the trip), time frames, any special abilities or physical level required, what to wear, what to bring, how you apply to the program, etc. As far as deductions go, you will need to find out what's eligible from the IRS and your tax advisor. At a minimum, the organization must be nonprofit and tax exempt, which many of these organizations are. Items that may be deductible (assuming you itemize on your tax return) include auto mileage, tolls, parking, food, and lodging. Of course, this only applies if the purpose of the travel is volunteering. Keep careful records! You can call the IRS for help at 800-829-1040; if hearing-impaired, call 800-829-4059.

A volunteer vacation is not an oxymoron. There are hundreds of volunteer organizations around the world just waiting to hear from you!

true LIFE **Joanne Edgar, a consultant for foundations and nonprofit organizations who lives in New York City, has enjoyed numerous Earthwatch expeditions.**

When I was a child, I used to catch holy hell from my mother for digging holes in our front yard. I needed the dirt for the mud pies I served at tea parties for my friends. I'm beyond mud pies now, but my long-forgotten hole-digging abilities came in handy when I found my way to an outpost in northern Manitoba to dig for science.

It was the summer of 2000, and I was one of a slew of intrepid Earthwatch volunteers helping to gather baseline data for a long-term study of global warming. Hole digging was about the only "skill" I brought to this effort, but Earthwatch is used to taking laypeople like me who show up with energy and will. They know how to make us useful.

In this case, we showed up in Churchill, Manitoba, a sparsely populated outpost on the shores of Hudson Bay. The town is known for its polar bears, birds, and the 25,000 Beluga whales that surface every summer. There is no road to Churchill; you fly in or take a 36-hour train from Winnipeg to the end of the line.

Churchill may be far from anywhere, but as our principal investigator, Peter Scott, told us, it is in the center of the North American continent if you don't count Mexico. And as such, it is an ideal place

from which to study global warming. It is home to a rich ecosystem and a large diversity of plants. It has the widest temperature range on earth (from 40 degrees below zero to 90 degrees above).

We were based at the Churchill Northern Studies Center on the grounds of a former rocket-testing site, now one of the premier research institutions of its kind in the world. Our volunteer tasks were varied, but the aim of most everything we did was to calculate carbon content, an indication of global warming.

We learned the true "art" of digging holes: With a machete, we neatly sliced 20-centimeter- by-20- centimeter squares in the tundra at 10-meter intervals. We dug hundreds of these holes. Except for the places where we took samples back to the lab, you could hardly tell we had been there.

We collected every living thing we found in 5-by-5-meter plots (and I mean *everything*, except moss). We took the plants back to the lab, identified the species, weighed and dried them, ground them up, and then fired them in special ovens and weighed the ash to get our measure of carbon content.

We rotated tasks in the field, with one volunteer, whistle at the ready, always on bear watch. Polar bears come ashore in the summer when the ice melts in Hudson Bay, and they usually hang out on their own until the bay freezes again in the fall, a span of time that has been growing as temperatures rise. We couldn't take tuna sandwiches to the field, for example, because bears have a strong sense of smell. And we were not allowed to walk around outside by ourselves. Peter Scott always had a gun in the field, just in case. Since it was light until almost midnight, we had plenty of time to see the sights after our duties were done for the day. Peter knows every nook and cranny of the area, and we saw most of them.

The 5 Earthwatch teams in 2000 set up 5 of the 6 sites for the Long-Term Ecological Research Program study. Peter reported that after only 1 summer's work, they were halfway through the baseline tasks, a process he had expected to take 3 years. That was praise indeed for this volunteer hole-digger. ⒧

true LIFE Charles Morlock of Lake Zurich, Illinois, shares his thoughts on an American Hiking Society volunteer vacation.

At noon, 11 strangers met at the Tyler Creek Campground of the Buffalo National River in north central Arkansas. After brief introductions, everyone set about erecting tents and getting organized. Though most projects involve tenting and alfresco dining, some provide indoor accommodations for those who prefer a bed and roof.

Our host, Zed, the National Park Service ranger, outlined the scope of our project. The needs of the host agency can change during the half year or more between submission of a project and its commencement. In fact, 5 of my 10 projects differed from what had been advertised. We were to build 2 flights of stairs up a steep embankment at one of their historic sites, the old mining community of Rush. The National Park Service had tried several fixes for the problem, but storms kept washing out the steeply sloped gravel trail, so we were to construct the ultimate solution: large steps framed on three sides with 8-by-8-inch timbers.

Next, we all planned the week's meals, divided up kitchen chores for the week, drove into nearby Marshall, purchased 5 grocery carts of food, and organized our provisions in coolers and animal-proof boxes. Food is generally provided by the host agency, so the only cost to volunteers is the $80 registration fee (2002 price). The day ended with a roaring campfire providing a backdrop as the 11 strangers conversed and became acquainted.

We came from Illinois, South Carolina, Alabama, Arizona, and New York, were aged 45 to 75; our group included three married couples, one of whom was honeymooning. Occupations included engineer, teacher, mechanic, housewife, computer programmer, forester, and retirees. The mix was as diverse as on my other projects, and I was the second oldest at 57; it is not atypical to have half the group over 60, with some volunteers well into their seventies and even eighties. I pray that I will still be doing these projects into my seventies!

To fill one afternoon, we were assigned to hike the 10 miles of local trails, clearing them of encroaching underbrush and fallen limbs and trees. Carrying bow saws and loppers, we split into groups and enjoyed the sunny afternoon of trail work. Over the next 3 days, we lugged the 8-by-8 timbers, measured and cut them into 76 sections about 6 feet long, notched their ends, dug parallel troughs for the side pieces across which we placed the notched steps, leveled them, drilled holes through the notched steps and hammered reinforcing bars deep into the earth to secure them,

filled the 6-foot-by-3-foot step area with gravel, and then began the next higher stair. Later, as we stood on the finished stairs and took our group photo, we proudly proclaimed that no storm would ever again wash away this trail, and the 11 former strangers experienced a familial kinship impossible to describe—a feeling I had felt at the conclusion of my 9 prior projects—for laboring cooperatively as we problem-solved, engineered, carried, cut, and dug, and as we cooked, ate, washed dishes, and talked together, invariably creates a new "family," as is evidenced by teary-eyed goodbyes at week's end.

But these projects are not just about hard work. And, as with many of the projects, one "off" day was provided. Usually they are for hiking, but Zed took us for an 8-mile canoe trip down the beautiful and scenic Buffalo River, complete with a picnic on a small island. Quite a day!

More rugged projects are available, which could require backpacking all your gear as many as 10 miles into a wilderness area, setting up a base camp, purifying all drinking water, abstaining from showers, and laboriously digging new trail tread, often on a steep mountainside. The requirements of each project and amenities available are always detailed in the literature, so you can choose whatever type of project appeals to you, and projects are available all over the country.

What better way is there to spend a week? You meet interesting adults from all over the country, people whose love of the outdoors matches yours and whose giving spirit impels them to volunteer and work cooperatively and productively to accomplish important work, which improves our magnificent country's natural resources. Though men tend to outnumber women, the mix is usually well-balanced. All projects are designed so everyone works to one's own limitations as determined by themselves. Only once have I witnessed a volunteer quit and leave early.

After years of backpacking, hiking, and mountain biking on thousands of miles of trails built and maintained by others, I take great pride in creating new trails or substantially improving an existing trail, and I believe my volunteer work is appropriate recompense to the hiking community for the immense joy I derive from backpacking. I hope my efforts help foster a lasting wilderness legacy and ethic to bequeath to future generations. ⓛ

TRAVELING WITH GRANDCHILDREN

Traveling with your grandchildren can deepen relationships and create lifelong memories. This type of travel ranks high on the trips mature travelers would like to take. In fact, in a survey of group travelers by the National Tour Association and Group Leaders of America, travel involving grandparents and grandchildren ranked ninth out of the top 50 tours and destinations available.

The leader in grandparent/grandchild travel is Grandtravel (www.grandtrvl.com or 800-247-7651). This organization has been around for over 15 years and is owned and operated by a grandmother, Helena Konig. Grandtravel offers national and international itineraries designed to be enjoyed by both generations; teachers or leisure counselors escort the trips. Tours, scheduled primarily in the summer months, include New York, Alaska, Kenya, Australia, and France. The Sierra Club (www.sierraclub.org or 415-977-5500) offers "Getting to Know Your Grandchildren" trips for kids between the ages of 6 and 12 (no age restrictions on the grandparents!). Enjoy hiking, swimming, and sightseeing in west-central Massachusetts. The Sagamore Foundation

(315-354-5311) offers a grandparent/grandchild summer camp in New York's Adirondack Mountains that includes hikes, indoor and outdoor activities, and campfires. Elderhostel also offers a large number of intergenerational trips of varying lengths and destinations (www.elderhostel.org or 877-426-8056).

Another avenue is to sign up with groups that offer family vacations. Although not specifically for grandparents/grandchildren, these trips still offer a cross-generational mix. Check out Rascals in Paradise (www.rascalsinparadise.com or 415-921-7000) or The World Outdoors (www.theworldoutdoors.com or 800-488-8483); both of these offer trips solely for families.

If planning a trip on your own, consider a cruise. The more family-oriented cruise lines include Disney, Carnival, Princess, Norwegian (especially the *Norwegian Dawn*), and Royal Caribbean. (See phone numbers and Web sites in this chapter's Resources.) Destinations such as dude ranches (for example, the Triangle C Dude Ranch in Wyoming, www.trianglec.com or 800-661-4928), resorts that cater to families, spas that allow adult indulgence yet provide activities for kids, and fascinating cities are other possibilities.

The financial costs of traveling with grandchildren can vary, but the emotional rewards can be priceless!

TRAVELING WITH PHYSICAL DISABILITIES

It's estimated that between 50 million and 65 million Americans have some type of disability. The travel industry is responding to this huge market. Don't let the fact that you need a scooter or wheelchair to get around slow you down. If you're hearing or vision impaired, need dialysis, require oxygen, or have other disabilities, you can still enjoy travel. You may need to do more homework than others, but accessible travel is out there.

Various travel organizations specialize in meeting access needs. Accessible Journeys (www.disabilitytravel.com or 800-846-4537) organizes group trips and cruises, helps with independent travel, and can provide a health care professional as a travel companion. Nautilus Tours and Cruises (www.nautilustours.com or 800-797-6004) and Flying Wheels Travel (www.flyingwheelstravel.com or 507-451-5005) also assist with disabled travelers, both nationally and internationally. Access-Able Travel Source (www.access-able.com or 303-232-2979) disseminates information on travel agents, cruises, accommodations, equipment rental, etc. They have a great drop-down box on their Web site that that helps you choose a travel professional based on your specific needs. Wilderness

Inquiry (www.wildernessinquiry.org or 800-728-0719) has been in business since 1978 and promotes inclusion of all ability levels and ages in the exploration of "wild" areas. One example: hiking and kayaking in Misty Fjords National Monument, Alaska.

If you have physical challenges, taking a cruise can be one of the better ways to vacation. The leading cruise lines for the physically impaired are Royal Caribbean, Celebrity (which is owned by Royal Caribbean), and Princess. New ships are being built with accessibility in mind, and older ships are being retrofitted to ensure smooth sailing with staterooms and hallways that accommodate wheelchairs and scooters; pools with lifts; newsletters, elevator buttons, and menus in Braille; amplified telephones; close-captioned TVs; roll-in showers; and lower closet bars and sinks. Ports of call and shore excursions are becoming more accessible as well. Contact the access desk at the appropriate cruise line to discuss your needs: Royal Caribbean (800-327-6700), Celebrity (800-437-3111), or Princess (800-421-0522). Now you don't have to miss the boat!

What if you'd like to participate in a home exchange? The Institute on Independent Living, founded in 1993, is headquartered in Sweden. It provides, for free, the ability to post ads or search ads for home exchanges (nationally and internationally) for those with access needs. The ads describe the types of accommodations provided in the home, condo, apartment, etc. For more information, contact the Institute at www.independentliving.org/vacaswap.html.

On a broader note, resource organizations for the disabled include Mobility International (www.miusa.org or 541-343-1284) and the Society for Accessible Travel and Hospitality (SATH), which can be contacted at www.sath.org or 212-447-7284. One of the goals of Mobility International is to promote "the inclusion of disabled people in all types of exchange, community, and volunteer service programs." SATH works to provide barrier-free travel both nationally and internationally, provides tips on travel (such as how to travel with a speech impairment), and provides a good resource list for the disabled traveler.

"Travel and change of place impart new vigor to the mind."
—Seneca

So, now you're ready, willing, and able. Take the attitude of Pastor Charles Swindoll, who said, "The longer I live, the more convinced I become that life is 10 percent what happens to us and 90 percent how we respond to it." Bon voyage!

true LIFE **Priscilla M. has multiple sclerosis. She lives in Vermont with her husband, Andy, and they travel extensively. These are her thoughts.**

I have MS and have difficulty walking distances. I usually do not require a wheelchair or assistance with stairs or a handicap-accessible room, but I do move slowly and walk with a cane, even on a good day. Many places are equipped to serve those with more severe physical challenges, but what I have found is that they are not always ready for those of us who just move slowly and tire easily. On that note, I have learned some things the hard way:

* When I inquire about elevators in hotels, I make sure the room is not what seems like five miles from them.

* Tours to Europe or Israel are too fast paced, and the bus stops too far away for me to maneuver, so we opt for a private guide with a car.

* On an Alaskan cruise, we traveled on Princess Cruise Lines. We found this worked well because I could stay on the ship and gaze out on fabulous scenery while the others could be more adventurous. It was nice to travel with friends, so Andy had someone to walk the towns with if I didn't feel up to going.

* I love to swim laps. We were in the Bahamas recently, and there was a gorgeous lap pool on the brochure. I never thought to ask where the lap pool was—it was quite a hike from our room, and there were comparable rooms nearby we could have requested.

* Airports can also be a challenge, as can public transportation in general, particularly trains and subways if stairs are involved. Many do not have elevator access, especially in New York. The last trip we took, we allowed plenty of time for me to walk to the departure gate at the airport.

* Andy seems to find European cities overwhelming, as they often have cobblestone streets that are not only hard for me to walk on but are not wheelchair friendly. ⒧

TRAVEL THOUGHTS AND TIPS

If we still haven't exhausted you with all there is to do during your 168 hours each week, here are some further ideas and suggestions about travel that don't fit neatly into one of the categories we've already discussed.

Lodging

If you'd rather stay in a European castle, cottage, or apartment than in a hotel, consider subscribing to the *Countryside Vacation Newsletter* (www.countryside-vacations.com or 888-505-8800). Properties are rated by people who have actually stayed at them, and the newsletter includes suggestions on restaurants, shopping, and sightseeing. Each issue also includes articles on four European countries. The introductory rate is $38 for five issues. Another option would be Hideaways International (www.hideaways.com or 800-843-4433). For $55 (mini-membership) or $145 (full membership) per year, you are given access to information on villas, yachts, condos, castles, etc., all over the world. Hideaway International has been in business for over 20 years.

There are a number of sites that allow potential renters to contact owners directly. A1 Vacations (www.a1vacations.com or 540-721-9915) lists more than 4,000 places throughout the world that can be rented directly from the owner. Their "two strikes and you're out" policy eliminates any property from being advertised if more than one complaint has been lodged against it. A1 is an advertising service, but they will provide assistance in finding your perfect vacation place. Other sites include EscapeHomes (www.Escape Homes.com or 800-937-9090); about 25 percent of their listings are vacation rental properties, and there are also timeshares and vacation homes for sale. Beachhouse.com (or 949-863-0050) is for those who believe life is better at the beach. Try Unusual Villas (www.unusualvillarentals.com or 800-846-7280) for over 3,500 villas or 400 yachts worldwide. Of course, if you own a place in a desirable location, you may also list your own property on these sites.

"Cuchi-cuchi!" Maybe you want to stay in a celebrity villa. You can rent homes owned by Charo, Jane Seymour, Merv Griffin, Randy Travis, Mick Jagger, and others through Overseas Connection (www.villasoftheworld.com, and click on "Celebrity Villas," or 888-72-VILLA). Gulp! Prices are all over the place, with a 74-acre Caribbean island with one home on it owned by Richard Branson going for $141,000 a week during high season—but hey, it sleeps 24, so just prorate it among your friends. Of course, more reasonable rates exist for other celebrity villas.

If you've already stayed at the Ritz or Four Seasons and are looking for something more over the top, consider these far-out places (your grandkids will thank you!):

Treehouses: Cedar Creek Treehouse (www.cedar creektreehouse.com or 360-569-2991) has a fabulous view of Mt. Rainier in Ashford, Washington, for $250 per night for two. Out 'n' About Treesort (www. treehouses.com or 541-592-2208) in Takilma, Oregon, offers 14 different treehouses that range in cost from $90 to $160 per night, depending on treehouse style and number of people. In Australia, check out the wallabies and tree frogs from your rainforest treehouse located 90 minutes from Cairns (www.rainforesttreehouses. com.au). Prices range from $205 to $240 per night for two depending on the time of year.

Ice hotels: The Ice Hotel Quebec and the Ice Hotel in Sweden have similar amenities including art galleries, an Absolut Ice Bar, spa, wedding chapel, and movie theater. The Ice Hotel in Canada (www.icehotel-canada.com or 877-505-0423), for example, takes 5 weeks to build, opens around the first of January, and is open for about 3 months. Temperatures range between 23 and 28 degrees Fahrenheit, and you'll snuggle in a sleeping bag on top of deer pelts. One night's lodging, including dinner and breakfast, starts at $229 Canadian (about $176 U.S.) per person, double occupancy.

Caves: Kokopelli's Cave Bed & Breakfast is located north of Farmington, New Mexico. Carved out of sandstone that is 65 million years old, this 70-foot-below-the-surface cave apartment has one bedroom, hot and cold running water, a hot tub, washer and dryer, and kitchen. Located near Mesa Verde National Monument, there are mountainous vistas of Arizona, Colorado, New Mexico, and Utah from the cliff face where you enter to descend to the dwelling. Rates are $220 for one or two persons per night. Contact www.bbonline.com/nm/kokopelli or 505-326-2461 for pictures and more details. The Desert Cave Hotel (www.desertcave.com.au) is located in the opal-mining town of Coober Pedy in the northern outback of South Australia. Built into a sandstone hill, the hotel opened in 1988 and has 50 suites, 19 of which are underground. With the cool, constant underground temperatures (71 to 78 degrees Fahrenheit), lodgers experience a delightfully cool sleep in the middle of the desert.

Under the sea: The Jules' Undersea Lodge in Key

When business travelers leave the big city after their meetings, you can often negotiate a good price for a first-class hotel room.

Largo, Florida (www.jul.com or 305-451-2353), is the world's only underwater hotel. You'll need to SCUBA dive to access this unique lodge 21 feet below the surface, but once there, you'll enjoy hot showers, comfy beds, and a kitchen. Your view out the windows, however, will be quite different from a regular hotel! The lodge was originally a research lab, but it has operated as an underwater hotel since 1986. Different packages are available, beginning at $250 per person including dinner and breakfast. If you're not certified in SCUBA, no problem—you can take a 3-hour course at Jules' ($80) that will allow you to enjoy this memory-making experience.

Scary: Double your fun—stay on the *HMS Queen Mary* (www.queenmary.com or 562-435-3511), and you'll be sleeping on a ship as well as an allegedly haunted floating hotel. Now permanently docked in Long Beach, California, the ship has several "hot spots" where apparitions and strange smells, noises, and temperature variations have been reported. One of the cabins (B340) is no longer used for passengers because of inexplicable oddities. A ghost tour by a paranormal researcher is even available. The liner has 365 staterooms that range from $109 to $500 per night.

Various other hotels are allegedly visited by ghosts, including the Hilton Hotel in Honolulu, Hawaii (808-949-4321), the Lizzie Borden Bed and Breakfast in Fall River, Massachusetts (508-675-7333), and Cloudcroft the Lodge in Cloudcroft, New Mexico (800-395-6343). Restaurants aren't immune either—check out the spectral beings that supposedly haunt Portland White Eagle Café and Saloon in Portland, Oregon (503-282-6810), Pirate's House Restaurant in Savannah, Georgia (912-233-5757), or Asheley's Restaurant in Rockledge, Florida (407-636-6430).

Lighthouses: There are quite a few lighthouses, many privately owned, that allow overnight stays. Several examples: Big Bay Point Lighthouse Bed and Breakfast (www.bigbaylighthouse.com or 906-345-9957) in Big Bay, Wisconsin, hugs a cliff on Lake Superior. More than a century old, its rates range from $99 to $185, depending on room and time of year.

With the Selkirk Light House (315-298-6688) in Pulaski, New York, you rent the entire lighthouse, consisting of two floors and four bedrooms. Rates begin at $125 for two people, with additional charges for extra people and certain days of the week. Part of the rental income goes toward the lighthouse's renovation. For additional lighthouse lodging, go to www.lighthouse.cc.

Vineyards: Want to see the birthplace of that

Chardonnay or Merlot? Chateau Darmagnac (www.france-plus.com and click on "Holiday") is in France's Bordeaux country. Experience wine making and tasting right on the premises, as well as golf, tennis, fishing, proximity to other vineyards, and visits to the nearby Atlantic coast. Prices range from 300 to 400 euros per week (to convert euros to dollars, go to a currency converter site such as www.xe.com). Or, consider a stay at Carriage Vineyards (www.carriagevineyards.com or 805-227-6807) on California's central coast, midway between San Francisco and Los Angeles. Prices begin around $180 per night during high season.

Air, Sea, and Auto Travel

For the best seats on a plane, try to get an exit row since these seats offer more legroom. If there are two rows of exit seats, choose the second row—the first row doesn't recline. If there are two of you traveling, and there are three seats across, reserve the aisle and window seats. The middle seats will be the last to be assigned, so the two of you may have the row to yourself. Conversely, if only middle seats are available when you book, ask to be put in a middle seat between two people with the same last name. Obviously, they are banking on the former tip! If they really want to sit together, one may switch with you, and you can end up with a window or aisle seat. If you want to try to get a different seat than the one assigned, call your airline after midnight on the day of departure. Seats may open up because of cancellations. Of course, you can also ask about changing your seat when you check in. For seating arrangements on various airlines and comments about seating on American, Continental, Delta, United, and US Airways, look at www.seatguru.com. It's a very helpful site.

For better seats, you can also try getting bumped on purpose. If time is not of the essence in arriving at your destination, ask at the gate to be put on the list of people volunteering to be bumped. Obviously, the earlier you're at the airport, the better your priority on the list. Airlines routinely overbook to ensure as full a plane as possible. Joyce L. and her daughter, Jessica, were ready to return

---

The top U.S. airports, according to a recent *Condé Nast Traveler* readers' poll, are Tampa, Orlando, West Palm Beach, Las Vegas, Pittsburgh, Providence (Rhode Island), Portland (Oregon), Washington, D.C. (Reagan National), Honolulu, and Salt Lake City.

to Chicago from a vacation in France when American Airlines announced it was looking for volunteers to be bumped. Not needing to get back immediately, Joyce and Jessica volunteered. They were put up at EuroDisney for the night (sent by cab), about 40 minutes from the airport, and were given a generous voucher for dinner and breakfast, as well as airline vouchers for $2,000. The only snag to the plan was that their luggage had been checked through to Chicago, and Joyce's carry-on luggage, which held toiletries, was now replaced by a gargoyle that she had bought on their travels! Moral: Having a carry-on bag containing toiletries and a change of clothes is a good move if you're hoping to be bumped. (The flight they took out the next day was also overbooked, but they passed on that opportunity.) Different airlines have different deals; make sure you understand what you're being offered before accepting! For more information, check out www.bumptracker.com.

And here's a tip regarding bargain fares: Discount fares are released on the Internet on Wednesdays at 12:01 A.M. Sign up for automatic notifications through your preferred airline, or through a site such as www.smarterliving.com.

Since airlines have become more stringent about extra luggage (right now Delta charges $40 for an extra bag, Northwest $80) or extra-heavy bags, it may be cost effective to send that extra luggage ahead. Or, if you just don't want to lug your luggage, consider shipping it ahead. If you want pickup service at your residence/business and quick delivery to your journey's end, you'll pay for the convenience of this door-to-destination service. Two to consider: Virtual Bellhop (www.virtualbellhop.com or 877-235-5467) and SkyCap International (www.skycapinternational.com or 877-775-9227), which is associated with FedEx. Less costly alternatives, but more work for you since you must pack and deliver your luggage, are the U.S. Postal Service, Federal Express, or Amtrak. Or, compare shipping rates from multiple carriers at www.iship.com.

You could also look into repositioning cruises. When cruise ships move from one region to another to reposition for a new itinerary, they often offer steep discounts as well as longer times at sea since they are on

---

Most automobile rental agencies start their weekend rates at noon on Thursday and end at midnight on Sunday. You can often obtain better rates during this time frame.

"one-way" cruises and frequently have fewer ports of call than do regular cruises. If you want to stretch your travel dollars, it's worth considering.

Entertainment

You can do a myriad of things on your getaway, some of which you can enjoy again and again.

Discount tickets. Join (for free) the Playbill Club at www.playbill.com, and become eligible for reduced Broadway, off-Broadway, and regional theater tickets, as well as restaurant, hotel, and merchandise discounts.

Disney Park Hopper passes. Remember, these passes never expire. One of the author's sons and a friend recently visited Disney World using remaining portions of 1993 Park Hopper tickets. Just don't forget where you put them!

Golf, anyone? The John Jacobs Golf School (www.jacobsgolf.com or 800-511-1639) provides accommodations, meals, and golf lessons in 40 locations. For ex-

ample, a 3-day/3-night session at the Solvista Golf and Ski Ranch in Granby, Colorado, includes 5 hours of instruction a day, 3 lunches, greens fees, cart, and a social hour for $995 (double).

Amusement parks and casinos. Tuesdays, Wednesdays, and Thursdays are usually the least crowded days to visit, with Wednesdays being the best of the three.

Other Assorted Points

There may come a time when you need to find a doctor when you're traveling. The International Association for Medical Assistance to Travelers (IAMAT) at www.iamat.org or 716-754-4883 provides free membership (although they would appreciate a donation) that includes a directory with physicians in 125 countries. The doctors speak English and have been trained in North America or Europe. A set schedule of fees has been established (for example, $55 for an office visit). In existence since 1960, the organization also provides infor-

---

Freedom Paradise Resort (www.freedomparadise.com or 866-LIVEXXL), near Cancun, Mexico, caters to the plus-size customer. Reinforced furniture, extra-large towels, broader chairs, wider walkways, king-size beds, boutiques with plus-size clothing, and easily accessed swimming pools make this a welcoming vacation spot for those who aren't comfortable around the bikini set.

mation about disease outbreaks, sanitary conditions, and required immunizations.

For the upscale traveler who wants all the fun without the hassles of planning a trip (and is willing to pay for the service), consider using a personal tour guide. Hiring a personal escort—someone who is an expert in the area you plan to visit—is becoming a more common option for a small group or family. This type of travel can be expensive; indeed, the cost is about what it takes for an additional person to go on the vacation. But having a guide who is familiar with the customs, history, food, and culture of an area (and who may also serve as a driver) can be a great boon to a trip. To hire a travel escort, try Abercrombie and Kent (www.abercrombiekent.com or 800-323-7308). A&K can make any of their general escorted tours into a personal tour, or you can create your own itinerary. You could also contact colleges or tour companies to see if they can provide an expert in the area you wish to visit. The guide may go with you, meet you there, or be with you for all or part of each day.

How much do we love to travel? A study by the National Tour Association found that almost 90 percent of us would choose an experience that enriches us over material goods. So, let's go!

How to Decode a Travel Brochure

Brochure Term	Translation
Tropical	Rainy
Secluded hideaway	Impossible to find or get to
Explore on your own	Pay for it yourself
Standard	Substandard
Deluxe	Standard
Light and airy	No air conditioning

4

WHAT AND WHERE IS HOME?

"Where you are is who you are."
—*Virginia Woolf*

"Home" conjures up many images. Defined as "the place in which one's domestic affections are centered," it has been celebrated by artists, poets, writers, and philosophers. With the number of multiple corporate relocations in our mobile society, "Where is home?" can become a difficult question to answer. Is it your current residence? Where you were born and grew up? Where most of your family lives? It's an important concept and a vital one to think about if you're contemplating moving upon retirement. Will there be a "Dinosaur Age," with retirees roaming the earth in search of nirvana?

According to Marjorie Garber in *Sex and Real Estate*, 50 percent of boomers think they'll move into a new home after they retire, 22 percent want to move to another state, and 44 percent want to move to the southern Atlantic coast. When you're talking about 78 million boomers, that's a lot of moving vans! Although many people "stay put" to be near family and friends, an interesting and surprising national survey by Clyde and Shari Steiner, authors of *Steiner's Complete How-to-Move Handbook*, found that the third most frequently cited reason for a move is to *escape* from family members and friends!

Whatever your reasons, will you pack up your things like a nomad and join the one in seven Americans who live along the East or Gulf coast? Will you ponder a second home? Which factors should you consider before relocating? How can you "try out" new places to live, and what housing possibilities exist? Should you consider renting? What if your adult kids decide to move back in with you? What is universal design, and how can it help you? And if you do decide to pull up roots, how do you increase your chances for a successful move? Enough questions—let's start answering them!

Currently, the majority of people do *not* move when they retire, but predictions about today's boomers paint a different picture. A 2003 survey by Del Webb, builder of active-adult communities, found that almost 60 percent of those between the ages of 44 and 56 plan to pull up stakes after they retire. If you've thought about the possibility of moving after retiring, take our survey, "To Relocate or Not to Relocate: That Is the Question" on page 453.

In addition to quality-of-life factors, Harry Dent, author of *The Roaring 2000s*, suggests you consider quantitative factors such as job opportunities, income growth, population growth, how much land and water is available for development, real estate appreciation, and office building vacancy rates. Dent also recommends using psychographics, or lifestyle analyses, in helping to choose a retirement location. One of these lifestyle analysis systems, called PRIZM, from Claritas, "classifies neighborhoods into one of 62 categories based on census data, leading consumer surveys and media measurement data, and other public and private sources of demographic and consumer information."

For example, on the Claritas Web site (www.claritas.com), we clicked on "Customer Segmentation Systems," then "You Are Where You Live." We then entered 33480, the zip code for Palm Beach, Florida, which we know is an expensive area. The three most common lifestyle segments that surfaced were "Gray Power" (affluent retirees), "Second City Elite" (college-educated

---

According to the U.S. Census Bureau, among the U.S. population in general, almost half of us (46 percent) lived in a different home in 2000 from the one we lived in during 1995! Why move? According to Monstermoving.com, the three biggest reasons were achievement of a different lifestyle, job requirements, and changes in size of household.

THE IDEAL SPOT TO LIVE

What are your requirements for the "good life"? What is nonnegotiable if you're choosing a place to live? In general, various authorities point to certain characteristics for an ideal retirement location. These factors mirror the results of a 2003 *Where to Retire* magazine subscriber survey. In order of importance, the factors to consider in choosing a retirement community are:

1. Low crime rate
2. Active, clean, safe downtown
3. Good hospitals nearby
4. Low overall tax rate
5. Mild climate
6. Friendly, like-minded neighbors
7. Scenic beauty nearby
8. Low cost of living
9. Good recreational facilities
10. Low housing cost
11. Active social/cultural environment
12. Nearby airport with commercial service
13. Major city nearby
14. No state income tax
15. Continuing-care retirement communities available
16. Friends, relatives in area
17. Full- or part-time employment opportunities
18. College town with adult education available

Perhaps you have one or two other criteria to add to the list (e.g. beach or lakefront property available, place of worship within walking distance, etc.).

professionals), and "Money and Brains" (educated professionals living in upscale neighborhoods). This is a thumbnail sketch of the type of information that PRIZM provides. Try putting in the zip code of your present locale or one you're considering, and see the demographics of people who live there!

Perhaps all these factors are not burning issues for everyone—some people love snow and cold weather, some are unconcerned with job opportunities or the quantity of available land, and for the very wealthy, a low cost of living may not be paramount. (When we and our spouses prioritized our own criteria, climate and prox-

...re paramount.) Each person has to ... important as he or she (and a signifi-...here is one) goes through the decision-...ess. You may realize you have the qualities ...ost important to you in your current location and decide you're already in the best possible location.

A HOME AWAY FROM HOME

One home or two? According to the National Association of Realtors, the second-home market represented 6 percent of real estate transactions in 2000; there were a total of 3.6 million seasonal homes by the third quarter of 2002. If you have the financial wherewithal and the desire for a second home, this is another path to consider—it's a hot trend. Perhaps you're very satisfied with your social group, you love your doctors, you know the maitre d's of the best restaurants by name—the only things you're missing are dramatic mountains to ski, a sandy beach to stroll, or a secluded cabin from which to enjoy Mother Nature. Or, maybe you'd like to be a snowbird (flee the cold winter weather for warmer destinations) or a sunbird (avoid the swelter of summer by going to a cooler location). A second home is also a way to sample an area as a future permanent retirement spot.

If you think you might want a second home, check out chapter 5, where we recommend some specific locations and communities. Or, take a look at Escape Homes (www.escapehomes.com and click on "Pressroom," or 800-937-9090), which released its 2003 list of "Top 100 Second-Home Markets." (You can also just browse on-line for a second home.) Escape Homes also compiled its 2003 list of "Top 10 Emerging Second Home Markets." Alphabetically, they are Burnside, Kentucky; Caribou, Maine; Ely, Minnesota; Island Park, Idaho; Ketchikan, Alaska; Lake Martin, Alabama; St. George, Utah; Sisters, Oregon; Waterville Valley, New Hampshire; and White Mountain, Arizona.

What if you want to buy some land at a good price on which to build your dream home? Robert Abalos, an at-

If you need some suggestions, try the free, easy survey at www.findmyspot.com, which asks you to choose from a number of lifestyle options and then generates a list of potential places to consider for relocation. Or, try www.bestplaces.net and click on "Find Your Best Place to Live."

torney who specializes in land investments and real estate development, gave these suggestions in the October 2, 2003, issue of *Fortune* magazine. Consider "buying lots from bankrupt or cash-starved developers, contacting out-of-state owners in resort areas who once intended to build but now just want to unload, and look into foreclosure auctions."

Pros of a Second Home

Real estate does tend to appreciate over time—you may be able to combine the best of both worlds (main home in a city full of cultural amenities with a second home in a laid-back beach area, for example). You may get away more often knowing there's a place waiting for you. You may be able to rent your place when you're not there to help defray costs. It may be a magnet for family and friends to visit (hmmmmmm . . . could this also be a con for some?). If you're not a planner, you'll always have a reservation at your seasonal destination. And you can double your social contacts by having two residences.

Cons of a Second Home

There are the issues of cost and maintenance—and of dealing with both from a distance. And, if you have a finite amount of money (and who doesn't?), would owning a second home tie up so much money that it would preclude travel or other expensive enjoyable activities? Some people have found it harder to make friends when shuttling between homes. Doris and Ken M., for example, own homes in St. Louis, Missouri, and Laguna Hills, California. Although friendly with both sets of neighbors, they found there was a readjustment period when they returned to either home. Plans had been made, groups had been formed, and it took a while to reintegrate themselves back into the social scene. Finding someone to keep an eye on each home in their absence was also critical.

A Few More Specifics

Consider distance. If getting to your second home becomes a major hassle in terms of time or cost, buying it may become a decision you'll regret. If you're looking for

---

According to the National Association of Realtors, in 2001, the median price of a primary home was $153,000—and of a *second* home, $162,000!

a weekend-type retreat, you may want to limit the driving distance to 3 hours or less (not more than a tank of gas away). If you're planning on living there for weeks or months at a time, however, this is less of an issue.

If you're thinking about a resort area for your second home (or even your primary home), find out the percentages of full-time and part-time residents, as well as rental restrictions. You may find your neighbors change from week to week.

Water damage can be a nightmare if you're not home. When you're leaving your house for an extended period, turn off the main water shut-off valve and drain the water lines at the lowest point. Don't forget exterior hose bibs and pipes, if the pipes could freeze. Claudia A. had a disaster while just picking up her dry cleaning. The rubber supply hose from the washing machine (located on the main floor) burst, causing water to ruin the hardwood floors in the kitchen, powder room, and hallway, and to pour into the basement. If the temperature where you live could go below the freezing point, add ethylene glycol (antifreeze or windshield washer fluid) to other drains with water-filled plumbing traps (tubs, showers, toilet bowls, floor drains, etc.) after you've removed as much water from them as possible.

Appliances can cause an electrical fire even if they are turned off. Switch off circuit breakers to everything but the lighting and heating you want to utilize while you're absent. Dishwashers have a little bit of water in the bottom to keep the seals pliable and protect the motor. To prevent that water from evaporating, add a half-cup of liquid bleach and three tablespoons of mineral oil. The bleach will kill bacteria, and the oil will float on top of the water, preventing evaporation.

Dispose of perishable foods, or take them with you. Safely store any valuable and/or sentimental items.

If your house is in a northern climate, when leaving for an extended period it's helpful to leave the windows cracked to allow the humidity to equalize inside and outside the house, preventing condensation and the growth of mold and mildew within your home. Ask someone

---

If one of your concerns about a second home is that it will curtail travel, Trade to Travel (www.vacationlink.com or 800-899-1096) allows you to trade your second luxury home (temporarily) for another one. Of course, there are fees for the service.

you trust to close and lock the windows after a few weeks. Also, installing a low-heat thermostat (set around 40 degrees) will prevent pipes from freezing while saving money over conventional thermostats, which typically have their lowest setting around 55 or 60 degrees. If you leave a southern home vacant during the summer, Pacific Gas and Electric Company recommends you set your air conditioner above 85 degrees and close the drapes.

You'll need a mechanism for receiving bills as you alternate between residences. Many companies can send bills over the Internet, a trend that's accelerating. It has the added plus of eliminating the paperwork that traditional snail mail entails. So, if you're comfortable with the computer, your bills are often only a click away, no matter where you are. Or, you can have the post office forward your mail.

There's nothing like the human touch. If you know someone who can periodically check on the house and get in touch with you if there's an issue, you'll feel much more relaxed about your second home. If you notify them, the police will also drive by to check things out.

FINDING A PLACE

So, you've decided to consider moving or maybe buying a second residence after retirement. How do you go about it?

First, reflect on *why* you're considering moving. Do you want to escape from something unpleasant in your current location (shoveling snow, meddling in-laws, high cost of living, a house that won't suit your needs as you get older)? Are you attracted to a place because of the lifestyle it offers (easy access to water, proximity to your children, low maintenance, etc.)? Usually, there is more than just one reason for contemplating relocation. Let's face it—most of us are living in a particular place because of job considerations. With this fact removed from the equation, it opens up a world of possibilities;

What's most important to you when looking for the best place to live? Money.cnn.com has an ongoing online poll. More than 70,000 people indicated the following order of preference: low crime rate, nice weather, low cost of living, outdoor activities/low taxes (tied), arts and culture/entertainment and dining (tied), and a slow pace.

you can now focus on lifestyle rather than livelihood!

Once you've completed the first step of thinking about why you'd like to move, reexamine the issues shown in "The Ideal Spot to Live" on page 93. Go ahead and prioritize them.

Now, the research part begins. You need to find communities that include your most important criteria, within the confines of what you can afford. Some of these, like proximity to friends and family (keep in mind that they could move, too!) or climate, are easy to determine. Others, such as safety issues, transportation, or property taxes, require more digging. The Internet is a fabulous resource to ferret out this information. A site such as www.money.cnn.com (type "Best Places to Live" in the search bar) allows you to input various criteria, then up pops a specific list! Or, let's say you want a place with tons of amenities (such as golf) or a gated community. Check out a site such as www.privatecommunities.com, where you can explore 16 states and three foreign countries from your home. Will an active adult community fit your lifestyle? Try www.retirementliving.com and look under "Retirement Communities." Or, you can take a look at chapters 5, 6, and 7, where we do the analysis for you, summarize the positives and negatives of specific places, and suggest places to live. (For some books and magazines that rate places to live, see the resources for this chapter). Solicit recommendations from neighbors, friends, and family who share a similar outlook to help devise a list of potential places.

If you're interested in Florida, Georgia, North Carolina, South Carolina, Tennessee, Virginia, or Nevada as a retirement spot, Live South (www.livesouth.com or 800-713-4263) offers the Live South Real Estate Show, with representatives from communities in these areas providing information and offering discovery visits to their locations. (We attended one of these free seminars, and though there was a bit of a hard sell from those manning the exhibits, lots of good information was provided all in one spot).

Another thought is to look where you have frequently traveled or vacationed. If you continue to return to the same place year after year, it's a sign that it could be the lo-

---

A cost-of-living calculator can help determine how far your money will go in a new location. Try the one at www.homefair.com (click on "Cost of Living Comparison").

cation for you. Linda and Michael D., for example, were drawn to the small-town beauty and sparkling summers of Charlevoix, Michigan, every summer from their primary home in Houston, Texas. When they decided they wanted to purchase a second home, it was a no-brainer.

As you investigate each area, it's helpful to take notes that reflect how each proposed community meets your most important needs. You can use a worksheet, such as "Compare Your Housing Costs" on page 455, to see how the costs of buying a home compare to your present home's costs. Most chambers of commerce are happy to send you information for free. A site such as www.touristinformationdirectory.com allows you to access the states' chambers of commerce with a click; you can then narrow it down to specific cities/towns within each state and request relocation information from them. Although you may also get mail from real estate agents, banks, and other businesses, we think it's a small price to pay for the valuable information you'll accumulate.

As you gather research on areas you're considering for relocation, it's important to document how they overlap with your lifestyle wishes. Again, taking notes as you go will save lots of time later!

TRYING A PLACE FOR FIT

Now that you've constructed a list that fits your lifestyle, at least in theory, it's time to visit! There's no way of getting around this part, unless you're choosing a place you already know. But, hey, this is the fun part! Many communities (especially the larger new ones with a long build-out time frame) offer discovery tours at reduced rates that allow you to take a tour, talk with residents, and sample such amenities as a round of golf or a meal at the clubhouse. Take advantage of these offers! You can get a real sense of the area and people and see if there's a good fit between you and the location. Perhaps you can either arrange a sabbatical from work to start your in-

---

Of course, you need to know what you'll have to spend on your next home. For a quick estimate of how much money you can expect to realize from the sale of your current home, go to www.houseandhome.msn.com and click on "Selling Your House," then "Home Values," or ask a local Realtor to do an analysis.

vestigation or volunteer in the areas you're considering.

After you've completed this vital step, you'll have a much better feel for what you want, and you'll be able to narrow your list to a few contenders. (If nothing grabbed you, maybe you need to either go back to the research stage or decide that, for you, "there's no place like home"—your current home, that is).

Here are a few more specific ideas.

Sample all seasons. If you find you're crawling along in traffic for hours with the thousands of snowbirds who have flocked to your potential new home, you might think twice about relocating there. Likewise, if you visit a place only in the winter, you could be in for a shock when the summer humidity sets in. The mountain community that is so beautiful in the late summer may strike you differently as you slide on black ice during the winter.

Get the local newspaper. You can access many newspapers online or at the library, or have a subscription sent to your home. Being in touch with the everyday events of your potential retirement haven clues you in on the events, issues, real estate prices, and flavor of a community.

Talk to the locals. Visit a community center or strike up a conversation at a park or casual restaurant. You can find out invaluable information that the chambers of commerce or Realtors may not offer. Lydia R., for example, was considering Brunswick, Georgia, when a resident told her about the factory that produces pine oil and the "aroma" that sometimes wafted over certain areas of the town. The existence of paper factories or rendering plants is worth finding out about beforehand!

Let your fingers do the walking. Get a copy of the area's Yellow Pages. You'll get a sense of the scope of restaurants, physicians, theaters, hospitals, parks, etc.

Rent or try a home exchange. It's a good idea to try out a prospective location for an extended period to ensure it's really for you. Companies such as Homelink (www.swapnow.com or 800-638-3841) or Intervac (www.intervacus.com or 800-756-4663) allow you to arrange a temporary swap of your home for one in a different location (you will pay a fee for the service).

Try out homesharing. If you have the right personality, you could try out an area by sharing a residence

---

"When you're 17, you dream of a summer romance. When you're 47, you dream of a summer house."
—Marjorie Garber, *Sex and Real Estate*

with another (unrelated) adult. This could allow you to sample an area while saving financially. If you're single, you might find the safety and companionship aspects attractive as well. Contact the National Shared Housing Resource Center (www.nationalsharedhousing.org).

Be a freeloader. Global Freeloaders (www.globalfreeloaders.com) is a free online service that allows you to stay at someone's home for free (though you need to be willing to reciprocate). The price is right!

Make sure there's a place for your "toys." Some developments include RV and boat storage on the premises. For example, the Villages of Westminster in Williamsburg, Virginia, provides on-site (hidden, fenced, and secured) storage for about 30 RVs and/or boats for a nominal yearly fee. This can be an attractive incentive for some buyers.

Practice retirement! Try living on your projected retirement income for a while, and try out those activities you're planning on doing when you actually do retire. It can be very instructive!

We realize people have many personality types. The methodical may go through all of these steps; others may stumble onto a place, fall in love, snap up the first home they visit, and live happily ever after (or not). We simply want to suggest ways to increase the chances of finding your ideal place.

TRENDS IN HOME BUYING

You've zeroed in on the perfect town. It's safe, close to a major airport, has great weather and terrific medical facilities—the top things on your personal priority list. You're ready to choose your residence. What are some recent home-buying trends of which you should be aware?

Given that there are 78 million baby boomers, builders need to know what they want so they can "build it, and they will come." Studies by the National Association of Home Builders and Countrywide Home Loans surveyed home buyers 50 and older and found that they are looking for:

* Energy-efficient and low-maintenance homes. And they want services to care for their yards and the exterior portions of their homes.

* Single-family, detached homes. More than half wanted these, with one-story layouts predominating.

* Secure homes/communities. Security systems, lighting, and limited access were important. There were more than 20,000 gated communities in the United States in the late 1990s, and the security trend is increasing.

* High-speed Internet connections. Homeowners want to be wired with broadband Internet service.

s. Buyers want to turn on some
c, turn off a few extraneous lights,
ıe house a bit warmer—all from
ʌ panel! Or close their garage door—
ʌr office; lower their oven tempera-
ıc ıth their cell phone; or see who's
ringing their doorbell—on their television.
That's the magic of "smart" homes, or home
automation. If you like high-tech gadgets,
explore a site such as www.smarthome.com
or call 800-762-7846.

* Proximity to shopping, restaurants, physicians,
  and places of worship.
* Quality workmanship.

Another survey of boomers, by Del Webb, found these
additional wants on boomers' "wish lists":

* New construction. More than 40 percent of
  boomers said they plan on moving into a new
  home after they retire.
* Great rooms, home offices, gourmet kitchens, and
  exercise rooms.

* Amenities such as computer labs, tennis courts,
  fitness centers, and pools.
* Intergenerational communities where children
  and grandchildren are welcome.

Another trend in new homes is the "his and her" house
with two master closets, two sinks at different heights,
two home offices, two retreat areas . . . you get the idea.
Outdoor fireplaces, summer kitchens, more outside living
areas, fountains, meditation rooms, and in-home theaters
are also attractive to those who can foot the bill.

Additionally, a substantial number of boomers would
like to move into active-adult, resort-style living environments without moving to another state or even far
from their existing community. They'd like to stay close
to their families and friends but still have all the bells and
whistles. In response, many developers are building
country club-style developments in what are not normally thought of as retirement havens. For example,
there are active-adult communities in New Jersey,
Massachusetts, and the Chicago area.

**As you outfit yourself and your dream house, try these Web sites to see whether you're getting the best
prices: www.PriceGrabber.com, www.Shopping.com, www.NexTag.com, or www.BizRate.com.
Comparison shopping is only keystrokes away!**

In a nutshell, boomers are choosing lifestyle, and it's pretty obvious they aren't planning on downsizing that!

RENT OR BUY?

The prevailing mantra has generally been that it's better to own than to rent your residence. Is this an ironclad rule?

Not always. If you're trying out a place for retirement, renting could make sense. That way, if you find out it's not really the place for you and decide to move within a few years, you won't risk losing some of your investment in a new home. Or, if you're not sure your future retirement income will support the cost of a house, renting could be an attractive option because you're not responsible for property taxes, upkeep, and possibly some utilities. If you're able to invest the money you save by renting, you could end up with a greater monthly retirement income. Buying, on the other hand, allows you to build equity, provides some tax breaks, and conveys the emotional pleasure of being a homeowner. Rents can increase annually, but you usually know your mortgage payment from year to year. As a homeowner, you are in control of changes to your home and not subject to the vagaries of a landlord or a lease.

To do the math on renting versus buying, use an online calculator such as www.fp.edu (click on "Financial Calculators," then "Should I Rent My Home or Buy?") or www.smartmoney.com/home/buying/ (go to "To Rent or to Buy?" under "Worksheets"). After you input the data, the calculator will help determine the right direction for you.

New or Resale?

Assuming you decide you want to own, not rent, is it better to buy new or purchase a resale? Again, it depends.

The pros of a new home include more choices, options, and upgrades; more energy efficiency; home-builder warranties; more modern layouts and use of

---

Almost 70 percent of potential home buyers surf the Internet to collect information. Sites such as www.realtor.com or www.rent.com are quite useful for doing preliminary research. You can plug in many different parameters to narrow a search to your specifications.

space; lower costs associated with repairs; and, in a new community, greater ease making friends since your neighbors are often new to the area as well.

The pros of a resale include more bang for your buck. On a square footage basis, resales are usually less expensive; may already have amenities such as mature landscaping, watering systems, and window treatments; have no surprises in terms of the neighborhood because what you see is what you get; are often closer to stores and restaurants; and often have larger lots.

Tanya and Bruce F. were transferred several times during their career with General Electric. When moving to an area, they always bought new. The main reason? They felt it was easier for their children (and them) to make new friends. Vicki and Brent S., on the other hand, like the traditional layouts and established landscaping of an older home. In addition, they are very handy at repairs and like to be within walking distance of town. The moral: There is no right or wrong. There is only what works for you.

CUSTOM BUILDING

We've discussed purchasing a residence, but what if you've found the perfect piece of land and decide to build your retirement retreat while you finish up your last year on the job?

First, take stock of your existing home and write down any "must-haves" for your new one. For example, Celia and Jim M.'s previous home had a garage with access directly into their kitchen. In their next home, they made it a point to have the entrance into the laundry room. Angela and Michael R. put a high premium on having a first-floor master bedroom. Bob and Paula F. looked for a flat driveway so they could install a basketball hoop for their four grandchildren. Karen and Rob L. wanted their kitchen sink to have a window above it so they could look outside while performing the unpleasant task of washing dishes. Caroline B. is not happy with the lack of outlets in her existing home; she vows to address this in her next one.

Be aware of any restrictions or covenants governing the building of your new home. Jasmine and Charles K. ended up having to move their driveway 18 inches because it was not installed the required distance from their lot line.

Contact the local homebuilders' association and obtain a list of local builders. Look through the real estate sections and see who is building homes in your price range. Check out any models or projects of potential builders. Get recommendations from your soon-to-be neighbors and from realtors, and contact references provided by the builders after you meet with them. Visit the referenced homes if possible; if not, at least check out the outside. Be aware of warranties and service after the completion of your home, find out how long the builder has been in business, and be sure you feel that your personalities click. Check out builders with the Better Business Bureau. Consider hiring an architect and interior designer, as well. Input from these professionals can be invaluable to this big investment. They should be willing and able to work as partners as your residence is planned.

Use technology. E-mail and digital photographs will go a long way toward keeping everyone apprised of issues and progress. Of course, you'll need to visit the site in person periodically to see how things are going. In addition, it would be helpful to hire someone to check things out on a regular basis; in some cases, the architectural firm may do this, or perhaps a trusted friend or neighbor can keep an eye on things.

HOUSING OPTIONS

Condos, modular homes, manufactured homes, zero-lot-line homes, apartments, carriage homes, single-family homes, townhomes—the list of housing choices is extensive. (If you're looking for a less typical arrangement, such as living in an RV, in a hotel, or on a ship, check out chapter 6.) Consider: What lifestyle are you seeking? Do you love gardening, or would you rather leave yard work to someone else? Does the thought of having someone sharing adjoining walls bother you? Do you want your community to be age restricted, or do you relish interacting with all age groups? Does the security of a gated community appeal to you, or do you feel you'd be living "behind bars"?

If you're contemplating a change (say, from a single-family home to a condo), it's a good idea to rent in your potential new spot to see if that style of living is for you. It will also provide you the opportunity to become better acquainted with the area. Some things to keep in mind as you decide on housing:

(continued on page 110)

If you're building your own home, you may want to consider the "New Home Construction Bidsheet" from nationally syndicated columnist Tim Carter at www.askthebuilder.com. It covers all aspects of construction and can be e-mailed to you as an Adobe PDF file for $30.

DESIGN TIPS FROM AN EXPERT

This list, adapted from nationally syndicated columnist Tim Carter (www.askthebuilder.com), contains excellent ideas whether you're buying new construction, considering a resale, or planning to remodel your present home.

1. Interior doorknobs: Make sure that the backset hole is drilled 2¾ inches, *not* the standard 2⅜ inches. Your knuckles will thank you.

2. Second sink: We have a regular double-bowl sink and a second small bar sink next to our refrigerator. The second sink has come in handy on many occasions!

3. High vanities: Who says you have to use low cabinets in a bathroom? Are you tired of bending over to brush your teeth? Use kitchen cabinets in a bath or ask whether your cabinet company makes a 34½-inch-high cabinet instead of the usual 30- or 31-inch-high bath cabinet.

4. Shower seats: Shower seats are luxurious. Make sure they are at least 16 inches deep and anywhere from 14 inches to 17 inches tall.

5. Dual shower heads: Forget about all those fancy shower devices. Just install two shower heads to hit you from opposite directions. You may need an extra-large water heater, so plan ahead!

6. Tall garage ceilings: The average garage has lots of wasted space. If you raise the ceiling to 12 feet, you can install a useful loft that will give you all sorts of wonderful storage opportunities.

7. Large entry with closet: Many entry halls are too small to comfortably greet two or more people. Make yours spacious if possible. Be sure to have a large coat closet somewhere in the space.

8. Nine-foot ceilings: You would be surprised what a difference tall ceilings make. If the rooms are really oversized, you had better consider 10-foot ceilings.

9. Kitchen space: The distance between rows of cabinets or an island should be at least 42 inches. You will love this roomy feel.

10. Indirect lighting: Indirect lighting can really set the mood in a room. It is not hard to achieve this goal. It is an excellent idea in a family room for nighttime TV viewing. Have you flown on an airplane at night? Airlines use the soft, indirect lighting technique above the windows.

11. Electrical outlets. You need to think this one

out by doing a furniture layout plan early in the job. Who wants outlets *behind* a couch or a bed? They are useless! Place outlets exactly where lamps, radios, and appliances are going to be. Place the outlets at a correct height so you don't have to bend over or see the cords under furniture.

12. Multilevel decks and patios: A two- or three-tiered deck or patio with large areas at each level makes a dramatic outdoor jewel. Plant colorful vegetation or place planters between each level.

13. Cookout area: If you have natural gas or propane, be sure that it's extended outdoors for your grill.

14. Garage outlets: Be sure there are electrical outlets on all four walls of your garage. Have the electrician place an outdoor outlet near the garage doors for easy access if you are working outside.

15. Wide garage: Most garages are not wide enough. Be sure each garage door opening starts at least 4 feet away from a corner. Five feet is even better.

16. Window seats: These items are charming and functional.

17. Laundry room counters: Where do you fold your clothes? A countertop in a laundry room is nice.

18. Slop sink: Every house needs one. They used to be in basements. Put it near or in the laundry room.

19. Hot-water loops: Do you wait for hot water at your plumbing fixtures? Install a simple recirculating loop.

20. Storage shelves: You simply can't have enough storage shelves. If you live in a slab home, make your garage extra large to house these shelves.

21. Attic storage: Many modern houses have steep roofs. Even if you don't, you can order cost-effective attic or storage trusses—the whole roof doesn't have to be made from these, which will save money as well!

22. Paper cutouts: You must do scale cutouts of furniture to make sure room sizes are correct and that you don't block interior pathways within rooms.

23. Wide driveways: Plan for a 12-foot width for single driveways and at least 20 feet for double driveways.

24. Large garage doors: Double doors should be 18 feet wide, and single doors should be 10 feet wide.

(continued)

25. Technology wiring: You must install category 5 wiring to each room. Put it where you think a computer, TV, or appliance might be. Some rooms may need multiple cable drops. All cable runs must be home runs. Do not loop wire through the house!

26. Central vacuums: They are a real treat. Get one that is fully cyclonic.

27. Outdoor conduits: Put multiple 3-inch PVC pipes under sidewalks, drives, and patios. This will allow you to get wires to remote locations in the future.

28. Hidden safe: You can buy affordable safes that can be hidden while you build. Buy a fire-proof one!

29. Access panels: Old homes had nice access panels to get to the backs of tubs and other critical plumbing areas.

30. Shower stalls: Minimum width should be 36 inches. Bigger is better here.

31. Outdoor vents: Vent all fans, dryers, etc. to the exterior of the home. Never dump this air into a crawlspace or attic.

32. Combustion air: The building code requires this, but make sure it is not forgotten. It is a safety issue.

33. Return air vents: If you have forced-air heating and cooling in each room, except in baths and kitchens, you must have return air vents!

34. Hidden hallways: Each room has these. They are where you walk within a room. Make sure they are big enough and that you don't have too many entrances into a room. More entrances mean more hallways, which means less space for furniture.

35. Dual staircases: Old homes often had a main and rear staircase. My house has two staircases into the basement. One leads directly to the garage. They are a treat.

36. Hillside foundations: Who wants to see an ugly triangular slab of concrete on the side wall of a house? Progressive foundation companies can install treated wood strips for siding or brick ledges so the foundation can be hidden. Ask about these.

37. Door covers/porches: Builders years ago knew it was nearly impossible to stop wind-driven rain from getting past doors. That is one reason large covered porches are common on old homes. Put covered porches over all your exterior doors.

38. Overhangs: While on the same subject, roof overhangs help protect windows and the sides of the house. They work like umbrellas. Make sure they are at least 2 feet deep.

39. Laundry chute: If your bedrooms are far away from the laundry room, you will love an old-fashioned chute. Make sure it is smooth inside and at least 8 inches in diameter or 8 inches square.

40. Soundproofing: This is a hidden design feature. You must do everything possible to minimize sound transmission.

41. Creature comfort: Consider radiant heating if possible. Go one step further if you have the right conditions and do geothermal. The best heating system is a mixture of radiant heating and forced air. The forced-air system allows you to move air and filter it.

42. Built-in speakers: Consider wall speakers for the dynamic new TVs, DVDs, etc. Wait till you see what you will be able to watch from the Internet in just 5 years or less!

43. Heated garage floor: Do you work on your own cars? Does it get cold? Part of your garage floor could have a radiant loop in it connected to a small water heater. Fire up the heater the day before you intend to work!

44. Wine storage: Many people are starting to admire and acquire wine. You need a place to store it to maximize its flavor.

45. Low-E glass/window films: These invisible features that prevent damage to furniture by blocking sun rays will save you money and keep your possessions in good shape.

46. Future expansion plans: Do you think you might do a room addition? If so, plan for it now to make sure a perfectly good room doesn't become a wasted space as it is transformed into the entrance of the room addition.

47. First-floor bath: Every two-story house needs a full first-floor bath. Someone might get hurt or sick and be unable to go upstairs.

48. Blocking: These hidden framing materials allow you to securely fasten grab bars, large pictures, holiday wreaths, etc. with confidence that they won't fall. You simply need to plan where to hang things. Use large 2-by-10 or 2-by-12 blocks to provide a large target area. Take photos before the drywall goes up to be able to locate them.

Full-time versus part-time residents. If you are a full-time resident living in an area of many part-time residents (or the other way around), there may be friction. The full-timers may want strict noise ordinances; the part-timers may not care if people are having parties in their absence. Part-timers may want liberal rental arrangements; full-timers may want renters who will be there a minimum of 3 months for more continuity. Mary Lou and Bill S. live full time in a condo in Myrtle Beach, South Carolina. They find that during high season they can sometimes go for days without seeing a familiar face. Also, the sounds of people pushing carts full of luggage while moving in and out can be quite loud. Although this doesn't bother them, for others it would be anathema. If there are covenants governing these issues, you need to be comfortable with them before committing to a purchase.

Fees. The cost of a home is just one factor in choosing your residence. Keep in mind all those amenities in a planned community (golf courses, spas, pools, tennis courts) have to be paid for by someone, and that someone is probably you and your neighbors! Association dues can be quite steep, depending on the community. Frank D. found that when he tried to sell his three-bedroom townhome in a good school district in Maryland, people were attracted by the listing price of $160,000 but were turned off by the high monthly association fees for repairs and maintenance. So, you'll need to be sure to account for these; keep in mind that associations can raise dues as well.

Restrictions. Besides such understandable issues as whether rentals are allowed, neighborhood covenants can include all kinds of things, such as what time your garbage cans can be put out for trash pickup, what color you can choose for the exterior of your home, what type of basketball hoop (if any) you can install, and what changes you can make to your landscaping. Of course, the idea is to protect the value of your property, but make sure you can live with the rules and regulations.

Low-dough options. If you're looking for a single-

Condos are hot! In 2002, prices rose 11 percent, compared to the 7 percent gain for single-family homes. The National Association of Realtors reported that sales also rose by nearly 11 percent in 2002, due to the increasing numbers of retirees and first-time buyers, as well as attractive interest rates.

family home but cost is a limiting factor, consider pre-fabricated housing. Modular homes, kit homes, and manufactured homes have come a long way, baby! Materials and looks have improved, they are better and more quickly built, and they can cost about one-fifth to one-third less than a "stick-built home." According to the Census Bureau, about 10 percent of all residences are manufactured homes, with an average home cost of about $50,000 (excluding the land). Take a look at some examples: Champion Enterprises (www.championhomes.net or 248-340-9090), Clayton Homes (www.clayton.net or 800-822-0633), or Fleetwood Enterprises (www.fleetwoodhomes.com or 909-351-3500).

Universal Design

Whether you stay put, buy new, buy a resale, rent, or re-model, you need to know about a concept called "universal design." According to the Center for Universal Design, the intent of this type of design "is to simplify life for everyone by making products, communications, and the built environment more usable by as many people as possible at little or no extra cost. Universal design benefits people of all ages and abilities." Translated into specifics (we love specifics!), it means 27-inch-high electrical outlets to minimize bending, rocker switches to make turning lights on and off easier, nonslip flooring, wider hallways to accommodate a wheelchair (if necessary), etc. In other words, universal design makes a home more accessible, no matter what your age or condition. For a terrific list of exterior and interior universal design ideas, see the "Smart Ideas Checklists" on page 437.

SELLING YOUR HOME

Let's say you decide to move and put your home up for sale. What are some tried-and-true methods for ensuring you get top dollar for it?

Choose your real estate agent wisely. It goes without

The land under your prefab housing may be purchased or rented. Be careful about renting: There have been cases where people owned their homes but rented the land, and the land was sold for redevelopment. This has happened in a number of older trailer parks. The homes often cannot be moved, or it's prohibitively expensive, and the owners end up having to abandon them.

According to the Clayton Homes Web site, a *manufactured home* has been "built entirely in the factory under federal code administered by the Department of Housing and Urban Development (HUD)," while a *mobile home* is "the term used for homes built prior to June 15, 1976, when HUD code went into effect. Voluntary standards were previously in effect." A *modular home* is "built to state, local, or regional code where home will be located. Multisection units are transported to sites and installed." A *panelized home* is "built in factory, where panels that include windows, doors, wiring & siding, are transported to site and assembled. Codes are set by state or locality where sited." Lastly, a *precut home* involves "materials that are factory cut to design specifications and then transported to the site and assembled. Examples are: kit, log, and dome homes. Standards are set by state and locality."

saying that he or she should be in good standing, belong to the Multiple Listing Service, and have a current real estate license. It's preferable if real estate is the agent's full-time profession and if he or she is a local resident and really knows the area. Choose someone who will be honest in his or her comments about your home and know how to show it off to its best advantage. Ask friends, neighbors, and relatives for recommendations, interview several agents, check their references, and be sure you feel comfortable working with your pick. Although your agent will market and advertise your home, the National Association of Realtors reports that more than 80 percent of sales are due to agent contacts, not advertising or open houses. (In one of the author's neighborhoods, FOR SALE signs go up infrequently. One agent knows the area so well and has so many contacts that a call to her usually results in a sale without a sign ever going up.)

Curb Appeal

First impressions count! If prospective buyers aren't enticed or excited about your home when they pull up to the curb and get their first look, you're already fighting an uphill battle. In fact, they may never even set foot inside. The idea is that the potential purchasers should become emotionally involved with your house, envisioning it as their own and relating to the lifestyle it projects.

Take stock of the yard. Trim your trees, shrubs, and bushes, and remove dead flowers, leaves, weeds, and other debris. Be sure landscaping hasn't overwhelmed the house and that windows aren't blocked by plants. Lay down a fresh layer of mulch. Keep the lawn (which should be healthy and weed-free) mowed at an attractive height (no scalping), and edge along driveways or sidewalks. Kill grass growing through sidewalks. Think color! If you're selling at the right time of year, plant flowers (yellow is particularly effective) or use hanging baskets—get blooming flowers from a nursery.

Paint, repair, and replace. Windows or outside trim that is peeling or a front door that is bleached out from the sun are turnoffs. Replace or polish doorknobs or knockers that have become dull or damaged from the elements. Repair any fences, shutters, roofing, porches, screens, cracks, etc. Make sure your mailbox or mailbox slot is in good shape. Replace your welcome mat.

Clean. Wash windows and any outside light fixtures (make sure all light bulbs are working, while you're at it). Sweep walkways, decks, and porches. Hose off the driveway, and try to remove any oil stains. If you have or can borrow a power washer, it's great for sprucing up outdoor furniture, decks, siding, and the driveway. If not, use your hose and extra elbow grease. Tidy up the grill and surrounding area, and clean out gutters.

Downplay pets. Not everyone will be as fond of your pets as you are! Remove any "presents" your dog may have left on your property. It might be a good idea to leave the dog with a neighbor or relative during showings.

Straighten up the garage. This is one of the author's own litmus tests when considering a home. Unclutter the garage. Remove cars during a showing so the buyers can see how spacious and well-maintained it is. Remove oil spots from the floor; painting the garage floor with an

---

If you hope to avoid a Realtor's commission and want to try to sell your own home, think about using one of these online assists (remember, about two-thirds of us use the Internet for home-shopping): www.SellYourHomeYourself.com, www.PrivateForSale.com, or www.ForSaleByOwner.com. Only about 9 percent of home sales are by owner, and, of course, you'll pay for the ad.

acrylic or latex paint can make the floor gleam. Consider painting the walls as well. Neatly arrange mowers and tools. Consider buying new trash cans.

Interior Fixes

Clean. The proverb "cleanliness is next to godliness" is so very true when it comes to selling your home. Cleanliness includes odor removal, so if you have pets or there's a smoker in the house, get out the Febreze or have carpets, window treatments, and furniture professionally cleaned. Sometimes you don't notice the odors in your home—ask the Realtor or a friend for an honest opinion. Windows, mirrors, and glass doors should sparkle, and floors should shine.

Minimize. Go through closets, basements, the garage, and other storage areas. Give away things you no longer use (you probably won't fit into those size-two jeans again) to a worthy cause, such as Goodwill, the Salvation Army, or St. Vincent de Paul (of course, document this for tax purposes), or have a garage/yard sale prior to putting the house up for sale. Or, put things outside with a sign that they are free for the taking. We've done this a number of times, with great success (because of our homeowners' association rules, we only do it the evening before and the day of trash pickup). Make your drawers, closets, bookshelves, cabinets, and countertops look spacious. Store excess personal items in another location. Remove furniture that makes a room look crowded, and arrange what's left to make the room appear larger.

Repair and replace. Again, go through your home and replace faded or ripped cushions, window treatments, and carpeting. Buy new towels, throw rugs, and shower curtains for bathrooms. Fix any nail holes showing in the drywall and replace missing screws, handles, and light bulbs. Be sure all windows open and close easily and that faucets and appliances, including your air conditioner and furnace, are in good working order.

Make it cozy. Have the smell of fresh-baked cookies or pie wafting through the house when people come to look. Put fresh flowers around the house, and have some

---

A Clemson University study that found "good" landscaping increased the selling price of a home by 4 to 5 percent over that of a home with "average" landscaping, and "excellent" landscaping increased the selling price by an additional 6 to 7 percent (or more).

soft music playing in the background. Leave lights on, even during the day. Keep shades open so the light comes in, and so that your home doesn't look foreboding from outside. Remove personal mementos (such as photographs or diplomas); it's easier for a potential buyer to imagine the house is his or hers without them.

Consider hiring a professional home stager. Ever go into a model home and notice how the lamps never have cords, the desks never have bulky computers, and the bedrooms often have no dressers? Stagers can make a home look spacious and attractive, but, of course, you'll have to pay for it. They may charge by the hour or the job; some bring in rented furniture to show your home to its best advantage. Ask neighbors or Realtors (especially the larger realty companies) for referrals. Or, find an accredited staging professional in your area at www.stagedhomes.com or 800-392-7161. While this can be a pricey way to go, it may increase the amount you'll get for your home.

Leave. Don't be in the house while it is shown. This makes it easier for everyone involved.

BUYING A HOME

We've already mentioned the factors to consider when choosing a new community. Once you've been sold on the area, here are a few tips for buying your home.

Construct a wish list. Know what you want in a new home (hopefully you made this list while living in your previous residence), so you can approach the process from a methodical, logical perspective rather than an emotional or seat-of-the-pants approach.

Consider using a buyer's agent. A buyer's agent represents the buyer, not the seller (unlike Realtors, who get their fee from the sale of the house and so are paid by the seller). Buyer's agents exclusively represent your interests. Ask friends for recommendations, call the larger real estate firms, or look under "Real Estate" in the Yellow Pages—companies will often advertise that they have buyer's agents.

Have the home professionally inspected. The American Society of Home Inspectors has more than

---

You can use the handy reference "Wood Wise House Hunting" to compare homes you're considering for purchase. Go to www.beconstructive.com and click on "Home Buyers," then "Home Buying Guide." Bring along your digital camera, to help jog your memory as you review your notes!

6,000 members and is the largest professional association of home inspectors in the United States. Locate an inspector on their Web site (www.ashi.com) or call them at 800-743-2744. If it's a new home, with many warranties, you may not need to do this, but you never know. . . . Pat and Phil D. had an inspection on their new home and found that their chimney flue had been improperly installed. The builder rectified it prior to their closing.

Know these things. Is your home under a flight path, or can you hear the sounds of the highway? If there is vacant land nearby, find out how it's zoned, as well as any developments in the pipeline. Be sure there are no paper plants, landfills, or businesses nearby that would be unpleasant neighbors. (One of our neighbors downsized and ended up moving close enough to a rendering plant to "enjoy" the smell.) Orientation of the house is important: Is the main living area on display to the neighbors if you have your shades up? Will cars shine their headlights into your home as they make a turn into your neighborhood? Is it impossible to make a left turn out of your neighborhood in the morning because of traffic? Are you situated on an embankment that could be subject to erosion? Even if you're an empty nester, is your home in a good school district? Are you buying the most expensive home in the neighborhood (not so good) or the least expensive home in a good neighborhood (better)? Keep in mind that if the house has been professionally staged, you may be falling in love with an unrealistic picture of how it will be lived in. Are there many renters in the development, which can depress property values? Is the area safe?

Have your loan preapproved. You'll be in a much stronger negotiating position if you've been preapproved by the mortgage company. Check out several mortgage companies before committing, and get written specifics, including your interest rate and for how long it's locked in.

Consider the future. Eventually, you or your heirs will most likely sell your home. Even as you're buying,

---

How long does the typical person or couple look at a home prior to making an offer? Usually less than half an hour, according to Realtors! On average, a buyer walks through fewer than a dozen homes, and the average search time is 8 weeks.

think in terms of what will sell later. The National Association of Home Builders reports that more than half of consumers want a home with at least 2,000 square feet (or more than three bedrooms), a two-car garage, and at least two bathrooms. Kitchens that open into family rooms or at least have a view of a family room are desired by most. Half want a library and/or sunroom, and 80 percent need a dining room. Three-quarters want a porch, patio, deck, trees, and a fenced lot. Almost half want a brick exterior. Amenities such as parks, walking trails, and open spaces are also high on buyers' lists.

See what happens in the rain. We have homes in our neighborhood that back up to a retention pond. Although the pond works as it should, the level of water becomes frighteningly high in a heavy rain. It's a good idea to visit the home you're considering purchasing during a downpour to check out the effects on the inside and outside of the house.

THE BUY-SELL CONUNDRUM

In most cases, you'll need the money from the sale of your existing home to buy your new home. You may have to put things in storage for a while or find temporary housing, but it's better than having two mortgages, unless you know you can carry two homes. Perhaps you can have a contingency on the sale of your house, but many potential buyers won't go for that; or maybe you can state in your contract that you'll remain in the house for a specified time after the sale, paying the new owners a daily agreed-upon "rent" while you find a new home. Maybe your buyers will agree to a far-off closing date. In actuality, you may just have to move out and make the best of it while you search for your new place! If you have grown children, perhaps you can temporarily move in with them. (This could be payback if they've boomeranged back to your home in the past!)

Warning: A number of problems have been associated with EIFS (Exterior Installation Finish System), or synthetic stucco. There are lawsuits against manufacturers, installers, and builders using this product. Water can get in, but not out, which may result in decay of the underlying wood and perhaps mold growth and termite infestation. If purchasing a home of this type, be extremely cautious.

Walk around. Talk to people living in the neighborhood. You'll get a good sense of the issues affecting the development and see whether you'd feel comfortable living there. Return at least three times over a 24-hour period to get a sense of the community at different times of the day. Finding out why the seller is listing the home can be important in negotiating the best price—loss of a job may be a big incentive, for example.

Ask a few questions. What did the seller pay for the house? This is a matter of public record and can help you estimate how much equity the sellers have in the house (you can find out through the local tax assessor's office, and the information is usually available online for free). For example, if the sellers bought their home for $300,000 2 years ago and they're now asking $500,000, you might well question the inflated asking price. Other questions: How old is the roof? Air conditioner? Hot water heater? Other appliances? Sellers fill out a disclosure form, but if they have lived there a relatively short time, they may not know those answers. Ask about the previous owners, and see if you can contact them.

Read everything carefully before signing!

Best advice? Caveat emptor (let the buyer beware).

MOVING DAY

Now you need to get from here to there. Will you move yourself, like more than half the population does (according to U-Haul), or use a professional mover for some or all of the work? Regardless, planning is imperative. To help plan your move, see the "Moving Planner Checklist" from North American Van Lines on page 441. They provide a handy list of things to do, from 2 or more months ahead of time through moving day.

If you go the do-it-yourself route by renting a moving truck, you will save money, but check into getting additional coverage on your homeowner's policy.

A reverse mortgage is a loan against your home that allows you to continue living there and to collect a monthly check until you die or sell your house. There are restrictions. For more information, see chapter 9.

Most rental companies exclude many items (such as jewelry and furs and damages due to improper packing).

How much will movers cost? Price is affected by the weight of your belongings, distance, location (moving to a rural area may be less expensive than moving to the middle of a city), time of the move (nonsummer months can be less expensive), amount of packing involved, and any other services you require, such as storage. Friends and relatives can be a good source of recommendations for moving companies, and it's a good idea to consult the Better Business Bureau to see if there are any complaints against the companies you're considering.

Experts recommend that you obtain estimates from at least three moving companies. Estimates can take several forms; most often, they are binding or non-binding. A binding estimate is just that—you are bound to pay the price in the estimate whether the final cost of the move is more or less. A nonbinding estimate approximates the cost of your move; you are then limited to paying up to 110 percent of the amount of the nonbinding estimate at delivery and must pay any additional charges within 30 days; your final cost is determined by actually weighing the shipment. There is a third type of estimate called a not-to-exceed estimate; it may go by other names (such as a price protection estimate). In this type of estimate, you pay the lower of the actual cost of the move or the binding estimate cost. Of course, if you tack on additional services (such as storage), or ship additional pieces of furniture, you will be charged extra!

Clarify with the mover how payment will be made. Some do not accept major credit cards; others do. Many do not accept personal checks. You may need a certified check, money order, or cash. Get everything in writing!

What if you have problems with the move? Is there any recourse? Short-circuit any problems by signing up with a reputable company, but if issues arise, you do have some rights. Federal law requires your mover to provide a pamphlet, "Your Rights and Responsibilities when You Move." You can read this information online at www.fmcsa.dot.gov and click on the link under "Moving." If you have a complaint about

---

If you need storage or assistance loading or unloading, check out www.emove.com to find help.

your mover you'd like to file with the Federal Motor Carrier Safety Administration, log on to their site at www.1-888-dot-saft.com/ or call them at 888-368-7238 anytime.

THEY'RE BAAAAAAAACK! (BOOMERANG KIDS)

What if your kids fly back to the nest? This phenomenon is referred to as "boomerang kids," and we didn't feel we could wrap up the chapter without discussing this not-so-uncommon event.

About 10 percent of adults between the ages of 25 and 34 live with their parents, according to the 2000 U.S. Census. A survey by Healthy Workplaces consulting firm found that 9 percent of respondents had an adult child living at home. Several explanations have been advanced for this increasing trend: the not-so-great job market; the need to pay back college loans; sky-high rents; boomer parents not wanting their children to grow up; kids having been overindulged and spoiled; marriages occurring later in life; divorce among young adults; changing parent-child dynamics (parents acting more like friends than parents); and a drawing out of the period before kids become fully functioning adults (*Newsweek* termed this "adultolescence").

What's a no-longer-empty nester to do? Some parents love the idea that their children are returning. It makes them feel younger, and they are gratified that their children feel comfortable using them as a safety net. Katie H., for example, moved back into her parents' home after college graduation during her first year of teaching. It enabled Katie to buy a car and save enough money to move into an apartment (with a roommate) during her second year of teaching. Her parents were delighted to have Katie living at home.

Others aren't quite so delighted. Cecilia and Kyle P.'s son also moved home after graduation. He's sleeping in until noon every day, barely contributes to the housework, and makes only a token effort to look for a job. In short, they are losing their minds!

To get a rough idea of the cost of a proposed move, go to the North American Van Lines Web site, www.northamerican-vanlines.com, and click on "Free Estimate."

Expert Advice

Discusss a time line. Adult children should understand this is a *temporary* arrangement. A specific move-out date should be determined (for example, 2 years would be pretty generous).

Develop house rules. We're talking adult children here, so the idea is to foster independence. Consider charging rent and/or having your children cook, contribute to the upkeep of the home, and wash their own clothes. Determine guidelines for such things as smoking in the house, having friends or significant others over, and/or people spending the night.

Be a cheerleader. In some cases, you may need to give a little nudge to get your bird out of the nest. Let your children know that you know they can do it. Encourage them to work toward independence, whether it's by sending out résumés, looking for a roommate, or getting counseling if they need it. You and your spouse or significant other should be in sync on the time line and house rules.

Examine your own agenda. If you're an empty nester, does having a child back in the home satisfy a need to be needed? Do you lack confidence in your child's ability to fend for himself or herself? Do you want your children to stay dependent forever? If that's the case, counseling may be helpful for you as well. *Psychology Today* termed this inability of parents to let go "permaparenting."

What is home? Where is home? It may be a no-brainer if you're not going anywhere, or finding your potential utopia may open up almost limitless possibilities that you'll need to whittle down. Keep in mind, though, that there could be many correct decisions—it's doubtful that only one place would fit your personal lifestyle requirements.

If you are one of those people who have a yen for the unusual, though, chapter 6, "What Are Some Niche Retirement Lifestyles?" is for you!

Century 21 offers a "Mature Moves" service. Targeted to those between 55 and 70 years of age, the service helps to clarify a client's psychological needs (such as proximity to relatives) and physical needs (such as universal design issues) and assists in purchasing a home that meets those goals. Find a "Mature Moves" professional at www.century21.com (type "Mature Moves" in the space bar) or 800-4-HOUSES.

"Chance favors the prepared mind." A wise man, that Louis Pasteur!

In researching retirement areas for our seminars and this book, we discovered a place in the southeastern United States that looked great on paper. We (along with our spouses) flew from Cincinnati to Florida in the morning, looked at oceanfront lots in a brand new golf community, made and had our offers accepted, and flew home that evening.

All our previous homework and legwork made a "snap" decision possible, and as a result we now each own a place on the ocean—a lifelong dream for both couples! Ⓛ

A woman walked into a pet shop and asked the clerk for several large rats and a few dozen cockroaches. By way of explanation, she said, "I'm moving out of my apartment, and my lease says when I move I must leave the apartment in the same condition as I found it."

PART II

WHERE SHOULD YOU SPEND
YOUR RETIREMENT YEARS?

5

WHERE SHOULD YOU MOVE?

Recommended Locations within the United States

"A problem becomes a pleasure when you come up with the solution."
—Anonymous

Where are the beautiful beaches? The gorgeous golf courses? The best boating spots? The places with the lowest cost of living? In other words, if you're thinking about relocating, where should you move?

Of course, we recognize that *most* people will remain where they are when they retire. But for those who do want to move, this is the chapter for you. The legwork to determine some of the most desirable places to live in the United States has already been done!

To accomplish this monumental task, we first examined current books, periodicals, Internet resources, and articles that rate the best places to retire. Cross-referencing these sources, we generated an extensive list of potential places to relocate, supplemented by additional locations garnered from our own and others' experiences. We then visited these areas, exploring neighborhoods and the towns' amenities, speaking to residents, and investigating trends. We interviewed retirees, people who were close to retiring, and well-traveled baby boomers to get additional information and insights. Our retirement seminars, "Searching for Nirvana," gave us the opportunity—via discussions, Q&A segments, and the preference inventories we gave the participants—to tap into the concerns and interests of those about to retire or recently retired. Finally, we narrowed down our list to those communities we simply liked the best, based on activities such as riding bikes on the beach on Hilton Head Island; playing tennis in Chapel Hill; patronizing restaurants in Santa Fe; golfing in Scottsdale; visiting the Thursday night farmers' market in San Luis Obispo; boating in Punta Gorda; and walking on the college campus in Tucson. (As you might guess, this was the toughest part of our job, but it had to be done!)

Is the list comprehensive? Of course not. New communities develop, revitalization occurs, and unforeseen circumstances, such as the moving or bankruptcy of a major employer, can change the complexion of a town. In addition, it would be impossible to visit every single community in the United States. What is desirable for one person (warm winters, for example) could be a negative for someone else. So, using the surveys of what people want in a retirement area as the basis for selection, and coupling them with other research and our own biases, we produced our final list. We know you may feel you're already living in the perfect location, and if it isn't included here, we're always open to suggestions and new locales to check out!

We should emphasize that our recommended locations are not all-inclusive, nor is there any such thing as the perfect retirement location. For example, you may have to balance fantastic weather with lots of traffic, or a wonderful beach area with mediocre medical facilities. We also realize some people want a second home in a place that wouldn't have to meet the same criteria as their permanent home. So, near the end of the chapter we provide a list of suggestions for second-home locations. We also present our "Honor Roll" of what we feel are the best of the best primary-home locations.

For each city we recommend, we provide assessments of the major features a person should consider before deciding to relocate. We'd like to point out a few

---

Harris Interactive, a marketing research firm, queried adults about which state they'd most like to live in (that's not their current state). Here are the 2002 results, in order: California, Florida (the first time Florida has not been number one since the poll began in 1997), Hawaii, Colorado, North Carolina, Arizona, Tennessee, New York, Washington, Oregon, Montana, Virginia and Alaska (tied), Texas, and Georgia.

things about some of our sources for each location.

Population figures, for the most part, are from the 2000 U.S. Census. If more recent population figures were available, we used them.

We've based the cost of living partly on the ACCRA (former acronym of the American Chamber of Commerce Researchers Association), which produces the Cost of Living Index. This is a measure of goods and services (transportation, medical costs, groceries, housing, utilities, and other miscellaneous items) for cities with populations of at least 50,000. The U.S. average Cost of Living Index is pegged at 100. For example, New York City had an ACCRA cost of living index of 216, while Raleigh-Durham in North Carolina was 101 for the same time period. Thus, it would cost more than twice as much to live in New York City as in the Raleigh-Durham area. If a city did not meet the size criterion (or did not elect to participate, since membership in ACCRA is voluntary), an-

other cost of living index is provided, if available. For example, Florida has the Florida Price Level Index. This index compares cost of living within counties in Florida, with 100 as the Florida state average. Finally, in some cases, cost of living is described more vaguely, such as "about average," "lower than average," or "above average." Hard numbers are provided, if available, and most data is from 2003.

As for safety, we generally included only locations with average or lower-than-average crime rates. If a recommended area has an unusually high (or extraordinarily low) crime rate, we comment on it; otherwise, you can assume the safety data is around the average.

Most of our safety statistics were published by the FBI in its Uniform Crime Report (2001 or 2002), which computes a crime index for cities with a population of more than 100,000. The FBI Crime Index is calculated from the combination of violent crime (murder, manslaughter, rape, robbery, and assault) and property

---

Which locations have the highest percentage of residents age 65 and older? A 2000 Brookings Institution analysis by William Frey lists these as the top five metropolitan areas: Sarasota, Florida (30%); West Palm Beach, Florida (24%); Tampa/St. Petersburg/Clearwater, Florida (21%); Scranton/Hazelton, Pennsylvania (19%); and Pittsburgh, Pennsylvania (18%).

crimes (burglary, larceny, auto theft, and arson) committed annually in a city. Violent crime accounts for about 12 percent of the total crime index, and property crimes account for approximately 88 percent. In 2001, the average U.S. crime index was 41.6 crimes per 1,000 inhabitants. Keep in mind, however, that reporting is voluntary, and you won't find FBI statistics on towns with populations under 100,000. Another source of our safety statistics was the Florida Department of Law Enforcement Uniform Crime Reports for 2001, which provides a crime index rate for each county in Florida.

We've attempted to provide the most recent unemployment data available, from 2003, and listed the largest employers for an area. Although not everyone plans to work after retirement, we believe that a good place to relocate is one where there is a reasonable amount of economic vitality.

When suggesting notable neighborhoods, we often, but not always, chose newer and larger communities with a long build-out time frame. In fact, some of the larger gated communities may have completion dates that extend a decade or more. Although we realize this type of neighborhood is not everyone's preference, investigating newer and larger communities provided more opportunities to interact with those who have relocated than did older, smaller neighborhoods. It also gave us insight into new building trends and demographic patterns.

At the end of each city discussion is a summary of what we think are the strengths and weaknesses. We also offer a "report card" that summarizes our overall assessment of each city. This is, of course, ultimately a subjective grade, but one that's grounded in fact, research, firsthand experience, and first-person consultations. Since we only included places we thought were worth considering for relocation, the report cards tend to have higher-than-average marks (not unlike all the above-average children in Garrison Keillor's *Prairie Home Companion*).

Let's take a look at some cities you may want to consider sinking new roots into.

You may have heard about the guy who had his head in an oven and his feet in a bucket of ice. When asked how he felt, he answered, "On average, I feel great!" Consider the statistical averages in this book in the same light.

ALABAMA

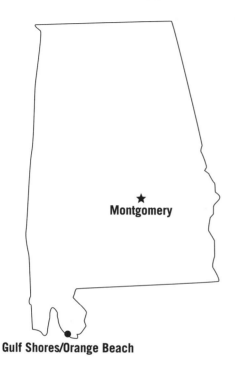

★ **Montgomery**

Gulf Shores/Orange Beach

Capital: Montgomery

Nickname: Yellowhammer State

Motto: "We dare defend our rights"

Flower: Camellia

Bird: Yellowhammer

Population: 4,447,100

Fascinating Fact: The Hall of History in Bessemer houses Hitler's typewriter.

Alabama's Gulf Coast: Gulf Shores and Orange Beach

REPORT CARD

Overall Rating:	B
Climate:	A-
Cost of Living:	A
Health Care:	B-
Transportation:	B
What's to Do:	B-

"Sweet Home Alabama" is a possibility if you choose this 32-mile stretch of beach on the Gulf of Mexico. Enjoying the same dazzling sugar-white sand and turquoise water as Florida's Panhandle, the adjoining coastal towns of Gulf Shores and Orange Beach are laid back, friendly, and growing. The permanent population of these two small communities increased about 60 percent over the last 10 years. Mild winters make this area a popular haven for snowbirds.

Cost of living is competitive and crime is low; unfortunately, the latter often holds true for wages. Alabama's lure for those in the second half of their lives is reflected in the fact that it is now one of the top states for retirees. Tourism is the engine that propels the local economy.

Access to Gulf Shores is fairly convenient: Interstates 65 and 10 are major arteries that connect to Alabama Highway 59 (Gulf Shores Parkway), and Pensacola and Mobile provide the airports, both within about an hour's drive. Jack Edwards Airport in Gulf Shores accommodates private and corporate planes. The area is a little light in the cultural realm; you may need to travel to a major city for a fix of the arts and theater.

If you're looking for world-class fishing; a serene, ecologically diverse environment; a pleasant climate (other than during the hot and humid Julys and Augusts); plenty of golf; and a polite southern ambience, take a look at Alabama's Gulf Coast.

Who Lives in Gulf Shores and Orange Beach?

Gulf Shores has about 5,000 permanent residents, and Orange Beach has approximately 4,000. About 40 percent of Gulf Shores residents are 50 or over; the percentage for Orange Beach is about 50 percent.

What's the Cost?

Alabama's property taxes are among the lowest in the country. The cost of living in Gulf Shores and Orange Beach is a little less than the national average of 100. The median home price averaged between $123,000 and $172,000 in 2001.

What's to Do?

Angling, golfing, beachcombing, boating, parasailing, diving, and enjoying the flora and fauna are all possible activities. Shop at the outlets in Foley, a 5-mile drive. Day trips include exploring Fort Morgan and Fort Gaines, Dauphin Island Estuarium, the 65-acre Bellingrath Gardens and Home, and the USS *Alabama* Battleship Memorial Park. Both New Orleans and Montgomery are less than a 4-hour drive away.

Where Are the Jobs?

Restaurants, real estate, golf courses—companies involved with tourism are the primary employers, in addi-

What's It Like Outside?	Jan.	Apr.	Jul.	Oct.	Rain (in.)	Snow (in.)
Average High (°F)	58	74	89	78	59	–
Average Low (°F)	44	63	77	65	–	–

tion to retail, medical care, and education. The unemployment rate for Baldwin County (where Gulf Shores and Orange Beach are located) is 4 percent, and it is one of the fastest-growing counties in the country.

Where Are the Doctors?

South Baldwin Regional Medical Center has over 200 physicians in this more than 80-bed hospital, located 5 miles away in Foley. There are also walk-in medical care centers in Orange Beach and Gulf Shores. Pensacola's Sacred Heart Hospital is 30 miles away, and the Mobile Infirmary Medical Center and the University of South Alabama's hospitals are located in Mobile, 50 miles northwest from the Gulf Coast.

Where Are Some Notable Neighborhoods?

As expected, cost varies according to location and type of home. For example, Summer Trace in Gulf Shores (www.rent.net/direct/summertrace or 251-968-1700) rents a one-bedroom apartment about a mile from the beach for $560 per month. Condos in the Bayshore Towers on the Bay at Perdido Pass in Orange Beach sell for around $400,000 (www.bayshoretowersrealty.com or 877-518-3008). Examples of prices in the gated golf and tennis community of Peninsula (www.thepeninsula.com or 800-646-5554) in Gulf Shores include homesites for around $100,000, condos for $225,000, and estate-sized homes for $800,000.

true LIFE **Ken and Rita W. live in Deer Park, Illinois, an upscale suburb of Chicago.** About 4 years ago, they purchased a beachfront condo at the Beach Club Towers (www.beach-clubal.com) in Gulf Shores, Alabama, which they discovered when Ken had business in the area. They were attracted by the sun, sand, weather, friendly people, manageable distance from their permanent home, and cultural diversity and activities in the area. Ken and Rita plan on keeping their condo as their second home and living in Gulf Shores during the winter months and while vacationing.

Thirty-three major hurricanes have affected the Gulf Coast (from Texas to the Florida Panhandle) over the past century.

Rita advises people looking for an ideal location to stay away from congested main roads, and Ken suggests checking out what the natives (not just the tourists) do for recreation and culture.

Perfect climate (great for golf!), a rural atmosphere, low crime, and the vitality that a variety of cultures bring to Gulf Shores make it a very desirable place to Ken and Rita. ⓛ

How Do I Pursue Lifelong Learning?

Faulkner State Community College/Gulf Shores Campus includes programs in culinary arts, hospitality services management, landscape operations management, and leisure facilities management on its 15-acre campus. The Baldwin County Campus of the University of South Alabama is located in Fairhope, about 35 miles from the Gulf Coast.

Strengths

Beaches, beaches, beaches! The 32 miles of Gulf Coast are nicely apportioned, with about one-third residential, one-third commercially developed, and one-third protected land. Lots of building and growth are happening in the Gulf Coast.

Weaknesses

Medical, educational, and cultural offerings are adequate, but not stellar. You may have to travel elsewhere to purchase major-ticket items.

FYI

Check out these sources for additional information: Alabama Gulf Shores Chamber of Commerce (www. alagulfcoastchamber.com or 251-968-6904); Gulfside Living (www.gulfsideliving.com); and *The Islander* local newspaper (205-968-6414). The Mobile and Pensacola daily papers also serve the Gulf Coast.

'Bama's top tourist attraction is the "Unclaimed Baggage Center" in Scottsboro. After 3 months, if the airlines are unable to find a bag's owner, both luggage and contents are sold to this unique, non-airline-affiliated shop. Over one million visitors a year scour this unusual department store. From suits of armor to snakes to surfboards (along with the more conventional stuff), this place has it all. It will take you about 7 hours to get there from the Gulf Coast.

ARIZONA

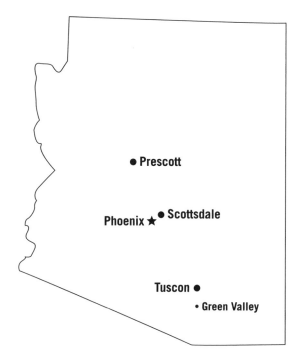

Capital: Phoenix

Nickname: The Grand Canyon State

Motto: "God enriches"

Flower: Saguaro Cactus Blossom

Bird: Cactus Wren

Population: 5,130,632

Fascinating Fact: Lake Havasu City is now home to the original London Bridge.

Prescott

REPORT CARD

Overall Rating:	A-
Climate:	A
Cost of Living:	A-
Health Care:	B
Transportation:	B
What's to Do:	A

Prescott's rich history dates back to the gold rush days of 1838 and is reflected by the fact that it has more than 500 buildings on the National Register of Historic Places. This western town is located in Arizona's central mountains, about 100 miles northwest of Phoenix and 90 miles southwest of Flagstaff. There's a small-town feel, the people are friendly, and the residents think their city has almost perfect weather. With an ideal four-season climate and summer temperatures that rarely top 85 degrees, they may be right!

In the hot summer months, "sunbirds" (including residents from the Phoenix/Scottsdale area) flock to Prescott to cool off. The airport, Ernest A. Love Field, provides commuter service to Phoenix Sky Harbor International Airport.

Arizona's natural beauty can be enjoyed with day trips to some pretty exciting places. Prescott National Forest, with

450 miles of scenic trails for hiking, backpacking, horseback riding, and mountain biking, provides the outdoor enthusiast with a great playground. The Grand Canyon is a 265-mile round-trip excursion. Or, take the Soldier's Trail to Flagstaff and visit Montezuma's Castle and Montezuma's Well, ancient Indian cliff dwellings from the 12th and 13th centuries. Alpine skiing in the Arizona Snowbowl, outside Flagstaff, is easily accessible and only about 90 miles away. And gorgeous Sedona is about an hour's drive away.

Prescott's elevation is 5,347 feet. The altitude, coupled with mountain breezes, abundant sunshine, and moderate year-round humidity of 45 percent, make the climate in this small Arizona town something to brag about. July and August tend to be the rainiest months, with cooling afternoon thunderstorms.

Who Lives in Prescott?

You will find a diverse population among Prescott's 35,000 residents. Caucasians comprise about 88 percent of the total, Hispanics about 8 percent, and Native Americans and Asians also have a presence. Over 40 percent of the population is over age 55.

What's the Cost?

In 2002, the Prescott-Prescott Valley area had an ACCRA average of 104.1.

What's to Do?

Much of the activity in the city of Prescott is centered in the downtown Courthouse Plaza. The white granite courthouse sets the stage for many a Prescott festival—Bluegrass Festival, Territorial Days, Fair on the Square, and Fall Fest, to name just a few. When you are downtown, it's hard to miss the friendly small-town atmosphere and easy to understand why Prescott has the nickname "Everybody's Hometown."

Community theater draws on local talent to provide a full season of drama, musicals, and slapstick. The 1,200-seat performing arts facility at Yavapai College hosts a variety of entertainment throughout the year and houses an

What's It Like Outside?	Jan.	Apr.	Jul.	Oct.	Rain (in.)	Snow (in.)
Average High (°F)	50	67	88	72	12	17
Average Low (°F)	21	34	56	37	–	–

art gallery and sculpture garden. Three museums—the Phippen, Smoki, and Sharlot Hall—will take you back to the days of the Old West in Prescott while you enjoy a fascinating history lesson through the eyes of the Anglos and the Native Americans.

The Prescott National Forest—home to the world's largest contiguous stand of Ponderosa pine—provides visitors with 20 recreational facilities, including an equestrian facility for campers with horses. At over 7,000 feet, the Granite Mountain Wilderness Area will challenge even the most experienced rock climber. Hiking, hunting, fishing, backpacking, horseback riding—it's all here if you're up for adventure.

Speaking of adventure, why not ride an authentic 1901 steam train to the Grand Canyon? Travel through Arizona's Old West on this 2½-hour trip from the town of Williams, which is about an hour's drive from Prescott, to the Canyon.

Where Are the Jobs?

The town, the school district, retail establishments, Prescott newspapers, and the Arizona Department of Transportation are among the biggest employers. Companies such as Better-Bilt Home Products, Printpak, Inc., and Ace Retail Support Center also provide a significant number of jobs. The unemployment rate is 5.1 percent.

Where Are the Doctors?

The Yavapai Regional Medical Center serves the Prescott area. It's an acute-care, comprehensive hospital. The Northern Arizona Veterans Administration Medical Center also has its main facility in Prescott.

Where Are Some Notable Neighborhoods?

Prescott Lakes (www.prescottlakes.com or 877-717-2300) is a gated golf community that sits on 1,150 beautiful acres with scenic views from almost any location. Hale Irwin built the par 72 golf course, and Del Webb is building The Cottages, a community within this existing neighborhood. The Cottages are priced from the $200,000s to the $300,000s; the Villages are luxury condominiums priced from the $140,000s, and estate homes are priced from $500,000. The Athletic Center offers indoor and outdoor

---

MSN House & Home ranked Prescott third on its list of 10 "Best Places to Retire."

swimming, a fitness center, and great mountain views.

Talking Rock (www.talkingrockranch.com or 866-433-4220) is a private, gated golf community 20 minutes from downtown Prescott that features over 1,000 acres of open space and an 18-hole golf course. The Ranch Compound offers fitness, swimming, and tennis. Cottages start in the high $300,000s, and custom homes start in the $600,000s.

Forest Trails (www.prescottgolf.com/wp or 928-776-1166), with custom homes from the $200,000s and up, is a neighborhood with quiet streets and great views. The Granite Oaks community offers 1-to-2-acre lots beginning around $150,000 and homes from the high $200,000s.

How Do I Pursue Lifelong Learning?

In addition to its degree and certificate programs, Yavapai College offers non-credit courses through its Retirement College, which also plays host to the largest residential Elderhostel program in the world. Prescott College is a small, private liberal arts college of about 1,000 students with an adult degree program; Northern Arizona University offers programs in conjunction with Yavapai College; and Embry-Riddle Aeronautical University (ERAU) specializes in aerospace and aviation.

Strengths

"Everybody's Hometown" has the allure of the Old West and the scenic beauty of the Granite Dells, freshwater lakes, and the surrounding mountains. This town is away from it all, yet close enough to big-city life—Phoenix is 100 miles away, and Las Vegas fewer than 300. The climate is hard to beat.

Weaknesses

Except for commuter service to Phoenix, air travel requires a drive or flight to the Phoenix Sky Harbor Airport. It does snow, and the temperatures on winter nights are often below freezing.

FYI

Check out these sources for additional information: Prescott Chamber of Commerce (www.prescottchamber.com or 800-266-2000); the *Daily Courier* (928-445-3333) and the *Arizona Republic* (928-445-4181).

Four beautiful lakes surround Prescott. Willow Lake and Watson Lake are minutes from downtown, Goldwater Lake is 8 miles south of the courthouse, and Lynx Lake is a 55-acre man-made lake 15 minutes away.

Scottsdale

REPORT CARD

Overall Rating:	A-
Climate:	B+
Cost of Living:	B-
Health Care:	A
Transportation:	A
What's to Do?	A

Are you ready for a move to the "Valley of the Sun"? Located in central Arizona in the Sonoran Desert, Scottsdale, "the West's Most Western Town," offers you quick access to the big-city life of Phoenix and the benefits of a college town in Tempe. Scottsdale is upscale and dynamic, with a mix of Southwestern and contemporary art galleries, great dining and nightlife, and shopping that—well, you need to see it to believe it!

Approximately eight million visitors come to Scottsdale each year, and golf is just one of the attractions. Scottsdale is one of the foremost golf destinations in the nation. The surrounding areas boast more than 200 courses that can be played 365 days a year. There are more than 65 resorts and hotels, 500 restaurants, and over 58 miles of bike paths. Think "relaxation and rejuvenation"—words used to describe Scottsdale's spa experience. Currently, 14 resort spas find their home in Scottsdale. There is no ocean, but there are mountains to climb and rivers to raft.

The Phoenix Sky Harbor Airport is a short 20-minute drive from Old Town Scottsdale. About 20 major airlines fly in and out of Sky Harbor. If you're looking for a diversion, the Grand Canyon is a 4½-hour drive, and Las Vegas is about 3 hours away.

Who Lives in Scottsdale?

This vibrant city continues to grow beyond its 215,000 official residents; Scottsdale has grown 56 percent since 1990. About 40 percent of the population is over the age of 55, with a median age of 42 years. There is a sharp seasonal increase in population when it's cold in other areas of the country.

More than half of the five million people who live in the state of Arizona reside in or near Scottsdale in Maricopa County.

With 330 days of sunshine each year, outdoor activities are a way of life, although sometimes it's necessary to enjoy the outdoors before dawn to avoid that searing sunshine in July and August!

What's the Cost?

When cost of living is calculated, Scottsdale is blended into the Phoenix metropolitan area. Accordingly, the ACCRA ranks the area as 99. (Scottsdale, however, is a fashionable resort town with expensive housing, dining, and shopping. Thus, the ACCRA is not a true reflection of the cost of living here.) Depending on the zip code, median home sale prices range from $163,000 to $546,000.

What's to Do?

Scottsdale offers an extensive list of action-packed outdoor activities. Off-road Jeep and Hummer tours, rafting, tubing and water sports, ecological outings, and hot air ballooning are activities that keep residents (and tourists) in love with the Valley of the Sun. If you start out hiking in one of many city or state parks, you may be ready to tackle 2,700-foot Camelback Mountain before you know it.

Folks in Scottsdale are not always horseback riding and hiking, though. They take tremendous pleasure in the arts as well. ArtWalk, a Thursday night tradition, finds the art galleries open late with special exhibits and artist receptions. One- to 3-hour tours and desert walks are available at Frank Lloyd Wright's Taliesin West. Arizona State University's Kerr Cultural Center offers musical and theatrical events, as well as visual arts exhibits.

Into sports? Scottsdale Stadium is home to the San Francisco Giants' spring training, and the Chicago Cubs train in Mesa, Arizona, just a short drive away.

Living in Scottsdale means all of Arizona is yours to explore. A short drive takes you to Sedona, the Grand Canyon, Monument Valley, the Petrified Forest, and Lake Havasu with its 23 miles of shoreline and that refreshing, cool blue water for swimming and waterskiing.

But save some energy for shopping! Fashion Mall's 225 boutiques, galleries, and department stores are a good

What's It Like Outside?	Jan.	Apr.	Jul.	Oct.	Rain (in.)	Snow (in.)
Average High (°F)	65	84	106	88	7	–
Average Low (°F)	41	55	81	60	–	–

place to start. It's the Southwest's largest shopping destination. Other unique shopping experiences await you at Borgata of Scottsdale and El Pedregal Festival Marketplace.

If this list of things to do has you exhausted, plan a visit to one of the many resort spas in the area.

Where Are the Jobs?

The tourism, retail, health care, and hospitality industries are the major employers. Prestigious companies such as Motorola, the Mayo Clinic, PCS, and Vanguard have a presence here as well. Scottsdale's average unemployment rate is 3.8 percent.

Where Are the Doctors?

The big name in Scottsdale is the Mayo Clinic. Need we say more? There is a hotel right on the campus grounds of this comprehensive facility. Healthsouth Scottsdale Rehabilitation Hospital and Scottsdale Memorial Hospital also contribute to health care, and there are a number of other facilities in the area.

Where Are Some Notable Neighborhoods?

Several of the suggested notable neighborhoods have a city address other than Scottsdale but are within a 30- or 40-minute drive of the amenities of the Scottsdale/Phoenix area. These new communities are great for retirees or for second homes.

Grayhawk (www.grayhawk.com or 800-GRAY-HAWK) is a diverse community with housing options for most budgets. The amenities include numerous parks, 30 miles of trails, two golf courses, restaurants, and medical facilities. And here are a few examples of residential areas: the Lofts is an apartment community renting from about $800 per month; the Enclave is a rental townhome community priced from about $950 per month; Tesoro is comprised of villas and townhomes priced from around $200,000; Homes by Towne is group of condominiums priced from around $200,000; and single-family homes are available from Columbia Communities from around $400,000—your choice!

Anthem Country Club (www.anthemcountryclub.com or 888-717-9777) has homes beginning in the $200,000s. Most of these residences have golf course views or views of the desert terrain. This community was voted "Best Master-Planned Community in America" by the National Association of Home Builders in 2001.

Trilogy at Power Ranch (www.mytrilogylife.com or 480-279-2100), in Gilbert, a 20-minute drive from

Scottsdale, is an active adult community with homes from around $130,000. It boasts a learning center, social clubs, and a wellness center, and don't forget the views of the San Tan Mountains.

Desert Mountain (www.desertmountain.com or 800-255-5519) is a gated golf community with 90 holes of Jack Nicklaus Signature Golf, as well as tennis, spa, fitness, and swim facilities. Desert Mountain is very exclusive, very expensive, and very beautiful. Available lots in this 8,000-acre enclave begin around $800,000. About 300 homesites remain, and there will be about 2,600 residences when complete. You'll need millions to live in this fabulous community of custom homes.

How Do I Pursue Lifelong Learning?

Arizona State University serves 57,000 students on three nearby campuses: Tempe, Phoenix, and Mesa. Scottsdale Community College offers 2-year associate degrees, and the Frank Lloyd Wright School of Architecture offers master's and bachelor's degrees.

Strengths

The warm, dry, sunny climate will encourage an active lifestyle. The beauty of the desert surroundings with the mountains as a backdrop is hard to beat. New communities are springing up in all the neighboring areas, making housing more affordable and adding to the growth of the city. The populace is highly educated, with almost half the residents having at least one college degree.

Weaknesses

One hundred and six degrees is hot, no matter what they say about the "comfort index"! The millions of tourists visiting the golf courses, spas, and restaurants create lots of traffic. Depending on where you're from, you could get homesick for green grass and trees with falling leaves.

 Ann and Joe H. live and work in Dayton, Ohio, and bought a second residence in Scottsdale 4 years ago.

They vacationed and had business in Scottsdale and always enjoyed their time there, savoring the fantastic weather (from September to May), cultural activities, and diversity of age groups. Ann and Joe's decision to purchase a condo was also influenced by Scottsdale's legendary shopping, restaurants, concerts, shows, and museums.

Scottsdale's low crime rate and the fact that the adjoining city of Phoenix is large but has a small-town feel and casual lifestyle were also factors in their choice.

Because of the distance, their time there is limited, and they do depend on friends to keep an eye on their residence. Ann's advice is to "spend time wherever you're considering, and see how it is to live there in all seasons." ⓛ

FYI

Check out these sources for additional information: City of Scottsdale (www.scottsdaleaz.gov or 480-312-6500); Business Chamber of Commerce (www.scottsdalechamber.com or 480-945-8481); Convention and Visitors Bureau www.scottsdalecvb.com or 866-475-0535); the *Scottsdale Republic* (800-332-6733); and the *Scottsdale Tribune* (480-946-5000).

Tucson

REPORT CARD

Overall Rating:	A-
Climate:	A-
Cost of Living:	A-
Health Care:	A
Transportation:	B+
What's to Do:	A

Located less than an hour from the Mexican border, Tucson is a diverse city that reflects its Native American, Hispanic, and Asian heritage. Surrounded by 9,000-foot mountains, this desert valley city is about 2,500 feet above sea level. *Tucson* is derived from a Native American word meaning "water at the foot of black mountain." Southern Arizona enjoys over 300 days of sunshine a year, and the convenient location of the University of Arizona contributes to the city's vitality. If you're into outdoor activities, affordable

---

The saguaro cactus can live up to 200 years. It's found only in southern Arizona, northwestern Mexico, and a small area in southeastern California. The saguaro is the largest cactus in the United States, and its bloom is Arizona's state flower.

housing, warm days and cool evenings, ample cultural opportunities, and a city that's very accessible through its International Airport, consider Tucson.

Who Lives in Tucson?

Though the population of Tucson has grown 20 percent since 1990, its year-round population is about 500,000, which increases seasonally with the influx of snowbirds. The median age of a Tucson resident is 36, with about 10 percent of residents between 50 and 60 years old. Tucson has an educated workforce—more than half have attended college, compared to the national average of only 38 percent.

What's the Cost?

Tucson's cost of living is 99. The average sale price of a single-family home is $202,000, and the average two-bedroom rental is $700 per month.

What's to Do?

Baseball fan? The Arizona Diamondbacks, Chicago White Sox, and Colorado Rockies all have their spring training in Tucson. There are several lakes near Tucson for water sports, as well as Biosphere 2, in nearby Oracle, Arizona. Tucson's offerings also include Colossal Cave Mountain Park; several museums; three observatories; snow skiing from December to April only 30 miles away at Mount Lemmon; 50 nearby golf courses; greyhound, horse, and NASCAR racing; excellent shopping; and a sizable number of major destination resorts such as Canyon Ranch and Miraval Resort & Spa. Ballet, live theater, a symphony, and opera are some of the cultural opportunities. If you yearn for a taste of the Wild West, visit Tombstone, "the Town Too Tough to Die," a preserved Old West town that is a "real" town as well.

Where Are the Jobs?

The largest employers in Tucson include the University of Arizona, Davis-Monthan Air Force Base, and Raytheon System (space vehicles and missiles). Unemployment in Pima County (where Tucson is located) is 4.3 percent, compared to the U.S. average of 6.1 percent.

Where Are the Doctors?

There are 15 hospitals in Tucson, with more than 1,700 physicians and 400 dentists. The University of Arizona

---

Tucson was awarded the dubious honor of being ranked the number one metropolitan area "hot spot" for asthma by Bert Sperling, an expert on quality of life matters and creator of BestPlaces.net.

in Tucson has the only medical school in the state and also has a transplant program.

Where Are Some Notable Neighborhoods?

Dove Mountain (www.dovemountain.com or 888-603-7600) is a master-planned residential golfing community 25 miles northwest of Tucson. Encompassing 5,600 acres, with close to 2,000 acres reserved as open space, it features homes from several builders and a wide swing in housing prices—from the $150,000s to several million dollars.

Saddlebrooke (www.robson.com or 800-733-4050) is an active-adult community developed by Robson Communities. Surrounded by the Santa Catalina Mountains, it offers several different housing options, with prices ranging from the $160,000s to the $300,000s. Its country club amenities include golf, a fitness center, restaurants, and tennis. In addition, Saddlebrooke has a host of conveniences on-site, including a post office, market, doctor's office, bank, and beauty salon. Saddlebrooke is about a 25-minute drive northeast of downtown Tucson.

If you're looking for more house for the money, Rancho Resort (520-648-9921) is an active-adult community of 350 manufactured homes that is integrated into the larger planned community of Rancho Sahuarita. Located 15 minutes south of Tucson, Rancho Resort has pre-constructed homes beginning around $50,000 and an extensive offering of activities centered on its 20,000-square-foot clubhouse.

Green Valley (www.greenvalley4sale.com or 877-273-2146), 25 miles south of Tucson, was established as a retirement community in 1964. Its elevation of almost 3,000 feet results in a delightful climate, with daytime temperatures averaging 80 degrees and evening temperatures hovering around 50. Nestled at the base of the Santa Rita Mountains, this community of 27,000 people in an area 12 miles long and 3 miles wide offers affordable housing, scenic vistas, and lots to do. Green Valley contains a variety of neighborhoods, such as Canoa Ranch, Madera Reserve, and Quail Creek.

What's It Like Outside?	Jan.	Apr.	Jul.	Oct.	Rain (in.)	Snow (in.)
Average High (°F)	65	82	100	84	12	–
Average Low (°F)	39	66	73	57	–	–

Housing prices and options vary—manufactured homes, condos, patio homes, townhomes, single-family homes, and La Posada at Park Centre—a continuing care retirement community—are all available, with prices ranging from $40,000 to over a half million dollars. The average price of a home is $126,000.

For resort-style apartment or condo living, consider the Golf Villas at Oro Valley (www.thegolfvillas.com or 520-219-2202), where you'll enjoy mountain views, golf, swimming, and a spa. One-bedroom/one-bath apartment rentals begin under $700 per month, and one-bedroom condos start at $115,000.

How Do I Pursue Lifelong Learning?

Tucson boasts the University of Arizona, a large university with its own medical school. Pima Community College serves around 60,000 students at multiple campuses and is one of the largest community college systems in the nation. University of Phoenix, Inc., is a private, online, accredited institution that caters to working adults and has a campus in Tucson.

Strengths

During the winter, the ability to bask in the sun in the morning and ski in the afternoon is pretty impressive. The Sonoran Desert beauty, lush compared to the other three deserts of the West, the lower cost of living, and the revitalization of the downtown are all plusses.

Weaknesses

Summers are hot, although the humidity is low. The intense rain during monsoon season can also temporarily disrupt travel on some low-lying roads due to flooding.

FYI

Check out these sources for additional information: Tucson Chamber of Commerce (www.tucsonchamber.org or 520-792-1212); Tucson Online (www.pima.com/magazine); the *Arizona Daily Star* (520-573-4511), and the *Tucson Citizen* (520-573-4561).

Tucson receives at least half of its annual rainfall during "monsoon season," which is July through August. This is a time of heavy rains and thunderstorms, during which the average rainfall is 6 inches in what is normally a dry region.

CALIFORNIA

Capital: Sacramento
Nickname: Golden State
Motto: "I have found it"
Flower: California Poppy
Bird: California Valley Quail
Population: 33,871,648
Fascinating Fact: California raises the most turkeys of any state.

San Luis Obispo

REPORT CARD

Overall Rating:	B+
Climate:	A
Cost of Living:	C
Health Care:	A
Transportation:	B
What's to Do:	A

San Luis Obispo (SLO), in the heart of California's central coast, is located roughly halfway between Los Angeles and San Francisco. The city is 8 miles from the Pacific Ocean and is situated between the peaks of the Santa Lucia Mountains.

If you've dreamed of the perfect California climate and the West Coast's scenic beauty but have been overwhelmed with images of L.A. and other major cities, consider this charming city. San Luis Obispo is the county seat of San Luis Obispo County and is the commercial and cultural hub of California's central coast. The town was established with the construction of the Mission de Tolosa in 1772, the fifth in California's chain of 21 missions. Many special events are held at Mission Plaza, with its charming creekside setting, including the

Mozart Festival in the summer and a Wine Festival in the fall. California Polytechnic State University is located in the community and is an integral part of everyday life. The university sponsors cultural and sporting events, often free to retirees. The San Luis Obispo Regional Airport offers service from three regional carriers—United Express (Skywest), American Eagle, and America West (Mesa)—with about 40 flights offered daily.

Who Lives in San Luis Obispo?

The population of SLO is about 44,000, with approximately 250,000 residents in San Luis Obispo County. About one-fourth of the city residents are 55 or older, and the median age is 26. In terms of demographics, the population is about 76 percent Caucasian and 16 percent Hispanic, with the balance a combination of African-Americans, Asians, and Native Americans.

If the temperatures don't impress you, how about 315 days of sunshine a year? Or, consider a growing season of 339 days—gardening could be a full-time job! Most of the rain falls between November and March.

What's the Cost?

The cost of living would be considered above average, at around 130. The median single-family home selling price is $368,000, and the average monthly rent for a two-bedroom apartment is about $1,300. The median household income is $50,000, compared to about a $52,000 average for California.

What's to Do?

With the Pacific Ocean about 10 minutes away, the pleasures of the sea are within your reach every day. You can swim, boat, kayak, fish, and surf, not to mention such land pursuits as biking, golf, tennis, hiking, and visiting vineyards.

The mild climate will encourage outdoor activities in town as well. Every Thursday night an average of 15,000

What's It Like Outside?	Jan.	Apr.	Jul.	Oct.	Rain (in.)	Snow (in.)
Average High (°F)	66	73	84	76	23	–
Average Low (°F)	43	47	56	50	–	–

residents enjoy the farmers' market. Listen to live music and entertainment and chow down on BBQ and other foods at restaurant booths while shopping for fresh-picked produce and flowers. The Mozart Festival, over 2 weeks long in late July and early August, celebrates all kinds of music with more than 30 concerts in various locations, including the Performing Arts Center and many outdoor venues.

San Luis Obispo County is home to five state parks and the Los Padres National Forest. The city has 21 parks, and there are five regulation-length golf courses within 15 minutes of SLO. With a world-class performing arts center, theater, shopping, and fine dining, as well as cultural and sporting events offered through the university, you would not find it difficult to be active in this community.

Where Are the Jobs?

The largest employers include the county government, as well as the university, Pacific Gas & Electric, health services, the school system, tourism, and retail. The unemployment rate is 3.7 percent.

Where Are the Doctors?

San Luis Obispo is served by two major hospitals: Sierra Vista Regional Medical Center and French Hospital Medical Center. (The latter may be sold or closed—no decision had been reached at press time.)

Where Are Some Notable Neighborhoods?

Home prices in California are very high, and SLO is no exception. In San Luis Obispo Country Club Estates, a 3,000-square-foot home with a three-car garage has an asking price of $990,000. A two-bedroom, one-bath home in Old Town, within walking distance of all downtown amenities, is listed for $550,000, while a similar-size home farther away from downtown is listed for $425,000. A beautiful 4,000-square-foot home on 1 acre, built in 1994, is listed for $1.4 million.

The abbreviation for San Luis Obispo (SLO) is well-suited to its laid-back pace. For a change of pace in the "land of the car," try Amtrak. Amtrak has reasonably priced service on the West Coast, and its California car has special bicycle racks, so bring your bike and explore SLO.

Recognizing that affordable housing is an issue, the city has a Web site that lists existing and planned affordable residences. Access it at www.slocity.org/community-development/housing.asp.

 Rich B. and his wife, Catherine, have retirement plans concerning SLO.

I currently live with my family in Santa Maria, which is approximately 40 miles south of San Luis Obispo. We own a lot in San Luis Obispo and plan to build a retirement home in about 5 years.

I have spent my share of time in cold-weather climates (New Jersey, Missouri, and Alaska)! San Luis Obispo has a great climate and is close to the Pacific Ocean, which I like.

From our lot, it is just 10 miles to Pismo Beach, 8 miles to Avila Beach, 13 miles to Morro Bay, 30 miles to Cambria, and 30 miles north to Paso Robles.

Since there is coastal fog, San Luis Obispo is an ideal location because it is close to the beach, but not affected by the fog bank. I like the downtown area with its creekside cafes and a lot of other neat and unique stores, all within walking distance of each other.

If I were a wine drinker, San Luis Obispo would be the ideal location. It is on the verge of surpassing Napa Valley in quality vineyards. Fine restaurants are opening in the area to cater to the people who are enjoying their trips to the many winery tasting rooms.

San Luis is a small college town with a lot of free concerts and other entertainment. The farmers' market, which takes place every Thursday night, is a very fun time with good food, good music, and lots of fresh country produce.

The only two points of concern about living in San Luis Obispo would be the price of houses and health care. The latest economic forecast projects

---

Forty-five minutes to the north of SLO is the Hearst Castle San Simeon State Historical Museum. This estate, built by William Randolph Hearst and architect Julia Morgan, is well worth the trip. The estate contains 165 rooms with 127 acres of pools, gardens, and terraces. The main house has 38 bedrooms and 41 bathrooms, for a total of 60,000 square feet.

the median home price in San Luis Obispo County to be $671,900 by the year 2008.

The second concern, health care, could be adversely affected by the proposed closing of French Hospital. The high cost of housing, together with the limits placed on reimbursements for services by HMOs, may affect the ability to attract quality doctors and other health care workers to the area. Hopefully, the health care concern will be addressed in the near future because other than that concern, San Luis Obispo is the place I want to live for a very long time. Ⓛ

How Do I Pursue Lifelong Learning?

California Polytechnic State University, one of the largest schools of engineering and architecture in the West, is located in SLO. With 18,000 full-time students, Cal Poly is a real presence in this town. It also houses the Osher Lifelong Learning Institute, which allows members unlimited access to classes within the institute for a yearly $150 membership fee. Another 10,000 students are enrolled in Cuesta Community College.

Strengths

If you have been dreaming of the West Coast, and California in particular, San Luis Obispo might be the spot for you. The reality is that this university town appears to have endless sunshine, mild temperatures, beautiful topography, and a strong sense of community. The Pacific Ocean is only 8 miles away, and a long weekend in San Francisco or L.A. is a beautiful 4- or 5-hour drive away. The California Crime Index ranks SLO as one of the safest communities in the state.

Weaknesses

A regional commuter airline will get you where you need to go, but not always as quickly as you would like. SLO, like all of California, is expensive, and the state appears to be in somewhat of a financial bind. There are not a wide variety of job opportunities here, and it's a ways from a major city. Some find the presence of the nearby Diablo Nuclear Power Plant unsettling.

FYI

Check out these sources for additional information: Chamber of Commerce (www.visitslo.com or 805-781-2777); SLO Downtown Association (www.downtownslo.com or 805-541-0286); County Visitor and Conference Bureau (www.sanluisobispocounty.com); the *Tribune* (800-288-4128); and the *New Times* (800-215-0300).

Temecula

REPORT CARD

Overall Rating:	A
Climate:	A
Cost of Living:	B
Health Care:	A
Transportation:	A
What's to Do:	A

All great places in California are not on the coastline. Temecula is located in a lush valley about 20 miles inland from the Pacific Ocean communities of San Juan Capistrano and Oceanside. Its location just 85 miles south of Los Angles and 60 miles north of San Diego makes visiting these great cities very accessible when the traffic permits! With more than 3,000 acres of picturesque wine country, Temecula is reminiscent of the Napa Valley. The geography, climate, and soil combine to produce award-winning wines. Stop by and visit any of the 16 wineries and enjoy a tasting, or visit a charming inn and restaurant. With an elevation of 1,500 feet above sea level, Temecula prides itself on clean air and more than 300 days of sunshine. The best news is that you will find less traffic and more affordable housing than in most southern California towns.

Who Lives in Temecula?

The population of Temecula is 75,000, with a median age of 31, and only 14 percent of the residents are over the age of 55. Demographically, approximately 70 percent are Caucasian, 19 percent Hispanic, 3 percent African-American, and 5 percent Asian.

What's the Cost?

One of the attractive aspects of living inland in California is the lower cost of housing—lower at least than the cost of housing in San Diego (about $65,000 less) or Orange County (about $220,000 less). Now for the bad news: Prices rose 18 percent in 2001 and another

What's It Like Outside?	Jan.	Apr.	Jul.	Oct.	Rain (in.)	Snow (in.)
Average High (°F)	72	72	90	84	19	–
Average Low (°F)	40	47	60	53	–	–

20 percent in 2002. The median price of a home in Temecula is $310,000, and rent averages $850 to $1,350 a month for a three- or four-bedroom home.

The Chamber of Commerce in Temecula reports that the overall cost of living is 126.

What's to Do?

Temecula's mild, dry climate provides great weather for a healthy lifestyle. Outdoor activities include golf (eight public and private courses in the area), tennis, hiking, and spending time in one of the 36 city parks.

Lake Skinner, 10 miles east of Temecula, offers great camping, including equestrian campsites. Diamond Valley Lake is the largest body of freshwater in southern California. Both lakes offer similar recreational activities, including swimming, fishing, and boating. Known as California's "other wine country," Temecula's 16 wineries and many wine festivals round out the list of outdoor fun.

Old Town boasts more than 640 antiques dealers, unique shopping, and fine dining. Be sure to visit the farmers' market on Saturday mornings or on Wednesdays at the Promenade Mall. The Arts Council of Temecula Valley helps the approximately 30 arts and cultural organizations support the visual and performing arts in the area.

Where Are the Jobs?

Between 1991 and 2001, the number of jobs in Temecula increased by more than 11 percent. In addition to the school system and health care, major employers include Guidant, International Rectifer/Hexfet, and Diversified, the Staffing Solution. Unemployment is 4 percent.

Where Are the Doctors?

Temecula Valley is located between the medical teaching institutions of Loma Linda University and the University of California, San Diego. The 80-bed Inland Valley Regional Medical Center, an acute care facility and trauma center, provides the residents of Temecula with very good medical care.

Although separated from the Pacific Ocean by the Santa Rosa Mountains, the Rainbow Gap allows mild beach breezes to flow into the Temecula Valley and helps moderate temperatures.

Where Are Some Notable Neighborhoods?

K. Hovnanian's Olde Orchard (www.khov.com or 909-302-0864) at Morgan Hill in Temecula offers one- and two-story single-family residences priced from the $400,000s. Twenty-five miles north of Temecula, K. Hovnanian's Four Seasons at Hemet (www.khov.com or 866-694-4293), an active-adult community, is priced from the $200,000s. This is a gated community situated along a public golf course and featuring an indoor recreational center.

Sterling Heights (www.alexandercommunities.com or 909-304-3240) features homes from 2,600 to 3,300 square feet, priced from the high $300,000s. Lake Skinner and the Santa Rosa Wildlife Preserve are nearby, in addition to several golf courses.

How Do I Pursue Lifelong Learning?

Residents of Temecula can attend Mt. San Jacinto Community College, and the University of California has a site in Temecula. California State-San Marcos is about half an hour away.

Strengths

The beauty of the green valley and snowcapped mountains all wrapped up in the southern California climate make this town of 75,000 a great place to retire. There are jobs to be had and tennis and golf to be played. The Pacific Ocean is only 20 minutes away. Homes are not cheap, but affordable (especially for southern California).

Weaknesses

I-15, a main artery between San Diego County and Riverside County, coupled with Temecula's affordable housing (for California), has created an increase in population and an increase in traffic. If you're considering relocating from a less expensive area, the cost of living at 126 is high.

FYI

Check out these sources for additional information: Temecula Valley Chamber of Commerce (www.temecula.org or 909-676-5090); and the *Press-Enterprise* (www.pe.com or 909-684-1200).

There are eight ballooning companies in Temecula, and every June the Temecula Valley Balloon and Wine Festival attracts thousands.

COLORADO

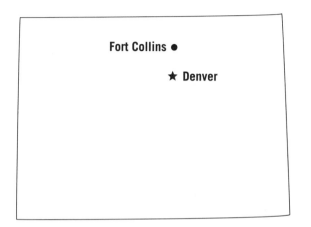

Capital: Denver

Nickname: Centennial State/Colorful Colorado

Motto: "Nothing without Providence"

Flower: Rocky Mountain Columbine

Bird: Lark Bunting

Population: 4,301,261

Fascinating Fact: The longest continuous street in the United States is Colfax Avenue in Denver.

Fort Collins

REPORT CARD

Overall Rating:	A
Climate:	B
Cost of Living:	A
Health Care:	A
Transportation:	B
What's to Do:	A

Fort Collins is located at the foothills of the Rocky Mountains in northeastern Colorado, about 65 miles north of Denver, on the Cache La Poudre River. It offers a small-town feeling but with the big-city amenities that many people desire. It also fits the bill if you are looking for a college town. Colorado State University is located in Fort Collins, and its 24,000 students bring vitality to this community that's located 5,000 feet above sea level.

Since 1997 Fort Collins has been recognized in many publications as a great place to live. Arts and Entertainment (A&E) television rated Fort Collins one of the "10 Best Cities to Have It All," Business Opportunity Index (2000) ranked it "Fourth Best for Business Opportunity," *Money Magazine* (2000) ranked it "One of the Top 10 Best Places to Retire," MSN.com (July 2003) rated Fort Collins as one of the "Top Five Places to Retire," and Loveland/Fort Collins is the number-one "Best Place to Reinvent Your Life," according to *AARP Magazine* (May/June 2003). With accolades like this, how can you go wrong?

Residents describe Fort Collins as "Fort Fun" as they brag about the long list of things to do in their city. With 300 days of sunshine and outdoor activities that include hiking and biking on 20 miles of trails and skiing in resorts (a 2- to 4-hour drive away), this Colorado town is enticing. If sports are your passion, take a short drive to Denver and cheer on the Denver Broncos, Colorado Avalanche, Colorado Rockies, and Denver Nuggets.

The Denver International Airport is about 1½ hours from Fort Collins, and the Airport Express operates hourly bus service to the airport. It's also possible to take a commuter plane between Denver and the Fort Collins-Loveland Airport.

Fort Collins enjoys an average of 300 sunny, low-humidity days each year. Fifty inches of snow seems like a lot, but the brilliant sunshine and mild temperatures melt a great deal of that snowfall early in the day.

Who Lives in Fort Collins?

About 120,000 people live in the 50 square miles of Fort Collins, the county seat for Larimer County. The median age is 28, and about 16 percent of the population is over the age of 55. About 85 percent are Caucasian and another 13 percent Hispanic. You will find a large number of Californians fleeing the crowded lifestyle of their home state for the sunshine and beauty of this small Colorado town.

What's the Cost?

Cost of living in Fort Collins is equal to the ACCRA national average of 100. The median price for an older home is $260,000; for a new home, $272,000.

What's to Do?

While you can't see the ocean from Fort Collins, there is the Cache La Poudre River, which is a National Wild and Scenic River. Poudre Canyon is a great spot for whitewater rafting, kayaking, camping, fishing, and hiking. Visit Rocky Mountain National Park and view elk, mule deer, black bear, and more, or enjoy mountain hiking. If you're into skiing, the popular ski resorts of Beaver

---

The Cache La Poudre River allegedly gets its name from a stash of gunpowder hidden along the river's banks by French trappers in the 1800s.

Creek, Breckenridge, Copper Mountain, and Keystone, with their own picture-perfect towns, are just a few hours away. Or, enjoy the New West Fest in Fort Collins's Historic Old Town every August. This event showcases more than 300 arts and crafts and food booths, as well as concerts throughout the afternoon and evening.

Moving indoors, there are scores of local groups to inspire your more artistic side. Canyon Concert Ballet offers dance training and performances, and the Fort Collins Children's Theater stages live plays using local actors and actresses. There are several art galleries, and the Lincoln Center has programs that include professional theater, dance, and children's programs. And don't neglect the shopping. There is a pedestrian mall in the historic downtown that includes fine restaurants, bars, and lots of shops.

Where Are the Jobs?

Fort Collins is considered the regional employment and retail hub for northern Colorado, southern Wyoming, and western Nebraska. Major employers include such presti-gious names as Hewlett Packard, Agilent Technologies, Anheuser Bush, and Waterpik Technologies. Colorado State University, the Poudre school district, and Poudre Valley Health Systems are big employers as well. The unemployment rate is 5.4 percent.

Where Are the Doctors?

The Poudre Valley Hospital provides medical care and serves as the regional trauma center. The hospital was named to *US News and World Report*'s annual list of top 50 U.S. hospitals for the quality for its orthopedic surgery and its treatment of diabetes. With close to 40 specialties, this hospital provides excellent health care.

Where Are Some Notable Neighborhoods?

If you're interested in renting, the upscale apartments at Argyle of Willow Springs (www.argyle-willowsprings.com or 970- 229-1882) will be of interest. The monthly rent starts at about $800 for a one bedroom and about $1,300 for three bedrooms and two baths.

What's It Like Outside?	Jan.	Apr.	Jul.	Oct.	Rain (in.)	Snow (in.)
Average High (°F)	41	59	86	64	15	50
Average Low (°F)	12	31	54	34	–	–

Observatory Village (www.observatoryvillage.com or 970-226-1560), a new community, includes a real working observatory and offers maintenance-free homes, as well as single-family homes, starting from the $200,000s.

Maintenance-free townhouses and patio homes, as well as estate-size residences and single-family homes, are available at Water Valley (www.watervalley.com or 970-686-5828). This community is situated on a golf course and surrounded by five scenic lakes (with sandy beaches) and 7.5 miles of recreational trails. Condominiums are priced starting at $140,000, and the Pelican Bay Boardwalk Luxury Lodges are priced from $230,000.

Morningside Village (www.chateaudevelopment.com or 970-223-2200) is located 12 minutes from downtown Fort Collins and has a community pool with expansive parks and walking paths. The Cottage Series is priced from $130,000 to $200,000, with townhomes priced from $180,000 to $220,000.

In the Multiple Listing Service, new construction in Highland Meadows, with four bedrooms and three baths (2,170 square feet) is selling for $307,150.

How Do I Pursue Lifelong Learning?

This is an easy question to answer! Colorado State University is a land-grant institution with 24,000 full-time students, and it's waiting for you to enroll. To encourage life-long learning, students over 60 pay only half the tuition cost. Another institution, Front Range Community College, with about 4,000 students, offers classes in more than 100 subjects, as well as a host of continuing education classes.

Strengths

Panoramic views of the snowcapped Rocky Mountains, the proximity of some of the country's best ski resorts, sunny days, a beautiful river, and the benefits of living in a town where learning is a high priority make Fort Collins hard to beat.

Weaknesses

Snow. If it doesn't melt early in the day, you are stuck with it! The Denver airport, your best means of air travel, is 1½ hours away. Traffic delays and lack of public transportation are issues in Fort Collins. The economy in Fort Collins has softened over the last few years.

FYI

Check out these sources for additional information: Chamber of Commerce (www.fcchamber.org or 970-482-3746); City of Fort Collins Web site (www.ci.fort-collins.co.us); the *Fort Collins Coloradoan* (970-493-6397); and the *Northern Colorado Business Report* (970-221-5400).

FLORIDA

Capital: Tallahassee

Nickname: Sunshine State

Motto: "In God we trust"

Flower: Orange Blossom

Bird: Mockingbird

Population: 15,982,378

Fascinating Fact: Clearwater has the highest number of lightning strikes per capita of any city in the country.

Boca Raton

REPORT CARD

Overall Rating:	A-
Climate:	A-
Cost of Living:	B-
Health Care:	A
Transportation:	A
What's to Do:	A

Boca Raton is an upscale community located on the east coast of Florida between Fort Lauderdale and West Palm Beach. The city has 5 miles of ocean frontage, and the rejuvenated downtown area has many lush green parks. Bordered by Atlantic beaches on the east and the Everglades on the west, the city has purchased countless acres of environmentally sensitive land, including half of the Boca shoreline. Mizner Park has been renovated to include new restaurants, theaters, and an amphitheater and is home to the International Museum of Cartoon Art.

The culturally inclined will enjoy a feast of activities in Boca, including the Boca Pops, Boca Ballet, and the Caldwell Theatre Company, as well as performances at the Kravis Center, 30 minutes away in West Palm Beach. The climate is tropical, and outdoor activities can be enjoyed year-round. Your friends and family will be celebrating your choice of Boca Raton, especially when they come to visit in January and February! Boca's rainy season is May through October.

Getting to Boca is not a problem, with international airports in Palm Beach (25 miles), Fort Lauderdale (20 miles), and Miami (45 miles).

Who Lives in Boca Raton?

The population of Boca Raton is approximately 75,000, with about 30 percent over the age of 55 and a median age of 43. It is 84 percent Caucasian, 9 percent Hispanic, and 4 percent African-American.

What's the Cost?

The cost of living is 108. Housing is expensive, with the median cost of a home at $253,000.

What's to Do?

Palm Beach County, where Boca Raton is located, has almost 150 golf courses and, with such great weather, close to 365 days a year to play them! If golf isn't your game, try fishing on Lake Okeechobee, the second largest freshwater lake located entirely within the contiguous United States. Visit Loxahatchee Everglade Park and see the gators, or go snorkeling in Red Reef Park. The list of outdoor activities includes biking, hiking, tennis, and relaxing on a sunny beach. There's also the fine dining in Mizner Park, the pops and the ballet, the Harid Conservatory, and the Caldwell Theatre Company. You'll be wishing there were more than 24 hours in the day! When all else fails, there's always outlet shopping! Sample Sawgrass Mills, 10 miles west of Fort Lauderdale. With more than 400 stores and 30 places to eat, you should find something to fill your bags or stomach. Twenty-five million shoppers a year can't be wrong!

Where Are the Jobs?

The largest employers are education, health care, government, and the hospitality industry. Boca is sometimes

---

There is some controversy about what the name "Boca Raton" means. While some say its Spanish translation is "mouth of the rat," others insist this is a misconception and that residents in Raton, Mexico, say that *raton* is more accurately described as something to do with rocks. Either way, Boca is beautiful.

called "Silicon Beach" because of its many high-tech companies, including IBM, Siemens Information and Communication Networks, NCCI, Database Technologies, Rexall Sundown, and Sony Professional Products. The unemployment rate is 5.4 percent.

Where Are the Doctors?

The Boca Raton Community Hospital, with almost 400 beds, and the West Boca Medical Center are two examples of the excellent providers of health care for the Boca area. The Mae Volen Senior Center and the Ruth Rales Jewish Family Services provide assistance for seniors in the Boca area.

Where Are Some Notable Neighborhoods?

You could try out Boca for possible relocation by renting an apartment. For example, the Royal Colonial Apartments (www.royal-colonial.com or 561-395-3080)

are on the Intracoastal Waterway and rent monthly for about $2,000 to $3,000 for a furnished apartment during high season, and from $1,000 to $1,600 per month from April to December. Regular annual rentals begin around $1,000 a month.

There are a number of communities throughout the Boca area. Some have resales; others have pockets of new building going on.

Addison Reserve (www.addisonreserve.com or 800-317-2289) is a gated, 650-acre country club community comprised of 19 "villages." Homes begin in the $400,000s and escalate to over $5 million, with each lot having a water, golf, or open space view.

Broken Sound Country Club (www.brokensound-properties.com or 561-776-6653) has 1,600 single-family homes, patio homes, townhomes, and villas in 27 "villages" on 1,000 acres. Homes begin in the $200,000s.

Mizner Country Club (www.miznercountryclub.com

What's It Like Outside?	Jan.	Apr.	Jul.	Oct.	Rain (in.)	Snow (in.)
Average High (°F)	75	82	90	84	60	–
Average Low (°F)	55	65	72	70	–	–

or 561-658-5500), created by the nationally recognized builder Toll Brothers, is located north of Boca in nearby Delray Beach and is 15 minutes from the ocean. Homes begin around $500,000, and the sky is the limit!

The Polo Club (www.poloclubboca.com or 786-853-6162) is a mix of single-family homes, villas, and condos, with prices beginning around $200,000. You could also rent in this community.

How Do I Pursue Lifelong Learning?

Boca Raton is home to Florida Atlantic University, which offers baccalaureate degrees as well as master's and doctoral degrees. The Boca campus is also proud to house the Lifelong Learning Center, the largest organization of its kind in the country, offering non-credit classes to over 22,000 seniors over age 60. In addition to FAU, Palm Beach Community College, South Campus, has a branch in Boca.

Strengths

Boca is a great small city located near three big cities: Fort Lauderdale, Palm Beach, and Miami. The weather is warm all winter, and the list of things to do is endless. Residents tend to be educated and affluent.

Weaknesses

The word "upscale" is almost always used in conjunction with Boca. Life is expensive here. This is also a location frequented by great throngs of visitors from the north in January and February. Watch out for the traffic. The population increases by 12 percent to 15 percent every winter.

FYI

Check out these sources for additional information: Greater Boca Raton Chamber of Commerce (www.bocachamber.com or 561-395-4433); the *Boca News* (561-893-6400); and the *Palm Beach Daily News* (800-654-1231).

Addison Mizner began developing Boca in the 1920s, and he is also the architect of the beautiful Boca Raton Resort & Club, one of Florida's best hotels. This incredible pink building, designed to look like a Mediterranean castle, is a landmark in Boca Raton. (In fact, one of Boca's nicknames is "the Pink City.") Amenities include two 18-hole golf courses, a half-mile of private beach, a marina, and almost 50 clay tennis courts.

Naples

REPORT CARD

Overall Rating:	B+
Climate:	B+
Cost of Living:	B+
Health Care:	A
Transportation:	B+
What's to Do:	A

If you are driving south along the west coast of Florida on Interstate 95, the last exit before the Everglades is Naples, considered by many to be the crown jewel of southwest Florida (although a few folks in Sarasota might disagree). Naples is in the subtropical zone, where you'll find a Mediterranean-type climate with warm breezes and endless sunshine. The sugar-sand beaches and the great fishing and boating make Naples an outdoor paradise. This city is also a cultural treasure in southwest Florida. The Philharmonic Center for the Arts, for example, offers more than 400 events each season.

Southwest Florida attracts thousands of snowbirds seeking warmth from the cold winters of the north, and Naples is the choice for many of them, as well as for retirees looking for a full-time location. A short jaunt (35 miles) will take you to Southwest Florida International Airport serving Naples, Fort Meyers, Bonita Springs, and Marco Island.

In Old Naples, all the streets running east to west end at the beach. Sounds like this is a town that has its priorities straight!

Who Lives in Naples?

The population in Naples is about 24,000. The median age is 44 years. About 93 percent of the population is Caucasian, 5 percent is African-American, and 2 percent is Hispanic. Naples is one of the nation's fastest-growing metro areas; Collier County grew 65 percent during the 1990s.

What's It Like Outside?	Jan.	Apr.	Jul.	Oct.	Rain (in.)	Snow (in.)
Average High (°F)	74	85	91	85	57	–
Average Low (°F)	52	62	75	67	–	–

You can expect high humidity and late afternoon thunderstorms on a daily basis during the summer.

What's the Cost?

Naples can be upscale living, that's for sure. Shopping, dining, and housing lean in the direction of "expensive." Shopping for decorator items, furniture, antiques, and clothing in the great boutiques or larger shopping areas of Naples, as well as experiencing the wide variety of cuisine, could qualify as a part-time job. The average sale price of a home is high—about $400,000. The Florida Price Index for Naples, however, is close to average at 103. Reasonably priced homes are available, although they tend to be farther away from the water, and you can choose to live more inexpensively.

What's to Do?

The United Arts Council of Collier County is comprised of more than 40 organizations that bring culture to Naples and the rest of the county. The Philharmonic Center for the Arts/Naples Museum of Art entertains residents of Naples with Broadway plays, opera, classical and popular music, lectures, and dance. Or, get out of the audience and join one of the many community theaters for a production—either onstage or behind the scenes.

Enjoy the Florida sunshine while golfing, boating, or playing tennis. Watch a swamp buggy race, or go fishing. Indulge in a day of shopping, interrupted by a lunch in an outdoor café in Old Naples. Experience the beauty of the sun setting over the Gulf of Mexico. Explore the 1.5 million-acre Everglades National Park—just not all in one day! Ask about their Golden Age Passport, which allows free entry for life, free access to most federal recreation areas, and other discounts to those over 62 for a one-time fee of $10.

Where Are the Jobs?

The major employers are the schools, retail, county government, health care, and tourism. The unemployment rate in Naples is 4.7 percent.

March is considered the peak of the tourist season, and the population generally increases by one-third in Collier County, where Naples is located. Approximately 500,000 tourists descend on Naples between January and March.

Where Are the Doctors?

The Naples Community Hospital Healthcare System operates two hospitals with more than 500 physicians and 26 outpatient facilities in the area. The prestigious Cleveland Clinic operates in Naples as well.

Where Are Some Notable Neighborhoods?

There is a huge range of housing types and prices in Naples—from the $100,000s to millions and millions of dollars. Lots of building and renovation are happening in this area—there is a development for almost every letter of the alphabet: Aqualane Shores, Bay Colony, Collier's Reserve, Eagle Creek, Fiddler's Creek, Gordon Drive, Grey Oaks, Hunter's Ridge, Kensington, The Moorings, Old Naples, Pelican Marsh, Port Royal, Quail West, Royal Harbor, Stonebridge, Vineyards, and Wyndemere, just to name a few.

Tarpon Bay (www.wcicommunities.com or 800-924-2290), located in north Naples, is built by WCI, a company with more than a half-century of experience. The community has low-rise condominiums, villas, carriage homes, and patio homes priced from the low $200,000s. Tarpon Bay's amenities include membership in the athletic center, a beach club, swimming and tennis, and a marina where boat slips are available for rent or purchase.

Beautiful lakes, a nature preserve, and an Arnold Palmer Signature Golf Course surround the Toll Brothers' Naples Lakes community (www.napleslakes.com or 239-732-2000), located on the south side of Naples. The clubhouse offers tennis, fitness, and swimming. Full membership to the golf course and country club is included with every home. A variety of housing styles are available, beginning in the $200,000s.

About 15 miles north of Naples is Bonita Springs (www.bonitabay.com or 888-875-8782), a great place to live and still enjoy the amenities of Naples. Bonita Bay is a spectacular, 2,400-acre gated community in Bonita Springs with lots of resale homes, villas, and high-rise condominiums overlooking the Gulf of Mexico.

Another outstanding development, The Brooks (www.thebrooks.com or 888-875-8782), also in Bonita

---

Collier County is the largest of Florida's 67 counties, covering about 2,000 square miles. Everglades National Park and Cypress Swamp State Park take up a sizable portion of the county's land.

Springs, is a 2,500-acre development (over 50 percent will remain open space), minutes from the Southwest Florida International Airport. There are many housing options at The Brooks—some homes are new, and there are many resales within its four separate communities. Prices range from the $200,000s to $1 million-plus.

Another possibility is to head to Marco Island, Florida, about 20 miles south of Naples, but still within Collier County. Marco Island's 6 miles of beach and its more than 100 miles of waterways throughout its 14 square miles enable many homes to have a canal in their backyard. With its approximately 15,000 residents (this number will swell by about 20,000 during the winter), this is a laid-back, friendly island, with many people owning second homes and others converting from snowbirds to full-timers. Home prices vary tremendously depending on type and location.

How Do I Pursue Lifelong Learning?

There are several opportunities for lifelong learning in the Naples area. The Florida Gulf Coast University is actually located in nearby Fort Meyers and offers noncredit courses in addition to degree courses. Edison Community College offers classes in Naples and Fort Meyers.

Strengths

The subtropical climate in Naples translates to warm, sunny winters, and the city's location on the Gulf Coast translates to breathtaking sunsets. Great fishing, boating, and beaching, coupled with fine dining, shopping on the waterfront, and more cultural events than days in a year, give Naples a well-deserved wonderful reputation.

Weaknesses

Exceptionally hot, humid summer days make outdoor activities somewhat difficult. Traffic and snowbird crowds in restaurants and at the airport make winter months a challenge.

FYI

Check out these sources for additional information: Chamber of Commerce (www.naples-florida.com or 239-262-6376); Naples/Marco Island and the Everglades Web site (www.visit-naples.com or 239-262-6141); and the *Naples Daily News* (800-404-7343).

Azure, a new 25-story luxury high-rise in Bonita Bay, breaks ground in 2004.

Ocala

REPORT CARD

Overall Rating:	A
Climate:	B+
Cost of Living:	A+
Health Care:	A
Transportation:	B
What's to Do:	A-

While driving through north central Florida, taking in the beauty of the green, gently rolling topography, beautiful horse farms, and countless old oak trees, you might ask, "Where are we? This can't be Florida!" Oh, but it is! Ocala, a small town in a rural setting, reminds many people of the Midwest or the Northeast. The beaches are 60 miles in either direction, and Orlando, at about 100 miles away, is still accessible when visitors come.

Ocala is a draw for retirees because it has a great deal to offer, and the cost of living is relatively low. You can be a part of a state-of-the-art retirement community, play a little golf, go fishing, and enjoy college football at the University of Florida, while living in a laid-back small town with a mild, four-season climate. And remember, no hurricanes!

Who Lives in Ocala?

The population of Ocala is about 46,000. The population of Marion County, where Ocala is located, is approximately 260,000, up 32 percent since 1990. About half the population of Marion County is over 45 years old, with one in four over 65.

What's the Cost?

The cost of living is good, reported to be about 93.14 by the Florida Price Index, compared to a Florida average of 100. Housing represented the lowest category, at 87. The median price for a home in Ocala is $88,200.

What's to Do?

For starters, the 383,000-acre Ocala National Forest is a vast area filled with ecological sites, trails, springs, and lakes for the outdoor enthusiast. Or, go camping or canoeing in Silver River State Park. The waters you find in

Ocala was voted "One of America's Best 100 Towns" by *Where to Retire Magazine* in 2001.

Ocala are crystal-clear rivers and freshwater springs, and there's great fishing and boating on the many lakes and rivers. Visit Silver Springs—Nature's Theme Park—and take a glass-bottom boat to explore the artesian spring system and abundant underwater life. The public El Diablo Golf Course was voted "Best New Course in America" by *Golf Digest* in 1999, and the 47-mile Willacoochee State Trail begins in Citrus Springs and stretches to Dade City for biking, walking, and jogging.

Enjoy the Victorian homes of the town's historic district, or patronize the Appleton Cultural Center, a complex that includes Ocala Civic Theater and the Pioneer Garden Club and serves as the hub for cultural activities in Ocala. Have lunch at Carmichael's Café and enjoy the art museum in the afternoon. The Ocala Civic Theater has presented almost 400 productions and performs for over 50,000 people each season. You will also find ballet and a variety of musical offerings, from jazz to symphonic music.

Driving to the famous Florida attractions is a popular pastime for Ocala residents. A short drive south will take you to Orlando, the Kennedy Space Center, and any number of spring-training baseball games. Ocala is within half a day's drive to any of the Sunshine State's major cities, and Amtrak also serves the area. The Gainesville Regional Airport, a nonhub airport about 40 miles from Ocala, provides the closest air transportation. Delta Connection, ASA, US Airways, and Piedmont Airways provide service to hub cities close by. Four international airports are located within 100 miles of Ocala.

Where Are the Jobs?

The top employers in Ocala are within health care and manufacturing. Private employers include Emergency One, Cingular Wireless, Kmart Corporation, Closet Maid, and Lockheed Martin. The unemployment rate is 4.7 percent.

Where Are the Doctors?

Several facilities serve the medical needs of Ocala residents, including Munroe Regional Medical Center,

What's It Like Outside?	Jan.	Apr.	Jul.	Oct.	Rain (in.)	Snow (in.)
Average High (°F)	66	81	91	81	52	–
Average Low (°F)	42	56	70	60	–	–

Ocala Regional Medical Center, and West Marion Community Hospital. The University of Florida in Gainesville, a 40-minute drive from Ocala, has a teaching hospital as well.

Where Are Some Notable Neighborhoods?

Colonnades at On Top of the World (www.colonnadesfl.com or 800- 421-4162), is a gated, age-restricted community with two 18-hole golf courses available to everyone. The residents have created more than 200 clubs, and you can start one if you can come up with a new idea! Golf, tennis, and fitness, as well as the full-service Friendship Shopping Center, make living here fun and easy; they're all within walking distance or just a golf cart ride away. Prices vary from around $110,000 for a villa to $200,000 for a single-family home.

Oak Run Country Club (www.oakrunflorida.com or 800-874-0898) is a gated, age-restricted community with recreational facilities including indoor and outdoor swimming, fitness, and tennis. There are two golf courses, one 18-hole and one 9-hole executive course. Homes (not including lot) are priced from the $120,000s, and homesites begin under $20,000.

Oriole at Stonecrest (www.oriolehomes.com or 800-245-2770) is in Summerfield, about 20 miles south of Ocala. It's an active-adult community on about 850 acres featuring 18 holes of championship golf, as well as swimming and fitness, and is close to Ocala amenities. When fully built-out, there will be about 900 homes; prices of existing homes begin in the $130,000s.

West Wind Trails (www.banyanhomes.net or 352-861-9800) and Bent Tree (www.banyanhomes.net or 352-861-8777) are planned communities 3 miles from I-75 in Ocala, minutes from the town's downtown amenities. Single-family homes are priced from the $120,000s at West Wind Trails and from the $140,000s at Bent Tree.

Although 25 miles north of Ocala, Gainesville is more than a notable neighborhood—it's a college town of nearly 120,000 residents, home to the University of Florida. While it provides excellent health care and low

---

Often referred to as the "Horse Capital of the World," Marion County employs about 30,000 people in some capacity in its thoroughbred industry.

unemployment (2.4 percent), it does have a higher cost of living (104). A community in Gainesville worth checking out is Haile Plantation (www.haileplantation.com or 888-226-8802). As an example of new urbanism, Haile Plantation offers the possibility of living, playing, and working all in the same place. Homes begin in the $100,000s and go to $600,000 and up; apartment rentals for about $1,000 per month are also available.

How Do I Pursue Lifelong Learning?

Central Florida Community College has an Ocala campus that confers A.A. and A.S. degrees, and Elderhostel and Senior Institute programs are part of its offerings.

Webster University has over 90 locations, including one in Ocala. The university caters to adult learners, offering evening and weekend programs in five 9-week terms per year. And, of course, the University of Florida is just 40 minutes away!

Strengths

Living in Ocala means warm, sunny Florida weather (without the threat of hurricanes), green grass and oak trees, horses grazing, and freshwater lakes. The cost of living and the active-adult communities are real pulls. The medical facilities are top-notch and include a major university hospital 40 minutes away. There is no state income tax in Florida.

Weaknesses

Ocala does not have a tropical feel—it has few palms and no ocean. The rural setting and the lack of a major airport might make one feel isolated.

FYI

Check out these sources for additional information: Ocala Chamber of Commerce (www.ocalacc.com or 352-629-8051); City of Ocala (www.ocalafl.org); Gainesville Chamber of Commerce (www.gainesvillechamber.com or 352-334-7100); the *Ocala Star Banner* (352-867-4010) and the *Gainesville Sun* (800-443-9493).

Definitions of "age-restricted" vary from community to community, but generally, there is a minimum age of 55 (although it may be as low as 50 or as high as 62) for at least one member of a couple. Check age restrictions prior to purchase.

Palm Coast

REPORT CARD

Overall Rating:	B+
Climate:	B+
Cost of Living:	A
Health Care:	B
Transportation:	A-
What's to Do:	B

Palm Coast is a diamond in the rough, located about an hour's drive south of Jacksonville, halfway between quaint St. Augustine and lively Daytona Beach. From the exit off Interstate 95, you can be on a golf course, boating on the Intracoastal Waterway, or strolling on the beach within 10 minutes. Three airports triangulate Palm Coast, with Jacksonville International 1 hour north, Orlando 1 hour west, and Daytona 30 minutes south. Developed by ITT in the 1970s as a planned commu-nity, Palm Coast incorporated as a city December 31, 1999, yet retains the feel of a small town.

Relatively unknown, Palm Coast has the amenities of a resort area—beautiful beaches with cinnamon-colored sand, great boating, Players Club Tennis, endless hiking and biking trails, and eight championship golf courses. Its location above the frost line, however, precludes Palm Coast from becoming a mecca for snowbirds, creating a community that is less transient than many in Florida. Things are happening in Palm Coast—two new super-markets and a new Flagler County Library are part of the new construction that is making this city a very desirable place to live.

Most rain falls during the summer months in the form of afternoon thunderstorms.

Who Lives in Palm Coast?

More than 38,000 people live in an area that covers about 50 square miles. The median age of a Palm Coast

What's It Like Outside?	Jan.	Apr.	Jul.	Oct.	Rain (in.)	Snow (in.)
Average High (°F)	71	84	89	75	50	–
Average Low (°F)	50	65	72	57	–	–

resident is 51, and 15 percent of the population is between 55 and 64 years old. About 85 percent of residents are Caucasian, 10 percent African-American, and 5 percent Hispanic. According to the Census Bureau, Flagler County is the fastest-growing county in Florida and the eighth fastest-growing in the nation.

What's the Cost?

According to the Florida Price Level Index, Flagler County is 94.5. The mean selling price of a single-family home is about $127,000; some lots are available in Palm Coast for as little as $10,000, and rental homes range between $600 and $1,500 per month.

What's to Do?

Year-round outdoor activities include biking, hiking, boating, golfing, fishing, beach sports, and tennis. State parks and wildlife preserves are plentiful in Flagler County. The Washington Oaks Gardens State Park spreads over more than 390 acres, from the Atlantic Ocean to the Matanzas River.

Disney World is an easy 90-minute drive, a possible day trip when the grandchildren visit. Titusville, about an hour south of Palm Coast, is home to the Kennedy Space Center. St. Augustine, about 25 miles north, the nation's oldest city, is a great place to find a gourmet restaurant or a bargain at the Designer Outlet Mall. From St. Augustine, you are a short drive from the World Golf Village and the World Golf Hall of Fame. If you are a sports enthusiast, Daytona Beach and NASCAR are neighbors of the Palm Coast, about 25 miles south, or you can travel to Jacksonville for a Jaguars football game. If you're a patron of the arts, visit the Jacksonville Symphony or the Florida Theater in Jacksonville.

Meet your neighbors on Fridays at an outdoor farmers' market at Flagler Beach in Veterans Park. Enjoy fresh produce, bright flowers, and fantastic crafts.

Historically, the Jacksonville area has been affected by the fewest number of hurricanes in Florida. Cooler water temperatures and less favorable wind conditions make it more unlikely to sustain hurricane-strength winds. In addition, this part of the state does not protrude into the Atlantic, which makes northeast Florida less of a target for hurricanes.

Where Are the Jobs?

Palm Coast is the home of Sea Ray Boats and Palm Coast Data, two of Palm Coast's major employers. The construction, health, and service sectors have had the most growth. Flagler County's unemployment rate hovers around 5.4 percent.

Where Are the Doctors?

The new Memorial Hospital-Flagler opened in the fall of 2002. Services include the Memorial Heart Institute, Memorial Cancer Care Center, Women's Health Care Center, Outpatient Services, and Emergency Medical Care Center. The famed Mayo Clinic is about an hour's drive north in Jacksonville, though, as of 2003, the clinic "no longer accepts Medicare assignment for professional and physician services covered under Medicare Part B," according to its Web site.

Where Are Some Notable Neighborhoods?

Hammock Beach (www.HammockBeach.com or 888-556-5570) and Ocean Hammock (www.oceanhammock.com or 888-515-4579) are contiguous developments on a spectacular piece of property that includes 2 miles of pristine Atlantic beach, an acclaimed Jack Nicklaus Signature Golf Course featuring six holes on the ocean, two oceanfront beach clubs, and miles of bike paths. Homesites begin under $200,000 and can reach a million dollars or more.

Grand Haven (www.grandhavenfla.com or 800-957-0213) is situated on 1,400 acres of woodland along the Intracoastal Waterway. The centerpiece of Grand Haven is a Nicklaus Signature golf course, with three holes overlooking the Intracoastal. Homesites are priced from the low $40,000s, and homes begin in the upper $200,000s. A new neighborhood, The Crossings at Grand Haven, will have 133 patio homes beginning in the $140,000s.

How Do I Pursue Lifelong Learning?

There are a number of colleges/universities within an hour's drive of Palm Coast, including the Palm Coast campus of Daytona Beach Community College. In addition, you can satisfy your intellectual cravings at Bethune Cookman College (Daytona Beach), Embry-

---

Volunteering to monitor the beach for the Flagler Sea Turtle Preservation Society sounds like a great way to spend the day in Palm Coast.

Riddle Aeronautical University (Daytona Beach), Flagler College (St. Augustine), Jacksonville University (Jacksonville), University of Central Florida (Orlando and Daytona Beach), and the University of North Florida (Jacksonville).

 Mary Ann and Mike M. explain their decision to move to Palm Coast.

The authors of this book get the credit for introducing us to Hammock Beach in Palm Coast, Florida. Several years ago, during their research, they discovered this oceanfront community, which was just beginning to be developed. It sounded great—wide beaches, a beautiful golf course with several holes along the ocean, and near a smaller town with a plan for its future. The northeast Florida location also offered a change of seasons—which meant it wouldn't be a huge snowbird destination.

We finally visited and bought a lot, not knowing if we would really ever build in Hammock Beach.

For three years, we visited frequently and watched the development grow into a community with world-class amenities. We played golf on the Ocean Hammock golf course and stayed at the magnificent Club at Hammock Beach, with its multimillion-dollar swimming complex. We even talked with prospective builders on a couple of visits.

We decided that Hammock Beach and the surrounding area had everything we wanted—sunny skies most of the year, golf, a beach, biking, tennis, nature preserves, friendly people, and a new hospital. The smaller-town life seemed like the right fit, so we chose a builder, and here we are. The fact that our two sons and daughter-in-law live about an hour and a half away didn't hurt either!

We think Hammock Beach is one of the hidden gems in Florida. ⓣⓁ

Strengths

Palm Coast enjoys three seasons and, fortunately for retirees, winter is the missing one! The climate is subtrop-

---

Flagler County received a statewide award for its Coastal Greenway, a countywide network of bike paths that connect its greenways and other parts of the county.

ical, and the population does not double or triple with seasonal tourists. You are a 30- to 90-minute drive from many of Florida's major attractions when company comes. The area has not been hit by a major hurricane since 1990. Crime rates are lower than the national average.

Weaknesses

The closest upscale shopping is in Daytona Beach or at the Avenues Mall, which is about 45 minutes north off I-95. The cultural amenities of a big city are an hour away in Jacksonville, and the best restaurants are often a drive as well.

FYI

Check out these sources for additional information: Flagler County Chamber of Commerce (www.flaglerpc-chamber.org or 800-881-1022); Flagler County information (www.flagleronline.com or www.flaglercounty.org); and *Palm Coast News Tribune* (386-437-3877).

The Panhandle (The Emerald Coast)

REPORT CARD

Overall Rating:	B
Climate:	A-
Cost of Living:	A-
Health Care:	B-
Transportation:	B
What's to Do:	B

The Emerald Coast of Florida spans about 100 miles, called the "Miracle Strip," from Panama City west to Pensacola. Like pearls on a necklace, towns are strung along the Gulf of Mexico. Communities include Fort Walton Beach, Destin, Niceville, Sandestin, Seaside, Grayton Beach, Seagrove Beach, Santa Rosa Beach, Navarre, and Pensacola. Panhandle beaches are regularly ranked among the best beaches in the country, where you'll find the softest, white-gold sand and water that really does look like the sparkling gem this area is named after.

The Panhandle's sand gets its wonderful texture from its amazing journey. Originating in the Appalachian Mountains, the tiny quartz particles are smoothed and polished as they bounce along streams and rivers en route to the Gulf of Mexico.

A four-season climate results in quiet, cool winters and a bustling summer tourist season, though the Panhandle is becoming more of a year-round tourist spot. Airports in Pensacola, Fort Walton Beach, and Panama City make the Emerald Coast accessible, but nonstop flights from certain cities are only seasonal. There is a plethora of city, county, state, and national parks. It may be the perfect place if you're looking for a second home, though four hurricanes (Opal, Erin, Earl, and Georges) have affected the Panhandle since 1995, causing millions of dollars in damages and contributing to beach erosion.

Who Lives in the Panhandle?

The Panhandle's proximity to Georgia and Alabama gives it a real southern flair. The people are unfailingly polite and helpful, and southern accents are not uncommon. The population of the Panhandle is growing; for example, Santa Rosa County and Walton County both increased in size between 40 percent and 60 percent from 1990 to 2000. Using Pensacola as an example, approximately 30 percent of the population is between 35 and 54 years old, and another 22 percent of the population is 54 or older. Destin has about 11,000 residents, Fort Walton Beach about 20,000, and the city of Pensacola approximately 56,000. In general, other than the far western counties, the laid-back counties of the Panhandle are not experiencing the rapid growth that many other Florida areas are experiencing. There's also a strong military presence—both active and retired.

What's the Cost?

Fort Walton is 100.6, Panama City is 99.9, and Pensacola is 97.3. Pensacola is a particularly good bargain for home prices, averaging almost 10 percent below the national average. Of course, there is a tremendous range of prices, from million-dollar homes fronting the Gulf to inexpensive condos in the interior.

What's to Do?

As expected, the Panhandle boasts all things water related, including boating, swimming, and fishing (Destin

What's It Like Outside?	Jan.	Apr.	Jul.	Oct.	Rain (in.)	Snow (in.)
Average High (°F)	61	77	89	80	60 in	—
Average Low (°F)	42	60	74	60	—	—

is nicknamed the "World's Luckiest Fishing Village"). Other outdoor activities include hunting, horseback riding, hiking, camping, and golfing. There are several museums, including the unique Air Force Armament Museum, a community theater group in Fort Walton Beach, and a performing arts center at Okaloosa-Walton Community College. Spend the day strolling around Seville Square, Pensacola's historic district, or enjoying Gulf Islands National Seashore. Snowbirds longing for a bit of winter sport can watch the Ice Pilots, a minor league hockey team that plays at the Pensacola Civic Center. The "Big Easy" (New Orleans) is a 4-hour drive from Pensacola, and the Mississippi casinos are less than 3 hours from Pensacola. Shop at the Santa Rosa Mall in Fort Walton Beach or the Silver Sands Factory Stores in Destin. A number of entertainment and retail projects are in the planning/development stages on the Panhandle. On a more laid-back note, enjoy a scenic drive: Highway 30-A winds along the coast sans adver-tising, fast-food restaurants, or miniature golf courses. A big plus—construction height along this lovely stretch of road is limited to 50 feet.

Where Are the Jobs?

Service, retail, and government are the three largest job sectors. Eglin Air Force Base, Tyndall Air Force Base, and Whiting Field Naval Air Station are examples of military installations that employ thousands of civilians and con-tribute to the area's economy and low unemployment rate, which hovers around 3 percent.

Where Are the Doctors?

Sacred Heart Hospital in Pensacola is a 430-bed facility. A 50-bed medical center, Sacred Heart Hospital on the Emerald Coast, opened in Santa Rosa Beach in January 2003. Tallahassee, less than an hour away, has two major hospitals, Tallahassee Community Hospital and Tallahassee Memorial HealthCare.

St. Joseph Peninsula State Park, located near Panama City, was ranked the number one beach in the United States for 2002 by "Dr. Beach" (Dr. Stephen Leatherman, an environmental scientist and re-searcher at the International Hurricane Center). He does an annual ranking of America's beaches, using 50 criteria to evaluate each beach.

Where Are Some Notable Neighborhoods?

If you're considering a second home on the Gulf, WaterColor, WaterSound, and Rosemary Beach are newer communities directly on the water that are predominantly rental/second homes. WaterColor (www.arvida.com or 877-459-4537) is in Seagrove Beach (next to Seaside) and will include approximately 1,000 residences (multifamily residences and single-family homes) on almost 500 acres. Western Lake provides boating, and the community also offers a town center, tennis, pools, footpaths, a beach club, fitness center, golf (about 6 miles away), and restaurants. Build-out is anticipated in 2008. Fractional ownership (one-eighth interest) begins just under $200,000; lofts, bungalows, and cottages are all available; and homes can go for as much as $2 million.

WaterSound (www.arvida.com or 888-499-7767) is also located in Seagrove Beach. WaterSound will consist of approximately 500 multi- and single-family residences on 250 acres that include Camp Creek Lake, and the community will offer the same kind of amenities as WaterColor. The latest release of homesites sold from $325,000 to $415,000, and multifamily residences sold from $850,000 to $1.5 million. An additional release of multifamily residences from around $1.2 million to $1.7 million will be offered.

Rosemary Beach (www.rosemarybeach.com or 800-736-0877), established in 1995, is an example of new urbanism, with West Indies-style and southern cottages and homes characterized by small lots, front porches, and interesting architectural touches. An integration of green space, a town center with lofts, and a neighborhood designed for walking (you can get anywhere within 5 minutes) makes this a most aesthetically pleasing coastal village. According to one Realtor, approximately 85 percent of the homes are either second homes or rentals. There will be approximately 440 homes, and build-out is slated for 2008. Resale homesites begin around $325,000; available homes start around the mid-$500,000s, and those fronting the Gulf can cost more than $5 million.

If the Panhandle seems like a location you'd want for

Try the highly rated Cuvee Beach Cellar and Wine Bar Restaurant in Destin—enjoy Chef Steven Vanderpool's fabulous Provence- and Tuscany-influenced cooking.

a *primary* retirement home, consider living in an area with a sense of community, rather than the condos and homes along the Gulf that are chiefly seasonal or rental homes. There are a number of neighborhoods tucked away from tourist activity, yet close enough that you can enjoy the amenities of a resort town. In Destin, there is the 900-acre Kelly Plantation (www.kellyplantation.com or 800-837-5080), complete with 18 holes of golf, tennis, a fitness and equestrian center, and bay-front property. Sample prices: a homesite with a golf course view at $125,000 and a waterfront homesite on Jones Bayou for $500,000. Regatta Bay (www.regattabay.com or 800-648-0123), also in Destin, is a 525-acre gated golf and country club community on the Choctawhatchee Bay. Wetlands and nature areas are incorporated into this master-planned community, and residences range from condos and golf villas (upper $300,000s) to estate homes; lots are also available.

On the bay side of Route 98, across from the Hilton Sandestin Beach Golf Resort & Spa, is the Village of Baytowne Wharf, replete with retail, restaurants, condos, townhomes, lodging, and a marina on the Choctawhatchee Bay. There are a number of gated communities near the village center, including Anchorage (condos), the Fountains of Sandestin, and Augusta. Farther inland are towns such as Niceville or Crestview, which are about a half-hour drive from the beaches but are more residential and give more bang for the buck on home prices.

How Do I Pursue Lifelong Learning?

Several institutions of higher learning dot the Panhandle, including Gulf Coast Community College in Panama City, Troy State University Florida Region in Fort Walton Beach, Okaloosa-Walton Community College in Niceville, and the University of West Florida in Pensacola. There are also several vocational-technical schools. Florida State University is located in Tallahassee,

Santa Rosa Island on the Panhandle is known as the "worst place in the nation for drowning," according to the United States Lifesaving Association. Riptides in this area accounted for more than 50 percent of Florida's surf drownings and were responsible for 13 percent of national drownings over the 5-year period ending in 2000.

in the big bend area of Florida, about a 45-minute drive from the Gulf of Mexico.

Strengths

The gorgeous beaches and pleasant temperatures are the strong points. A lower cost of living is also attractive. There are a number of retail and entertainment facilities in the planning stages. Plus, it's tough to compete with seeing both the sunrise and sunset over the same glittering body of water!

Weaknesses

The Gulf on one side, and East Bay, Choctawhatchee Bay, and air force bases on the other side limit the development of the area (some would consider this a strength). Route 98, although undergoing widening in several places, is the single artery across the Panhandle. Panama City is a big spring break destination. The area is light on cultural activities, and the threat of hurricanes can't be ignored.

FYI

Check out these sources for additional information: Crestview Chamber of Commerce (www.crestview-chamber.com or 850-682-3212); Destin Chamber of Commerce (www.destinchamber.com or 850-837-6241); Fort Walton Beach Chamber of Commerce (www. fortwaltonbeachfl.org or 850-244-8191); real estate information (www.gulfsideliving.com); Pensacola Chamber of Commerce (www.pensacolachamber.com or 850-438-4081); Pensacola Beach Chamber of Commerce (www.pensacolabeachchamber.net or 800-635-4803); Santa Rosa Beach (www.waltoncountychamber.com or 850-267-0683); the *Destin Log* (850-654-8400); the *Northwest Florida Daily News* (800-863-2212); and the *Pensacola News Journal* (850-435-8500).

Florida residents 50 years of age and older are responsible for about 50 percent of consumer expenditures in Florida but comprise only one-third of its population.

Punta Gorda

REPORT CARD

Overall Rating:	A
Climate:	A
Cost of Living:	A
Health Care:	A-
Transportation:	A
What's to Do:	B+

Punta Gorda is about 100 miles south of Tampa and 25 miles north of Fort Myers on the banks of the Peace River and the Gulf of Mexico. Punta Gorda is Spanish for "broad point" and refers to the wide point of land extending out into Charlotte Harbor. The town streets are lined with huge royal palms. This community receives a lot of praise and has been included on "best of" lists by *Forbes*, *Where to Retire*, and MSN.

If you are into boating or fishing or have always dreamed of having your boat docked outside your back door, you might vote Punta Gorda number one on *your* "best of" list! With more than 85 miles of navigable canals, access to the Gulf of Mexico is easy if your boat is in your backyard. Beautiful public beaches are a short drive away in Boca Grande, and Captiva and Sanibel islands are about an hour's drive away. When you're not using your boat for transportation, the Fort Myers Airport is 45 minutes away and the Sarasota Airport, 1 hour.

Who Lives in Punta Gorda?

The population of Punta Gorda is about 14,000 and of Charlotte County is about 147,000, with a median age of 64. Demographics show that approximately 93 percent of the population is Caucasian, 4 percent African-American, and 3 percent Hispanic.

What's the Cost?

When you hear that residents in Punta Gorda often enjoy the privilege of docking their boat on a canal in

---

The history of Charlotte County dates back to 1513, when Ponce de Leon first arrived here in the midst of his Florida exploration. When he returned in 1521 to establish a colony, he met his fate during a battle with the Calusa Indians.

their own backyard, you may think that sounds like big bucks. Not always so. The cost of living is reported to be 90.4, well below the national average of 100. Housing is even better news—that segment of the cost of living is only 78.8. The median price of a home is $168,000.

What's to Do?

The residents of Charlotte County enjoy what they refer to as "pure Florida": clean air, sunshine, and the beauty that is South Florida. The Charlotte Harbor/Gasparilla Sound Aquatic Preserve is comprised of 80,000 acres of costal areas and barriers islands. Don Pedro Island State Recreation Area is a private barrier island with 7 miles of white, sandy beach. This island, accessible only by boat, is great for game fishing, year-round swimming, and shelling. Visit Palm Island via a car ferry and explore its 7 miles of beaches. The Port Charlotte Beach complex in-cludes a beach club, fishing pier, and boat ramps and is a short drive from the shopping and restaurants of Fisherman's Village. There are more than 70 parks and recreational sites in the Punta Gorda area, including Audubon-Pennington Nature Park, a bird-watching paradise.

The Charlotte County Art Guild sponsors year-round art exhibits and provides classes and workshops to all residents. There is a Historical Center and a Performing Arts Center, as well the Charlotte Symphony to keep you entertained. And don't forget, the Cultural Coast (Sarasota), is less than 1 hour away.

Where Are the Jobs?

The city and county governments, school system, retail, and health care are the major employers in Punta Gorda. The economy is healthy, with an unemployment rate of 3.7 percent.

What's It Like Outside?	Jan.	Apr.	Jul.	Oct.	Rain (in.)	Snow (in.)
Average High (°F)	74	85	91	85	52	–
Average Low (°F)	53	62	74	67	–	–

Where Are the Doctors?

Punta Gorda is served by the Charlotte Regional Medical Center, an acute care medical facility with more than 200 beds. The hospital has received national recognition for its patient care.

Where Are Some Notable Neighborhoods?

Burnt Store Marina and Country Club is a 640-acre development that will have around 2000 residences by the end of 2005. The community offers waterfront condominiums that include amenities such as 27 holes of golf, tennis, fitness, and a 500-slip, deep-water marina, which is the largest private marina on Florida's west coast. Use your golf cart to get around the community. New condos with harbor views begin around $500,000; single-family homes and resale condos are also available beginning in the upper $100,000s. Contact a realtor such as Prudential (888-358-8330) for homes and lots, or, for the new condos, contact WCI Communities (800-237-4255).

Heron Creek (www.heron-creek.com or 877-334-3766) is a master-planned community located on almost 700 acres of beautiful island property 15 miles from Punta Gorda. The development includes an Arthur Hills golf course, all the amenities of a country club community, and a town center for shopping. Single-family homes, villas, and townhomes are priced beginning in the $180,000s.

How Do I Pursue Lifelong Learning?

Edison College offers credit and noncredit continuing education courses for residents of Punta Gorda on its Charlotte County campus. Florida Gulf Coast University, in Fort Myers, also provides options for lifelong learning.

Strengths

This is laid-back Florida, with sunshine, golf, and boaters enjoying the Gulf. Housing is affordable, and there is so much to enjoy close by, including Sarasota, Fort Myers,

---

If you're concerned about your golf game, don't be! There are 16 golf courses in the immediate area where you can practice your sport.

and Tampa. According to the Florida Crime Report Index, Charlotte County has the lowest crime index of any county in Florida.

Weaknesses

Because it is a small town, Punta Gorda is working on "big-city amenities." The median age of 64 for residents could be viewed as a positive, a negative, or neutral (of course, it does help explain why the crime rate is so low). Goes without saying, but summers are hot!

FYI

Check out these sources for additional information: Charlotte County Chamber of Commerce (www. charlottecountychamber.org or 941-639-2222); and the *Sun Herald* (www.charlotte-florida.com or 941-629-8256).

Sarasota

REPORT CARD

Overall Rating:	A
Climate:	A-
Cost of Living:	A-
Health Care:	A
Transportation:	A
What's to Do:	A

Located on the west coast of Florida, about 60 miles south of Tampa, Sarasota might have that small beach town/big-city feel you're looking for. Three international airports serve Sarasota County—Sarasota Bradenton International, Tampa International, and St. Petersburg-Clearwater International. Interstate 75 is the main corridor for the southeastern United States and provides easy access to Sarasota for family and friends.

Siesta Key has some of the most beautiful beaches in the world, often found on the "top 10" lists of the most sought-after beaches. In addition, there are more than 50 miles of inland waterways and canals for your boating pleasure.

With 35 miles of pristine Gulf beaches and all the amenities of city life, the combination is irresistible for many retirees and young families alike. Sarasota County includes the communities of Sarasota, Englewood, North Port, Venice, and St. Armand's Circle, as well as the barrier islands of Casey Key, Lido Key, Longboat Key, and Siesta Key. More than 60 public and private golf courses and white, powdery sand beaches not more than a 15-minute drive from almost anywhere in the county make enjoying the tropical weather a snap! If you are looking for more than sun and sand, Sarasota is also known as the cultural coast of Florida.

From June through September, rainfall averages about 8 inches per month.

Who Lives in Sarasota?

The population of Sarasota County is about 345,000, with about 55,000 in the city of Sarasota. About 45 percent of the population is 45 or older; among metropolitan areas whose suburbs have the highest percentage of residents age 65 and older, Sarasota ranks first with about 30 percent. About 92 percent of the population is Caucasian, 4 percent African-American, and 4 percent Hispanic.

What's the Cost?

Sarasota comes in a little above the national average at 104. The median cost of a home is $150,000, and average rent is about $700 per month.

What's to Do?

Sports fans will have an opportunity to enjoy some old-fashioned baseball every February and March when the Cincinnati Reds come to Sarasota for spring training, the Pittsburgh Pirates are in Manatee County, and the Yankees and Devil Rays hold camp in Tampa. If baseball's not your game, enjoy Reggae by the Bay at Marie Selby Botanical Gardens or check out the Sarasota Film Festival. You can also enjoy performances at the Van Wezel Performing Arts Hall, the Asolo Theatre

What's It Like Outside?	Jan.	Apr.	Jul.	Oct.	Rain (in.)	Snow (in.)
Average High (°F)	72	82	91	85	60	–
Average Low (°F)	51	60	73	65	–	–

Company, the Sarasota Ballet of Florida, the Florida West Coast Symphony, the Jazz Club of Sarasota, or the Ringling Museum of Art. Visiting the 30 renowned art galleries is always stimulating and especially fun on the one Friday night a month when the galleries host the artists and local musicians and serve wine and hors d'oeuvres. This is just a sampling of the indoor activities that might appeal to you in Sarasota. The beautiful white sand beaches and the Gulf of Mexico should take care of any additional spare time, unless, of course, you want to go shopping and out to dinner on St. Armand's Circle!

Where Are the Jobs?

The major employers in Sarasota are related to education, health care, social services, and retail. Sarasota is also home to many corporations, including AM Engineering, ASO Corporation, Boar's Head Provisions, and PGT Industries. The unemployment rate is 3.7 percent.

Where Are the Doctors?

There are close to 70 hospitals in the Tampa Bay/Sarasota region. Sarasota Memorial Health Care System has more than 800 beds and is the second largest acute care center in any public hospital in Florida.

Where Are Some Notable Neighborhoods?

Lakewood Ranch (www.lakewoodranch.com or 800-30RANCH) is an award-winning, 7,000-acre master-planned community situated on the line between Sarasota and Manatee County. There are over 30 neighborhoods located in five residential villages with prices ranging from the upper $100,000s to well over a million dollars. Everything is provided in one location: recreation, schools, shopping, and restaurants—even a polo club and an osteopathic medical school!

River Wilderness (www.riverwilderness.com or 888-776-8080) offers "privacy, access control, championship golf, and classic Southern Living . . . on the river."

Both the Amish and the Mennonites visit Sarasota each winter, and their favorite restaurants offer the best fried chicken and homemade pies in the world! Try Yoder's Restaurant on Bahia Vista Street.

Located on the north shore of the Manatee River, close to both I-75 and Sarasota, this beautiful 1,400-acre gated golf community has a lot to offer, including direct boating access to the Gulf of Mexico. Home prices range from the $200,000s to more than a million dollars.

University Park (www.universitypark-fl.com or 800-394-6325) is conveniently located between Sarasota and Bradenton, just west of I-75. This community is composed of individual neighborhoods with a great variety in style and cost: Kenwood Park from the $350,000s, Warwick Gardens from the $600,000s, and Sloane Gardens from the $900,000s. All communities enjoy the four-star golf course, 11 lighted tennis courts, and the social amenities of the clubhouse, which offers duplicate bridge, bocce ball, bingo, and a book club.

Rosedale (www.Rosedalegolf.com or 800-881-9080), located in Bradenton and only 15 minutes from the Sarasota airport, is comprised of detached, single-family, maintenance-free homes in a master-planned golf and country club community. Rosedale offers a wide range of housing options, priced from the $200,000s to over a million dollars.

Condos or manufactured homes in the Sarasota area are also available, beginning below $100,000. Of course, depending on location, the condo prices can be reasonable or astronomical.

How Do I Pursue Lifelong Learning?

There are an impressive nine colleges and universities in the Sarasota area, including Manatee Community College, Sarasota County Technical Institute, Keiser College, Ringling School of Art and Design, the University of South Florida, and the International College. The International College is the home of the Creative Retirement Center, an Elderhostel affiliate, committed to helping its members enrich their lives by active participation in the process of lifelong learning through the study of history, religion, art, opera, or the American short story (to name just a few).

Strengths

Living in a tropical climate in the "cultural center" of Florida, in a real working city that feels like a small town, appeals to many. The beaches (especially Siesta

---

Don't miss the outdoor farmers' market every Saturday morning from 7 A.M. until noon. Enjoy the Caribbean-style baked goods and the Gulf of Mexico shrimp.

Key) are among the most beautiful to be found anywhere, and the views and sunsets over the water are spectacular. A great airport and easy highway access make travel a breeze.

Weaknesses

The downside to a tropical paradise is usually cost, and so it is here as well. The average new home on Siesta Key is priced at $500,000, and most homes close to the water will be extremely expensive. Some 350,000 tourists descend on the area every winter and create traffic gridlock and long lines at the restaurants. If you are looking for a year-round location, consider spending the summer months in a rental before you make a full-time move.

FYI

Check out these sources for additional information: Greater Sarasota Chamber of Commerce (www.sarasota chamber.org or 941-955-8187); the *Sarasota Herald Tribune* (941-953-5171); and the *Longboat Observer* (941-383-5509).

Vero Beach

REPORT CARD

Overall Rating:	A-
Climate:	A
Cost of Living:	A-
Health Care:	B+
Transportation:	B
What's to Do:	A

Vero Beach is the largest of five incorporated municipalities in Indian River County. Located in the south-central portion of the east coast of Florida, Vero Beach is part of the "Treasure Coast" that includes Port St. Lucie, Stuart, and Jupiter Island.

With the Kennedy Space Center 70 miles north and Miami 135 miles south, Vero Beach is the midpoint of growth in Indian River County. Commercial airline service is provided by Melbourne International Airport's 14 daily jet flights. It's located 35 miles north of Vero Beach. Vero Beach Municipal Airport

---

The name Treasure Coast originates from the gold doubloons that washed ashore from sunken Spanish vessels making their way from Havana to Spain in the 1500s.

provides service to corporate jets and small aircraft.

If you like water, you will love this part of Florida—it seems water is everywhere, with homes on canals, lakes, the Sebastian River, the Indian River Lagoon, and the Atlantic coast. Golf and tennis are available to everyone in Vero Beach; both Pocahontas Park and Riverside Park offer active tennis programs. The Sandridge Municipal Golf course has received national acclaim as one of our country's best public courses. Indian River County boasts 26 miles of sandy beaches and all the water sports and activities that can be enjoyed in the beautiful Florida sunshine. Most of the rainfall in Vero Beach occurs between June and October.

Vero Beach becomes Dodgertown when the Los Angeles Dodgers come to Holman Stadium for spring training. What a great way to enjoy our country's pastime on a more intimate level—6,500 fans instead of 50,000! In 1995, the Cultural Council of Indian River was created to support many area organizations; the Center for the Arts, the Vero Beach Art Club, and the Riverside Theatre are just a few groups that have benefited from the council. It appears that Vero Beach has it all.

Who Lives in Vero Beach?

More than 112,000 people live in Indian River County, with 17,700 living in Vero Beach. The median age is 48, and over 40 percent of the population is 62 or older.

What's the Cost?

The cost of living in Vero Beach is 97.3. Apartment rentals average $680 per month, and the average price of a home is about $200,000.

What's to Do?

Water, water, everywhere. With more than 20 parks that have access to the ocean or lagoon, everyone has entrée to swimming, fishing, kayaking, boating—virtually every water sport. There are myriad ecological attractions, including Pelican Island National Refuge, the En-

What's It Like Outside?	Jan.	Apr.	Jul.	Oct.	Rain (in.)	Snow (in.)
Average High (°F)	75	85	90	79	50	–
Average Low (°F)	53	66	72	60	–	–

vironmental Learning Center, Riverfront Conservation Area, and Harbor Branch Oceanographic Institution. Visit the UDT Navy SEAL Museum, or join the Vero Beach Art Club, the Theatre Guild, or the Choral Society. Take the grandkids to Orlando—it's only 100 miles away.

Where Are the Jobs?

Services, retail, government, and agriculture account for most of the jobs in Indian River County. New Piper Aircraft is the largest private-sector employer. The unemployment rate is about 7.6 percent.

Where Are the Doctors?

Indian River Memorial Hospital provides service to the Vero Beach area, and there are a number of emergency care clinics as well. Holmes Regional Medical Center is in Melbourne, 40 miles away.

Where Are the Notable Neighborhoods?

Pointe West (www.pointewestflorida.com or 561-794-9912) is a neo-traditional community with 750 single-family homes and 449 attached villas, priced from the $140,000s to the $350,000s. Enjoy semiprivate championship golf with a learning center, world-class equestrian facilities, and a pedestrian-friendly, practical town center, all in one location. A new "Lakes at Pointe West," described as "a unique retirement campus in a country club setting" is under development.

The Indian River Club (www.indianriverclub.com or 800-575-0005) is a gated golf community that holds the great distinction of being a Designated Audubon Signature Sanctuary. There are only two other such sanctuaries worldwide. Homes are priced from under $300,000 to over $750,000.

Grand Harbor (www.grandharbor.com or 800-826-8293) offers a resort lifestyle with amenities that include two championship golf courses, a 144-slip protected marina, a mile of intracoastal waterway, tennis, fitness, and a beautiful beach club. A variety of housing styles are available, and resales begin around $200,000, while new homes start at $400,000 and can exceed $1 million. Oak Harbor is an independent-

---

The Gulf Stream's water generally maintains daytime air temperatures of at least 70 degrees, thus giving this area the nickname "Gateway to the Tropics."

living retirement community located adjacent to Grand Harbor and offers its own nine-hole golf course, world-class clubhouse, and health center. Condos start in the $300,000s, and villas and cottages are also available beginning around $400,000.

Old Orchid (www.channingcorporation.com or 561-589-3505) was voted Best New Residential Community by the Indian River County Chamber of Commerce. Single-family homes are priced from the $280,000s. Enjoy lakefront views as well as a beautiful swim and tennis club just steps from the Atlantic Ocean.

How Do I Pursue Lifelong Learning?

Indian River Community College has a campus in Vero Beach. Career training, professional and personal development, customized business training, classes that will transfer to a four-year university, and free adult education/GED preparation are offered. The Florida Institute of Technology has more than 100 degree programs and is located 35 miles north in Melbourne.

Strengths

Vero Beach is a well-established small town with all the amenities to draw a diverse population. If you enjoy water sports, the arts, the theater, and ecological attractions (not to mention a 7-day-a-week bridge club!), you will want to consider Vero Beach.

Weaknesses

The closest big city is Orlando, about 100 miles away. Miami is 135 miles from Vero Beach.

FYI

Check out these sources for additional information: Indian River County Chamber of Commerce (www.vero-beach.fl.us/chamber or 561-567-3491); and the *Vero Beach Press Journal* (866-707-6397).

Indian River County has one of the largest bridge clubs in the nation. Vero Beach Duplicate Bridge Club has almost 2,000 members in its database and is housed in a 10,000-square-foot building that is open 7 days a week.

GEORGIA

★ **Atlanta**

Savanah •
Skidaway Island ●

Capital: Atlanta

Nickname: The Peach State

Motto: "Wisdom, justice, and moderation"

Flower: Cherokee Rose

Bird: Brown Thrasher

Population: 8,186,453

Fascinating Fact: Coca-Cola was invented in 1886 in Atlanta by Dr. John Pemberton.

Skidaway Island

REPORT CARD

Overall Rating:	A-
Climate:	A-
Cost of Living:	A-
Health Care:	A-
Transportation:	A-
What's to Do:	A

When is an island not an island? When it's Skidaway Island, which was probably oceanfront 40,000 years or so ago during the last ice age but is now an inland barrier island surrounded by the Wilmington and Vernon rivers, Skidaway Narrows, and Romerly Marsh. Eight miles long and 3 miles wide, Skidaway Island is a nature lover's dream, with a wonderful state park, great hiking trails, and rich marshland. It is also home to the Landings, a large residential area that's only 12 miles from Savannah.

You can have your cake and eat it, too—enjoy the close-by amenities of a wonderful southern city, bask in warm weather, revel in the natural beauty of the island, and have easy access to the area through the Savannah/Hilton Head International Airport.

Who Lives in Skidaway Island?

Skidaway Island, as well as the city of Savannah, are in Chatham County, which has about 230,000 residents; about 19 percent of the population is 55 or older. The composition of the county is about 55 percent Caucasian, 40 percent African-American, and 2 percent Hispanic. On the island itself, there are around 7,000 residents who are 97 percent Caucasian and about 1 percent Hispanic. The median age is 61 years old.

What's the Cost?

The cost of living in Savannah is 99.3.

What's to Do?

Skidaway Island State Park encompasses more than 500 acres of this 6,300-acre island. Swim, picnic, camp, or hike through the forest or along a boardwalk trail through the marsh. Enjoy the flora and fauna of the area—fiddler crabs, herons, egrets, ferns, palmettos, and pines are your companions. The University of Georgia's Marine Extension Center and the Skidaway Institute of Oceanography are on the island, and both are open to the public. Living on Skidaway Island allows you to combine the pleasures of water, wildlife, and a wonderful city.

When you crave city life, drive a short distance to Savannah and take advantage of all that it has to offer. Visit the pedestrian-friendly historic district, explore the sizable number of museums, stroll along the pedestrian promenade at the city market, take a ghost tour, and investigate the old cemeteries, forts, parks, and churches. Savannah has a Greek Festival, Jazz Festival, and Film Festival, just to mention a few of its almost 200 festivals. Attend a live production at the 1,000-seat Savannah Theater, or attend a performance of the Savannah Symphony or Ballet South, followed by some "low-country" cuisine. Fewer than 25 miles from Skidaway Island (less than 20 from Savannah), you can saunter along the 3-mile swath of beach at Tybee Island.

Where Are the Jobs?

Health care, education, manufacturing, tourism, and retail are among the largest employers. Gulfstream,

What's It Like Outside?	Jan.	Apr.	Jul.	Oct.	Rain (in.)	Snow (in.)
Average High (°F)	60	78	91	78	48	–
Average Low (°F)	38	54	72	57	–	–

Aerospace Corporation, International Paper, Fort James Corporation, and Great Dane Trailers also employ a sizable number of residents. The unemployment rate is 4.1 percent.

Where Are the Doctors?

There are several hospitals in Savannah, including St. Josephs/Candler Health System, Memorial Medical Center, and the Georgia Regional Hospital.

Where Are Some Notable Neighborhoods?

The Landings on Skidaway Island (www.thelandings. com or 800-841-7011) is a private, gated community that spreads over almost 4,500 acres. Six golf courses, more than 30 tennis courts, four clubhouses, two deep-water marinas, fitness facilities, swimming pools, social clubs, and hiking trails are found in this coastal development that is the largest one in the Savannah area.

Lots on Skidaway Island range from around $60,000 to $600,000, and a variety of housing styles range from around $200,000 to $3 million-plus.

How Do I Pursue Lifelong Learning?

There are several institutions of higher learning in the Savannah area, including Armstrong Atlantic State University, the Savannah College of Art and Design, Savannah State University, Savannah Technical College, and South College.

Strengths

Oaks dripping with Spanish moss are just one more thing to admire about this area. Cost of living is within reason, and people are hospitable and friendly.

Weaknesses

What can you say—you're in the South! You'll have heat and humidity in the summer. Although the location lends itself to the threat of hurricanes, the last major hit was in 1979 (David), when winds approached 100 miles per hour.

FYI

Check out these sources for additional information: Savannah Area Chamber of Commerce (www.savannah chamber.com or 912-644-6400) and the *Savannah Morning News* (912-236-0271).

Midnight in the Garden of Good and Evil by John Berendt has Savannah as its setting; the film version of Berendt's book, *Forrest Gump*, and *The Legend of Bagger Vance* were filmed there.

NEVADA

Reno

★ **Carson City**

Las Vegas

Capital: Carson City

Nickname: The Silver State

Motto: "All for our country"

Flower: Sagebrush

Bird: Mountain Bluebird

Population: 1,998,257

Fascinating Fact: The ratio of slot machines to Nevada residents is about 1 to 10.

Las Vegas

REPORT CARD

Overall Rating:	A
Climate:	B
Cost of Living:	A
Health Care:	A
Transportation:	A
What's to Do:	A

Las Vegas is located at the southern tip of Nevada between the Sierra Nevada and Wasatch mountain ranges. This big city is described by the Chamber of Commerce as "One City, Two Stories." On one hand, the entertainment industry and casinos are known worldwide, and the shopping is legendary. On the other hand, Las Vegas is much, much more than its downtown. The mountains, lakes, and desert surrounding the city provide residents with scores of opportunities for recreational activities—more physical than sliding on and off your chair at the casino! Lake Mead, the largest man-made lake in the world, is perfect for water sports, and the fish are biting year-round. Mount Charleston is a great place for snow skiing, and Red Rock Canyon is a photographer's dream and a hiker's paradise. Las Vegas is dotted with dozens of golf courses, and the Grand Canyon is only 300 miles away. McCarran International Airport is opening more than 20 new gates, and the city has purchased 6,500 acres near Jean, south of Las Vegas, for a proposed second airport to open around 2010.

Las Vegas enjoys about 320 days of sunshine a year.

Who Lives in Las Vegas?

Nevada is our fastest-growing state. Clark County is home to 1.4 million people, and the population of Las Vegas is about 650,000. Each month 2.5 million people visit Las Vegas, and the city welcomes about 10,000 new residents annually. Retirees make up the largest segment of people currently moving to Las Vegas.

What's the Cost?

The cost of living in Las Vegas is 106. The median cost of a home is $171,300, and you can rent a small apartment for about $750 per month. Nevada does not have a state income tax. Median household income is about $50,000 a year.

What's to Do?

Blackjack, slot machines, poker, roulette: gambling, gambling, everywhere! Shopping is becoming somewhat of a sport in Las Vegas as well. With Lord & Taylor's opening in 2003, the Fashion Show Mall had eight anchor stores—the most of any mall in the country, with a size equivalent to 33 football fields.

Visit Lake Mead, the Hoover Dam, Red Rock Canyon, and the Grand Canyon and enjoy all the outdoor activities they have to offer. Or soak in a hot spring at Gold Strike Hot Springs, about an hour from Vegas. But be sure to be back in the city for the evening to enjoy the great restaurants and entertainment.

Where Are the Jobs?

Education, gaming, government, medical, high-tech services, retail, and construction are big employers. Las

What's It Like Outside?	Jan.	Apr.	Jul.	Oct.	Rain (in.)	Snow (in.)
Average High (°F)	56	77	105	84	4	–
Average Low (°F)	33	49	75	53	–	–

Vegas has a pro-business environment that exempts companies from a variety of taxes. Las Vegas has ranked number one in high-tech job growth since 1990. The unemployment rate is 5.3 percent.

Where Are the Doctors?

Sunrise Hospital and Medical Center is the state's largest comprehensive medical complex. Las Vegas has a total of 12 hospitals with a combined medical and support staff of over 13,000.

Where Are Some Notable Neighborhoods?

Lake Las Vegas (www.lakelasvegas.com or 800-564-1603) is a resort containing several gated communities centered on a beautiful lake, about 17 miles from the Las Vegas Strip. Enjoy the amenities of a Hyatt Regency and Ritz-Carlton and three world-class golf courses, or build a custom home on the lake. Condos and homes begin at $350,000. Porto Villagios offers a private yacht and beach club.

Summerlin is the fastest-growing master-planned community in the country and has been for the past 8 years. Homes, condominiums, townhomes, and custom homes range in price from under $200,000 to over $2 million. Red Rock Country Club (www.redrock countryclub.com or 702-360-3100), by Sunrise Colony Company, is a gated golf community within the 30-village Summerlin. Homes are priced from $350,000 to over $2 million.

If you want to be in the middle of all the excitement, live at Turnberry Place (www.turnberry-place.com or 800-616-2120), and have the world-famous Bellagio casino right around the bend. Condos in these four, 40-story-high towers boast outstanding amenities and range in price from $500,000 to over $5 million. You can join the Stirling Club at Turnberry Place and enjoy the spa, restaurants, and entertainment. Construction should be complete in 2005.

In the December 2002 issue of *Money Magazine*, Las Vegas was at the top of the charts in the rankings of "Best Places to Live."

How Do I Pursue Lifelong Learning?

The University of Nevada, Las Vegas, is located in the middle of the city and has many programs to offer its more than 18,000 students. On a space-available basis, seniors 62 and older are invited to take credit classes tuition-free. The Community College of Southern Nevada has three campuses in the Las Vegas area.

Strengths

This part of the country is growing at an incredible rate; so much of everything is new—the homes, the roads, the shopping. The sunshine and the entertainment will make this a very popular place for friends and family to visit.

Weaknesses

How much of a good thing is too much? Is Las Vegas growing too fast? Are 2.5 million visitors a month a few too many? What will that glorious sunshine feel like in July and August? The crime rate in Las Vegas is higher than the national average for both personal and property crime.

FYI

Check out these sources for additional information: Las Vegas Chamber of Commerce (www.lvchamber.com or 702-735-1616); the *Las Vegas Review Journal* (702-383-0400); and the *Las Vegas Sun* (702-385-3111).

Work as a table games supervisor and make an average of $22 an hour. Better yet, as an Elvis impersonator, you can earn $650 a day!

Reno

REPORT CARD

Overall Rating:	B+
Climate:	B-
Cost of Living:	B
Health Care:	A
Transportation:	A
What's to Do:	A

Reno is known as the "Biggest Little City in the World." It sits between the majestic Sierra Nevada Mountains and the Cascade Mountains, which provide a scenic background for the city. The Truckee River winding its way through town and the surprising red brick construction of the historic section provide quite a contrast to the glitzy casino town that many people envision. Located in the northwestern part of the state, Reno is 230 miles from San Francisco, 470 miles from Los Angeles, and a 45-minute drive from beautiful Lake Tahoe, the largest alpine lake in North America.

The Reno/Sparks/Lake Tahoe area has a lot to offer, with close to 20 world-class ski resorts, more than 40 golf courses, and around 60 gaming locations. Summer or winter, inside or outside, you have options, including an international opera company and ballet. The Reno/Tahoe International Airport makes travel to and from this city easy.

After the temperatures hit 90 in the summer, it'll cool off early in the afternoon, and you can expect to be under the covers at night!

Who Lives in Reno?

The population of Reno in 2002 was 190,000, up 5.4 percent from the 2000 census; about 35 percent of the residents are over the age of 45. Approximately 77 percent of the population is Caucasian, 14 percent is Hispanic, 2 percent is African-American, and 5 percent is Asian.

What's It Like Outside?	Jan.	Apr.	Jul.	Oct.	Rain (in.)	Snow (in.)
Average High (°F)	46	63	90	71	8	26
Average Low (°F)	19	29	48	31	–	–

What's the Cost?

Reno's cost of living index is 106. An average single-family home is priced at $224,000. The city boasts more than 100 residential neighborhoods priced from $120,000 to over $500,000 with an easy commute (under 30 minutes) to downtown and the airport.

What's to Do?

The casinos provide not only gaming but also great entertainment and fine dining. Reno is home to the 80-lane National Bowling Stadium and an IMAX Theater. The National Automobile Museum, the Championship Air Races, and the Reno Rodeo are additional attractions. Or, meander along the River Walk that winds along the Truckee River.

For activities of a more cultural nature, patronize an event at the McKinley Arts & Cultural Center or at the Wingfield Park Amphitheater, or visit the Nevada Museum of Art.

Lake Tahoe, about 50 miles away, provides year-round outdoor fun for the entire family. There is skiing and snowboarding in the winter, and Lake Tahoe has about 30 public beaches to help you enjoy water activities in the summer. Flume Trail at Lake Tahoe is rated among the top 20 mountain bike trails in the United States.

Virginia City, an authentic western town, complete with plank sidewalks and saloons, is 35 miles north of Reno and will give you a real flavor of the Old West. Or, take a day excursion to Nevada's capital, Carson City, or travel to Yosemite National Park and enjoy the beauty of the area.

Where Are the Jobs?

The largest employers include education, health care, tourism, and the gaming industry. Many prestigious companies have operations in the area, including Cisco, Microsoft, Oracle, Michelin, and John Deere. The unemployment rate is 3 percent.

Where Are the Doctors?

Washoe Medical Center, a level II trauma center with 529 beds, and St. Mary's Regional Medical Center (367

Mark Twain described the beauty of Lake Tahoe as "surely the fairest picture the whole earth affords."

beds) provide excellent care for the residents of Reno. There are additional health facilities, such as the HealthSouth Rehabilitation Hospital and the U.S. Veterans Medical Center.

Where Are Some Notable Neighborhoods?

Double Diamond Ranch (www.tanameratownhomes.com or 775-852-2800) offers a selection of housing choices among its 3,500 units, as well as almost 30 miles of walking and biking trails, a clubhouse, pool, and views of the Sierra-Nevada Mountains. Consider Fleur de Lis townhomes in a gated neighborhood, priced from the $200,000s. Tanamera Luxury Apartments (www.tanamera.net or 775-852-8989) are available if you would rather rent. Tanamera has 440 apartment homes priced from around $1,100 a month, and amenities include a clubhouse, a full gym, and a beautiful swimming pool. Wyndgate Village and Waterford are communities of single-family homes within Double Diamond Ranch (www.tanamerahomes.com or 775-850-4200); listings begin in the $200,000s.

Arrow Creek (www.arrowcreek.com or 888-702-7769) is a 3,200-acre, master-planned, gated community with homes priced from the $500,000s to $2 million and up. Enjoy miles of natural trails and two 18-hole championship golf courses. The closest ski resort is only 14 miles away.

Somersett (www.somersett.com) is a master-planned golf community that, when complete, will have close to 2,700 homes, a network of 25 miles of hiking trails, a town center, and two golf courses. Attached duet homes are priced from the high $200,000s, and single-family homes are priced from the $300,000s. Most of the community is not age-restricted. Del Webb, however, is building the active-adult community Sierra Canyon (www.delwebb.com or 866-252-9322) within Somersett, which will be Del Webb's first age-restricted community in northern Nevada. The plans include 850 single-family homes on 300 acres, with recreational amenities that include access to the par-3 Canyon Golf Course. Sierra Canyon will open sometime in 2004.

How Do I Pursue Lifelong Learning?

Reno offers a number of opportunities for lifelong learning, including Truckee Meadows Community College; Morrison University; the University of Nevada, Reno; and the Career College of Northern Nevada. And don't forget the Reno Professional Bartending School.

Strengths

Three hundred-plus days of sunshine is almost always a good thing, especially when it helps to melt the snow. Access to Lake Tahoe and the ski resorts makes this a great place to enjoy the outdoors. And if you like to gamble, well, watch out!

Weaknesses

Even with a great airport, Reno seems to be a little "out of the way." Evenings are cool or downright cold. Winter will bring snow, and not just to the ski slopes. And if you like to gamble, well, watch out!

FYI

Check out these sources for additional information: Reno-Sparks Chamber of Commerce (www.reno-sparkschamber.org or 775-337-3030); the *Reno Gazette Journal* (775-788-6200); and the *Reno News and Review* (775-324-4440).

NEW MEXICO

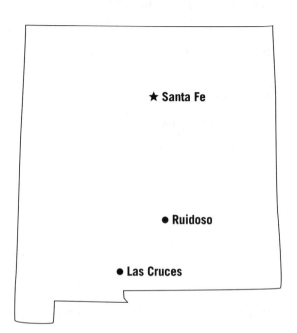

Capital: Santa Fe

Nickname: Land of Enchantment

Motto: "It grows as it goes"

Flower: Yucca

Bird: Roadrunner

Population: 1,819,046

Fascinating Fact: Santa Fe, with an altitude of 7,000 feet, is the highest state capital in the nation.

Las Cruces

REPORT CARD

Overall Rating:	B+
Climate:	A
Cost of Living:	A
Health Care:	B+
Transportation:	B+
What's to Do:	B+

Las Cruces means "the crosses" in Spanish and is thought to have been named after the crosses raised in remembrance of those who died during an 1830s raid by the Apaches. Las Cruces is the second largest city in New Mexico (after Albuquerque) and is less than an hour's drive from Mexico. The airport in El Paso, Texas, is also about an hour away. The rugged Organ Mountains and the meandering Rio Grande bound the city. A strong agricultural base of cotton, chili peppers, and pecans is related to Las Cruces's location in the fertile Mesilla valley.

Las Cruces has cultural and educational amenities, coupled with an outstanding cost of living, nice climate, and scenic beauty. Having recently celebrated its 150th anniversary, Las Cruces is growing rapidly yet retains its "Old West" flavor.

Average relative humidity is a pleasant 27 percent, and Las Cruces boasts 350 days of sunshine a year.

Who Lives in Las Cruces?

The population is 74,000, with 15 percent 62 years or older. Anglo, Hispanic, and Native American cultures predominate.

What's the Cost?

Las Cruces is an excellent value, with a cost of living at 93. Housing and health care costs are exceptional, with housing rated a very attractive 84 and health care 85. The average price for a new three-bedroom home is $195,000; for an existing three-bedroom home, it is $132,000. Rentals average $600 per month for an unfurnished three-bedroom apartment.

Money, *Where to Retire*, *Family Digest*, and *Hispanic* magazines have all rated Las Cruces among their top places to live and/or retire.

What's to Do?

Activities include playing virtually year-round golf, mountain hiking and biking, and exploring historic sites and museums. The adobe buildings and plaza in the close-by community of Old Mesilla make it the top visitor destination in southern New Mexico. Day trips include the Gila Cliff dwellings, recreation areas such as Elephant Butte Lake and White Sands National Monument, and the Juarez City Market in Mexico. Theater, symphony, art galleries, and ballet round out the cultural offerings. And, of course, the Mexican influence is a bonus for those who love Mexican food!

Where Are the Jobs?

The largest employers are affiliated with education, health, and government. The unemployment rate for the Las Cruces metropolitan area is 6.5 percent.

Where Are the Doctors?

The Memorial Medical Center, Memorial Health Plex, Mt. View Regional Medical Center, and Mesilla Valley Hospital, as well as several clinics, serve Las Cruces. There are approximately 400 physicians in 30 specialties in town. Assisted living, Alzheimer's care, and home health care are also available.

Where Are Some Notable Neighborhoods?

The big push for growth is to the east of the city. Sonoma Ranch (www.sonomaranch.com or 877-700-7210) is an example of a relatively new golf course community located in this direction, with the jagged Organ Mountains as the backdrop. Begun in 1999, this planned community covers more than 900 acres, and the first two phases alone are zoned for more than 3,000 residences. There is a mix of residential styles, and commercial and professional amenities will also be integrated into the community. Homes range from $200,000 to $600,000. Within the confines of Sonoma Ranch is the gated Boulders, an active-adult community with its own golf course and clubhouse. Homes begin in the $170,000s, and homesites (which aren't in-

What's It Like Outside?	Jan.	Apr.	Jul.	Oct.	Rain (in.)	Snow (in.)
Average High (°F)	59	77	97	77	9	3
Average Low (°F)	27	42	62	44	–	–

cluded in the cost of the home) begin in the $40,000s. For information on the Boulders, contact Sonoma Ranch.

You can travel northwest, cross the Rio Grande, and arrive at the community of Picacho Hills (www.picacho-living.com or 505-526-3818), a private country club community located in the hills above Las Cruces. Here, you'll find panoramic views of the city and the mountains, though the part of the city you go through to get to Picacho Hills is not very attractive. Although Picacho Hills has been around for about a decade, there is still a lot of building going on with many homesites available. Land/home packages can start under $150,000 and go up to the $600,000s.

If you're looking for a manufactured home community, investigate Trails West (www.trailswest-nm.com or 877-924-9226), a tidy, gated adult community near the historic plaza of Old Mesilla, with a community center and pool. You lease the lot ($300 to $375 per month) and purchase your own manufactured home. When fully developed, there will be approximately 440 homesites; presently, about half of these are occupied.

How Do I Pursue Lifelong Learning?

New Mexico State University and Dona Aña Branch Community College provide adult and continuing education classes in addition to credit classes and degrees.

The Munson Senior Center, Eastside Community Center, and Mesilla Park Recreation Center also offer a wide array of programs.

Strengths

Cost of living, transportation, scenery, and climate are all plusses. Medical facilities are good. The fact that Las Cruces is the fastest-growing city in New Mexico—and one of the fastest growing in the United States—is no accident!

Weaknesses

The crime rate in Las Cruces is higher than the national average. According to the 2001 FBI crime reports, Las Cruces had an overall rate of 77 crimes per 1,000 people, compared to a national average of 51 crimes per 1,000 people. The higher crime rates are in the categories of rape, burglary, and larceny/thefts. Downtown Las Cruces is not that attractive, but it is undergoing revitalization.

FYI

Check out these sources for additional information: Chamber of Commerce (www.lascruces.org); relocation guide (www.lascrucesrelocation.com); visitors' guide (www.lascrucesvisitors.com); the *Las Cruces Bulletin* (505-524-8061); and the *Las Cruces Sun News* (505-541-5400).

Ruidoso

REPORT CARD

Overall Rating:	B-
Climate:	B+
Cost of Living:	B
Health Care:	B-
Transportation:	C
What's to Do:	B-

Ruidoso is a small, laid-back town (except in summer), located in south-central New Mexico. Its 7,000-foot altitude provides a cool but fairly mild climate with low humidity; beautiful aspens and evergreens afford a different look from much of New Mexico's desert flora. Ruidoso snuggles at the base of 12,000-foot Sierra Blanca in the Sacramento Mountains.

The town is an outdoor playground. Skiing, hiking, fishing, golfing, and horse racing are on the menu of activities. There are also several museums, two casinos, and a performing arts center. The town is fairly isolated—the nearest interstates are more than 100 miles away, Las Cruces is a 2½-hour drive, and flying in or out of Ruidoso using a major airport is a hike— Albuquerque International Airport is about a 4-hour drive, and El Paso International Airport is over 2 hours away. There is a regional and a municipal airport as well.

Who Lives in Ruidoso?

Ruidoso has about 8,000 permanent residents, but this number can swell to 30,000 in the summer, as people escape the heat of the Southwest for this cooler mountain town, many coming to enjoy the horse racing. About 20 percent of the population is at least 62 years old, and between 1990 and 2000 the population increased by about 70 percent. About 90 percent of residents over 25 have a high school diploma,

Ruidoso comes from the Spanish name for "noisy" and refers to the small
Rio Ruidoso River that flows through the village.

and approximately 30 percent have at least a bachelor's degree.

What's the Cost?

The median household income in Ruidoso is about $40,000, and the mean price of a home is $140,000. Although exact numbers aren't available, according to one Realtor, the cost of living "is cheaper than California, but more expensive than west Texas."

What's to Do?

If you want to hit the slopes, Ski Apache is owned and operated by the Mescalero Apache tribe. It's open between Thanksgiving and early spring and boasts the largest lift capacity in the state. Or, take in a horse race and wager a few bets at the Ruidoso Downs Race Track and the Billy the Kid Casino. Golf, fishing, camping, and hiking are available in Ruidoso as well as nearby towns. If you're looking for something more elegant, enjoy a ballet or the symphony at the Spencer Theater for the Performing Arts. The beauty of Lincoln National Forest and White Sands National Monument can be appreciated year-round.

Where Are the Jobs?

Tourism, retail, local government, and health care are the largest employers. The unemployment rate for Lincoln County is 3.6 percent.

Where Are the Doctors?

The Lincoln County Medical Center has a hospital, clinic, and nursing home associated with it. Home health care is available, as well as a mental health program for seniors.

What's It Like Outside?	Jan.	Apr.	Jul.	Oct.	Rain (in.)	Snow (in.)
Average High (°F)	45	62	82	66	23	47
Average Low (°F)	19	27	47	30	–	–

Where Are Some Notable Neighborhoods?

Alto Lakes Golf & Country Club is a bit north of Ruidoso, and homes are available starting around $300,000. Homes in the village of Alto average approximately $250,000. Kokopelli (www.kokopelliclub. com or 877-336-1818), also located in Alto, is a new, gated golf community comprised of garden homes and custom homesites. Villas sell for about $515,000, and garden homes around $800,000. Lots range from $113,000 to $300,000. There are a number of manufactured homes in the Ruidoso area for under $100,000.

How Do I Pursue Lifelong Learning?

Eastern New Mexico University offers 2-year degrees at its Ruidoso location. Online courses and noncredit courses are also available.

Strengths

If you're into the outdoors and are looking for small-town western living in a beautiful, secluded setting, Ruidoso may be your place.

Weaknesses

Ruidoso's isolation could be a negative factor. The mixture of older manufactured homes next to single-family homes might be a concern. Health care could be an issue if there are complex medical problems. If you're a shopaholic, you may have to leave town to really feed your addiction.

FYI

Check out these sources for additional information: Chamber of Commerce (www.ruidoso.net/chamber); and the *Ruidoso News* (505-526-3818).

Ruidoso's Lincoln County is the birthplace of Billy the Kid, Smokey Bear, and Kit Carson.

Santa Fe

REPORT CARD

Overall Rating:	A-
Climate:	B
Cost of Living:	B
Health Care:	A
Transportation:	A
What's to Do:	A

Founded in 1610, Santa Fe is the oldest state capital in the country. It's nestled in the foothills of the Rocky Mountains at an elevation of 7,000 feet. Located in a valley above the Rio Grande and surrounded by thousands of acres of national forest, it is a 37-square-mile city and has a full-service airport 60 miles south in Albuquerque. If you want a day at the beach, it will be necessary to drive 12 hours to either Padre Island in Texas or Los Angeles. That's the bad news. Everything else about Santa Fe is good news! You will enjoy four seasons, with at least partial sunshine 300 days each year. This high desert country is greener than most due to the ample rainfall and melting snows. If you like a lot of space, the population of the entire state of New Mexico is 1.8 million (close to the population of Houston, Texas)!

With horse racing, hiking, biking, river rafting, cycling, skiing, not to mention golfing 365 days a year, you'll never have a dull moment. If outdoor adventure is not your thing, the variety of cultural opportunities in Santa Fe is vast. The opera performs at an outdoor theater and is almost never interrupted by weather. The Santa Fe Symphony Orchestra and Chorus and the Desert Chorale provide a year-round calendar of great musical events. Walking from the main, downtown plaza in any direction will take you past sculpture gardens, tons of art galleries, an impressive number of museums, and Native Americans selling handcrafted jewelry. With more than 200 restaurants, you'll never want to cook again (if it weren't for the great cooking

---

The architecture of Santa Fe is very distinctive. The Spanish pueblo style predominates, and strict building codes require all new buildings to be constructed of adobe or adobe-looking material in varying earth tones.

schools in downtown Santa Fe). With one to two million tourists each year, too many visitors could be your biggest problem.

Who Lives in Santa Fe?

About 26 percent of the 66,500 people living in Santa Fe are over the age of 55.

What's the Cost?

Santa Fe's cost of living is 116. The cost of housing is the main culprit, with the median price of a home about $270,000. Many homes are priced from $500,000 to over a million dollars. The median household income in Santa Fe is about $43,000.

What's to Do?

Santa Fe appears to offer more opportunities to active retirees than a city four times its size! Art classes and cooking classes are available if you're looking for a new challenge. Music, theater, and dance thrive in Santa Fe year-round. The Santa Fe Opera, Chamber Music Festival, Sangre De Cristo Chorale, Shakespeare in Santa Fe, and the Santa Fe Festival Ballet are just a sampling of what the city has to offer. With 250 art galleries and museums, those who love cultural endeavors will certainly get their fill.

For the outdoor enthusiast, there are several exceptional public golf courses in the area, as well as the opportunity for fly-fishing, rock climbing, snow skiing, snowboarding, river rafting, horseback riding, hiking, bicycling, and more. Take a day trip to one of eight Northern Indian pueblos, or volunteer with the Literacy Volunteers of Santa Fe or the Food Brigade of Santa Fe. The only limiting factor is your energy level!

Where Are the Jobs?

Government (local, state, and federal), along with retail, tourism, health care, and construction are the biggest em-

What's It Like Outside?	Jan.	Apr.	Jul.	Oct.	Rain (in.)	Snow (in.)
Average High (°F)	40	60	91	63	14	32
Average Low (°F)	19	35	57	38	–	–

ployers in Santa Fe, though one in six people is employed in the arts. Unemployment is low, averaging around 3.4 percent. The Santa Fe City Council voted to enact a minimum wage of $8.50 per hour for all large businesses in the city (with 25 or more employees), which will gradually increase to $10.50 per hour by 2008.

Where Are the Doctors?

Santa Fe has four hospitals; the largest is St. Vincent Hospital, with about 270 beds, and it is the only level III trauma center in northern New Mexico. St. Vincent is nonprofit, nonaffiliated, and proudly states its mission "to care for all the people of Santa Fe, northern New Mexico, and southern Colorado regardless of their ability to pay."

Where Are Some Notable Neighborhoods?

Aldea (www.aldeadesantafe.com or 800-586-1032), on the northwest side of Santa Fe, is a neo-traditional village designed by acclaimed new urbanist architect Andres Duany. Homes are gathered around a central commercial and civic plaza. The community includes a mix of housing types, priced from around $300,000, with lots beginning around $100,000.

The master-planned development of Tierra Contenta (www.tierracontenta.org or 505-471-4551) will have almost 6,000 residences on 1,400 acres when complete. This is a city initiative to provide affordable housing, a major issue for Santa Fe. As their Web site states, "Tierra Contenta is designed to emulate the traditional villages of northern New Mexico in both layout and architecture. Tierra Contenta is designed to be a place where people live close to each other around neighborhood centers with shopping, work, schools, and community facilities within walking distance. Tierra Contenta also features large open space areas connected by pedestrian and bike paths." Two neighborhoods of note are Highlands East and Highlands West—they offer single-family homes with stunning mountain views.

The Georgia O'Keeffe Museum in Santa Fe is the home of the world's largest permanent collection of works by Georgia O'Keeffe. Although O'Keeffe was born in Wisconsin, she lived the latter portion of her life in New Mexico, inspired by the area's beauty.

Las Lagunitas (www.laslagunitas.com or 505-989-3573) is a private, gated community several miles south of Santa Fe that includes natural spring-fed ponds, family picnic areas, and private parks, as well as more than 130 acres of open space. Homesites begin around $120,000.

Las Campanas (www.lascampanas.com or 800-992-4250) is the premier private, gated golf community in Santa Fe, set at the southern tip of the Rocky Mountains. About 1,700 homes are planned on 4,800 acres (more than 1,000 homesites have been sold already). Amenities include two Jack Nicklaus Signature golf courses, an equestrian center featuring a 30,000-square-foot indoor riding rink, and a spacious spa and tennis facility with an outdoor pool and indoor lap pool. Homesites begin around $250,000, and homes, mainly resales, average around $1.2 million. Pricey, but beautiful.

How Do I Pursue Lifelong Learning?

A number of educational opportunities await you in Santa Fe. The College of Santa Fe is near the top of *U.S. News and World Report*'s list of best regional liberal arts colleges in the West; St. John's College awards both bachelor of arts and master of arts degrees; Santa Fe Community College offers a variety of programs as well as classes just for seniors; and New Mexico Elderhostel provides educational and travel opportunities for seniors 55 and older.

Strengths

The beauty of Santa Fe is surpassed only by its multitude of museums, festivals, art galleries, restaurants, music, and theatrical performances. If you're the outdoor type, stay in good shape for all the adventures that await you. Enjoy all four seasons and the low humidity.

Weaknesses

The architecture is fabulous, but housing prices are high. Though it melts fairly quickly, there is snow, and you'll need that winter coat.

FYI

Santa Fe Chamber of Commerce (www.santafechamber.com); and the *Santa Fe New Mexican* (800-873-3372).

Taos, New Mexico, a great ski town, is just 70 miles from Santa Fe and a great place to visit (www.taoschamber.com).

NORTH CAROLINA

Capital: Raleigh

Nickname: Tar Heel State

Motto: "To be, rather than to seem"

Flower: Dogwood

Bird: Cardinal

Population: 8,049,313

Fascinating Fact: Fayetteville is home to the first miniature golf course.

Asheville

REPORT CARD

Overall Rating:	A
Climate:	B
Cost of Living:	A
Health Care:	A
Transportation:	A
What's to Do:	A

Nestled between the Blue Ridge Mountains and the Great Smoky Mountains, Asheville is viewed by many to be a near-perfect retirement location, whether you're married or single. The city sits at an elevation of 2,200 feet on a plateau divided by the French Broad River and surrounded by beautiful mountains with elevations of 5,000 feet and more. Asheville is said to be a "manageable size" with the advantages of big-city amenities. It's 125 miles west of Charlotte, 113 miles east of Knoxville, and 200 miles north

---

Asheville has enjoyed an impressive list of accolades over the past 10 years,
and was most recently chosen one of the "Best Places to Retire" (MSN.com, July 2003),
one of the "15 Best Places to Reinvent Your Life" (*AARP Magazine*, May/June 2003), and among
the "Top Safe and Cheap Getaways" (*USA Today*, April 4, 2003).

of Atlanta. It's the largest city in western North Carolina, and it is the regional center for manufacturing, transportation, health care, banking, professional services, and shopping. There is a "Real Shindig" almost every Saturday night between July 4th and Labor Day, and downtown Asheville comes alive with musicians celebrating Appalachian music and dance in the City-County Plaza.

The mountains and rivers provide outdoor enthusiasts with wide-open spaces for white-water rafting, kayaking, canoeing, rock climbing, and hiking. There are more than 250 waterfalls in western North Carolina, and you can see them by heading to the Blue Ridge Parkway for hiking trails, including those at Craggy Gardens, Great Smoky Mountain National Park, Yellowstone Falls, and Graveyard Fields. But if the shore is really your thing, it's about a 5-hour drive to Myrtle Beach, South Carolina.

Asheville could be called a college town. Although not the home of a major university, several colleges have a real presence here. The University of North Carolina, Asheville, opened the Reuter Center in September 2003,

the new home of the North Carolina Center for Creative Retirement.

The mild, four-season climate appeals to most people, with the exception of the 16 inches of snow and possibly "black ice" on the mountain roads when the temperatures hover around the freezing point.

Who Lives in Asheville?

Asheville's population has grown 25 percent in the past two decades. Full-time residents enjoy the opportunity to make new friends but do not enjoy the increased traffic. The population in 2002 was estimated at about 70,000, and the demographics show that 89 percent are Caucasian, 7 percent African-American, and 3 percent Hispanic. The median age is 39, and about 35 percent of the population is over 55.

What's the Cost?

Asheville's cost of living is 97.9. Utility costs are about 16 percent higher but health care is about 15 percent lower

What's It Like Outside?	Jan.	Apr.	Jul.	Oct.	Rain (in.)	Snow (in.)
Average High (°F)	46	65	83	71	46	16
Average Low (°F)	26	41	62	42	–	–

than average. The cost of housing is about 10 percent to 15 percent higher than the national average, with an average new home costing about $145,000 and the average two-bedroom apartment renting for about $750 per month.

What's to Do?

If you imagine yourself taking to the trails with a group of new friends for a trek through the Blue Ridge Mountains to absorb the beauty of the fall colors or the new spring wildflowers, Asheville may be the spot for you. Just call Asheville Parks and Recreation Outdoor Programs and sign up for Senior Treks or Hikes for Seniors, offered every Friday. If you are someone who enjoys winter, there are more than eight resorts/spots for snow skiing, snowboarding (you, too, can be one of the "grays on trays"), and snow tubing around Asheville. Why not try your hand at rock climbing at Looking Glass Rock, about an hour from Asheville, known as the best rock climbing spot in the state? If that sounds a little strenuous, you might like to try "rockhounding": looking for rubies, sapphires, and other precious stones. Whitewater rafting, kayaking, canoeing, and floating are popular water activities in Asheville.

If you are ready to volunteer, try the World Market, a nonprofit, volunteer-based program that helps market handmade crafts from low-income craftspeople in developing nations. Or shop at the Woolworth Walk, where more than 150 artists and artisans make and sell fine arts, crafts, and jewelry.

History, art, and music are a big part of what makes Asheville a special place to live. The Carl Sandburg Home is located here, as is the Biltmore Estate. The latter covers 8,000 acres, including 75 acres of gardens, a winery, and the 250-room Biltmore House. The Pack Place Education Arts & Science Center is home to the Asheville Art Museum, Colburn Gem and Mineral Museum, Diana Wortham Theater, and Health Adventure. Indoors or out, summer or winter, you will find plenty to do and new adventures in Asheville.

Asheville Regional Airport is served by US Airways, Comair, ASA, and Continental Express.

Where Are the Jobs?

The top employers include education, government, and health care. Blue Ridge Paper Products, Ingles Markets, and G.E. Lighting Systems are also big employers in the area. The unemployment rate is about 4 percent.

Where Are the Doctors?

The doctors, more than 600 physicians practicing 50 specialties, are at Mission St. Joseph Hospital in Asheville. Mission Medical Center, the largest medical center in western North Carolina, is the largest employer in the area with more than 5,600 employees and close to 1,000 volunteers. *U.S. News & World Report* named Mission one of the top 50 heart hospitals in the nation.

Where Are Some Notable Neighborhoods?

We would be remiss if we did not mention two delightful small towns that are close to Asheville that you may also want to consider: Brevard and Hendersonville.

Brevard is small (7,000 residents), charming, and beautifully situated among the streams, forests, and waterfalls of the Blue Ridge Mountains. Thirty-five miles from Asheville, the town is known for its music and fine arts (it's home to Brevard College) and boasts that it averages only five days of snow per year. Sixty percent of new arrivals to Brevard are retirees.

Hendersonville is about 25 miles south of Asheville and has an attractive historic downtown with antique stores, specialty shops, and restaurants. A number of festivals and events are offered year-round. This scenic mountain town has about 10,000 residents, and the presence of Blue Ridge Community College adds vitality to the area.

Brevard and Hendersonville are only 20 miles apart. In Hendersonville, check out Champion Hills (www.championhills.com or 800-633-5122) as a neighborhood—homes begin in the upper $200,000s and go to about $4 million, and lots start around $50,000 and go to the upper $300,000s.

The Craft Heritage Trails of Western North Carolina guidebook (800-331-4154)
includes seven driving tours with almost 450 recommended stops including craft shops, studios,
galleries, and historic inns and restaurants.

Now, some specific places in and around Asheville.

If you are looking to rent, the Monarch Woods Apartments (www.monarchwoods.com or call 828-670-8030) offers two-bedroom apartments on wooded sites. Rent is about $600 to $700 per month.

Kenmure (www.kenmure.com or call 800-345-1860) is actually in Flat Rock, a 15-mile drive from the Asheville airport. This beautiful neighborhood, on 1,400 acres surrounded by the Blue Ridge Mountains, has an antebellum clubhouse, an 18-hole golf course, swimming, tennis, and fitness. Residences begin in the $200,000s and go up to around $800,000. Rentals are also available.

Blue Mist Farms (www.bluemistfarms.com or 888-707-3276), located 8.5 miles from downtown Asheville at elevations from 2,000 to over 4,000 feet, asks the question, "Why live at the bottom when you can live at the top?" Blue Mist Farms celebrated their grand opening in the fall of 2003, with 1-acre home sites priced from the $40,000s and sites up to 11 acres or more available.

Avery Park (www.landresourcegroupnc.com or 888-387-9070), a beautifully forested, private 300-acre community surrounded by the Pisgah National Forest, offers swimming and tennis and is a 5-minute drive to great public golf. Avery Park offers approximately 1-acre homesites about 15 minutes from Asheville and 15 minutes from Hendersonville, with lots ranging from under $200,000 to about $500,000.

The Cliffs (www.cliffscommunities.com or 800-884-2958) is a community that has it all, from mountains to valleys to lakes to meadows. It is actually four communities with four distinct settings, all offering tennis, swimming, fitness, and wooded trails for hiking. Walnut Cove is home to a Jack Nicklaus Signature golf course and is surrounded by the Pisgah National Forest. Cliffs Valley, bordered by thousands of acres of protected forest, has a Ben Wright golf course and a new wellness center and includes indoor and outdoor swimming. The Cliffs at Glassy is the home of the Tom Jackson golf course that holds the honor of being ranked fourth best in the nation, according to *Golf Digest*. The Cliffs at Keowee Vineyards is surrounded by two beautiful lakes and boasts a Tom Fazio-designed golf course. Membership at

Two additional places in western North Carolina that are more secluded are Cashiers and the Highlands, located southwest of Brevard.

one Cliffs community gives you privileges in all four. Homesites are available from $150,000 and homes from $400,000. Additional cottages, homes, and villas are also under development.

If you're interested in a cohousing community (see chapter 6 for a description of this type of living), you may want to check out the Westwood Cohousing Community (www.ndbweb.com/westwood or 828-250-9339) in Asheville. Although it's completed, there are a few resales beginning around $120,000. More cohousing projects are being developed in western North Carolina by Neighborhood Design/Build.

How Do I Pursue Lifelong Learning?

The University of North Carolina (UNC) at Asheville (www.unca.edu or 828-251-6140) is one of only six public universities in the country classified as a National Liberal Arts University and has received accolades from the *Fiske Guide to Colleges*, the *Princeton Review*, and *U.S. News & World Report*. The North Carolina Center for Creative Retirement (NCCCR) is a part of UNC Asheville. With over 1,600 participants in 2000, NCCCR serves as a "laboratory for exploring creative and productive roles for a new generation of re-tirement-aged people, many of whom blend education with postretirement careers." NCCCR offers some interesting ways to get ready for the second half of your life: College for Seniors, Community Service and Volunteer Programs, Creative Retirement Weekends, Uncertain Times Workshop, and an Un-Retirement Option.

Montreat College is a private Christian college located 15 miles east of Asheville with an enrollment of about 1,500 students. It offers the Montreat Center for Adult Lifelong Learning. Western Carolina University, Warren Wilson College, and Asheville-Buncombe Technical Community College are additional options.

Strengths

The mountains, valleys, lakes, and streams provide unparalleled beauty, a real feast for the eyes. Asheville is the regional hub for western North Carolina, and the town itself offers great shopping, restaurants, theater, and music. The neighborhoods are surrounded by forests and often have great mountain views. Mild summer temperatures make outdoor activities a pleasure and promote a healthy lifestyle. Asheville is also known as a welcoming town for singles.

Weaknesses

Seeing the words "black ice" and "mountain roads" in the same sentence may strike fear in some! Winters are mild, but certainly not free of snow and ice. Housing costs can be high, and some of the neighborhoods seem isolated, although not far from town.

FYI

Check out these sources for additional information: Asheville Chamber of Commerce (www.ashevillechamber.org or 828-258-6101); travel information (www.exploreasheville.com); Mountain Area Information Network (www.main.nc.us); North Carolina Center for Creative Retirement (www.unca.edu/ncccr or 828-251-6140); the *Asheville Citizen-Times* (828-252-5611); and the *Mountain Xpress* (828-251-1333).

The Research Triangle (Raleigh, Durham, and Chapel Hill)

REPORT CARD

Overall Rating:	A
Climate:	B+
Cost of Living:	B+
Health Care:	A+
Transportation:	A
What's to Do:	A

The Research Triangle, or Triangle, gets its name from the geographic region anchored by three outstanding universities: University of North Carolina (Chapel Hill), Duke University (Durham), and North Carolina State (Raleigh). These universities and several other institutions of higher learning help define this area. There are more Ph.D.s in the Triangle than anywhere in the world! Residents are often involved in lifelong learning and are stimulated by the vitality of the students in these college

Ladies' Home Journal included Durham and Raleigh in their list of "Best Cities for Women 2002."

towns. At the center of the Triangle is Research Triangle Park, founded in 1952, home for 136 companies that employ roughly 45,000 people.

Air transportation is a snap—The Raleigh-Durham International Airport is located in the heart of the Research Triangle, equidistant from downtown Raleigh and Durham.

Living here lets you get to the beaches of the Atlantic or the Blue Ridge Mountains of western North Carolina in several hours. And, living near the center of the state means very few hurricane watches and no mountain roads with black ice!

The Research Triangle has received impressive accolades over the years, including ranking number two in the A&E Channel's "Top Ten Cities to Have it All" and being ranked as *Money Magazine's* "Best in the South."

Who Lives in the Triangle?

Chapel Hill is the smallest of the three cities with a population of about 50,000, including 26,000 students at UNC. Residents of Chapel Hill are 78 percent Caucasian, 11 percent African-American, and 7 percent Asian, with a median age of 28. Durham is the home of 187,000 people, with approximately 48 percent Caucasian, 46 percent African-American, and 4 percent Asian. Raleigh has a population of 280,000, with about 70 percent Caucasian, 23 percent black, and 7 percent Hispanic. The median age is about 30 for both Raleigh and Durham.

What's the Cost?

The Raleigh-Durham-Chapel Hill metropolitan area had a cost of living of 98. The average home sells for $211,000, but housing costs and rents are higher in Chapel Hill than in Raleigh or Durham. Median family income is high—around $70,000, perhaps proving that education pays.

What's to Do?

University sports come to mind—the North Carolina State Wolfpack, the Tar Heels of UNC, and the Duke

What's It Like Outside?	Jan.	Apr.	Jul.	Oct.	Rain (in.)	Snow (in.)
Average High (°F)	50	72	88	72	42	4
Average Low (°F)	30	48	68	47	–	–

Blue Devils . . . just their names can make you think of basketball and their team colors! There are other sports teams in the Triangle, however, including the Durham Bulls, a minor league baseball team that has been a Triangle tradition for more than 100 years. The Carolina Hurricanes, an NHL team, also resides here.

The universities are also a resource for nonsports activities. Duke Continuing Studies offers hundreds of classes for retirees, including molecular biology, Gorbachev to Yeltsin, belly dance fitness, and photo editing. Music and theater are part of each campus and help enrich the lives of everyone in the area.

Raleigh is known as the "Smithsonian of the South." It is the home of several outstanding museums, including the North Carolina Museum of Natural Sciences, the North Carolina Museum of Art, and Exploris—the world's first global experience center. The North Carolina Symphony, The Opera Company of North Carolina, and the Carolina Ballet make their homes in Raleigh as well.

The Morehead Planetarium and the North Carolina Botanical Gardens are in Chapel Hill, as are the quaint shops on Franklin Street. The Eno River provides opportunities for canoeing and floating, and there are miles of hiking trails around the river. The Festival on the Eno brings great music to the river every year on the 4th of July. Jordan Lake and Falls Lake, with miles of shoreline and beaches, set the scene for all types of water-related activities. Add more than 20 local public golf courses and a mild, four-season climate, and you will find that spending quality time outdoors is a breeze.

Where Are the Jobs?

The list is impressive. The largest employers are the universities and the hospitals. (The area ranks in the top 10 for physicians per capita nationwide.) You will surely recognize these well-respected corporations operating in the Triangle: SAS Institute, Blue Cross/Blue Shield, IBM, General Electric, Cisco Systems, GlaxoSmithKline, and Nortel Networks. The unemployment rate for the area is 4.2 percent.

Can you define "half-back?" Half-back not only refers to football, but also refers to retirees coming "halfway back" from Florida and settling in central North Carolina to escape the heat in South Florida!

Where Are the Doctors?

Duke University Medical Center, recognized as one of the world's best health care providers in publications such as *Time* and *U.S. News and World Report*, serves the Triangle with three of the finest hospitals in the state: Duke University Hospital, Durham Regional Hospital, and Raleigh Community Hospital.

Where Are Some Notable Neighborhoods?

Relocating to the Triangle could be a difficult (but fun) task because there are so many options from which to choose. With three cities, all university towns with great amenities, deciding which one to live in may be tough. Should you live on a tree-lined street in the historic section of Chapel Hill within walking distance of shopping and the university? Or choose a lakeside setting in the rolling hills of Durham or Raleigh with nature surrounding you? It could be a daunting choice.

An apartment may be the place to start. Summermill Falls River (www.summermillliving.com or 888-882-0743) in the Raleigh area has one-, two-, and three-bedroom apartments. Rent is about $800 a month for two bedrooms.

The Preserve at Jordan Lake (www.thepreserve.ws or 800-252-5263) is a magnet for retirees. This community is located in the middle of the Triangle region around a 14,000-acre lake, which means that swimming, boating, and fishing may compete with your tee times. The championship Davis Love III golf course adds to the beauty of the area. Prices for homesites begin around $75,000, and homes begin in the $400,000s.

In Raleigh, the Wakefield Plantation (www.wakefield-plantation.com or 919-556-6300) is set on 2,200 acres and includes a Hale Irwin, 18-hole TPC golf course, as well as swimming, tennis, and another nine-hole golf course. Villas, townhomes, and single-family homes are available from around $130,000 to over $2 million.

Anderson Creek Club (www.andersoncreekclub.com or 866-465-3568) is located in a 1,700-acre pine forest,

---

Volunteerism is alive and well in the Triangle. The YMCA Service Corps of Retired Executives (SCORE) and the Retired Senior Volunteer Program (RSVP) are both very active organizations in the area.

a short drive from Pinehurst, Raleigh, and the Research Triangle. In addition to the beautiful forest, complete with waterfalls and nature trails, this community offers a Davis Love III championship golf course. Homesites begin in the $40,000s, and homes start in the $180,000s.

Bedford at Falls River (www.privatecommunities.com, and click on "Bedford at River Falls" under "Find a Community by Name" or call 919-792-0100), in Raleigh, offers a recreation center with swimming and tennis. Patio homes, townhomes, and custom homes are priced from around $150,000 to $750,000 and up.

Governor's Club (www.governorsclub.com or 800-925-0085), in Chapel Hill, is a community that is a must-see, even if you are just looking! The rolling hills are enhanced by 27 holes of Jack Nicklaus golf, wooded trails, swimming, fitness, and a spectacular golf club-house. Homesites are one-quarter acre to 3.5 acres and are priced from $40,000 to $500,000, with homes priced from around $300,000 to $2 million-plus.

How Do I Pursue Lifelong Learning?

If you plan to take classes as part of reprogramming your time after retiring, the offerings for seniors in the Triangle may overwhelm you. But remember, they can be non-credit, without homework or prerequisites. All that is necessary is the desire to learn.

North Carolina State offers the Encore Center for Lifelong Enrichment. A wide range of classes includes Civil War Leadership of Abraham Lincoln and Music of World War II. The University of North Carolina offers continuing education and noncredit classes at the Friday Center. Classes in art, language, computer technology, literature, public issues, and government are offered. As mentioned earlier, Duke also has extensive course listings.

Strengths

Central North Carolina, with its rolling hills, beautiful lakes, and mild four-season climate attracts many who want to work, as well as many who don't. If you are

---

Dukehealthline is a free quarterly publication that reports up-to-date health trends in a reader-friendly format. For a free subscription, visit www.dukehealth.org.

looking for more than just sunny days and great scenery, you will find it here. The universities provide a stimulating atmosphere, and the health care is hard to beat.

Weaknesses

If the beach is a priority, you have to drive a few hours to get there. Housing in Chapel Hill is pricey. The college students often gobble up the part-time jobs and may compete for restaurant tables. Traffic can be an issue.

FYI

Check out these sources for additional information: Chapel Hill-Carborro Chamber of Commerce (www.carolinachamber.org or 919-967-7075; Greater Durham Chamber of Commerce (www.durham chamber.com or 919-682-2133); Greater Raleigh Chamber of Commerce (www.raleighchamber.org or 919-664-7000); the *Chapel Hill Herald* (919-967-6581); the *Chapel Hill News* (919-932-2000); the *Durham Herald Sun* (919-419-6889); and the *Raleigh News and Observer* (919-829-4500).

SOUTH CAROLINA

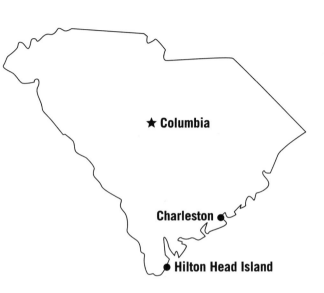

Capital: Columbia
Nickname: Palmetto State
Motto: "Prepared in mind and resources"/ "While I breathe, I hope"
Flower: Yellow Jessamine
Bird: Great Carolina Wren
Population: 4,012,012
Fascinating Fact: The shag is the official dance of South Carolina.

Charleston and the Low Islands

REPORT CARD

Overall Rating:	A-
Climate:	B
Cost of Living:	B
Health Care:	A
Transportation:	A
What's to Do:	A

The Charleston area, with its coastal islands of Kiawah, Seabrook, Sullivan's Island, and the Isle of Palms, presents a winning combination—island living coupled with the rich history and cultural opportunities of a city with a nice climate. The three islands are about 20 miles away from Charleston and boast beautiful beaches, abundant wildlife, and breathtaking marshlands. Charleston is regarded as the "cultural capital of the South," and justly so. It is an attractive tourist destination, with more than four million visitors contributing close to $5 billion annually to the economy.

This area of the country is often described as "low country." This means that the approximately 200 miles of low-lying land between Charleston and St. Mary's, Georgia, is intricately linked with lakes, marshes, and ocean.

Who Lives in Charleston?

The Charleston metropolitan area is comprised of Berkeley, Charleston, and Dorchester counties, with a population of almost 550,000 people. About 65 percent are Caucasian, 30 percent African-American, and 2 percent Hispanic. Average household income is about $43,000.

What's the Cost?

The cost of living for the Charleston metro area is 100. The average price of a home in the Charleston area is around $220,000, and the average rent for a two-bedroom residence averages around $580 a month.

What's to Do?

Art, theater, ballet, the symphony, museums, restaurants, shopping, and the Atlantic Ocean, combined with mild

---

This coastal city has the fourth busiest container port nationally and is ranked sixth (by dollar value) in international shipments. The Charleston area is served by Charleston International Airport.

weather, provide the ingredients for a rich, active lifestyle. Parks, gardens, the Francis Marion National Forest, plantations, Fort Sumter and other historic landmarks, architectural tours, and the aquarium will help keep you busy as well.

Where Are the Jobs?

The largest employers include the military, health care, and the school system. Bayer, Dupont, Westvaco, and Alcoa also provide a sizable number of jobs. Unemployment is 4.4 percent.

Where Are the Doctors?

You'll find medical facilities almost everywhere you look in Charleston! Hospitals include Bon Secours-St. Francis Xavier Hospital, Charleston Memorial Hospital, Medical University of South Carolina Medical Center, Roper Hospital, and East Cooper Regional Medical Center (in Mt. Pleasant), to name a few. There is a naval hospital and a Veterans Affairs Medical Center as well.

Where Are Some Notable Neighborhoods?

Prices on the low islands vary widely: $110,000 for a one-bedroom/one-bath condo on Seabrook Island, $490,000 for a three-bedroom/two-bath single-family residence on Kiawah with a wooded lot, and up to $6 million for an estate home on the ocean.

Sullivan's Island doesn't allow condos, nor does it have motels or hotels. A half-acre oceanfront *lot* sold for $3 million in August 2003, which created a new price record for a homesite. The lowest home prices are around $400,000, with homes on the ocean going for $3.5 million and up.

Isle of Palms residences range from $65,000 for a one-bedroom/one-bath condo, to $500,000 for a single-family, three-bedroom/two-bath home on a cul-de-sac, to $3.2 million for a 5,000-square-foot home on the ocean. About 5,000 people call the Isle of Palms home.

Wild Dunes is a 1,600-acre gated community on the

What's It Like Outside?	Jan.	Apr.	Jul.	Oct.	Rain (in.)	Snow (in.)
Average High (°F)	58	76	90	77	50	Trace
Average Low (°F)	38	54	73	56	–	–

northeast tip of the Isle of Palms with golf, tennis, and its own harbor. Prices begin under $200,000 for a condo and can escalate into the several millions for oceanfront property. There are vacation rentals as well as year-round residences.

Daniel Island is a relatively new 4,000-acre island town, located 15 minutes from Charleston, with its own businesses, shops, schools, and neighborhoods. Daniel Island isn't on the ocean, but it is bordered by the Wando and Cooper rivers and Charleston Harbor. Examples of homesites include $340,000 for a marsh view and $420,000 for a lot with a view of the golf course. Residences range from around $220,000 for a condo to $400,000 for a four-bedroom/2.5-bath single family home, up to $2 million for an almost 6,000-square-foot home.

Other popular places to live in the Charleston area include Mount Pleasant and Summerville.

 **Ann and Bill S. moved to Daniel Island, near Charleston, South Carolina, in April 2003.**

How did they choose Daniel Island? They were looking for a place with milder winters than they had experienced in the Midwest, a golf community, proximity to some of their four grown children, and a smaller community yet one that was close to an airport, medical facilities, and cultural amenities. After researching and visiting places from Virginia to Florida, they decided on the community of Daniel Island.

Ann and Bill enjoy the great weather (other than the occasional hurricane threats!), the charming and historical city of Charleston, and the hospitable neighbors. They especially like that it's a new, vital neighborhood of full-time residents.

They're happy with the Medical University of

An earthquake in Charleston? Yes, it happened in 1866—more than 100 lives were lost, and 90 percent of the brick buildings in the city were damaged. The quake was felt as far south as Cuba, as far north as New York, as far west as the Mississippi, and all the way east to Bermuda.

South Carolina, traffic that is reasonable compared to that in other metropolitan areas, and the unlimited number of recreational and cultural activities the area has to offer, which has them convinced they'll never be lacking for things to do. As for safety, Ann says, "Many people do not lock their doors—but keep that a secret!" Ⓛ

How Do I Pursue Lifelong Learning?

The College of Charleston, the Military College of South Carolina (the Citadel), the Medical University of South Carolina, and Charleston Southern University are all located in Charleston.

Strengths

Beach living with a charming nearby city is a strong pull. The cost of living is reasonable (unless you want a house on the ocean).

Weaknesses

Humid, hot summers, and you'll need to like a city steeped in Southern tradition!

FYI

Check out these sources for additional information: Metro Charleston Chamber of Commerce (www.charlestonchamber.net); the *Post and Courier* (843-577-7111); and the *Charleston Regional Business Journal* (843-849-3100).

The Family Circle Cup, the longest-running tennis tournament for women, has its home on Daniel Island.

Hilton Head Island

REPORT CARD

Overall Rating:	B+
Climate:	B+
Cost of Living:	C
Health Care:	A-
Transportation:	B+
What's to Do:	A

This beautiful, foot-shaped barrier island is located off the Atlantic coast of South Carolina and is wildly popular with permanent residents and visitors alike. Hilton Head Island is located 90 miles south of Charleston and 45 miles north of Savannah, Georgia.

An English sea captain named William Hilton gave the island its name in 1663, and most folks believe Mr. Hilton would be amazed and delighted to see his island today. The blue heron, dwarf deer, and alligators coexist with the human urban environment as a result of very careful planning by city officials. Keep your binoculars handy; there are more than 250 species of birds on the island.

This 12-mile-long barrier island with its semitropical climate has much to offer in the way of sun and sand. The island is connected by an intricate system of bike paths, and when a traffic jam is reported, it could be made up of bikers! Bicyclists are found on the beach when the tide is low, and there are never tie-ups on the hard-packed, extra-wide beaches of Hilton Head Island. Other outdoor activities include tennis, boating, fishing, crabbing, and did we mention golf? There are more than 20 golf courses on the island, most of which are public, and dozens more in proximity to the island.

The history, ecology, and art of the Low Country can be explored in many museums located throughout the island. U.S. Airways Express flies directly onto the island from Charlotte, and the Savannah-Hilton Head Island International Airport is 45 minutes away and is serviced by many of the major airlines. Average relative humidity is 79 percent.

Hilton Head Island employs a council-manager form of government, with six council members and one mayor.

Who Lives on Hilton Head Island?

The population of Hilton Head Island is about 35,000 year-round residents and more than 150,000 summer residents. About 85 percent of the population is Caucasian, 11 percent are Hispanic, and 8 percent are African-American. Twenty-three percent of the residents are 65 or older, and the median age of residents is 45. Visitors number more than two million each year.

Hilton Head Island is in Beaufort County, the fastest-growing county in South Carolina; its population has increased nearly 40 percent in the past decade.

What's the Cost?

The cost of living on Hilton Head Island is 105.3. Groceries and housing are a bit higher (106), with health care a tad lower (95). The median price of a new, three-bedroom home on Hilton Head Island is $350,000.

What's to Do?

Let's start with the obvious: the beach! The water temperature is warm from April to September and almost bathlike in July. At low tide, this exceptional beach is 600 feet wide and hard-packed enough to ride a bike or play soccer, baseball, or football on. Low tide brings waves gentle enough for a toddler to enjoy.

Residents and tourists alike spend time whale watching, crabbing, kayaking, parasailing, or choosing their favorite yacht (to dream about) at Harbor Town. Hilton Head Island is a top tennis destination, with 145 public courts and more than 20 tennis clubs. Golf is king, and the big event is the Heritage Golf Classic at the Harbor Town Links in Sea Pines, drawing a whopping 100,000 spectators each year.

Located in the heart of Hilton Head Island is the Arts Center of Coastal Carolina, the centerpiece for visual and performing arts. The Center includes a 350-seat center stage auditorium and a permanent art gallery. The Hilton

What's It Like Outside?	Jan.	Apr.	Jul.	Oct.	Rain (in.)	Snow (in.)
Average High (°F)	59	79	89	78	47	–
Average Low (°F)	40	56	74	58	–	–

Head Island Orchestra, Choral Society, Dance Theater, and The Barbershoppers provide musical entertainment year round. The Coastal Discovery Museum offers exhibits, classes, tours, and cruises to help visitors understand the history and ecology of the island. The Hilton Head Art League supports the visual arts and has more than 800 members; the Art League maintains a gallery that showcases the work of more than 100 local artists.

Where Are the Jobs?

The big employers on the island are the schools, hospitals, and resorts, including the Marriott, the Hilton, the Westin, and the Crowne Plaza. Beaufort County's unemployment rate hovers below 3 percent, one of the lowest in the nation.

Where Are the Doctors?

Hilton Head Medical Center and Clinics, a privately owned acute-care hospital, serves the island, along with a number of urgent care centers and medical centers.

Beaufort Memorial Hospital, 40 miles away, is licensed for 182 beds and is one of the few hospitals in the country with its own emergency boat dock; it's the largest medical facility between Savannah and Charleston. Islanders also utilize the Memorial Health University Center in Savannah, Georgia, which is less than an hour away.

Where Are Some Notable Neighborhoods?

The island was originally developed with the concept of gated golf communities within the confines of 11 "plantations." These plantations are named after the southern farms that once occupied them; rice, cotton, and indigo have been replaced with expensive homes, bike paths, restaurants, and full-time residents. Sea Pines was the first plantation to be developed on Hilton Head Island and has the longest stretch of beach of any of the 11 plantations. Finding a place to live on any of these plantations is rewarding, but challenging. There are many op-

**Hilton Head Island has the largest Hispanic population
of any municipality in South Carolina.**

tions for the prospective buyer: some new construction, some teardowns, resale lots, homes, and condos. Off the island, between Beaufort and Hilton Head, new construction is springing up. If you can live with a 30-minute drive to the beach, you should take a look at the many off-island communities this area has to offer. We'll take a look at some on- and off-island possibilities.

On the Island

Long Cove (www.longcoveclub.com or 843-842-5580) is a residential area that does not allow short-term rentals. Of the 569 full-sized residential homesites, close to 400 are complete and occupied. All available lots are resales at this time. The number-one ranked golf course in South Carolina surrounds this private, gated community, and membership is automatic for all property owners. You will find lots priced in the $200,000s and resale homes priced from $400,000.

Sea Pines Plantation (www.seapines.com or 800-846-7829) covers 5,200 acres on the south end of the island and offers three championship golf courses, a 605-acre wildlife preserve, 5 miles of Atlantic Ocean beaches,

miles of great bike paths, wonderful shopping, and fine dining. It's easy to see why new property is hard to find in Sea Pines! Resales include villas and townhomes as well as single-family residences, priced from $175,000 to $8 million.

Spanish Wells Plantation is a wonderful Hilton Head Island community offering a variety of housing possibilities, from expensive estates to modest homes. Many residences have deep-water lots with private docks. Check out Timbercrest by D.R. Horton homes (www.drhorton-homes.com or 843-689-2400), priced from the $200,000s.

Off the Island

Oldfield (www.oldfield1732.com or 866-653-3435) is located between Beaufort and Hilton Head Island in Okatie, South Carolina. This beautiful community overlooks the Okatie River and is home to Greg Norman's first low-country golf course. Homesites range from $150,000 to $900,000, and homes and cottages start around $800,000. The activity center includes a pool, tennis courts, and other amenities.

The Prince of Tides by Pat Conroy was set in the Colleton River marshlands of this area.
Conroy lives on nearby Fripp Island.

Belfair (www.belfairhiltonhead.com or 800-587-7710) is located 5 miles west of the bridge to Hilton Head Island and 11 miles east of I-95 in Bluffton, South Carolina. Enter this private, 1,000-acre gated community on the Avenue of the Oaks and visit the 25,000-square-foot clubhouse, home to two Tom Fazio golf courses and the Jim Ferree Golf Learning Center. Enjoy a good workout in the pool or the fitness center and the convenience of shopping at the Belfair Towne Village. Homesites begin at $140,000, and homes begin at $550,000.

Callawassie Island (www.callawassieisland.com or 800 221-8431) is situated in Beaufort County, along the headwaters of the Colleton River, midway between Hilton Head Island and Beaufort. This private residential community offers golf, tennis, and a variety of water-related activities. Homesites are priced from $65,000 and homes from $250,000.

Sun City Hilton Head (www.delwebb.com; click on "Active Adult," then "Sun City Hilton Head" or call 800-978-9781), an active-adult community, was voted one of America's 100 Best Master-Planned Communities in 2003 by *Where to Retire* magazine. With two 18-hole golf courses, a fitness center, indoor and outdoor swimming, a 17,000-square-foot social hall and a 6,250-square-foot, fully equipped ceramics, painting, sewing, and computer workshop, this Del Webb retirement location (it's actually in Bluffton) has something for everyone. Home prices begin at $130,000.

How Do I Pursue Lifelong Learning?
The University of South Carolina at Beaufort offers free undergraduate classes for credit or audit if you are 60 or older. Classes are offered in Beaufort as well as on Hilton Head Island. On July 3, 2003, the University of South Carolina broke ground for a new south campus (planned opening in late summer 2004), located halfway between Beaufort and Hilton Head Island. The University of South Carolina at Beaufort also offers classes in Hilton Head and Beaufort through the Learning Exchange,

---

**How about a new career in the hotel business? No, not as a bellboy!
You can work toward a 4-year degree in hotel management on Hilton Head Island
when you enroll in classes offered by the University of South Carolina.**

which was formerly called the Creative Retirement Center. The class schedule changes three times each year, and for $150, Learning Exchange members can choose to take any of 60 to 90 classes in either location. For information, go to www.sc.edu/beaufort and type "Learning Exchange" in the search box, or call 843-521-4113.

Strengths

This island has the feel of a huge family resort. The two million tourists that visit yearly are mostly families, and they do contribute to the energy of the town. The beach is like no other if you like to play on the sand and not just recline with a good book. The beauty of the moss-covered live oaks, the many lagoons (some with alligators and some without), and the exquisite birds and other wildlife make Hilton Head Island a special place for those who live here. If you are looking for a four-season climate with a short, mild winter, Hilton Head Island might be it!

Weaknesses

The island itself is rather remote, and the traffic generated by the two million tourists is a thorn in the side of the full-timers. Many of the homes are rental properties, and the price of buying a home or villa makes this community unrealistic for many. The summers are very hot and humid, and several major hurricanes have hit South Carolina.

true LIFE **Jeannie and Jim H. lived all their lives in Maryland, vacationing every year at Hilton Head Island, South Carolina, with their two children.**

When Jeannie and Jim considered where they would like to live when they retired, their thoughts immediately gravitated to Hilton Head, since they were familiar with the area, climate, and amenities of this resort town and had many fond memories of time spent there. They bought a second home, four rows back from the ocean, and now divide their time between their homes in Maryland and Hilton Head. (tL)

FYI

Check out these sources for additional information: the Beaufort Chamber of Commerce (www.beaufortsc.org or 800-638-3525) Hilton Head Island/Bluffton Chamber of Commerce (www.hiltonheadisland.org or 800-523-3373); the *Beaufort Gazette* (www.beaufortgazette.com or 843-986-5507); and the *Island Packet* (www.island-packet.com or 843-760-8222).

TENNESSEE

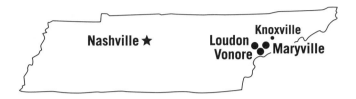

Capital: Nashville

Nickname: Volunteer State

Motto: "Agriculture and commerce"

Flower: Iris

Bird: Mockingbird

Population: 5,689,283

Fascinating Fact: Tennessee is bordered by eight states.

Maryville, Vonore, and Loudon

REPORT CARD

Overall Rating:	B+
Climate:	B+
Cost of Living:	A
Health Care:	A-
Transportation:	B+
What's to Do:	B

If you don't live there or aren't into country or bluegrass music, Tennessee seems to be one of those states you never read or hear much about. Maybe it's because there are only three large cities in the state—Memphis, Nashville, and Knoxville. If you're considering relocating, though, you may want to change that thinking pattern.

The eastern section of Tennessee nestles in the foothills of the Great Smoky Mountains, close to Knoxville and the University of Tennessee. This area basks in the beauty of the Appalachians, is a haven for outdoor enthusiasts,

---

Maryville is on a number of "best of" lists. It placed among the top dozen recommended places in *Your Money* magazine. The A&E (Arts & Entertainment) channel named Maryville one of the "Top 10 Cities to Have it All," and the National Strategy Group called it one of "America's Select Cities."

enjoys a four-season climate with fairly mild winters, and has the additional lure of Great Smoky Mountains National Park, Gatlinburg, and Dollywood. Snow tends to melt quickly because of the milder temperatures. McGhee Tyson Airport is a dozen miles south of Knoxville and has over 120 daily departures and arrivals. As far as cost of living, the Volunteer State ranks in the upper echelons of states offering the best financial deals.

Who Lives in Maryville, Rarity Bay, and Tellico Village?

Maryville, as well as the communities of Rarity Bay in Vonore and Tellico Village in Loudon, are all close to one another. And the people in these communities are very friendly!

About 20 percent of Maryville's 23,000 residents are 62 or over, and the median age is about 38. The area is approximately 16 square miles. About 38 percent of Maryville residents have a bachelor's degree or higher. Vonore has a population of about 1,200 in an area that is fewer than 9 square miles. This small town has a median resident age of 37, and about 20 percent of its population has at least a bachelor's degree. Loudon has a population of about 4,500 in an area of about 9 square miles. The median age is 42, and about 13 percent of the residents have at least a bachelor's degree.

What's the Cost?

This is where Tennessee really shines. The Tax Foundation (www.taxfoundation.org) analyzes states by tax burden. Tennessee comes out smelling like a rose (or should we say an iris, the state flower?). It has the fourth-lowest state tax burden, both with and without federal taxes considered.

There is no broad-based state income tax, although Tennessee does tax most interest and dividends. If that's the source of most of your income, your numbers will not be as good. In fact, Kiplinger used a hypothetical retired couple living in the state capital and ranked Tennessee the 19th highest in taxes of the 50 states.

What's It Like Outside?	Jan.	Apr.	Jul.	Oct.	Rain (in.)	Snow (in.)
Average High (°F)	45	70	87	70	48	12
Average Low (°F)	26	44	66	46	–	–

For Maryville, property taxes are about $1,075 per $100,000 of assessed value; in Loudon County, property taxes run about $450 per $100,000 of assessed value (that's one-fourth the authors' tax rate in Cincinnati, which isn't considered a high cost of living area); and in Monroe County, the rate is about $570 per $100,000.

Tennessee is often touted as a retiree-friendly state, and these facts certainly support that contention.

What's to Do?

Think outside. Boating, fishing, hiking, enjoying wildlife, tennis, year-round golf, swimming; Great Smoky Mountains National Park with its whitewater rafting, camping, and horseback riding; Ober Gatlinburg Ski Resort and Amusement Park . . . your imagination is your only limit.

The University of Tennessee, about a 45-minute drive away, provides cultural opportunities, and Knoxville itself offers shopping, dining, museums, historical sites, theater, ballet, and opera.

Where Are the Jobs?

There are a number of large employers in the Knoxville area. Health care (Covenant, Fort Sanders, University of Tennessee Medical Center, St. Mary's) is a biggie, as well as the University of Tennessee, UT-Battelle and BWXT Y-12 (national security), ALCOA, and Sea Ray Boats. Unemployment for the Knoxville metropolitan statistical area is an attractive 3.2 percent.

Where Are the Doctors?

There are several health care options, including the University of Tennessee Medical Center (a teaching hospital with more than 600 beds), Blount Memorial Hospital, Baptist Hospital, Fort Sanders Medical Clinics, and St. Mary's Health System.

Where Are Some Notable Neighborhoods?

In addition to the town of Maryville, check out the developments of Rarity Bay and Tellico Village. Both Rarity Bay and Tellico Village are on 16,000-acre

---

Great Smoky Mountains National Park is the most visited national park in the country.

Tellico Lake, which was created in 1979 by the completion of the Tellico Dam. Both neighborhoods are sizable and offer golf, boat docks, tennis, and swimming. Of course, both communities charge association dues, and several different types of golf memberships are available.

Rarity Bay (www.raritybay.com or 888-RARITY BAY) encompasses 960 acres and is the newer of the two developments. There is an equestrian center located just inside the entrance of this lovely community, beyond which is the gatehouse. There will be approximately 1,500 residences; about 400 of them are presently occupied. Condos average around $180,000 to $225,000; villas average between $290,000 and $400,000; and building a custom home costs between $100 and $150 per square foot. Lot prices vary—again, location is key. A lot with a view of the water is priced at $135,000, a site with Tellico Lake in the backyard is listed at $430,000, and a lot with sweeping water vistas on three sides is listed for over $1 million. Three other Rarity communities in Tennessee (Rarity Pointe, Rarity Meadows, and Rarity Ridge) can be accessed through the Rarity Bay Web site.

Tellico Village (www.tellico-village.com or 800-Tellico) has been around since 1986. It's more spread out (the development is on both sides of Tellico Parkway) and larger (about 4,600 acres) than Rarity Bay. There is less of a community feel than in Rarity Bay, but the plus side is that you can get a home for less in Tellico Village. There are about 2,800 homes and townhomes built out of a projected total of around 6,500. Residences can be found in the mid-$100,000s, although the average is closer to the $200,000 to $300,000 range. Homes on Tellico Lake begin around $500,000. Lots in the interior areas go for as low as $10,000; sites on the golf course run in the $40,000s to $70,000s; and lakefront lots go from about $200,000 and up.

How Do I Pursue Lifelong Learning?

The University of Tennessee in Knoxville, a 45-minute drive away, has about 28,000 students on its 550 acres. Pellississippi Technical Community College is also in Knoxville.

Strengths

The west side of Knoxville, which is the area closer to Maryville, Rarity Bay, and Tellico Village, is growing, which will add more vitality to the area. And, how cool would it be to have a lot on the lake and drive your boat right into its own boathouse? Financially, Tennessee is a bargain.

Weaknesses

If you have to be near the ocean to be happy, keep in mind it's about a 7-hour drive to get to the Atlantic and 9 hours to the Gulf of Mexico. And, although the people are very friendly, you'll find the highest educational level attained by the general population of this area may be lower than in other parts of the country.

FYI

Check out these sources for additional information: Blount Chamber of Commerce (www.blountchamber.com or 865-983-2241); Knoxville Chamber of Commerce (www.knoxville.org); and the *Knoxville News Sentinel* (www.knoxnews.com or 800-237-5821).

VIRGINIA

Capital: Richmond

Nickname: Old Dominion State

Motto: "Thus always to tyrants"

Flower: Dogwood

Bird: Cardinal

Population: 7,078,515

Fascinating Fact: Eight presidents were born in Virginia, and seven are buried there.

According to the 2000 Census, Charlottesville and Williamsburg were listed among the areas with the biggest influx of older residents in the United States.

Charlottesville and Williamsburg

REPORT CARD

(both towns received identical ratings)

Overall Rating:	B+
Climate:	B
Cost of Living:	B
Health Care:	A-
Transportation:	A-
What's to Do:	A-

"Virginia is for Lovers." This has been this state's advertising slogan since 1969, but is Virginia for retirement as well? We think so.

Situated halfway between New York and Miami, Virginia boasts good highways, 11 commercial airports, close to 60 private aviation airports, as well as railway and ferry service. Its location, according to Virginia's Visitor Information Center, enables you to drive to any city east of the Mississippi in under a day. Beaches, mountains, parks, gardens, skiing, colleges, factory outlets, theme parks, museums, battlefields, historic buildings—Virginia is a smorgasbord of things to do and see.

We especially like two places in Virginia: Charlottesville and Williamsburg. Let's take a look at these two locations and see if you, too, think that "Virginia is for Retirement."

Charlottesville, centrally located in Virginia on the Rivanna River, is situated at the foothills of the Blue Ridge Mountains, about 100 miles southeast of the nation's capital. Its residents enjoy four distinct seasons, numerous parks, a low unemployment rate, and the prestigious (not to mention beautiful) University of Virginia. The area is noted for its horses, fox hunting, and fruit orchards. Old estates and the rolling countryside are visual feasts. The Charlottesville-Albemarle Airport provides nonstop service, mainly to cities on the

---

What's It Like Outside in Charlottesville?

	Jan.	Apr.	Jul.	Oct.	Rain (in.)	Snow (in.)
Average High (°F)	45	69	88	70	47	23
Average Low (°F)	26	45	66	47	–	–

East Coast. Williamsburg did sustain some damage from Hurricane Isabel in Fall 2003.

Steeped in history, Williamsburg is the colonial capital of Virginia. You can be at the beach or skiing within an hour, take classes at The College of William and Mary, or go to Norfolk, 35 miles away. Shopping in Williamsburg is legendary—there are outlets galore, craft and pottery shops, and boutiques, and even though there are more than 800,000 yearly visitors to Colonial Williamsburg, you'll enjoy small-town living (on fewer than 9 square miles) in this scenic area. Newport News/Williamsburg Airport, Norfolk International Airport, and Richmond International Airport service the area.

Who Lives in Charlottesville and Williamsburg?

Of the approximately 45,000 residents of Charlottesville, about half are between the ages of 20 and 45, with a median age of 26 years. About 70 percent of the population is Caucasian, 22 percent African-American, and 3 percent Hispanic. About 40 percent of the residents have at least a bachelor's degree.

Williamsburg has about 12,000 residents, with an average age of 36. About a fourth of the population is older than 45; Caucasians represent about 80 percent of the population, African-American about 13 percent, and Hispanics approximately 3 percent. Almost half of Williamsburg's residents have a bachelor's degree or higher.

What's the Cost?

In Charlottesville, the median household income is $31,000; in Williamsburg, it's $37,000 (compared to the national average of $42,000). Unemployment in Williamsburg is about 6 percent. The median price of an existing home is about $169,000, and a new home costs about $194,000. For Charlottesville, unemployment is 3.5 percent, and the median cost of a home is $175,000;

What's It Like Outside in Williamsburg?	Jan.	Apr.	Jul.	Oct.	Rain (in.)	Snow (in.)
Average High (°F)	51	68	90	68	39	10
Average Low (°F)	34	48	82	60	–	–

for Albemarle County it's $269,000. Average rent for a two-bedroom apartment in Charlottesville runs about $700 to $800 per month, and you can rent an apartment in Williamsburg beginning around $650 per month.

Both Charlottesville and Williamsburg have overall costs of living slightly higher than the national average. (There are no ACCRA figures available.)

What's to Do?

There is a full menu of activities to choose from in either town. Both offer art, culture, and history. Charlottesville offers Monticello, James Monroe's home, the pedestrian-friendly Downtown Mall, concerts, museums, wineries, diverse dining, and the University of Virginia. Williamsburg offers the colonial experience, Busch Gardens and Water Country USA, the nearby Jamestown Settlement, historic plantations, Yorktown, and shopping.

Of course, outdoor activities such as golf, rafting, fishing, hiking, tennis, biking, and canoeing are available in both Charlottesville and Williamsburg. Wintergreen, an all-seasons resort with skiing, golf, nature hikes, rock climbing, and a spa is only about 30 miles from Charlottesville and 150 miles from Williamsburg.

Where Are the Jobs?

Not surprisingly, the largest employers in Charlottesville are involved with the University of Virginia. The university itself employs around 20,000 people, and the University of Virginia Health Systems has about 4,500 employees.

The Colonial Williamsburg Foundation employs more than 3,000 people, although recently they have experienced some budget shortfalls, which they attribute to 9/11, the Washington D.C-area sniper attacks, the war in Iraq, and the economy. The College of William and Mary provides jobs to almost 5,000; Anheuser Busch, which operates Busch Gardens and Water Country USA., is another large employer, and its Web site specifically solicits older workers.

Where Are the Doctors?

Charlottesville is home to the premiere University of Virginia Health Sciences Center and the Martha Jefferson Hospital, in addition to several clinics.

**Sissy Spacek, Dave Matthews, Rita Mae Brown, Howie Long, and John Grisham . . .
these are some of the notables you may see around the streets of Charlottesville.**

Williamsburg has Sentara Williamsburg Community Hospital and Eastern State Hospital (which emphasizes mental health care), urgent care facilities, and Williamsburg and Norge medical centers.

Where Are Some Notable Neighborhoods in Charlottesville?

Forest Lakes (www.forestlakes.com or 804-817-9400) is a newer neighborhood with townhomes, village homes, and estate homes ranging from $125,000 to $500,000. Amenities include pools, a clubhouse, walking trails, lakes, ponds, and open space.

Glenmore (www.glenmore.com or 434-977-8865) is 8 miles east of Charlottesville in Keswick. This gated community of more than 1,000 acres provides country club living as well as an equestrian center. Homesites range from $140,000 to $600,000, and homes from $450,000 to almost $2 million.

There are also many lovely, older homes in the area. Contact the Chamber of Commerce (www.cvillechamber. org or 434-295-3141) to recommend a Realtor.

Where Are Some Notable Neighborhoods in Williamsburg?

Colonial Heritage (www.colonialheritageva.com or 866-456-1776) is a new, active-adult community built by Lennar. This brand-new gated neighborhood, with home prices ranging from the low $200,000s to $400,000 or more, will have a golf course, pools, fitness center, tennis, hiking trails, and clubhouse.

Ford's Colony (www.fordscolony.com or 800-334-6033), a gated community stretching over almost 3,000 acres, has been around for almost 20 years but is still developing. With 1,600 homes already built and a final total of 2,400 homes, you can find a home or homesite in this beautiful award-winning enclave of three golf courses and five-star dining. Homesites begin under $100,000, and most homes are in the $300,000 to $1.5 million range. About one-third of the residents are retired, with the other two-thirds semiretired or still working.

According to a national survey released by Manpower, the Newport News-Williamsburg area is one of the top 10 best areas in the nation for employment.

How did Jennie and Bob C. decide on Ford's Colony in Williamsburg as their retirement location?

Having relocated a number of times during Bob's career, Jennie and Bob didn't feel there was any one "logical" place to retire. They discussed desires and options and agreed on a few things: It made sense to have only one home in order to more easily establish a local social network and avoid issues relating to absentee ownership. And, since they were going to build their dream home, they wanted to be in it full time! Jennie loves the beach and Bob loves golf, but neither relished the thought of having sand in virtually everything they own. Having a change of seasons was also important, as was avoiding the extreme temperatures of the far North or South.

With all that in mind, they decided to seek an area that gave them that nebulous but important "right feel" but "would not be in the middle of other people's vacations."

As a result, Bob and Jennie narrowed their search to North Carolina and Virginia and found Ford's Colony in Williamsburg. The area appealed to them for a number of reasons: It isn't a large population center, so it fit their size requirements; it has a terrific local college (William and Mary); it is a magnet for tourists, which has the benefit of supporting a good selection of restaurants and a number of excellent golf courses (the traffic that tourists bring can be avoided by local residents); it enjoys a strong sense of community spirit; the Richmond airport is less than an hour away; and Bob and Jennie found the residents of Williamsburg open, accepting, and welcoming.

By discussing what they wanted in their ideal location, Jennie and Bob were able to shape what their retirement location should look like and geographically shrink the potential places down to a manageable search.

How long did their search take? It lasted a little over a year, but Bob and Jennie started the process almost a decade in advance of Bob's expected retirement so that they wouldn't feel any pressure to make a decision before they knew they had found what they were looking for. ⓛ

The Governor's Land at Two Rivers (the rivers are the James and Chickahominy) has 734 homesites with about 525 families already living in this community, which has been around for about a dozen years. A private golf course, marina, clubhouse, and wildlife sanctuary are some of the amenities of the neighborhood. Lots range from around $90,000 to $1 million, and homes range from $400,000 to $3 million. The Governor's Land (www.govland.com or 800-633-5965) has a lower density than most communities in the area.

Kingsmill (www.kingsmill.com or 800-392-0026), on the James River, is a 3,000-acre community with country club amenities, including a spa, marina, four restaurants, and a variety of residences, including condos, townhomes, patio homes, cluster homes, and estate homes. There are some new homes, even though this community is approximately 30 years old. Prices range from around $125,000 (resale condos) to close to $4 million.

(true LIFE) Diane P., 59, moved from the Washington, D.C., area to the Villages of Westminster in Williamsburg, Virginia, after retiring from a career with the federal government. For the past 4 years, she has lived in Williamsburg with her significant other. Diane had visited Williamsburg regularly for many years, and on one visit, she and her mate decided to look at some model homes. Before they left, they had signed on the dotted line to buy a single-family home!

Diane loves her "really great" neighbors and enjoys the lower traffic volume and slower pace than she experienced in the D.C. area, the free concerts in Merchant's Square, and the four seasons and a bit milder winters Williamsburg offers. The historical atmosphere of Williamsburg and Busch Gardens (the number three-ranked park in the United States) are wonderful assets when guests visit. As she says, the downtown shopping area is "packed with gray-headed people—we love free stuff!"

Diane feels safe in Williamsburg, and she is happy with the health care. Being the vivacious person she is, she recommends, "Just do it. Move, make new friends, and enjoy them. It's nice to buy in a new area because everyone is new." (tL)

How Do I Pursue Lifelong Learning?

Both of these towns provide ample opportunities for lifelong learning, which is one of the reasons we recommend them.

As already noted, Charlottesville is home to the University of Virginia, founded by Thomas Jefferson in 1819. A variety of noncredit courses is offered through the university's School of Continuing and Professional Studies. Piedmont Virginia Community College and the Institute of Textile Technology also have a home in Charlottesville.

Williamsburg has its own historic college, William and Mary, as well as Thomas Nelson Community College and Christopher Newport University, both a little more than 20 miles away.

Strengths

If you're a history buff, either Charlottesville or Williamsburg could be a good fit. Milder winters, yet four distinct seasons, are also appealing. Add scenic, small-town living in a college town, and did we mention history? If you love the beach, Williamsburg is about an hour away from Virginia Beach. And if you love to read, Charlottesville, according to *American Profile* magazine, is credited with having "more households per capita engaging in 'avid book reading' than any other place in the United States."

Weaknesses

You'll have to travel to get to a larger airport. If you are snow averse, some white stuff does fall in both these towns, and there's a little bit more of it in Charlottesville than in Williamsburg. To get to a beach from Charlottesville, you'll need to travel more than 2 hours. The cost of living for both places is higher than the national average, and traffic can be daunting at times.

FYI

Check out these sources for additional information: Charlottesville Chamber of Commerce (www.cvillechamber.org or 434-295-3141); Williamsburg Area Convention and Visitors Bureau (www.visitwilliamsburg.com or 800-368-6511); the Charlottesville *Daily Progress* (www.dailyprogress.com or 434-978-7283); and the Williamsburg *Daily Press* (www.dailypress.com or 757-247-4800).

WASHINGTON

San Juan Island
● Bellingham
● Whidbey Island
Port Townsend
Sequim ●
Port Ludlow
● Seattle
Bainbridge Island
★ Olympia

Capital: Olympia

Nickname: The Evergreen State

Motto: "By and by"

Flower: Pink Rhododendron

Bird: Willow Goldfinch

Population: 5,894,121

Fascinating Fact: Starbucks had its beginnings in Seattle.

Bellingham

REPORT CARD

Overall Rating:	B
Climate:	B
Cost of Living:	A-
Health Care:	B
Transportation:	B
What's to Do:	A-

Bellingham is located halfway between Seattle and Vancouver on the northern edge of Puget Sound, the last city before the Canadian border and about 20 miles away from our northern neighbor. Bellingham's active waterfront includes Squalicum Harbor, the second-largest harbor in Puget Sound, home to 2,000 boats and the hub for port services. Passenger ferries leave from Bellingham ports for Victoria, British Columbia; the San Juan Islands; and Alaska. Three freshwater lakes and several streams add to the beauty of this area. *Money Magazine* has this to say

---

**For all you gardeners out there, the growing season begins
in April and continues into October.**

about Bellingham: "There are few places where you can walk out of a 20-story building, cast a line into a creek, and catch a salmon. Bellingham is one. . . ."

The historic Fairhaven district is a real draw for those looking for pubs, boutiques, and shops. Western Washington University, with its renowned outdoor sculpture collection, provides cultural events year-round, contributing to Bellingham's vibrancy. The climate is very mild, though it tends to be rainy. Majestic 10,000-foot Mount Baker and all that it has to offer is just an hour away.

Bellingham has an average of 93 days of rain a year. But the good news is that between March and September, it rains fewer than 3 inches per month. The warmest day in July rarely exceeds 80 degrees.

Who Lives in Bellingham?

The population of Bellingham is about 68,000 with 18 percent age 55 and over. The median age is 30, and 90 percent of the residents are Caucasian, 5 percent Asian, 3 percent Native American or Alaska Native, and 2 percent African-American.

What's the Cost?

Bellingham's cost of living is 102.6 overall. The cost of groceries is a little higher than the national average at 111.9, as is health care, which is 109. Residents get a break when purchasing a house (101) and paying utilities (94). The median price of a home, according to the Multiple Listing Service (MLS), is $183,500. There is no state income tax in Washington.

What's to Do?

Every Memorial Day, weekend teams of athletes assemble from around the world to participate in the 82.5-mile relay race from Mount Baker to the shore. This "Ski to Sea" festival puts competitors to the test in all areas of outdoor activity: cross-country and downhill skiing, running, mountain biking, canoeing, and sea kayaking. If you are more than just a "weekend warrior" athlete, you'll

What's It Like Outside?	Jan.	Apr.	Jul.	Oct.	Rain (in.)	Snow (in.)
Average High (°F)	45	55	70	55	36	7
Average Low (°F)	40	40	50	40	–	–

have the remainder of the year to enjoy these activities in Bellingham! If golf is your game, there are plenty of public courses, one described as "sculpted in the windswept, wide open Scottish tradition." About an hour east, in the beautiful Cascade Mountains, you will find the Mount Baker Ski Resort with its fantastic skiing, remote snowmobiling in the winter, and excellent hiking and biking in the summer.

In addition to the natural beauty of the area, Bellingham has many cultural offerings. The Whatcom Museum of History and Art, built in 1892, consists of a four-building campus that includes a children's museum. The Mount Baker Theater, a local treasure, has been in the business of producing local theater and hosting professional touring acts since 1927. The downtown is full of specialty shops, fine restaurants, coffee shops, and art galleries and has a manageable small-town feel. The Northwest Washington Fair, a tradition dating back to 1872, is an outdoor event that showcases local music and art.

Two scenic drives have their beginnings in Bellingham. For exceptional views of Samish Bay, the San Juan Islands, and the Olympic Mountains, take State Route 11 or the Chuckanut Drive. If you are in the mood for waterfalls, vineyards, and mountains, take State Route 542, the Mount Baker Scenic Highway.

Where Are the Jobs?
Bellingham's major employers include Georgia Pacific, Western Washington University, St. Joseph's Hospital, and the Bellingham schools. Bellingham's unemployment rate is 5.4 percent.

Where Are the Doctors?
St. Joseph's Hospital, with more than 250 beds, is a non-profit facility that provides a complete array of emergency and diagnostic services, as well as a cardiac care unit.

Where Are Some Notable Neighborhoods?
Meyers Estates (www.bellinghamhomes.com or 360-739-7779), located in North Bellingham, will consist of 42 new homes on quarter-acre lots. Some sites will have a view of Mount Baker.

Amtrak travels to Seattle and Vancouver and is available from Fairhaven Terminal.

Other homes available in Bellingham are priced from $150,000 to $2 million. Cost depends on the view and the location; prices soar when property is waterfront.

How Do I Pursue Lifelong Learning?

Western Washington University is home for 13,000 full- and part-time students. The university plays an active role in the life of the community and provides many cultural opportunities for the residents of Bellingham, including dramatic presentations, concerts, and other educational programs. The Whatcom Community College and Bellingham Technical College also serve the community. The Bellingham Senior Center offers programs for its more than 1,200 members.

Strengths

You won't find extreme temperatures in Bellingham, and the rainy days are not common during spring and summer. You can enjoy the natural beauty of the surrounding mountains, lakes, and ocean, and opportunities for outdoor recreation are endless. Bellingham has many large-city amenities but maintains a small-town ambience.

Weaknesses

Bellingham is a bit out of the mainstream since it's located in the far corner of the Pacific Northwest and at least an hour from a major airport (it does have a small regional airport serviced by Horizon Air). Transportation to other parts of the country may take extra time and money. To paraphrase The Carpenters, if rainy days and Mondays always get you down, 93 days of rain a year may be too much!

FYI

Check out these sources for additional information: Bellingham/Whatcom Chamber of Commerce (www.bellingham.com or 360-671-3990); the *Bellingham Herald* (www.bellinghamherald.com or 360-676-2600); and the *Bellingham Business Journal* (www.businessjournal.org/bbj or 360-647-8805).

Reader's Digest, AARP, CNN, and *Money Magazine* have all put Bellingham on their "Best Places" lists.

Port Townsend

REPORT CARD:

Overall Rating:	B
Climate:	A-
Cost of Living:	B
Health Care:	B
Transportation:	C
What's to Do:	B

Located in the northeast corner of Washington's Olympic Peninsula, Port Townsend is one of only three U.S. Victorian seaports listed on the National Historic Register. With the Olympic Mountains on one side, Port Townsend Bay on the other, and the Strait of Juan de Fuca to the north, Port Townsend is surrounded by water.

Visitors take a step back in time just walking around this quaint, historic town. So many of the Victorian homes and buildings are restored and open for lodging that Port Townsend is sometimes thought of as the un-official bed-and-breakfast capital of the Pacific Northwest. Most travel to and from Port Townsend is on the Washington State Ferries. Although no longer the thriving seaport it was in the 1800s, its commerce is still centered on manufacturing, tourism, and timber.

Whether hiking in Olympic National Park, boating on Puget Sound, bird-watching in the Dungeness River Center, or whale-watching in the San Juan Islands, residents soak up the natural beauty of the area and enjoy the mild climate provided by the rain shadow of the Olympic Mountains (in other words, the mountains help to block the rain). The Pacific Ocean helps to moderate the temperatures throughout the year, and the Olympic Mountains provide the barrier that results in much less rainfall than is the norm for the Pacific Northwest.

Who Lives in Port Townsend?

Port Townsend has a population of approximately 8,300 with about one-third of the residents over the age of 55.

What's It Like Outside?	Jan.	Apr.	Jul.	Oct.	Rain (in.)	Snow (in.)
Average High (°F)	44	59	76	61	18	4
Average Low (°F)	30	33	53	45	–	–

The median age is 46, and about 95 percent of the residents are Caucasian, 1 percent African-American, 2 percent Native American and/or Alaska Native, and 2 percent Asian.

What's the Cost?

Although specific numbers are unavailable, the cost of living is considered lower than the national average. Depending on location, home prices can be reasonable (a four-bedroom/two-bath in Port Townsend for $187,000) to high (a three-bedroom/two-bath in Kala Point for $625,000).

What's to Do?

With so much water around, the obvious outdoor, water-related activities spring to mind, including boating, hiking along the lakes and coastlines, and fishing. You can do all of these things in town or close by in Olympic National Park, with its 900,000 acres of land and 60 miles of Pacific coastline.

In addition to the natural beauty of the area, Port Townsend, known as "the City of Dreams," was a national prizewinner for its Main Street program of renovating and restoring historical buildings. Many art galleries, clothing boutiques, and fine restaurants are housed in these historic buildings. The Chetzemoka Park, named for the Native America chief Chetzemoka, is one of two dozen city parks in Port Townsend. This park has something for everyone: beach access, hiking paths, a 1905 bandstand, gardens, a picnic area, and a children's playground. The Port Townsend Marine Science Center offers visitors a hands-on marine life experience. There are music festivals to enjoy, featuring fiddle music, jazz, and country blues.

Although not considered a major wine-producing area, Port Townsend's wineries produce some outstanding wines as well as a few unusual ones: Strawberry rhubarb and plum wines are available for the tasting if you take the winery loop driving tour.

For a small town, Port Townsend has a lot to offer.

Where Are the Jobs?

Jefferson County's largest manufacturing employer, Port Townsend Paper Corporation, is located here. This is also

---

The *City Guide to Port Townsend* states, "Jobs are scarce, so creativity is encouraged."

a major boat-building and logging town. Health care and tourism are the other large employers. The unemployment rate is 5.1 percent, and the median household income in Jefferson County is $36,500.

Where Are the Doctors?

The medical needs of Port Townsend are served by Jefferson General Hospital. There are also several health clinics in Port Townsend.

Where Are Some Notable Neighborhoods?

You will not find retirees living in Port Townsend in one particular area, as there are no planned retirement communities per se. Some will choose to live in a Victorian home or a bungalow in town, close to restaurants, movies, and shopping. Others will choose the seclusion and wide-open spaces of the country, while still others prefer a planned community open to all age groups.

There are two planned communities for all ages close to town. Kala Point is 6 miles from Port Townsend and is situated on almost 400 acres with 1½ miles of sandy beach. The community includes swimming pools, boat docks, hiking trails, and some beautiful views. Lots are available from about $40,000, and there are a variety of homes with prices beginning under $300,000. You'll need to contact a Realtor in the area for available lots and homes.

Cape George, another private community, has a full-service marina and breathtaking views. Lots are available from $25,000, and homes sell for $250,000 and up. Again, contact a Realtor for more information.

Another area to consider is Port Ludlow. Located just 25 minutes south of Port Townsend, this is a 2,000-acre planned residential and resort community. Port Ludlow Associates (www.ludlowhomes.com or 800-872-1323) developed the land, owns the resort, and also builds some of the homes in the neighborhoods, which are both single-family and townhomes. The plan is to build 2,250 homes, and about 1,500 have been completed. Homes are priced from the $200,000s up to $1 million-plus. There are approximately 2,000 residents in Port Ludlow.

Take a drive through Kala Point and Cape George to experience the natural beauty of this heavily wooded area—you'll be impressed with the majestic mountain panorama and views of the sparkling waters and rugged coastline of the Pacific.

Residents enjoy 27 holes of golf; a 300-slip, full-service marina; and the Resort at Port Ludlow. Property owners enjoy automatic membership in the Owner's Association, which includes membership in the beach club with over 1 mile of sandy beach, tennis, squash, pickle ball courts, and heated indoor and outdoor swimming pools, as well as preferential annual rates at the golf course.

How Do I Pursue Lifelong Learning?

Several opportunities for higher education are available in the Port Townsend area, including Peninsula College at Port Townsend, a comprehensive community college. The Community Learning Center (360-379-5610), a Washington State University cooperative extension in Port Hadlock, offers classes toward several 4-year degrees. Distance learning through the University of Washington is another option (800-543-2320).

Strengths

The charm of living in a small town is magnified by the fact that the entire town is part of the National Historic Registry. The Victorian homes, the restored Main Street, the busy harbor, all accented with a backdrop of majestic mountains, make this a beautiful location for retirement. The climate is very mild, with little rain and even less snow.

Weaknesses

The ferry system may not be considered a desirable mode of transportation for some (although others may love it). Sometimes you can detect the smell from the paper plant. Port Townsend is remote; for some, that is part of its charm, but for others, it's not! If you need a job, pickings are pretty slim.

FYI

Check out these sources for additional information: Port Ludlow Chamber of Commerce (www.portludlow-chamber.org or 360-437-0120); Port Townsend Chamber of Commerce (www.ptchamber.org or 360-385-7869); Washington State Ferries (www.wsdot.wa.gov/ferries or 800-843-3779); the *Port Townsend & Jefferson County Leader* (360-385-2900); and the *Peninsula Daily News* (www.peninsuladailynews.com or 800-826-7714).

When traveling to Port Ludlow from Seattle, it is necessary to take the Washington State Ferry to Bainbridge Island and then cross over the mile-long Hood Canal floating bridge.

Sequim

REPORT CARD

Overall Rating:	B
Climate:	A
Cost of Living:	B
Health Care:	C
Transportation:	B
What's to Do:	B

Sequim, pronounced "skwim," is one of Washington State's most popular retirement locations. The Sequim-Dungeness Valley is located between the Olympic Mountains and the calm waters of the Strait of Juan de Fuca. Because of Sequim's location in the "rain shadow" of the Olympics (where the mountains block the rain), the city enjoys mild year-round temperatures and an average rainfall of only 17 inches, much less than in other cities in the Pacific Northwest. The sun shines at least part of the day about 300 days a year, and if it's overcast in Sequim, it's raining for sure in Seattle and the surrounding areas! But Sequim has more to offer than climate. The city has more than 160 service, fraternal, and special interest groups, offering something for everyone. The senior center is a great place to meet people and sign up for a trip to Victoria, British Columbia; enjoy an art class; or take aerobics or yoga. Golf can be played year-round on any of the three golf courses in the valley—Dungeness, Sunland, and Sun Ridge.

The Dungeness Spit is the world's largest sand spit at 5 miles long. This narrow ribbon of sand, which projects into the Strait of Juan de Fuca, has been designated a national wildlife refuge and is home to the Dungeness crab. It is a popular location for clamming, boating, kayaking, and horseback riding. The Railroad Bridge Park, habitat for 250 bird species, has been named Washington State's first Audubon Center.

Who Lives in Sequim?

There are about 25,000 people living in the Sequim-Dungeness Valley, with about 4,500 people living in the city. Within the city limits, 55 percent of the residents are 55 years of age or older, and the median age is 59. Nearly 95 percent of the population is Caucasian, 2 percent are Native American or Alaska Native, and 2 percent are Asian.

Sequim means "quiet waters" in the native language of the S'Klallam tribe.

What's the Cost?

The cost of living is a little lower than the national average, which is helped by the lack of a state income tax. The average new, three-bedroom home will cost about $185,000, and the average family income is around $36,000. There are several manufactured home communities in Sequim. If you'd like to live in a country club/golf course setting, the prices will be higher, from $200,000 to half a million dollars or more.

What's to Do?

This is a very laid-back, quiet community, with no tall buildings in sight.

Walking on the sandy shores of the Dungeness Spit, clamming, sea kayaking, fishing, and enjoying golf any day, year-round, top the list of things to do. Gardening is very popular due to the sunshine and extra-long growing season. Residents of Sequim treasure their slow-paced life, knowing they can travel to Port Angeles or take a trip on the Washington State Ferries to Seattle to enjoy the amenities of city life. If you love lavender, you're in luck. Sequim calls itself "the lavender capital of the United States" and has an annual lavender festival that draws people from all over. Or, enjoy an open-air market featuring local produce and crafts every Saturday morning from April through October. You can also go skiing in the almost one-million-acre Olympic National Park or gamble at the Seven Cedars Casino.

Where Are the Jobs?

Getting a job is not out of the question, but the job market is tight. Look for work opportunities in the service areas: health care, schools, or tourism. Perhaps with the recent approval for constructing a new Wal-Mart, more choices will be available. The unemployment rate is a very high 8.7 percent.

Where Are the Doctors?

A 126-bed, full-service medical center, the Olympic Medical Center (OMC), is located in Port Angeles, about

What's It Like Outside?	Jan.	Apr.	Jul.	Oct.	Rain (in.)	Snow (in.)
Average High (°F)	57	56	72	59	17	–
Average Low (°F)	24	39	46	42	–	–

20 minutes away, and provides all the hospital needs for the Sequim area. Some services are available in Sequim through the OMC—lab services, physical therapy, radiation/oncology, and health education. Specialists from Seattle come to OMC often to serve the residents of the area

Where Are Some Notable Neighborhoods?

While there are no huge, gated golf communities being built in Sequim, there are many established neighborhoods with some lots available for new construction, as well as resales. Take a look at SunLand Golf & Country Club (www.sunlandgolf.com or 888-289-4314), Jamestown, Bell Hill, and Happy Valley. Prices vary from around $150,000 to over $1 million. More than 700 residents live in SunLand Golf & Country Club, where you can enjoy a par 72 golf course with views of the Olympic Mountains. Tennis, swimming, and friendly people are also a part of this Sequim community.

How Do I Pursue Lifelong Learning?

Peninsula College is part of the state Community College system and offers adult classes in Sequim and also at the main campus in Port Angeles, including Elderhostel programs.

Strengths

Living a quiet, slow-paced lifestyle away from the big city but still close to city amenities appeals to many seniors. Add 300 days of sunshine, scenic beauty, and affordability, and you have a winner.

Weaknesses

Some may feel that traveling to Port Angeles for hospital care is a negative. Others may feel that taking a ferry to the city sounds like a lot of trouble! And still others may feel the slow, quiet lifestyle—even in such a beautiful place—lacks excitement.

FYI

Check out these sources for additional information: Sequim-Dungeness Chamber of Commerce (www.cityofsequim.com or 800-737-8462); the *Peninsula Daily News* (www.peninsuladailynews.com or 360-452-4507); and the *Sequim Gazette* (www.sequimgazette.com or 360-683-3311).

Because of its plentiful sunshine, Sequim has earned the nickname "Banana Belt."

ISLAND LIVING IN WASHINGTON STATE:

The San Juan Islands, Whidbey Island, and Bainbridge Island

Finally, we'll take a look at three of the islands of Washington State. We're deviating from our normal pattern of describing a city, because, frankly, these places are different and don't lend themselves to that format. The big question is, do you want to live on "island time," and rely on ferries for transportation to and from your home?

The State of Washington has several islands that lie in the far northwestern corner of the United States and one close to Seattle worth considering for relocation. Fidalgo Island, about 90 miles from Seattle, is the easternmost island in what is known as the San Juan chain of islands. It's known as the "drive-to" island and is home to the Washington State Ferry Terminal. The only other islands accessible by car are Whidbey Island at Deception Pass (the northern edge of the island) and Bainbridge Island (which is close to Seattle). Most residents of Whidbey and Bainbridge travel by ferry, and the remaining Washington State islands are accessible only by ferry or small private planes or charters.

The Washington State Ferries are the main mode of transportation for the islands, and they are considered part of the State Highway System. Actually, the Washington State Ferry System is the largest in the United States, carrying 25 million passengers in 2002, more than some major airports!

If you are a person who is always in a hurry and feels the need for speed, you may find ferry travel a challenge. There are many drawbacks to overcome—waiting in line, mechanical problems, rising costs, and huge crowds, not to mention the 30 minutes to 2 hours it may take to get from place to place.

Fortunately, the positive side of traveling on these ferries far outweighs the negative for the 25 million passengers traveling each year. When you look around, the veteran travelers are playing cards with their kids, reading, enjoying a snack or a beer from the restaurant, and taking in the amazing natural beauty that is part of every ferry crossing: the snow-capped Olympic Mountains, Mount Rainier, the blue-green water, rocky beaches, and the trees that have given this state its nickname, the Evergreen State. There is always something extraordinary happening: eagles soaring, whales breaching—not your everyday mass transit! If you can picture yourself relaxing and enjoying the ride, explore this part of the country for retirement.

Friday Harbor, San Juan Island

The San Juan Archipelago consists of about 700 islands, only about 170 of which have names. Only four islands are populated enough to have ferry service: San Juan, Orcas, Lopez, and Shaw. Friday Harbor, located on San Juan Island, is the business hub and county seat for San Juan Island. This quaint, historic fishing village has a population of 2,000 (total population of San Juan Island is about 6,500) and is a destination for visitors or retirees looking for a getaway.

Surrounded by ocean waters and mountains, Friday Harbor's daily temperatures rarely dip below freezing or rise above 80 degrees. The people who live here take advantage of these mild temperatures and the 250 days of sunshine while enjoying activities centered on the outdoors: watching orcas and other marine and land animals, SCUBA diving, sailing, sea kayaking, and bicycling. The interior of the island has a diverse terrain where you will find lakes, prairie land, lavender and alpaca farms, vineyards, and beautiful parks. Lime Kiln State Park is the only whale-watching park in the contiguous United States. If you tire of outdoor activities, Friday Harbor has a theater, art galleries, fine restaurants, and plenty of shopping. Don't miss the Saturday morning outdoor farmers' market and the musicians in the parks.

There are no large, gated golf communities currently under construction (although there is plenty of golf). When you look at the real estate ads, you read enticing descriptions of panoramic vistas, pastoral acreage, views of the San Juan Channel and Mount Baker, and waterfront estates with docks. Homes are listed from $140,000 to $3 million-plus.

The Friday Harbor Clinic has family physicians and provides emergency care; if a hospital is needed in an emergency, however, patients are airlifted to Anacortes or Bellingham. Most residents pay about $100 for an insurance policy that provides their family with medevac helicopter service.

Living on an island accessible only by air or water means getting away from it all for sure. *Travel and Leisure* named the San Juans the second most popular island destination in the continental United States and Canada in September 1999. The beauty of the San Juan Islands is

---

The Washington State Ferries have never had a ferry-related fatality in their 50 years of operation.

breathtaking, as are the ocean temperatures if you're a swimmer! Seattle is only a few hours away if you need a big-city fix, but the cost of living is higher on the islands than in surrounding areas of the state.

Whidbey Island

Whidbey Island, the longest island (55 miles) in the continental United States, is also located at the northwestern tip of Washington State, with the Cascade Mountains to the east and the Olympic Mountains to the west. The Olympic Mountains protect Whidbey from temperature extremes and excessive rainfall. Temperatures rarely fall below freezing in the winter and rarely rise above 80 in the summer. Rainfall varies from 18 inches to 28 inches, thanks to the rain shadow provided by the mountains.

The total population of Whidbey Island is about 60,000 people, with Oak Harbor (population 20,000), home of the Naval Air Station, the largest community. The Naval Air Station is the island's largest employer, with about 10,000 active duty and civilian employees. Boeing Company's large plane plant in Everett is a short commute from Whidbey.

Oak Harbor is a bustling small town, with busy streets, fast food, a historic section called Pioneer Way, and City Beach, a park right downtown for swimming and recreation. Oak Harbor's public marina is home to Whidbey Island Race Week, one of the top 20 sailing regattas in the world.

Deception Pass State Park is Washington's most popular state park, with freshwater swimming and a sandy beach at Cranberry Lake, 38 miles of trails, boat ramps, complete camping facilities, and an underwater park for SCUBA diving.

Driving around the island (don't worry about getting lost, as one road connects the entire island), you will find much smaller communities, such as Coupeville, with about 1,300 people, and Langley, with about 1,000 residents. Langley, sitting on a bluff overlooking the southeastern shore of Whidbey Island, is a quaint small town complete with art galleries and home to the island's art council. Enjoy shopping, dining, or a stroll on the beach in this village by the sea.

Whidbey Island General Hospital, located in Coupeville, has more than 50 beds and a 24-hour emer-

---

Washington State (particularly around the San Juan Islands) is rated among the best places for SCUBA diving in North America by *Scuba Diving* magazine.

gency room. The Whidbey branch of Skagit Valley College offers 2-year associate degrees, and Western Washington University has a branch campus in Oak Harbor.

There are no new golf communities or retirement communities under construction at this time, but there are plenty of opportunities to purchase a part-time or full-time residence on Whidbey Island. Oak Harbor has homes listed from $150,000 and also for $600,000 and more on 2-plus acres with water and mountain views. The average home sells for about $180,000 in North Whidbey, and the average cost in the south is about $238,000. Useless Bay Colony (love that name!), located near Clinton on the southern end of the island, is an existing community with a golf course and country club and more than 200 homes already built. Homes are for sale from the $250,000s, although those residences with some acreage and great views of the Sound and the mountains will have a much higher price tag. Condominiums are also available from the $150,000s to about $350,000, some with golf course views and some with water views.

For more information on real estate in Whidbey Island, contact a realty company such as Whidbey Pacific Realty (www.whidbeypacificrealty.com or 800-543-5405).

Many working people live on Whidbey Island. The ferry commute is like any commute to a big city; at peak times it's awful, and midweek or midday it's a lot more enjoyable than other types of mass transit—fast and exceedingly beautiful.

Bainbridge Island

Bainbridge Island, known as a "suburb" of Seattle, is home for some 20,000 people, half of whom commute to Seattle on a daily basis. The commute, by ferry, takes about 35 minutes. The homes in this Seattle suburb are expensive, with a median value of $335,000. The climate is mild, but unlike the other islands protected by the Olympic Mountains, Bainbridge has more rain and snow (about 38 inches of rain and 11 inches of snow each year). The average temperature in the summer is 70 degrees and, during the winter, 42 degrees.

If you plan to work in Seattle or visit the city amenities regularly, Bainbridge has a lot to offer as a home base. You can enjoy walking on the beach, kayaking, bicycling, hiking, or golf. There are art galleries, antique shopping, island-grown produce at a weekly farmers' market, a historical museum, and a performing arts theater. Olympic College opened a branch campus 15 miles from Bainbridge Island for the 2004 winter quarter. You may not need to go to Seattle after all!

FYI

Check out these sources for additional information: San Juan Island Chamber of Commerce (www.sanjuanisland.org or 360-378-5240); San Juan County Visitors Bureau (www.guidetosanjuans.com or 888-468-3701); and the *San Juan Journal* (www.sanjuanjournal.com or 360-378-5696).

Connect to Chambers of Commerce (www.islandweb.org/chambers.html); Whidbey newspapers (www.whidbeynewstimes.com or 360-675-6611 and www.southwhidbeyrecord.com or 360-221-5300); and Island Transit (360-678-7771).

Bainbridge Island Chamber of Commerce (www.bainbridgechamber.com or 206-842-3700); and the *Bainbridge Island Review* (www.bainbridgereview.com or 206-842-6613).

HONOR ROLL

In keeping with the report card motif, we thought it only fitting to create an honor roll of the places we found to be particularly outstanding or unique. Although we realize that priorities and values differ, this is our alphabetical top 10 list of A+ retirement locations.

1. Asheville, North Carolina: scenic mountains; small town with big-city amenities; single friendly; great summer golf.

2. Daniel Island, South Carolina: new island community close to historic Charleston with a wide variety of housing possibilities and price ranges.

3. Hilton Head, South Carolina: tropical island feel; family oriented and friendly; successfully combines resort and community living (and you can ride your bike on the beach, too!).

4. Palm Coast, Florida: affordable communities; quick access from the highway to waterfront neighborhoods and public beaches; few seasonal tourists.

5. Port Ludlow/Port Townsend, Washington: new master-planned community (Port Ludlow) near a quaint, Victorian bayside town (Port Townsend); snowcapped Olympic mountains.

6. Prescott, Arizona: beautiful freshwater lakes; cool summer days; small western town; known as "everybody's hometown."

7. Research Triangle (Durham, Raleigh, Chapel Hill), North Carolina: university towns; educated populace; four mild seasons; outstanding medical centers.

8. San Luis Obispo, California: almost perfect weather; 10 miles to the Pacific Coast; vibrant downtown; college town.

9. Santa Fe, New Mexico: pedestrian friendly; vital arts community; great southwestern cuisine; mild climate with close proximity to skiing.

10. Sarasota, Florida: cultural center of Florida; powdery white-sand beaches with great public access; diverse housing options; proximity to airport.

A SECOND HOME

We mentioned near the beginning of this chapter that some people who will keep their primary residence might be interested in a second home. Here is a list of possible locations. Of course, any of the places already recommended could be considered for a second home as well, just as these places could be your ideal setting for a primary home.

Escape from the City

These places could be a drivable distance from your primary residence or a reasonable drive from a major airport.

* Bethany Beach, Delaware
* Breckenridge, Colorado
* Lake Norris, Tennessee
* Lake of the Ozarks, Missouri
* Long Beach Island, New Jersey
* Poconos, Pennsylvania

Sunbirds

If you're looking to escape the heat and humidity of the summer months, one of these towns might fit the bill.

* Brunswick, Maine
* Charlevoix, Michigan
* Door County, Wisconsin
* Petoskey, Michigan

Snowbirds

If the winters are too cold for you, then head south. Located below the frost line, these places will provide sun and warmth during the coldest of months.

* Boca Grande, Florida
* Captiva and Sanibel islands, Florida
* Jupiter, Florida
* Palm Desert/Palm Springs, California
* Rockport, Texas

Q: "Why are you moving out of your house?"

A: "Because, according to statistics, most accidents happen at home."

WHAT ARE SOME NICHE RETIREMENT LIFESTYLES?

"If you cannot change your life, then why not change the way you live it?"
—Dr. David J. Demko, Age Venture News Service, www.demko.com

For some people, choosing a new retirement spot is much more about *lifestyle* than about area. If you're looking for a *way* of living, rather than a particular *place*, here are some niche retirement lifestyle choices that may appeal to you.

ACTIVE-ADULT COMMUNITIES

Tired of hearing the pitter-patter of little feet in your existing community? Longing to be surrounded by like-minded neighbors? You may want to explore living in an active-adult community. If a more age-homogeneous lifestyle with facilities and social activities that allow you to do as much or as little as you'd like sounds like your cup of tea, there are many choices, some probably close to your present home. Some communities have age restrictions, such as that at least one resident must be 55 or older and that no one under 19 may live full time in the community. Other communities are marketed to people over 50, without age restrictions. Although Florida and Arizona boast the most active adults, there are more than 760 active-adult communities in the United States, and this number is increasing! Today's active-adult community residents are more affluent, more educated, more computer literate, more intellectually curious, healthier, and more physically active than ever. Below are some of the "big guns" in active-adult living.

Del Webb, now owned by Pulte Homes (www.del-webb.com or 800-808-8088), is the country's largest builder of active-adult communities for those 55 and better. During the last 3 years, sales have shot up almost 30 percent. There are three types of Del Webb communities: active adult (which are age restricted), country club (which feature a resort setting), and family living (which cater to all ages). Amenities may include golf, tennis, fitness centers, swimming, special-interest clubs, and numerous planned activities. Del Webb's active-adult communities are located in 11 states: Arizona, California, Florida, Illinois, Maryland, Massachusetts, Nevada, New Jersey, South Carolina, Texas, and Virginia. Home prices range from the $100,000s to the $700,000s.

Hovnanian Enterprises (www.khov.com or 877-HOV-HOME), building communities for more than 40 years, has active-adult communities in California, Maryland, New Jersey, Pennsylvania, South Carolina, Texas, and Virginia. Hovnanian also has an assisted-living community at Sunrise at Mt. Laurel and at Sunrise at Woodbury Lake, both in New Jersey. Depending on the type of home and location, prices can vary from the $100,000s to $1 million or more.

Leisure World, a concept that began in California in the 1950s, has several active-adult communities; they are located in Mesa, Arizona; Laguna Woods and Seal Beach, California; Silver Spring, Maryland (near Washington, D.C.); and Lansdowne, Virginia. All Leisure Worlds have gated security, full-time professional management, and a plethora of facilities and activities that cater to virtually every desire and need. The Leisure World in Laguna Woods is incorporating as a city, Laguna Woods, becoming California's newest (in terms of cities) and oldest (in terms of population) place! Prices in Leisure World range from the $70,000s to over $600,000, with a variety of housing styles. For

For a listing of active-adult communities in the United States, you can subscribe to a directory through www.activeadultliving.com or 702-614-9120. For $20 or $25 (depending on the format) you'll have access to current as well as developing active-adult communities.

more information, contact the individual Leisure World location:

❋ Arizona: www.leisureworldarizona.com or 480-832-7451

❋ California: www.lwlagunawoods.com or 800-711-9273 (Laguna Woods), or www.lwsb.com or 562-598-1388 (Seal Beach)

❋ Maryland: www.idigroup.com/maryland.html or 800-398-0085

❋ Virginia: www.idigroup.com/virginia.html or 703-581-1711

Lennar Corporation (www.lennar.com or 305-559-4000) has combined with U.S. Homes to create another formidable presence in the active-adult niche. Lennar has communities in 12 states: Arizona, California, Colorado, Florida, Georgia, Michigan, Missouri, New Jersey, North Carolina, Ohio, Texas, and Virginia. One of their newest communities is Colonial Heritage in Williamsburg, Virginia. Prices range from the $80,000s to $1 million.

Robson Communities (www.robson.com or 800-732-9949), headquartered in Arizona, is another heavy hitter in active-adult communities. Robson has five communities in Arizona: Sun Lakes (Phoenix metro area), Sunbird (Phoenix metro area—both manufactured and frame-constructed homes), Quail Creek (south of Tucson), Pebble Creek (Phoenix area), and Saddle Brooke (Tucson). Robson's newest community is Robson Ranch in the Dallas/Fort Worth area. Home prices in these communities range from the $140,000s to the $300,000s. Amenities may include golf, fitness facilities, swimming, tennis, organized activities and clubs, shopping, medical facilities, banks, etc.

Sun City Center (www.suncitycenter.com or 800-633-0871) is a self-contained, 40-year-old community located between Tampa and Sarasota, Florida. Originally developed by Del Webb, it is now managed by Florida Design Communities. Sun City Center has about 16,500 residents out of a planned 20,000, and about 300 new homes are built per year with build-out anticipated in 2010. Sun City Center provides more than 200 activities/clubs. Condos, duplex villas, and single-family homes range from the $70,000s to over $400,000. Golf carts compete with

---

**Check out www.retirementresorts.com for the "World's Finest Active-Adult Retirement Living,"
according to the Senior Housing Hospitality Institute.**

cars as the prime mode of transportation. There is something for everyone in this all-inclusive retirement city, including an assisted-living facility and skilled nursing care.

AN AFRICAN-AMERICAN COMMUNITY

Ivy Acres, presently under development, is described as the only African-American-sponsored continuing care retirement community in the United States. This 48-acre nonprofit community will be located east of Winston-Salem, North Carolina, with frontage on Winston Lake. Plans include about 200 independent apartments, 50 independent-living cottages, and 80 units for assisted living. Skilled nursing care may also be provided. Residence sizes range from just under 700 square feet to around 1,500 square feet, with prices ranging from $800 to $1,100 per month. A community center, meals, housekeeping, some utilities, and linen service are available on an a la carte basis. For more information, call 800-362-9959.

AWAY-FROM-IT-ALL ISLANDS

Does the idea of seclusion and limited access appeal to you? If so, you may wish to investigate island living.

Refer to the South Carolina and Washington sections of chapter 5, or check out some of these island towns, which are more get-away-from-it-all than others.

Bald Head Island (www.baldheadisland.com or 800-234-1666) is on the southeastern tip of North Carolina, where Cape Fear River meets the Atlantic. Development is allowed on only 2,000 of its 12,000 acres. Four and a half hours from Charlotte, the island does not permit cars—electric carts, bikes, and feet are the modes of transportation. Access to Bald Head Island is via a 22-minute ferry ride from Southport, North Carolina, or by private boat. Bald Head Island's beaches have been included among the top 20 beaches in the United States in annual rankings. Additionally, the island offers golf, restaurants, and shopping. Neighborhoods include the Peninsula, Cape Fear Station, and The Hammocks (vacation homes). Prices vary, depending on location. For example, an oceanfront four-bedroom/three-bath home is listed for $900,000, while a three-bedroom/two-bath home on the golf course lists for $575,000. One caveat of island living in North Carolina: Due to its protruding coastline, North Carolina is susceptible to hurricanes. In 1996, the North Carolina coast was hit by an unprecedented four tropical systems. On average, a tropical storm or hurricane affects North Carolina once every four years. And, of course, there was Isabel in 2003!

Benthaven Island (www.bentwater.com or 800-313-7529), located about 60 miles from Houston, Texas, is connected to Bentwater on the mainland by a 450-foot gated bridge. Benthaven Island is on 22,000-acre Lake Conroe and will have approximately 70 estate homes. Lots on the island begin at $300,000. Residents of the island will be able to use the Bentwater amenities, including golf, tennis, dining, and swimming.

Callawassie Island (www.callawassieisland.com or 800-221-8431) is close to charming Beaufort, South Carolina, the second-oldest city in South Carolina. If you're interested in South Carolina Low-Country living and want the relative convenience of two nearby big cities (Savannah is 50 miles south, and Charleston is 75 miles north), consider this island. Callawassie has 880 acres, with homes averaging less than one residence per acre. Club cottages, townhomes, and single-family homes are offered in this community, which began in 1981. They range from $210,000 to over $1 million. Equity club membership (where you apply for membership, pay an initiation fee, and get back some or most of your money when you resign) is available.

Dataw Island/Distant Island/Polawana Island (www.discoverdataw.com or 800-848-3838) are also close to Beaufort (6 miles versus 5 miles for Callawassie) and have the same sort of Low-Country beauty. Accessible by land or water, Dataw Island is a pristine 870 acres and will have 1,100 homesites when completed. Distant Island offers deepwater homesites, and Polawana Island has only 32 lots available. Real estate examples: Homesites can begin at $50,000; a waterfront lot with dock is offered at $650,000; homes are listed for sale beginning around $250,000. Amenities include golf, a marina, and tennis. A private equity club membership entitling you to all the amenities is currently $35,000.

Daufuskie Island is located about 50 miles east of Savannah, Georgia, and 100 miles south of Charleston, South Carolina. As with Bald Head Island, cars are not allowed. Haig Point on Daufuskie Island (www.navigator.com/haigpoint/ or 800-993-3635), a private residential community on more than 1,000 acres (only 30 percent of the land will be developed), has a top-rated Rees Jones golf course ($65,000 equity membership), tennis, beach club, equestrian center, fitness, and more. Homesites can range from $100,000 to $1.2 million; homes, including cottages, townhomes, patio homes, and estate homes, also vary tremendously in price (from $500,000 to $4 million). There are two other private communities on the island (Melrose and Bloody Point), as well as "outback" homes and homesites with a much wider range of prices (interior lots from $10,000 and less, for example). Dafuskie Island (it means "sharp feather" or "land with a point") is surrounded by the Atlantic Ocean, the New River, Cooper River, Calibogue Sound, and Mongin Creek.

Fisher Island (www.fisherisland-florida.com or 800-624-3251) is an exclusive 216-acre island off Miami Beach. Accessible only by ferry, private boat, or helicopter, it is/was home to such notables as Julia Roberts, Sylvester Stallone, Pete Sampras, and Oprah Winfrey. Access to this "island without bridges" is very tightly controlled. Amenities include perfect beaches, golfing, tennis, a spa, marinas, and restaurants. Membership in the Fisher Club is by invitation only, and residences, among the most expensive in the United States, range from $525,000 to $7 million. Prices on new Bayview or Oceanside condos range from $1.65 to $5.2 million. In total, there will be approximately 600 residences on Fisher Island.

Sailfish Point (www.sailfishpoint.com or 800-799-7772), over the causeway from Stuart, Florida, is a gated, 532-acre private community at the southern tip of Hutchinson Island. Located 45 miles north of Palm Beach, Sailfish Point offers golf, tennis, an oceanfront beach club, marina, and its own heliport. Exclusivity does not come cheaply here: Listings of condos and homes range from $800,000 to $7 million; homesites range from $575,000 to $4 million. Warning: Not only does Hutchinson Island have two Florida Power & Light nuclear power plants, but it also has Blind Creek Beach, which has a tradition of nudity!

San Juan, Lopez, Orcas, Whidbey, Camano, and Shaw islands are some of the many islands in Washington State near Seattle. Located in Puget Sound, these Pacific Northwest islands are accessed by water and/or air and allow cars. Lots can range from $55,000 to $5 million, residences from $80,000 to $7 million. For more information, check out www.sanjuanweb.com, or www.whidbey.net, or chapter 5.

COLLEGE TOWNS

Question: Where can you be assured of plenty of cultural activities, stimulating intergenerational discussions,

---

Want to *really* live like Gilligan? If you've got the money, purchase (or rent) your own private island. Close to 200 islands are available on www.privateislandsonline.com.

sports, entertainment, restaurants, bookstores, libraries, stable housing prices, a well-educated community, and perhaps top-notch medical facilities? Answer: college towns. For those who would rather hit the books than hit a golf ball, it's worth consideration. For many baby boomers, living in an academic community provides the vitality of college life without the hefty tuition. Colleges are responding to this trend with lifelong learning opportunities for retirees, such as the North Carolina Center for Creative Retirement in Asheville, and the more than 200 peer-driven Institutes for Learning in Retirement at various college campuses nationwide. In addition, essentially all state universities offer reduced or free tuition (space permitting) and auditing of classes for those desiring the knowledge (without the exams!). Contact the admissions office or continuing education office for specifics. (Also, check out chapter 2 for more information about lifelong learning.)

Approximately 50 colleges or universities across the United States have developed communities to attract retirees, and about the same number are examining the possibility of doing so. The concept is not new—more than 20 years ago, Indiana University built Meadowood Retirement Community for retired faculty and staff—but the idea has become more encompassing. Many alumni return to their old college stomping grounds; after all, their college years were some of their best years!

Some college retirement communities require entrance fees as well as monthly fees (the entrance fee is often partly or fully refundable upon leaving the community). Just as you might pay more for a house located on a golf course or lake, you may pay more for housing with access to a college campus. Some communities are Continuing Care Retirement Communities (CCRC; see page 269), with housing ranging from independent living to assisted living. Regular housing in the college town of your choice may be an attractive financial alternative if you don't desire a CCRC. If your plans don't involve purchasing a home, however, finding rental property could be difficult because of stiff competition from students.

Kendal Corporation (www.kendal.org) manages a number of retirement communities associated with col-

---

For the past several years, the percentage of retirees in college towns has been greater than the percentage of retirees in the general population.

leges, including Hanover, New Hampshire (2 miles from Dartmouth); Oberlin, Ohio (1 mile from Oberlin College); and Ithaca, New York (2 miles from Cornell University and Ithaca College). The Granville community, 2 miles from Denison University in Ohio, is in development.

Other college retirement communities include Oak Hammock (a CCRC) at the University of Florida in Gainesville; University Commons at the University of Michigan (offers condos for alumni and retired faculty); Holy Cross Village at Notre Dame (will offer a nursing care center); Villa St. Benedict (a CCRC) at Benedictine College in Lisle, Illinois; Classic Residence by Hyatt (a CCRC) at Stanford University in Palo Alto, California; University Place (a CCRC) at Purdue in West Lafayette, Indiana; and Capstone Village at the University of Alabama (will welcome its first residents in 2005).

If you want to get in on the ground floor of a new university and town, consider Ave Maria University. Thomas Monaghan, founder of Domino's Pizza, is building Ave Maria University, a Catholic university 15 miles east of Naples, Florida. The new town of Ave Maria will be integrated into the 750-acre campus. Completion of the 5,000-student campus (golf course included) is slated for 2006, although 101 students began the fall 2003 session at a temporary site.

CONTINUING CARE RETIREMENT COMMUNITIES

If you're looking to make only one move that will provide for whatever care needs may develop, a Continuing Care Retirement Community may fit the bill. A CCRC offers a continuum of care and allows you to "age in place"—you can segue from independent living to assisted living to nursing care, all within the same facility. A variety of housing options is usually available, and there is often a community dining area where you can purchase meals if

---

The American Association of Homes and Services for the Aging publishes the *Consumers' Directory of Continuing Care Retirement Communities,* which lists more than 500 CCRCs, indexed by state, and details fees, services, contract options, and accreditation status. Cost is $30; call 800-508-9442 to purchase.

you wish. If your goal is to remain in the same geographic area, the sizable number of these facilities throughout the country may enable you to stay close to your present community, yet receive the help you need.

There is a menu of choices in CCRCs. Residences may be condos, apartments, single-family homes, or duplexes. In general, residents may either pay an entrance fee along with monthly fees or be charged a monthly rental fee that covers certain services. CCRC contract options are typically either extensive (monthly payments stay the same regardless of services); modified (a set number of days of nursing care is provided, beyond which the resident is financially responsible); or fee for service (you pay a la carte for nursing services and other health-related costs). Entrance fees can range from $10,000 to $500,000, and monthly fees from $600 to $4,000. In some CCRCs, domiciles can be passed on to heirs; in other communities, a portion of the entrance fee is refunded if the resident leaves or refunded to his or her estate if he or she passes on. CCRCs can be pricey; if you are in poor health, you could pay a hefty entrance fee for little time. There is often a wait to get into these types of communities, although more are opening all the time. The 154-acre River Landing at Sandy Ridge in High Point, North Carolina; the 190-acre Inverness Village in Tulsa, Oklahoma; and the Kahala Nui in Honolulu, Hawaii, are examples of new CCRCs. Here's a sampling of a few existing ones.

Carlsbad by the Sea (www.carlsbadbythesea.com or 800-255-1556) is located on the Pacific Coast in the delightful village of Carlsbad, California, north of La Jolla and Del Mar. This renovated 4-acre CCRC has 147 independent-living apartments (some oceanfront or with an ocean view), 13 assisted-living studio residences, and a 33-bed care center. A full complement of services and amenities is provided in this intimate, scenic setting. Two commuter rail lines in Carlsbad facilitate travel. At

---

The Continuing Care Accreditation Commission (sponsored by the American Association of Homes and Services for the Aging) is the country's only independent accrediting agency for CCRCs. To contact them and/or access the list of accredited communities, log on to www.ccaconline.org or call 202-783-7286. This organization has merged with the Commission on Accreditation of Rehabilitation Facilities (CARF), but both will use their separate names and facilities for a few more years.

Carlsbad by the Sea, entrance fees for residential living range from the $170,000s to $500,000 and monthly fees from $2,200 to $3,900. An additional person is $695 per month. Assisted-living fees range from $3,600 to $5,000, with a charge of $1,100 for a second person. The Care Center operates on a daily fee of $200 to $280. The fees include the residence. There is no Alzheimer's facility.

Twin Lakes (www.twinlakes.org or 513-719-3500) is located on 56 acres in Montgomery and borders the Village of Indian Hill, upscale suburbs of Cincinnati. Twin Lakes is affiliated with the United Methodist Church and is open to anyone 62 years or older. The 400-resident community will be completed by autumn 2004. Twin Lakes will have 115 villa homes, 91 apartments, and a health care pavilion with 27 assisted-living units and 38 full-care nursing accommodations. There is no Alzheimer's facility. Twin Lakes is located close to shopping, dining, and parks, as well as the amenities of downtown Cincinnati. The monthly fees for the apartments start at $2,100, villa homes begin at $2,300, and skilled nursing care will run about $7,500 a month.

Hyatt Corporation, with its affiliate, Classic Residence by Hyatt (www.hyattclassic.com/naples or 888-945-1121), entered the retirement community arena in 1987. Hyatt has 18 upscale retirement communities in ten states, and 7 of the 18 include a care center. Bentley Village in Naples, Florida, provides a continuum of care and, in addition, offers an Alzheimer's/memory support care facility. Its 156 acres include apartments, homes, golf, lakes, walking paths, and a 400-seat auditorium. Plus, you're minutes away from Naples, an outstanding location in its own right.

TidePointe (www.hyattclassic.com/hiltonhead or 800-386-8433), also by Hyatt, adjoins Sea Pines on Hilton Head Island, South Carolina, and provides access to the beaches, golf, and tennis of Sea Pines Resort, as well as TidePointe's own million-dollar spa. Broad Creek, within the gated community of TidePoint, provides assisted living, a rehabilitation center, and skilled nursing care. Penney and Jonathan P. moved to Hilton Head Island in 1987. Their plan is to stay in Sea Pines, and then, when they feel the time is right, move into Broad Creek.

To compare facilities covered by Medicare or Medicaid, log on to the government's Web site, www.medicare.gov, then click on "Nursing Home Compare."

TidePointe is located on 63 acres, and residents purchase their homes (beginning around $190,000 for a villa). Those living independently pay a monthly fee (ranging from $1,400 to $2,900), depending on the type of home they have; those who need assisted-living care pay a monthly fee beginning around $3,000; and those needing semiprivate skilled nursing care pay $170 per day. For a single, there is also a one-time membership fee of 10 percent of the purchase price of a home or $24,000, whichever is less; for a couple, the membership fee is 10 percent of the purchase price or $30,000, whichever is less.

GAY AND LESBIAN COMMUNITIES

According to the U.S. Census, almost 3 million gays and lesbians will be 55 by 2005; by 2010, that number will be closer to 4 million. Many gays may feel that a tradi-tional active-adult community or other communities may not welcome them. To serve this growing niche market, a number of gay/lesbian communities are now open, are being developed, or have been proposed.

The Palms of Manasota (www.palmsofmanasota.com or 941-722-5858) is in Palmetto, Florida (between Sarasota and St. Petersburg). Its Web site calls it "America's first gay and lesbian adult living community." Villas are available for under $160,000.

The Resort on Carefree Boulevard (www.resort-oncb.com or 239-731-7109), for women only, is located in Fort Myers, Florida. The community has 278 manu-factured homes and a number of RV sites. Homes range from $80,000 to $140,000, and typical lots are in the $40,000s.

Stonewall Communities (www.stonewallcommuni-ties.com or 617-369-9090) will consist of 75 to 100 one- and two-bedroom apartments in central Boston.

You can now buy a gussied-up golf cart that is "street legal." Known as low-speed vehicles (LSVs) or neighborhood electric vehicles (NEVs), they work on rechargeable batteries and have brakes, seat belts, lights, windshields, and roofs. They can go up to 25 miles an hour and are usually restricted to roads where the speed limit is 25 miles per hour or less. Global Electric Motorcars, a Daimler-Chrysler divi-sion, produces the GEM car, and Canadian Bombardier produces the NEV; both cost about $7,000.

The community's residents, middle- to upper-income gays, lesbians, and their friends who are 55 and older, will be offered a host of amenities, including health services, fitness facilities, meals, and transportation. Since it's still in the planning stages, prices have not yet been determined.

Birds of a Feather (www.flock2it.com or 888-425-3121), right outside Santa Fe, New Mexico (in Pecos), is a 140-acre development; "casita" lots (ranging from one-fourth to one-half acre) begin under $60,000, and single-family lots (of approximately 1 acre) begin at $110,000.

Our Town (Lundberggroup@ourtownvillages.com or 415-566-4100), still in the planning stages, will be a group of communities for lesbian, gay, bisexual, and transgendered people. Peter Lundberg of the Lundberg Group hopes to make this a reality in 3 to 5 years. Lundberg has more than 1,500 people on a waiting list and envisions both large urban communities and resort-style retirement communities within driving distance to major cities. One of the first communities is planned for the northern California wine country, perhaps followed by San Francisco and southern California locations. Amenities would include some assisted-living components so that residents could age in place.

Rainbow Vision Properties (www.rainbowvision-prop.com or 505-474-9696) is building 40 condos with an average price of $235,000 and 80 independent-living and 26 assisted-living rental apartments in downtown Santa Fe, New Mexico. Scheduled to open in early 2005, this community will welcome gays, lesbians, and straights. Amenities will include a fitness center, spa, and wellness services.

GOLF COMMUNITIES

Itching to trade in the weed whacker for a Big Bertha? If you want to focus on the fairways, consider living in a golf course community. Around 200 new neighborhoods sporting links have opened over the past 2 years, and this trend shows no sign of slowing. Even though the number of golfers in the United States (about 27 million) has remained relatively stable over the past

---

Looking for golf on a smaller scale? Myrtle Beach is considered the "mini-golf" capital of the world with more than 45 miniature golf courses; the U.S. ProMiniGolf Association is located here.

THE BEST GOLF COURSES IN THE BEST RETIREMENT STATES

Below, we've listed the best golf courses from *Golf Digest*'s "America's 100 Greatest Golf Courses" (2003–2004) that are located in several of the more popular states for retirement. Complete lists can be downloaded at www.GolfDigest.com.

Alabama: Shoal Creek (#64), Shoal Creek

Arizona: Desert Forest G. C. (#80), Carefree
The Estancia Club (#97), Scottsdale
Forest Highlands G. C. (Canyon) (#72), Flagstaff

California: Pebble Beach Golf Links (#5), Pebble Beach
Cypress Point (#3), Pebble Beach
Los Angeles County Club (#27), Los Angeles
The Olympic Club (Lake) (#16), San Francisco
Pasatiempo G. C. (#91), Santa Cruz
The Quarry at La Quinta (#88), La Quinta
Riviera (#26), Pacific Palisades
San Francisco G. C. (#18), San Francisco
Spyglass Hill (#43), Pebble Beach
Valley of Montecito (#59), Santa Barbara
Colorado: Castle Pines G. C. (#68), Castle Rock
Cherry Hills County Club (#21), Englewood
Sanctuary G. C. (#89), Sedalia

Florida: Black Diamond Ranch G. C. (Quarry) (#95), Lecanto
Jupiter Hills Club (Hills) (#75), Tequesta
Pine Tree G. C. (#81), Boynton Beach
Seminole G. C. (#14), North Palm Beach
TPC at Sawgrass (Stadium) (#67), Ponte Vedra Beach
World Woods Golf Club (#97), Brooksville

several years, the number of courses has increased. Even those who aren't golfers like to live where they can see lots of green grass and open space for which they're not responsible! Pinehurst, North Carolina, has eight courses, and Myrtle Beach, South Carolina, has 120. For specific information on golf course communities, click on www.golfcoursehome.net or www.golfcommunities.com.

You could also check out World Golf Village (www.wgv.com). Located less than half an hour south of Jacksonville, Florida, the community boasts two championship golf courses: the King & Bear (designed by

Georgia: Atlanta Country Club (#86), Marietta
Augusta National Golf Club (#2), Augusta
East Lake G. C. (#74), Atlanta
Ocean Forest G. C. (#96), Sea Island
Peachtree G. C. (#51), Atlanta

Nevada: Shadow Creek (#48), North Las Vegas

N. Carolina: Grandfather Golf & C. C. (#92), Linville
Pinehurst No. 2 (#12), Pinehurst
Wade Hampton G. C. (#37), Cashiers

Oregon: Bandon Dunes (#62), Bandon
Pacific Dunes (#44), Bandon
Crosswater (#96), Sunriver
Eugene Country Club (#83), Eugene

S. Carolina: The Dunes G. & Beach C. (#78), Myrtle Beach
Greenville C. C. (Chanticleer) (#94), Greenville
Harbour Town G. Links (#65), Hilton Head Island
Long Cove Club (#77), Hilton Head Island
The Ocean Course (#70), Kiawah Island
Greenville-Chanticleer (#95), Greenville

Tennessee: The Honors Course (#58), Chattanooga

Texas: Colonial Country Club (#35), Fort Worth

Virginia: Homestead (Cascades) (#39), Hot Springs

Washington: Sahalee C. C. (South/North) (#98), Sammanish

Palmer and Nicklaus) and the Slammer & Squire (for which Snead and Sarazen were consultants). Here, you not only play golf, but can also eat at a number of golf-themed restaurants, sleep, think, and shop golf. Homes range from condos to estate homes to Glenmoor, a retirement community whose offerings range from independent living to 24-hour nursing care. The World Golf Hall of Fame is located here, and the 30,000-square-foot PGA Tour shop offers about any golf-related accessory imaginable. Contact the Neighborhoods at World Golf Village (904-940-5000) or Glenmoor Adult Retirement Community (904-940-4800).

Or, if you're truly a diehard, live where the best-rated golf courses are located. *Golf Digest* ranked "America's 100 Greatest Golf Courses" for 2003-2004 (rankings are based on architecture), which includes both public and private courses, as well as a listing of "America's 100 Greatest Public Courses" for those who can't scale the gates (they do these rankings every other year). If you'd like to play at the best private courses, perhaps you can find a member who could take you as a guest; failing that, some of the courses (about 20) offer charity benefits that you may be able to access.

LIFESTYLE VILLAGES (OR DROP WHERE YOU SHOP!)

What is 51-year-old Chicago resident Jessica L.'s favorite leisure-time activity? It's shopping, followed by a latte at Starbucks! She's not alone. According to the Tourism Industry of America, shopping is a favorite vacation activity for most people. Couple this with the fact that boomers are the richest age group in the nation, and it's no wonder that a trend of "lifestyle villages," combining retail with residences, is taking off.

In more than a dozen places across the United States, plans are under way for mixing shopping and living, much like in a New York neighborhood. But the upscale retail spots found in these "lifestyle villages"—Gucci, Dean & DeLuca, Crate & Barrel, Banana Republic, and Starbucks—are designed to appeal to young professionals as well as empty nesters. "Living above the shops" is tailor-made for those retirees bored with suburbia, stressed out over traffic, and ready to move to an "urban" environment that requires little upkeep and driving. Rents can range from $1,000–$10,000 a month.

On the flip side, in many lifestyle villages there is a dearth of parks, schools, pets, children, and playgrounds. Also, noise, potential difficulty parking (for those who

---

Did you know that living in a golf course development designed by a "name architect" (think Nicklaus, Fazio, Palmer) increases the worth of a home? A 2001 Golf Research Group study, "The Value of U.S. Golf Architects," found this to be true. Interestingly, over 40 percent of golf course communities don't use an architect—the developer or a local pro plans the course.

own a car), loss of a sense of privacy and space, and inability to comparison shop may be drawbacks. Many people may not view these shopping and residential areas as true communities.

But, if you'd like to "drop where you shop," here are some options.

Birkdale Village (www.birkdalevillage.net or 704-895-7895), in Huntersville, near Charlotte, North Carolina, is a 52-acre mixture of offices, 320 apartments, retail, and entertainment built around a village green. Birkdale Village includes a Gap, Barnes & Noble, Starbucks, Talbots, and Banana Republic.

Phillips Place (704-553-7603) in Charlotte, North Carolina, was completed in 1998. It combines residential buildings (402 apartments), commercial enterprises, and retail establishments (130,000 square feet of restaurants and stores).

Santana Row (www.santanarow.com or 408-988-3600) in San Jose, California, opened in 2002. It's 17 city blocks with more than 100 shops, 20 restaurants, a hotel, and 1,200 lofts, flats, townhomes, and villas.

Will lifestyle villages be an enduring trend or a flash in the pan? According to Alex Krieger, chairman of the department of urban planning at the Harvard Graduate School of Design, "it's succeeding now because it's a novelty." Time will tell!

ON THE ROAD AGAIN

Over one million Americans call their RV "home." The largest contingent of recreation vehicle owners is 35-to-54-year-olds. If you're itching to be on the road, there are a few things to consider. Full-time RV living offers flexibility and convenience and the opportunity to visit many places; you can take your pets with you, provide your own guest quarters when you visit others, and meet lots of interesting people. It's also a lifestyle to consider if you're single. A typical RV can cost around $75,000 and gets around 7 miles per gallon. However, living the nomadic life makes it more difficult to form

---

Wal-Marts allow RVs to park for free (although there are no hookups or dumping stations). Some encourage only one-night stops; others are more liberal. In fact, if you want a list, Wal-Mart has its own atlas that lists every Wal-Mart store in the country.

a social support system and to develop deep and lasting friendships. There are several practical issues to address as well.

Tax considerations. Where will income from pensions and dividends be taxed? How do you determine your domicile? (See www.newrver.com/taxation.html for an excellent explanation of many of the tax issues affecting full-time RV living.)

Connections. Cell phones, message and mail forwarding services, and wireless technology to access e-mail make it easier to keep tabs on others (and to let them keep tabs on you!). More RV parks are also incorporating phone hookups.

Illness. This is a real worry, since many insurance policies don't take kindly to illness on the road. Even with coverage, it's often difficult to find a doctor and get an appointment. (The Escapees RV Club offers a CARE [Continuing Assistance for Retired Escapees] Center in Livingston, Texas. Its mission is to "to provide a safe haven at affordable prices for members whose travels are permanently or temporarily interrupted because of health reasons." See www.escapees.com and click on "CARE and VOW.")

Stuff. For some, the biggest drawback to living in an RV is lack of space. Of course, you can always rent storage space or lockers, but most find they have to live without the souvenirs.

Burnout. Discovering the right pace is critical. Generally, staying in the same place for at least a week will help prevent burnout.

Breakdowns. Thomas H., an RVer for many years, gives this advice: "Remember that you are in a house never meant to be on wheels and that you are traveling on wheels never meant to hold a house. When you marry the two, something is going to break as you travel down the highway. My wife and I have tried to take the mental frustrations out of the equation by simply looking at problems as part of the challenge of RVing—i.e., hey it's part of the trip! Luckily we have never broken down in an isolated area, mainly because I spend money up front on making sure my unit is well serviced by a local dealer whom I have trusted for the past 10 years."

Garage will travel: The Travel Supreme ME motor home comes equipped with a storage space that can hold a small car, motorcycle, or other must-haves and is operated by a hydraulic lift.

If you think you'd like life on the road, you may want to take a test drive first! For example, you could rent an RV through Cruise America (www.cruiseamerica.com) for 7 nights in the southern United States in June 2004 for about $1,200. This would include a standard RV (21 to 25 feet long, which sleeps a family of five), an estimated 700 miles of travel (you're reimbursed for the difference upon return of the RV), liability insurance, and damage deductibles.

 Ms. Doris Fletcher is a full-time RVer.

Doris became frustrated at "having to leave the fun and go back to work when others were able to stay a little longer or meander" on to other places, so she retired, put her New Jersey house up for sale, bought her 29-foot motor home, and "hit the road" in September 2000. Doris, who is single, does freelance medical editing. Prior to purchasing her current motor home, she progressed from a tent, to a pop-up, to a travel trailer, to a fifth-wheel trailer with slideout, to a small motor home. For Doris, home is "where she parks it." She likes "the freedom to go where I want when I want," and the fact that "if I don't like the weather, I can move. If I don't like my neighbors, I can move (haven't had to do that)."

Bill M. lives in Newport Beach, California, and is the owner of a company that provides plastic containers to major corporations. Bill and his wife, Kathy, have owned motor homes for more than a decade, and here are his thoughts about RVing:

Here I am, driving my motor home to Las Vegas (for work, honest), contemplating retirement. I've just turned 57, and this retirement idea seems to be on my mind.

My decision is easy. When the time comes, my wife and I will be hitting the road. For us, traveling in our motor home is the answer. We have owned

---

Quartzsite, Arizona, covering thousands of acres in the Sonora Desert, is most likely the biggest winter RV site. At fees of $25 per 2 weeks or $125 for 6 months, this Old West town attracts close to 200,000 recreational vehicles every winter.

motor homes for the last 14 years and are convinced this is the key to happiness when we retire. If you can say yes to any of the following statements, then motor home retirement may be for you, too.

✳ You want to see this country up close and personal.

✳ You want to travel at your pace, coming and going when you want.

✳ You want to renew old acquaintances and make new ones.

The vehicle can range in size from 20 feet to 45 feet and cost $10,000 to $1 million- plus. The big difference between a retirement home and motor home is that the old adage, "location, location, location," goes right out the window.

Your retirement motor home can be located wherever you want, whenever you want, along with your very own clothes, bedding, food, and entertainment.

This offers the best of all worlds, at a time in our lives when responsibilities, planning, and schedules should be a thing of the past (just like in college).

We don't plan to be "full-time" RVers; we enjoy our home and family too much. Hitting the highways for 2 weeks to 2 months at a crack makes for great adventures, and Canada and Mexico are within reach.

We've covered about 150,000 miles and can't wait to get the next 100,000 miles under our wheels. This is a very spontaneous way to live, see old friends, and make new ones. Hope to see you on the road! Ⓛ

PET-FRIENDLY PLACES

If Fido is your best friend, and you can't bear the thought of leaving him behind or subjecting him to the restrictions and unfriendly attitudes about pets found in so many communities, consider Harmony, Florida (www.harmonyinstitute.org, click on "Partnerships,"

Now you can get all decked out in your RV. SkyDeck has patented a system that involves a stairway leading to a rooftop deck. Grills, sound systems, lighting, a wet bar, and seating are accessed by an inside stairway. Everything collapses when not in use, adding only a half foot to the height of your RV.

then the "Town of Harmony," or call 866-498-1007). Research has shown that pets provide definite health benefits to their owners. The developing community of Harmony capitalizes on this idea with pet-friendly amenities: easy-to-reach waste disposal units, pet trainers, a pet park, and a pet concierge who coordinates pet care, services, and products. In this conservation-oriented master-planned community, homes begin under $200,000 and the most expensive model begins in the low $500,000s. Harmony is located in central Florida, east of St. Cloud in Osceola County. The "green" approach of Harmony preserves 70 percent of the 11,000-acre property as parks, woodlands, and wetlands.

ROOM SERVICE, PLEASE! OR, LIVING IN A HOTEL

Yearning for a roast beef sandwich at 2 A.M.? Call room service! Need reservations for that trendy new restaurant? Call the concierge! How would you like valet parking, housekeeping, fitness facilities, and the other amenities of a fine hotel just a phone call or steps away? Well, you could consider living in a hotel (or at least having the same privilege). Here is a sampling of full-time/shared-ownership (also called fractional ownership) opportunities available in fine hotels that you could call home. Warning: Luxury doesn't come cheap!

Acqualina (www.acqualina.com or 305-933-6666), located south of Fort Lauderdale, Florida, is slated to open in 2004. It is offered by the developers of Williams Island, where Acqualina is located. The services of this 51-story boutique hotel residence on 400 feet of Atlantic coastline are provided by Rosewood Hotels & Resorts. Not for the faint of wallet, prices range from about $1 to $10 million for three- to six-bedroom residences. Amenities include the use of Williams Island's tennis, golf, and marina facilities, as well as restaurants, a beach club, and a spa.

As of 2003, 16 states have passed laws that allow pet trusts to be set up. In 13 of these states (Alaska, Arizona, Colorado, Florida, Iowa, Michigan, Montana, New Jersey, New Mexico, New York, North Carolina, Oregon, and Utah), the trusts are legally binding; in the other three states (California, Missouri, and Tennessee), they are not. Average bequest? About $25,000.

The Atlantic (www.atlantichotelcondo.com or 954-630-1999), a 15-story, tiered oceanfront tower located in Fort Lauderdale, Florida, is scheduled to be complete in Fall 2004. The 124 fully furnished, turnkey condos start under $400,000. Developed by Luxury Resorts International and managed by Starwood Hotels & Resorts Worldwide, it allows owners to participate in the rental program when not in residence. Amenities include terraces, pools, indoor/outdoor dining, a fitness center, and a spa.

Carlson Hospitality Worldwide, in conjunction with Ryan Companies U.S., is developing Carlson Parks (763-212-5000), campuslike settings consisting of townhouses, condos, and a Carlson hotel. Carlson Park Lifestyle Communities are being designed for residents 55 and older, with recreational opportunities and resort amenities. Carlson Park Hill Country is the first of these communities and is located 20 minutes from San Antonio in the Texas hill country. The development consists of year-round residential housing and the full services of a 230-room Radisson hotel in the same community. There are 108 condos and 74 townhomes on the 27-acre San Antonio campus. A monthly fee will entitle residents to concierge services as well as housekeeping, transportation, fitness facilities, and general maintenance services. Over the next 15 years, 25 Carlson Park Lifestyle Communities are planned, including one in Savannah, Georgia, and one in Palm Desert, California.

Fontainebleau II (www.fontainebleau2.com or 866-531-8480), located at the Fontainebleau Hilton Resort, is located on 1,200 feet of Atlantic shoreline in Miami Beach, Florida. Construction should be complete in late 2004. All the perks of an upscale hotel, including 18 acres of recreational amenities, will be available in this 36-story, 462-unit condo/hotel, with furnished suites ranging from the $400,000s to over $1.3 million.

Four Seasons (www.fourseasons.com or 800-819-5053) has private residences and shared-ownership properties available both within and outside of the United States. Properties are located in Whistler, Canada; San Francisco; Scottsdale, Arizona; North San Diego; Punta

---

Find pet-friendly lodging, including hotels, condos, and vacation rentals in
the United States and Canada, at www.petfriendlytravel.com.

Mita, Mexico; Jackson Hole, Wyoming; Miami; and Sedona, Arizona. As you can imagine, the prices for a Four Seasons property are hefty. Lots at the Sedona location, for example, start at just under $1 million; condos in Miami, around $500,000.

Ritz-Carlton (www.ritzcarlton.com or 800-241-3333) also provides the option of purchasing a residence or sharing ownership, both within and outside of the United States. The company figures the Ritz-Carlton name and outstanding services translate into a 20 to 25 percent add-on to normal apartment prices. Owning a residence is possible in Boston; Coconut Grove (Miami); Grand Cayman Islands; Battery Park (New York City); Sarasota, Florida; Washington, D.C.; Georgetown; Jupiter, Florida; and their newest site in Berlin, Germany. "Private Club" memberships (fractional ownership) are available in Aspen, Colorado; St. Thomas, Virgin Islands; Jupiter, Florida; and Bachelor Gulch, Colorado (at Beaver Creek Mountain Resort). Sample costs: Condos in the Grand Caymans start at $2.1 million; condos are available in Washington, D.C., for under $600,000; in Jupiter, fractional ownership in the Private Club requires at least a ⅛ interest, with a cost of approximately $230,000 per deeded interest; and residences in Jupiter start at $1.8 million.

The Setai (www.setai.com or 877-997-3842), on the beach in Miami Beach, Florida, is a 40-story residential tower and a 90-room hotel, opening in 2004. With an emphasis on Asian serenity, the Setai will offer a spa, fitness center, concierge service, etc. The sister hotel to the Setai, the Datai, on the Malaysian island of Langkawi, was voted best overseas leisure hotel by *Condé Nast* (October 2001). Residences range from the $600,000s and up. Additional Setai Resort Clubs are planned for the Turks & Caicos in the Bahamas; Morocco; and Jackson Hole, Wyoming.

SEAGOING CITIES

What if you could travel around the world without ever leaving home? Imagine having a home in more than 40 countries! If this intrigues you, consider *The World of ResidenSea. The World* is a 43,000-ton Norwegian luxury ship that has 110 fully furnished residences and 88 guest suites. Prices start at $1.8 million for a one-bedroom apartment, and studio residences begin at $850,000. Amenities include 24-hour concierge and room service, a spa, restaurants, a full-size tennis court, golf (with real grass!), and swimming pools. The maiden cruise of *The World of ResidenSea* was in March 2002. For more information, contact www.residensea.com or call 305-264-9090 (Miami), or 310-887-7090 (L.A.).

Another project, not yet off the ground (er, water?!), is the proposed *Freedom Ship*, brainchild of Norman Nixon, engineer and CEO of Freedom Ship International. Envision a ship almost a mile long, 750 feet wide, and 350 feet high that will accommodate a population of about 100,000 (40,000 of these full-time residents). This seagoing community will circle the globe every 3 years and will boast parks, schools, shopping malls, hotels, a hospital, and an airport. Airplanes and hydrofoils will provide transportation between the *Freedom Ship* and ports. Residences (pre-construction prices) range from a unit without a kitchen (hmmm . . . no dirty dishes to wash—ever!) for $180,000, up to $44 million (yes, that second "4" is correct); there will also be monthly maintenance fees ranging from under $500 to $15,000. For more information, contact www.freedomship.com or call 941-539-6824.

SINGLES' TOWNS

If you're single and wish to relocate, what considerations should you weigh? Of course, whether you're part of a couple or going it alone, the same things—agreeable climate, ample cultural and recreational opportunities, good medical facilities, reasonable cost of living—are desirable. If you're unattached, however, you might want to look for specific places known to be hospitable to singles. These places tend to provide opportunities to make new friends and create social support structures. Consider areas that are growing rapidly. People new to an area tend to be more receptive to making new acquaintances than are those whose social circles have already been firmly established. Here are several suggestions for places particularly amenable to singles.

Asheville. Located in beautiful western North Carolina, Asheville has a four-season climate, the University of North Carolina-Asheville campus, and many opportunities to get involved.

Las Vegas. Beyond the strip, Las Vegas has affordable

Don't worry about slices or hooks! The golf balls on *The World* are ecologically correct "ecoballs" that biodegrade after 4 days; the tees are made from corn and also dissolve.

housing and a reasonable cost of living. About one-third of Las Vegas's population is retired, and there is a good job market. The desert beauty of Red Rock Canyon; boating, swimming, and fishing in Lake Mead; and the Hoover Dam are all a short distance away. Excellent transportation and numerous volunteer opportunities are also available.

Naples. With its 7 miles of beach on Florida's west coast, Naples is upscale and cosmopolitan, with an abundance of arts, entertainment, shopping, activities, and attractions.

Sarasota. As part of Florida's "cultural coast," this shining jewel on the state's west coast is "sophisticated yet laid-back, elegant, fun-loving and dedicated to the arts," according to its Web site.

Surprise, Arizona. This fast-growing city 19 miles northwest of Phoenix offers two active-adult communities especially good for singles: Arizona Traditions (www.aztraditions.com or 800-226-9214) and Del Webb

Sun City Grand (www.delwebb.com or 800-341-6121).

RV living is another possibility for singles. Approximately 10 percent of people in RV parks are single, so this could be an option if this type of living appeals to you. If you're a single woman, there is an organization especially for you: Rving Women, which has about 5,000 members (www.rvingwomen.com or 888-55Rving).

In general, if you're single, you might consider active-adult communities with their organized activities and/or gated communities for safety. Also, and perhaps most important, remember that a positive mental attitude will contribute to your enjoyment—wherever you decide to live!

THROWBACK COMMUNITIES

Three housing trends reflected in some new communities are throwbacks to decades-old styles of living: communal living, multigenerational (also called intergenerational) living, and new urbanism. All three of these

---

AOL Digital City (www.digitalcity.com) ranked the best cities for singles. Their top 10 for 2002: St. Louis, Missouri; Columbus, Ohio; Chicago; Atlanta; Cleveland; Detroit; Baltimore; Twin Cities, Minnesota; Milwaukee; and Las Vegas. Several criteria were used, including cultural opportunities, clubs, bars, and recommendations of AOL Digital City employees and visitors to their Web site.

"so old they're new" communities are designed to foster a sense of community, strengthen family or family-like ties, and encourage interaction among residents.

Communal Living/Cohousing

The commune concept is back! Now called cohousing, collaborative housing, or communal living, there are about 150 of these communities either completed, in development, or forming in the United States and Canada. This style of living was conceived in Denmark in the 1960s. Authors Kathryn McCamant and Charles Durrett, in the journal *In Context* (1989), describe four main characteristics of cohousing.

1. Participatory process: Residents organize and participate in the planning and design process for the development and are responsible as a group for all final decisions.
2. Intentional neighborhood design: The physical design itself encourages a strong sense of community.
3. Extensive common facilities: The common area is designed for daily use, to supplement private living areas.
4. Complete resident management: Residents—renters and owners alike—manage the development, making decisions of common concern at community meetings.

Who might consider this type of lifestyle? The average cohousing community is fairly small, often comprised of approximately 30 single-family homes, though some communities are larger and some are smaller. Thus, close-knit living would obviously have to be an attraction for you. In addition, if you enjoy sharing activities such as dining and laundry, *really* want to get to know your neighbors, and like the idea of being strongly involved in the decision-making process of shaping your community, this might be for you.

If this kind of living intrigues you, here are a few of the approximately 60 completed (or almost completed) places to check out.

East Lake Commons (www.eastlakecommons.org or 404-377-4893), 5 miles east of downtown Atlanta, was completed in 2001. It has 20 wooded acres, and according to its Web site, East Lake Commons is "designed to fulfill ideals of social diversity and environmental sustainability." A two-bedroom/one-and-one-half-bath townhouse was advertised for $175,000, and a one-bedroom apartment was renting for $600 per month.

Eno Commons (919-309-7924), in Durham, North Carolina, is a 22-home cohousing community on 11.2 acres. Of note is that homes are heated and cooled by geothermal heat pumps. A typical three-bedroom/two-bath home sells for $189,000.

Manzanita Village (www.manzanitavillage.com or 928-445-3015), still under construction in Prescott, Arizona, will have 36 homes on 12.5 acres. There are only a few homesites remaining, and home prices range from $150,000 to $275,000. There is a Common House ("the hub of the community"), and a "one-time allocation" charge of $10,000 for the first adult and $3,000 for additional adults in the same unit.

Multigenerational Living

How about having the whole gang living in the same neighborhood? Some developers are capitalizing on a trend of retirees wishing not only to have the swimming pool, golf course, and other resort amenities in a warm weather setting, but also the children and grandchildren. According to the Census Bureau, about 35 million Americans move each year, often separating relatives from one another. More than 30 percent of people no longer reside in the state where they were born. These are statistics some people are anxious to change. If you're interested in this "all in the family" approach to living, here are a few places worth considering.

Anthem by Del Webb (www.delwebb.com or 888-717-9777) is situated in the foothills of the Sonora Desert, 40 miles north of Phoenix. This master-planned community located on 5,800 acres is 2 years old, with 2008 as the projected completion date for approximately 12,000 residences. Recent asking prices range from $210,000 to $360,000. The community includes schools, water slides, rock-climbing walls, shopping centers, medical facilities, and community services.

Pelican Point (www.livethepoint.com or 877-735-7646) is located in Gonzales, Louisiana, between Baton Rouge and New Orleans. This is a master-planned, 800-acre multigenerational community of custom-built homes, patio/garden homes, and townhouses, with lot prices ranging from under $50,000 to $80,000, single-family homes from the $220,000s, garden homes beginning in the $160,000s, and townhomes starting below $200,000. There is also a 55-and-over adult community, The Greens, located within the community. Golf, parks,

---

**For a list of cohousing communities within the United States,
go to www.cohousing.org.**

playgrounds, and tennis courts are included in the amenities.

U.S. Homes, part of the Lennar Corporation (www.lennar.com or 305-559-4000), has multigenerational communities in Florida, California, and Texas. Prices range from under $200,000 to the high $600,000s and above. The communities offer a diversity of housing styles and amenities.

New Urbanism

Would you like to live, play, and work (if you're considering working!) all in the same place? If so, new urbanism (with its neo-traditional or traditional neighborhoods) may be for you. This style shares several principles: It is pedestrian friendly, which reduces residents' need for cars; offers a mix of shopping, homes, and offices; offers a variety of architecturally interesting housing designs with homes close to the street and lots of porches; and features narrow roads. New urbanism stresses increased density so that most everything is within a 10-minute walk. A neo-traditional neighborhood will have a well-defined edge to it—no "bleeding" into the next town or neighborhood. Its supporters claim the creation of compact, integrated villages fosters a sense of community, is environmentally friendly, raises the standard of living, and provides a better quality of life.

This type of neighborhood (old new urbanism!) can be found around the world in places like Capri, Venice, and Florence. In the United States, cities such as Annapolis, Maryland; Alexandria, Virginia; Saint Augustine, Florida; and Washington, D.C. reflect this type of configuration. There are approximately 150 of these neo-traditional neighborhoods either built or being developed in the United States. Sample towns that exemplify new urbanism include:

AQUA Allison Island (www.aqua.net or 305-867-5700). This is an 8.5-acre gated community on the tip of 40-acre Allison Island, just north of South Beach, Miami. Although not considered a "true" new urbanism neighborhood (because it will be gated), it has many of the other hallmarks of this type of community: a pedestrian-friendly layout, interesting architecture, and small parks interspersed throughout the 46 island homes and more than 100 condos. Prices begin at around a half million dollars and escalate. A promenade on the periphery of the island will allow all residents access to Indian Creek, part of the Intracoastal Waterway.

Celebration, Florida (www.celebrationfl.com or 877-696-TOWN). Just south of Orlando, Celebration is now a decade old. Developed by the Disney Corporation, it really sparked the new urbanism movement in the United States. A total of 12,000 residents is expected by completion of the community. Housing possibilities include apartments, terrace homes, bungalows, garden homes, cottage homes, townhomes, village homes, and estate homes. Prices range from the $170,000s to over $1 million. (One of us thought it was the perfect community; the other thought it was too "Stepford-like.")

Civano, in Tucson, Arizona (www.civano.com or 888-224-8266). For those looking for new urbanism combined with ecologically friendly living in the Sonoran Desert, Civano has 818 acres consisting of three neighborhoods integrated with commercial property. Neighborhood One will have approximately 650 homes, with a projected build-out in 2006; Neighborhoods Two and Three, developed by Pulte Homes, will have a total of 1,000 to 1,500 homes with an anticipated build-out around 2012. Homes reflecting Southwest-style architecture will range from the mid-$100,000s to the high $200,000s and will be engineered to use half the heating and cooling energy typically used by a home of similar size.

Habersham (www.habershamsc.com or 877-542-2377). Located 8 minutes from Beaufort, South Carolina, 30 minutes from Hilton Head Island, South Carolina, and 1 hour from Charleston, South Carolina, and Savannah, Georgia, Habersham's location is great. The Habersham Creek encourages boating, fishing, and swimming. Available homes begin around $310,000, and homesites begin in the $30,000s.

I'On (www.ionvillage.com or 866-330-8200). This is a 243-acre neo-traditional neighborhood in Mount Pleasant, South Carolina, 10 minutes from Charleston. This development, which will ultimately include about 760 homes, began in 1997. Lots begin in the $70,000s, and available homes start around $400,000. Porches are at least 8 feet deep to encourage rocking chair action and socializing with neighbors.

Kentlands and Lakelands in Gaithersburg, Maryland. These adjacent communities have condos, townhomes, main street homes, and single-family homes. Average condo prices are around $140,000, townhome prices are around $270,000, and single-family home prices are around $425,000. For more information, call 301-948-2071 (CMC, Kentlands' Management Company) or 240-631-8338 (CMI, Lakelands' Management Company).

Seaside (www.seasidefl.com or 866-891-4600). This is where the new urbanism movement was born. Located on Florida's Panhandle on the Gulf of Mexico, Seaside was the setting for the movie *The Truman Show*. Developed on 80 acres and begun in 1981, Seaside has 430 "cottages," many of which can be rented (for under $200 to over $1,000 per night). Want to purchase a cottage? Sale prices easily range from $1 million and up, with condos, townhomes, and some cottages also available.

SouthWood (www.arvida.com/southwood or 877-305-6365). After breaking ground in Tallahassee, Florida, in 2000, SouthWood is slated to have 4,700 homes on 3,200 acres by 2020. About 550 homes and/or homesites have been sold (as of 2003) in this community that has 1,000 acres of reserved green space, along with a golf course, 12 miles of walking trails, a community center, and a town center. Prices for SouthWood's townhouses and single-family homes begin under $200,000. SouthWood is close to campuses of the state university system, and the community has an Education Village to promote lifelong learning.

Sunset Island. This 37-acre developing neighborhood in Ocean City, Maryland, nudges up against the Assawoman Bay and is 2 blocks from the Atlantic Ocean. A mix of condos, townhomes, and single-family homes makes up this almost-600-unit property. Prices for condos begin in the upper $300,000s; townhomes,

in the upper $400,000s; and single-family homes, in the low $800,000s. A fishing pier, green spaces, a beach, pool, and walking paths are incorporated into the planning. Contact www.sunsetislandocmd.com or the three builders (Main Street Homes, 410-524-1245; NV Homes, 888-348-6060; or Ryan Homes, 888-343-7926).

WaterColor, Rosemary Beach, and WaterSound. These communities are on the same 8-mile stretch of the Florida Panhandle as Seaside. WaterColor encompasses about 500 acres with 1,140 homes; Rosemary Beach is on 119 acres and has a Caribbean influence; and the 256-acre New England-themed WaterSound is in the process of developing its first neighborhood, Bridges, which should be complete by Fall 2004. Some pricing examples: a ⅛ fractional interest in a WaterColor vacation home is about $200,000, and homes go into the millions; resale homesites at Rosemary Beach begin at $245,000, and parkside homes begin in the $700,000s. A Gulf-front home at Rosemary Beach is yours for $5.3 million. For more information, contact WaterColor at www.arvida.com/watercolor.com or 877-459-4537; Rosemary Beach at www.rosemarybeach.com or 800-736-0877; or WaterSound at www.arvida.com/watersound or 888-499-7767.

Windsor (www.windsorflorida.com or 800-233-7656). Nestled between the Indian River and Atlantic Ocean on 416 acres in North Vero Beach, Florida, Windsor will consist of a maximum of 350 homes. Lots range from $300,000 to $3.6 million and homes from $1 million to $8 million. In addition to the usual amenities, Windsor has an equestrian center, polo field, croquet, and a gun club. Many of the homes are second or third homes rather than primary residences.

 Jack C. is a retired partner in an international accounting firm.

About 7 years ago, he and his wife, Eileen, moved to the Kentlands in Gaithersburg, Maryland, from a spacious townhouse in nearby Bethesda. Jack's multiple sclerosis required that the master bedroom be located on the first floor. A ramp in the garage and a deck connecting the sunroom and master bedroom convinced them that the Kentlands was for them. Jack originally was concerned about the closeness of the homes (only 8 feet apart) and the decreased size of their new home, but he and Eileen quickly grew to love the friendliness and social aspects of their

"cozy village" and the proximity of Market Square, which contains the basics for day-to-day living. ⓣ

SPRING-TRAINING TOWNS

Ah, baseball, the great American pastime (although this is now a subject of debate). If you're a die-hard fan of the game, you could consider living where one of the 30 major league baseball teams conducts spring training. By moving to Florida, you could travel to two-thirds of the spring-training sites and also see the Florida Marlins and Tampa Bay Devil Rays at home when the regular season begins. Anne Marie and Joseph A. of Silver Spring, Maryland, were so enamored with their beloved Baltimore Orioles that they purchased a condo in Fort Lauderdale so they wouldn't miss any of the action!

The chart on the next page lists where the major league baseball teams hold spring training.

For schedules, tickets, and restaurant and hotel information regarding spring training, get *Spring Training Magazine* (919-967-2420) or log on to www.spring-trainingmagazine.com. Batter up!

Team	Spring Training Location	Box-Office Phone Number
Anaheim Angels	Tempe, AZ	480-438-9300
Houston Astros	Kissimmee, FL	407-933-2520
Oakland Athletics	Phoenix, AZ	602-392-0217
Toronto Blue Jays	Dunedin, FL	727-733-0429
Atlanta Braves	West Disney World, FL	407-939-1500
Milwaukee Brewers	Maryvale, AZ	623-245-5500
St. Louis Cardinals	Jupiter, FL	561-775-1818
Chicago Cubs	Mesa, AZ	480-964-4467
Tampa Bay Devil Rays	St. Petersburg, FL	888-FAN-RAYS
Arizona Diamondbacks	Tucson, AZ	520-434-1111
Los Angeles Dodgers	Vero Beach, FL	561-569-6858
Montreal Expos	Jupiter, FL	561-775-1818
San Francisco Giants	Scottsdale, AZ	480-990-7972
Cleveland Indians	Winter Haven, FL	863-291-5803
Seattle Mariners	Peoria, AZ	623-878-4337
Florida Marlins	Viera, FL	321-633-9200
New York Mets	Port St. Lucie, FL	561-871-2115
Baltimore Orioles	Ft. Lauderdale, FL	954-776-1921
San Diego Padres	Peoria, AZ	623-878-4337
Philadelphia Phillies	Clearwater, FL	727-442-8496
Pittsburgh Pirates	Bradenton, FL	941-748-4610
Texas Rangers	Port Charlotte, FL	941-625-9500
Cincinnati Reds	Sarasota, FL	941-954-4464
Boston Red Sox	Ft. Myers, FL	941-334-4700
Colorado Rockies	Tucson, AZ	520-327-9467
Kansas City Royals	Davenport, FL	863-424-2500
Detroit Tigers	Lakeland, FL	686-688-8075
Minnesota Twins	Tampa, FL	941-768-4279
Chicago White Sox	Tucson, AZ	520-434-1111
New York Yankees	Tampa, FL	813-879-2244

WATER, WATER EVERYWHERE

Looking to live on the water, but on a smaller scale than *The World of ResidenSea* or the proposed *Freedom Ship*? If you love the water, aren't susceptible to motion sickness, and think traveling where and when you'd like would be heaven, entertain the notion of trading in your home and car for a boat. Financial aspects of "living aboard" vary widely, as maintenance costs, insurance, and fees to dock your boat expand dramatically as the size of the vessel increases. Resources include Living Aboard (www.livingaboard.com or 800-355-5313; they also have a magazine); the Seven Seas Cruising Association (www.ssca.org or 954-463-2431); and books on the topic.

We've explored some niche retirement lifestyles, and the previous chapter looked at particular places within the United States, but if you want to consider relocating outside the USA, then the next chapter is for you!

Sailing Glossary

Tack: good manners

Heave to: What seasick sailors do

Rudder: More discourteous, as in "Bob was rude, but George was even rudder."

B.O.A.T.: Break out another thousand

WHERE SHOULD YOU MOVE?

Recommended Locations outside the United States

"Successful retirement depends on what you retire to, not from."
—Dr. David J. Demko, Age Venture News, www.demko.com

Approximately four million Americans live abroad, but how many people *retire* to another country? It's a good question, for which there is no definitive answer. The Social Security Administration sends about 400,000 Social Security checks out of the country each month, although it's estimated that many additional Americans living abroad have their checks deposited directly into a U.S. financial institution.

Perhaps the more important question is *why* consider relocating and retiring outside the United States? For many, money is a big incentive. Living in a low-cost-of-living country can stretch your retirement dollars. For others, becoming immersed in a different culture is exciting, becoming proficient in another language is enticing, and living in a locale with perfect weather and a laid-back approach to life is attractive. Some people feel safer escaping a high-crime area in the States, or they are intrigued by the novel recreational and cultural opportunities a new place has to offer. Many people who retire overseas have had positive experiences through travel, work, or study abroad. Others are ready to embrace a completely new way of life during the second half of their lives. The shrinking of the world through communications, computers, and improved transportation makes living abroad a more attainable possibility for many.

If having a home in another country sounds like a good idea, you'll need to prioritize your preferences and needs, suggests Kathleen Peddicord, publisher of *International Living* magazine. Think about these factors when considering another country: proximity to North America; cost of living; language barriers, if any; tax ramifications; recreational/cultural amenities; safety and political stability; medical care; climate; infrastructure (communications, roads, etc.); and special incentives for those who relocate. For example, if you never want to see another snowflake in your life, that would help narrow your list of possible locations. If you plan to stay only for several years and are in good health, top-notch, nearby health care may drop to the bottom of your list.

Some additional points to think about when contemplating another country for relocation:

Your personality. This may be the biggest issue. Remember, you're moving to another country, one with its own concepts of time, social interactions, politics, and ways of doing things. You can't expect the experience to be like moving to another area of the United States. If you're a "type A" personality, easily frustrated when appointments and schedules aren't kept, moving outside the United States—particularly to a Latin or southern European country that honors the tradition of an afternoon siesta—could be frustrating. (Of course, if that's your personality, living *in* the United States is probably frustrating as well!)

Health care. In general, health care tends to be less expensive in foreign countries. Doctors' visits, prescriptions, and hospitalization can cost less than comparable U.S. medical care. In many cases, however, your medical insurance will not be honored outside of the United States, and Medicare does not cover you overseas. You'll need to find out whether the insurance available in the country you're relocating to will serve your needs and whether you're eligible for low-cost government health plans; you might also be able to obtain national coverage in conjunction with private insurance. Some

---

To compare the costs of moving to other countries, try the international cost of living calculator at www.homefair.com (click on "Cost-of-Living Comparisons," then on "International Cities").

countries, such as Denmark, have a socialized health plan that will cover you once you've lived as a full-time resident for a set number of months. If you need to purchase some kind of international health insurance, consider Allnation Insurance Company (www.allnation.com or 800-342-0719), BUPA International (www.bupa-intl.com or 44-0-1273-208-181), or Health Insurance 4 Expatriates (www.health-insurance-4-expatriates.com or 877-982-522). As with all insurance policies, there are exclusions, deductibles, and different levels of coverage, so be sure to read the fine print before signing up. You may also want to include medical-evacuation coverage, which will cover transportation to an appropriate medical facility—even to the United States, if necessary. Health care quality can be excellent or poor (often within the same country); this is an important area to research.

Money matters. If your income and assets are in dollars, the amount available to you to spend will be tied to the exchange rate of your newly adopted country. If the dollar is strong, your purchasing power will also be strong; if the dollar is weak, your financial base will be weakened. You may want to set up a bank account at a local institution and keep several months' worth of expenses in that country's legal tender as a hedge against currency swings. Although you may be living outside of the United States, you are still responsible for filing U.S. federal tax returns because you are still a United States citizen—which, don't forget, also entitles you to U.S. Embassy privileges abroad. (Even if you renounce your U.S. citizenship—which we are not advocating!—you are still subject to the U.S. tax code for an additional decade after renunciation because the IRS will assume you are trying to avoid your tax liability.) You may also have to pay taxes in the new country as well. In some cases, you may be eligible for tax credits, deductions, or exclusions under U.S. and international tax laws. If you're seriously considering a move to a par-

---

If cost of living is your *primary* criterion for relocating, you'll be interested in Mercer Human Resource Consulting's 2003 ranking of 144 cities. The cheapest cities in the world include Asuncion, Paraguay; followed by Harare, Zimbabwe; Bogotá, Columbia; Buenos Aires, Argentina; and Blantyre, Malawi. Tokyo, Japan, ranked as the most costly.

ticular place, your best bet is to meet with both a tax professional in the new country who has expertise working with expatriate Americans and a U.S. tax planner with expertise in international tax. The four major U.S. accounting firms—Ernst & Young LLP, PricewaterhouseCoopers, KPMG LLP, and Deloitte & Touche LLP—are good resources. When determining your budget for living in the new country, don't forget to plan for trips back to the United States.

Legalities. What type of visa or residency permit is required? Can you become a citizen? How do you (and can you?) finance and purchase real estate? (This is a huge issue—people have lost their homes or have had to repurchase them due to changing political winds.) What about a work permit if you'd like to start your own business or get a job? What are the requirements for a driver's license? Can you take your pet with you? To help answer these questions, contact the embassy of the country where you're considering relocating or its closest consulate. "Foreign Consular

Offices in the United States" is available from the U.S. Government Printing Office (212-512-1800). You can also contact the U.S. Department of State Bureau of Consular Affairs at 202-647-4000. They produce a number of helpful pamphlets and provide assistance to those considering moving outside the United States and to those already living outside the United States.

Before deciding on a place to live, learn as much as you can about the country: Contact expatriates (U.S. citizens living in the places you're interested in), talk to a number of real estate agents, view actual properties to get the lowdown on where to live, and rent for several months to get a real feel for the place. Remember, different times of the year can feel distinctly different. Hurricane season in September may make you forget about those warm, sunny days in February when you knew your old neighbors back in Boston were digging out from under a nor'easter!

Countries with large numbers of U.S. citizens fre-

A helpful Web site, www.embassyworld.com, provides links to all U.S. embassies, foreign embassies, and consulates throughout the world. Many issues are addressed, from culture to employment to real estate to weather.

quently have a U.S. Chamber of Commerce or organizations or clubs for Americans that can provide information. The Department of State produces data sheets on every country called "Consular Information Sheets"; they include topics such as geography, government structure, safety, entry requirements, medical information, and real estate purchasing requirements. Of course, many books and magazine articles have been written about living in other countries; see the reference list for this chapter for some suggestions. To "talk" to expatriates over the Internet, try these Web sites: www.liveabroad.com, www.expatexchange.com, and www.expatforum.com. The Association of Residents of Costa Rica has developed a list of questions you should ask if you're considering locating to a foreign country. Their valuable "Relocation Checklist" is located on page 443.

Which countries outside the United States are best? Of course, "best" is a subjective term, but *International Living* publishes a yearly Quality of Life Index that attempts to quantify countries' infrastructures, health care, climates, costs of living, safety, freedom, and other important considerations. Their 2003 list ranks 194 countries; the top 10 include the United States (highest quality of life), followed by Australia, France, New Zealand, Canada, Denmark, Austria, Finland, Malta, and Germany. *International Living* also publishes an annual Global Retirement Index that not only considers the important factors one should consider if relocating, but also weighs "special benefits" (such as incentives for retirees) and real estate prices and ease of purchase fairly heavily—these two categories make up 35 percent of a country's ranking. *International Living*'s 2003 index ranks 29 countries; the top 10 include Panama, Malta, Australia, France, Canada, New Zealand, Cyprus, Mexico, Nicaragua, and Greece. (As a frame of reference, they rated the United States 28th). Needless to say, these lists are colored by the reviewers' biases, as is any list of what is "best," including ours throughout this book!

Now that you're aware of some of the particulars involved in moving to another country, let's take a look at a few specific desirable locations, as well as issues unique to each, such as how to purchase property, become a resident, and access health care. Based on our own Western slant, we suggest three countries to consider if you'd like to retire abroad: Canada, Costa Rica, and Mexico. Let's take a closer look.

CANADA

Capital: Ottawa

Population (July 2003): 32,207,113

Natural Resources: Nickel, copper, silver, zinc, iron ore, lead, potash, petroleum, diamonds, timber, coal, natural gas

Industries: Wood, paper, food, fish products, minerals, petroleum, natural gas, chemicals

Canada

REPORT CARD

Overall Rating:	B
Climate:	C
Cost of Living:	B
Health Care:	B
Transportation:	B
What's to Do:	B

"O Canada" is the name of this country's national anthem, but it may be what you appreciatively sigh as you experience the beauty of this land, the friendliness of its people, and its competitive cost of living.

At almost 4 million square miles, Canada is the second largest country (after Russia) by size, but it has about the same number of people—32 million—as California! Contrast this with the United States at 3.6 million square miles and a population of 290 million. Most of Canada's population (about 85 percent) is concentrated along its border with the United States, and the

---

International Living magazine ranks Canada fifth in its 2003 Quality of Life Index and fifth in its 2003 Global Retirement Index.

most-populated province is Ontario. There are close to two million (that's not a misprint!) lakes in Canada, and it boasts the longest coastline of any country in the world. Canada is divided into three arctic territories (Northwest Territories, the Yukon, and Nunavut) and 10 provinces (from the west to the east, they are British Columbia and Alberta; Saskatchewan and Manitoba; Ontario and Quebec; and New Brunswick, Labrador/ Newfoundland, Nova Scotia, and Prince Edward Island). In addition, each province and territory has its own capital city.

The topography of Canada varies from lowlands to mountains, and the climate ranges from temperate to arctic. Canada's large landmass encompasses six time zones. The country's government consists of a constitutional monarchy (Queen Elizabeth II is the chief of state and is presently represented by Governor General Adrienne Clarkson) along with a democratic parliament made up of the House of Commons (which has elected members) and a Senate (appointed members). The actual head of the government is the prime minister. Canada's economy is similar to our own; there is a high standard of living in this high-tech society, with an educated, skilled labor force and a great abundance of natural resources. The literacy rate (defined as the percentage of the population age 15 or older able to read and write) is 97 percent (same as in the United States).

Almost three-quarters of the labor force is involved in the service industry, with manufacturing, construction, and agriculture the other primary occupations. The Canadian dollar (CAD) is the official currency.

Who Lives in Canada?

The people of Canada are a diverse group, with 28 percent of British Isle descent, 23 percent of French origin, 15 percent from other European countries, 2 percent indigenous peoples, 26 percent of mixed background, and 6 percent of mostly Asian, Arab, or African descent. Almost half the population is Roman Catholic; Protestants make up about one-third of the total, and a

---

Though we often call Canada our "neighbor to the north," more than half of the U.S. states have at least a portion of their land north of Canada's most southern point, Point Pelee, which is about 40 miles southeast of Detroit!

variety of religions comprise the remainder. English and French are both official languages of Canada, with about 60 percent of the population having English as its mother tongue, and 23 percent claiming French. The median age is 38 years, and about 13 percent of the population is over 65.

What's It Like Outside?

This is tricky, since Canada covers such a huge area. Unless you're really into cold weather we *wouldn't* recommend the North, which has arctic and subarctic conditions—you'd have to like permafrost to consider living there! The two areas in Canada we would recommend for possible relocation or a second home would be either the west coast or the Nova Scotia area of the east.

For example, on the west coast, Victoria, British Columbia, experiences mild summers and winters, little snowfall, and an average rainfall of 27 inches per year (compared to New York's 50 inches of rain per year).

Average temperatures range from 44 degrees Fahrenheit in the winter to a delightful 71 degrees during the summer months.

Nova Scotia (latin for "New Scotland") has a climate that varies from place to place. The Atlantic Ocean helps moderate the climate; the average high summer temperature in southwestern Nova Scotia (the warmest part of the province) is about 72, with an average summer low of 54 degrees. Winter averages 25 degrees (which is 9 degrees warmer than Maine's winter average). Rainfall averages approximately 43 inches, and snowfall averages about 8.5 inches. You can expect fog and mist in Nova Scotia as well, and you can't rule out the occasional blizzard or the death throes from a hurricane in late summer or fall.

If you're looking for Florida temperatures, you obviously won't find them here, but many people are surprised at how moderate the seasons can be in certain areas of Canada. The pleasant summers could be a respite for those living in a hot, humid summer location.

Since Canada uses the metric system, it's helpful to know how to convert from Celsius to Fahrenheit. An approximate, easy way is to multiply the temperature in Celsius by 2, then add 30. For example, if it's 20 degrees Celsius, that would be about 70 degrees Fahrenheit.

What's the Cost?

The U.S. dollar has been strong against the Canadian dollar for the past several years. As a general rule of thumb, multiply Canadian dollars by .75 (the exchange rate as of January 2004) to get the amount of money you would pay in American dollars. For example, a home that costs $300,000 Canadian would translate to $225,000 American. Conversely, if you'd like to know the Canadian price, multiply the amount in U.S. dollars by 1.33. Thus, an item that costs $150 USD would cost about $200 CAD.

Canadians have less disposable income than Americans. According to KN&V, chartered accountants in British Columbia (www.knv.com or 800-761-7772), the 2003 marginal income tax rate for Canadians is higher at virtually all taxable income levels than the U.S. rate. The data from KN&V compared the marginal tax rates for a single person living in Washington State to the rates for a single Canadian living in British Columbia, with taxable incomes ranging from $5,700 to $313,000 USD. Of course, Americans who move to Canada will be paying those Canadian tax rates as well!

On the other hand, Canada's national health plan covers doctors' visits and hospitalization. Once you are an eligible resident, you can enjoy those services as well. The funding for this "free" service comes from—what else?—taxes! We've also been regaled with stories of how drug prices in Canada are less expensive because the Canadian government controls prescription prices, so you may save on costs there as well.

According to the Residential Multiple Listing Service, the average price of a home for the first half of 2003 in all of Canada was $151,000 USD. For the same period, the average price of a home in British Columbia was $189,000 USD; in Nova Scotia, it was $104,000 USD.

Both Canada and the United States have high standards of living. The bottom line is that people are paying for that standard through taxes one way or another. Don't consider moving to Canada solely as a cost-cutting measure—it won't work.

What about Property Ownership?

The good news is that there are no restrictions if you are a foreigner and wish to purchase property in Canada. If you purchase real estate as a nonresident, however (doesn't

---

In 2002, per capita personal income in Canada was $20,450 USD compared to $30,832 in the States.

there always seem to be a "however"?), you may still be considered a resident by Canada for income tax purposes.

In order to determine if you are a "resident" for income tax purposes in Canada, be sure to seek the assistance (prior to purchase) of qualified legal counsel both in the United States and in Canada to ensure the best tax position. If you decide to sell property in Canada, seek expert help to guide you through the U.S. and Canadian tax mazes.

What's to Do?

We could never do justice describing the activities of an entire country, so we'll look just at the two areas of Canada we're recommending: parts of British Columbia and several places in Nova Scotia. Since it's our opinion that it's nice to be somewhat close to city amenities, we'll discuss several of the major cities in British Columbia and Nova Scotia, then give examples of what the area in general has to offer.

Vancouver, one of the major cities in British Columbia, qualifies as one of the most picturesque cities in the world. With a backdrop of the glittering Pacific Ocean and coastal mountain ranges, this cosmopolitan city boasts scenic beauty, more than 100 museums and art galleries, performing arts centers, the 1,000-acre Stanley Park, golf, whale-watching, fishing, beautiful beaches, kayaking, international cuisine, good shopping, and heck, there's even a rainforest and skiing nearby! The Vancouver Canadians (minor league baseball), Vancouver Canucks (hockey), B.C. Lions (Canadian Football League—a bit different from the NFL!), and the Ravens (lacrosse) are some of Vancouver's sports teams. Whistler Blackcomb has won numerous awards as a skiing destination. It's a 75-mile drive from Vancouver on the incredibly scenic Sea to Sky Highway. There's a population of about 550,000 in the city and two million in the greater metro area. Vancouver has a mild climate, and most of its 49 annual inches of rain falls between October and March. In addition, the 16 hours of sunlight in the summer months provide plenty of time to enjoy this fabulous city.

Victoria, located on Vancouver Island, is the capital of British Columbia and enjoys the sunniest and mildest

---

Environics Research, a Canadian company, found that almost 90 percent of Canadians feel their quality of life is superior to that of United States citizens.

climate in Canada. The city abounds in restored or preserved Victorian (what else?) architecture and is pedestrian and people friendly. Next to San Francisco, Victoria has the most restaurants per capita in North America. The Royal B.C. Museum, the Maritime Museum of British Columbia, the Astrophysical Observatory, University of Victoria, live theater, the symphony, opera, golf, fishing, boating, hiking, parks, and beachcombing are enjoyed by tourists and the 300,000 residents of Victoria and the surrounding area. And we mustn't forget the flowers, flowers, flowers! Victoria is known as "Canada's Best Blooming City" for good reason. Grab a White Spot burger, and enjoy all this charming city has to offer.

Nanaimo is located on the east coast of Vancouver Island, 70 miles north of Victoria, and is a growing harbor city of approximately 80,000 people. Originally a coal-mining town, Nanaimo is now the second-largest city (after Victoria) on Vancouver Island and serves as the hub for the central and northern portions of the island.

It is a major ferry base for access to the mainland, and its growth is reflected in new housing (prices are lower than in Victoria), health care and retail additions, and increased community amenities. The mountainous area provides some great views, and all residents have access to the water via public paths. Go swimming at Qualicum Beach, just north of Nanaimo, take a class at Malaspina University-College, or take in a show at the 800-seat Performing Arts Theater.

Besides Victoria and Nanaimo, Vancouver Island itself has a lot to recommend it. There are a number of spectacular gardens, the most famous being the Butchart Gardens. You may also want to visit a winery, ski at Mount Washington or Mount Cain Alpine Resort, or learn about the First Nations culture by exploring a place such as Duncan, the "City of Totems." Access to Vancouver Island is via ferry, floatplane, helicopter, or boat from the mainland; this may be regarded as a plus or a minus.

Of course, in the majestic setting of British Columbia, all manner of outdoor activities are available. According

---

Vancouver tied (with Vienna and Geneva) for second of 215 cities worldwide in a quality of life survey by Mercer Human Resource Consulting in 2003. (In case you're wondering, Zurich was number one.)

to *Scuba Diving* magazine, British Columbia is among the best places for SCUBA diving in North America.

Switching to the East Coast, Halifax is the attractive capital of Nova Scotia. It's known as Canada's "smart city" because the greater Halifax area has the most colleges per capita in North America, and more than 55 percent of its residents have a degree beyond the high school level. More than 100 ethnic groups make up this diverse harbor city and its environs of 350,000 people, home to about 40 percent of Nova Scotia's population. Visit the Maritime Museum of the Atlantic or Halifax Citadel National Historic Site, or stroll the downtown's rehabilitated waterfront, with its casino, outdoor dining, shopping, and festivals. Point Pleasant Park, the Public Gardens, or one of the many art galleries will provide a calm counterpoint to the vibrant nightlife. Of course, being a harbor city, all things water related are popular as well.

You'll find other attractions in Nova Scotia as well. Cape Breton Highlands National Park is a feast for the eyes (assuming it's not foggy!); visit the historic reconstructed French fort in Louisbourg, descend into a coal mine in Sydney Mines, snap pictures at Peggy's Cove, stroll around postcard-perfect villages, golf, and eat lots of right-off-the-boat lobster.

What about Employment?

Unemployment in Canada was 7.4 percent in December 2003 (compared to the U.S. average at that time of 5.7 percent). Canada's primary industries include agriculture, fishing and trapping, forestry and logging, energy, construction, manufacturing, utilities, and the service sector. You can certainly be employed in Canada; in fact, having a job or being employable is highly desirable if you're thinking about emigrating from the United States. If you're seeking temporary employment, you'll generally need a work permit (though there are exclusions, such as for performing artists, public speakers, athletes, clergy, news reporters, and military personnel). Work permits are issued through Citizenship and Immigration Canada.

If you want a really unusual outdoor activity, try storm-watching. During the fall and winter months, watch the Pacific (from a safe vantage point, of course) do her thing as wild, 8-foot waves and intense winds assault the western coastline of Vancouver Island.

If you're looking for a long-term position, see the next section for more details!

What about Immigration Requirements?

Canada does not have a "retirement" category for those interested in immigrating. There are three basic classes of immigration to Canada: skilled worker class (you must have the desirable skills and education); business class (you must be able to become economically viable by becoming an investor, entrepreneur, or self-employed worker); or family class (you must be sponsored by a relative, family member, or common-law partner). To move to Canada, you must qualify in one of these categories. How do you find out if you're eligible?

Citizen and Immigration Canada (CIC) is the organization that evaluates applications and facilitates the process of immigration. Their Web site (www.cic.gc.ca) describes the various immigration classes in detail, fees, where to apply, and how to download guides and forms. If you don't have access to a computer, contact the Canadian embassy in Washington, D.C. (202-682-1740) for assistance.

Another method is to contact a law office in Canada that specializes in immigration and get a sense as to whether your background may qualify you to move to Canada. For example, www.immigration.ca allows you to complete a free assessment online and then e-mails you a report indicating your chances of being able to immigrate to Canada. One of the authors did this and was advised that she was "qualified to apply for Canadian permanent residence." Of course, this doesn't mean she *would* be able to retire to Canada; it only means she met enough of the criteria to be considered.

If you're interested in purchasing a second home in Canada, you may stay there for up to 6 months per year as a visitor without going through the immigration process. This is certainly something to consider, since you could enjoy the climate and beauty of the country during

---

Quebec and Manitoba have their own additional immigration guidelines, so if you're interested in relocating to these specific provinces, check out www.immigration-quebec.ouv.qc.ca/anglais/index.html (Quebec) and www.gov.mb.ca/labour/index.html (Manitoba). Also, if you're considering Quebec, it would be a good idea to brush up on your French!

its best months. Seeking residency will not affect your U.S. citizenship.

Where Are Some Notable Neighborhoods?

As we noted before, we would recommend two areas in particular to think about if you're considering Canada for retirement or a second home: the west (British Columbia) and the east (Nova Scotia).

If climate is the biggest consideration, "go west, young man" (or woman), as the journalist Horace Greeley liked to say. Although housing prices are higher in British Columbia than in Nova Scotia, the better climate may more than compensate for the extra cash you'll have to spend. Specifically, several places we have visited are worth looking into. All of these are located on Vancouver Island; the one caveat is that to take your car to Vancouver Island, you need to take a ferry—there are no roads connecting the island and mainland. This could be an issue for some, especially if you're a "type A" personality, don't like schedules, and like to be in control of your time. With that said, however, you may want to check out these places on Vancouver Island in British Columbia.

Longwood (Nanaimo). An attractive condominium community, with two-bedroom units for less than $150,000 USD. Amenities include a clubhouse, underground parking, and storage lockers. Contact 800-878-0588.

Arbutus Ridge (between Victoria and Nanaimo). This is a spectacular community that bills itself as a "seaside adult village"—at least one person must be 50 years of age. Many of the homesites have fabulous water views of Satellite Channel, with homes nestled in the hills. Arbutus Ridge offers golf, and you can also drive your golf cart to explore the Village Centre, boat ramp and dock, heated swimming pool, tennis, and fitness center. There are close to 700 residences in this 300-acre gated community, as well as almost a mile of waterfront. Prices range from $250,000 to $1 million USD. For more information, contact www.arbutusridge.com or 250-743-3000.

Fairwinds (north of Nanaimo in Nanoose Bay). The Fairwinds community is more than 1,300 acres with a golf

---

More Canadians move to the United States than vice versa; in 2001, close to 6,000 Americans moved to Canada, while 30,000 Canadians moved to the United States.

course, 360-berth marina, dining room, and the Fairwinds Centre with pool, fitness facilities, billiards, meeting rooms, and more. Purchase a homesite or home at Fairwinds through a builder. An example is Arbutus Hills or Observatory Point by Intracorp. Homes start at about $180,000 USD; homesites, around $70,000. For more information, check out www.intracorp.ca or 866-469-2799.

Craig Bay (north of Nanaimo in Parksville). Another Intracorp community, Craig Bay is a seaside village with a beach club, tennis, swimming, and library. Detached and semidetached homes sell from around $180,000 USD. See above for Intracorp's contact information.

Now, some specific ideas for Nova Scotia.

Fox Harb'r (Wallace). Located on the north shore of Nova Scotia, the 1,000-acre Fox Harb'r is fewer than 2 hours from Halifax, with gorgeous views of the Northumberland Strait. *Golf Digest* rated the golf course at Fox Harb'r "Canada's Best New Course for 2001." The gated community has a 5,000-foot runway, hangar, deep-water marina, clubhouse, and spa and wellness club. Real estate offerings have moved very slowly since Fox Harb'r has opened, so although the area is scenic and has potential, it's remote and seems somewhat of a gamble at this point. Real estate offerings include half-acre homesites beginning around $180,000 USD, townhomes for about $500,000, and one-quarter-interval ownership opportunities (fully furnished) available in the $150,000-and-up range. Fox Harb'r can be reached at www.foxharbr.com or 866-257-1801.

Chester, Lunenburg, and Mahone Bay. These are examples of quaint, picture-perfect harbor towns on the south shore of Nova Scotia (though sometimes they are hard to see because of the fog!). The farthest of the three towns from Halifax (Lunenburg) is about 60

Another place to consider on Canada's east coast is the new Humber Valley Resort (www.humbervalley.com) in the province of Newfoundland. Located on Deer Lake, with a golf course and clubhouse with amenities, properties are at least 1 acre, and lot prices range from around $98,000 to $300,000 USD; chalet building prices range from $150,000 to $300,000. Temperatures range from winter averages of 23 degrees Fahrenheit to summer temperatures of 80.

miles away. Prices are starting to escalate as both Americans and Canadians are buying up waterfront homes. Examples of recent housing prices: In Chester, the asking price for a 10-year-old, three-bedroom/two-bath 2,500-square-foot ranch with an attached double garage on .75 acres with views of Mahone Bay was $135,000 USD. In Lunenburg, the asking price for a 20-year-old, 2,600-square-foot home with three bedrooms and one and a half baths with an attached single garage with views of Lunenburg Harbor and the golf course was $120,000. And in Mahone Bay, the asking price for a recently renovated 100-year-old home with two bedrooms and one bath within walking distance of town and the wharf was $120,000. Of course, there are homes on private islands and on peninsulas, homes with lots of ocean frontage, etc., that can skyrocket into the millions of dollars (remember that .75 exchange rate rule).

You can find information on Chester through their Municipal Chamber of Commerce (www.chesterns.com or 902-275-4616); contact the town of Lunenburg at www.town.lunenburg.ns.ca/ or 902-634-4410; and contact Mahone Bay at www.mahonebay.com or 888-624-6151.

How Is Canada's Health Care?

Canada's national health care system is largely publicly funded through taxation. The gatekeepers are the primary care physicians who are usually the first point of contact for a patient and initiate referrals and hospital admissions. All eligible residents are given a health insurance card; no forms, deductibles, or co-pays are necessary. The provinces and territories also cover other types of health benefits such as prescriptions, eye care, and such medical equipment as walkers, for certain groups. While the United States leaves about one-third of its citizens without effective health care, the Canadian system theoretically provides for all its citizens. The World Health Organization published a report in 2000 that ranked 191 countries on health care, using criteria such as access, level of care, and cost. According to the WHO, Canada ranked 30th (the United States ranked

---

Lust for learning? Attend one of the almost 100 universities or 175 community colleges throughout Canada.

37th). The United States also had the dubious distinction of the highest per capita expenditure for health care costs among all ranked countries. On two other measures of health care, life expectancy and infant mortality, Canada ranks among the best in the world. If you become a permanent resident of Canada, you can receive health care services.

Because Canadians consider their health care "free," they don't tend to ration their visits as closely as those who pay deductibles and co-pays. As a result, their wait time for a referral to a specialist, to have surgery, or to receive lifesaving treatment is considerably longer than in the United States. The Frasier Institute, an economic think tank in Vancouver, found that the average waiting time from a family physician referral to treatment by a specialist averaged nearly 18 weeks in 2003; specifically, the waiting time for cancer radiation treatment was just over 8 weeks; for cancer surgery, just over 6 weeks; and for orthopedic surgery, 8½ months.

How Safe Is Canada?

The Canadian Centre for Justice Statistics for 2000 reported that the homicide rate is about five times less in Canada than in the United States, and aggravated assault rates are less than half the rate in the States. On the other hand, property crimes such as auto thefts and break-ins were about 30 percent higher in Canada than in the States. Canada's gun control laws are stricter than those in the United States.

Strengths and Weaknesses

We're combining the strengths and weaknesses for Canada, because, as in most of life, beauty (or ugliness) is in the eye of the beholder. The weather is not great (as far as we're concerned), but we realize not everyone wants warm, sunny weather year-round (although we can't figure out why). If you want a definite four seasons with some fog and storms, but also crystal-clear azure skies with low humidity, Canada's weather could be a strength. (And, if you choose to live in the inte-

---

Canada is a country without a death penalty. It's pro-choice, it's opened marriage to gay couples, it believes in a firm separation of church and state, and it is also looking at decriminalizing possession of small amounts of marijuana. If you're a liberal, you'll love it; if not . . .

rior provinces, expect winter temperatures to regularly dip below freezing—without the wind chill factored in!) Immigration to Canada is fairly difficult; the government is looking for educated people who can contribute economically to the country, which you may consider a blessing or a curse. Moving there permanently is not as easy as crossing the border! While the health care system is good, the wait to reap its benefits can be long.

We have to end with four definite strengths: the current exchange rate, lower prescription medicine prices (the government controls these costs), the fact that your U.S. car insurance is good when you're checking out the country as a tourist, and the friendliness of the people!

COSTA RICA

Capital: San José
Population (July 2003): 3,896,092
Natural Resources: Hydropower
Industries: Textiles, clothing, fertilizer, plastic products, construction materials, food processing, microprocessors

Costa Rica's stunning scenery results in its nickname:
"Switzerland of the Americas."

Costa Rica

REPORT CARD

Overall Rating:	B+
Climate:	A
Cost of Living:	A
Health Care:	B+
Transportation:	B-
What's to Do:	B

What country has fantastic weather, gorgeous scenery, a stable democratic government, a high standard of living, relatively low unemployment, a 96 percent literacy rate (defined as the percentage of the 15-and-older population who can read and write), and the highest percentage of Americans in any country outside of the United States? It's Costa Rica.

Costa Rica (Columbus named this country "rich coast") has about four million people in an area a little smaller than the state of West Virginia (just under 20,000 square miles). This Central American country is located between Nicaragua to the north and Panama to the south and is bounded by the north Pacific Ocean on the west and the Caribbean Sea on the east. Although Spanish is the official language, English is very commonly spoken in this highly educated, highly Catholic (more than 75 percent) country.

Costa Rica is a democratic republic with a president, a cabinet chosen by the president, a legislative assembly, and a supreme court. The country is comprised of seven provinces: Alajuela, Cartago, Guanacaste, Heredia, Limon, Puntarenas, and San José.

The international airport in San José makes Costa Rica very accessible from the United States, and major carriers include American, Continental, United, and Delta. The improvements and enhancements to the second major airport, Liberia International, on the Pacific coast, will open up this desirable country even more.

If you already know some Spanish or want to learn it and are ready to think metric, consider Costa Rica!

Who Lives in Costa Rica?

About 94 percent of Costa Ricans are Caucasian (this includes Mestizos, those with Native American-Spanish lineage); African-Americans make up about 3 percent of

---

International Living magazine ranked Costa Rica 52nd out of 194 countries in its 2003 Quality of Life Index.

the population; Chinese people and people indigenous to Costa Rica, about 1 percent each. It's estimated about 30,000 Americans live in Costa Rica. About 20 percent of the population is below the poverty line, compared to 12 percent in the United States (2001 data).

What's It Like Outside?

Costa Rica, located 8 to 11 degrees above the equator, contains coastal plains, rainforests, river valleys, and mountains. Whether you experience the subtropical or tropical climate of Costa Rica is a function of elevation rather than season. The central highlands remain in the 60s and 70s, while the coastal regions vary between the 70s and 80s. The dry season runs from December to April, and the rainy season from May to November. This is a bit simplistic, however, since rainfall can vary from more than 220 inches on the Caribbean coast to fewer than 60 inches in the northern part of the Pacific coast. In the wettest areas, it tends to rain at night.

The country is part of the Pacific "Ring of Fire" and experiences tremors from time to time. Arenal, Irazu, Rincon de la Vieja, Poas, and Tenorio are among Costa Rica's nine active volcanoes, and there are about 60 extinct or dormant volcanoes. The last major earthquake, 7.4 on the Richter scale, was in 1991, killing 27, injuring 400, and leaving 13,000 homeless.

Protected land accounts for almost 30 percent of Costa Rica. With its biodiversity of flora and fauna and its topography, it's an environmentalist's dream.

What's the Cost?

It's not as expensive to live in Costa Rica as it is in the United States, but the difference is not enormous. Housing is more reasonable, although prices have been steadily escalating as more people become aware of Costa Rica as a desirable place to consider for relocation. Prices on the beach can vary substantially, from fairly reasonable to "a bundle."

For some things, such as automobile and boat parts (which may also be harder to get), you will pay more, but the cheaper labor costs result in about the same repair costs as in the States. Cars (new or used) are also pricier.

Costa Rica abolished its army in 1948. It's the only Central American country without one, which is a major source of pride for this peace-loving country.

On the other hand, groceries are only about two-thirds of what you'd pay in America, and you can have a full-time maid for about $250 per month. Utilities, dining out, and lodging are also not as expensive as Up North. Property, corporate, and personal taxes are low, and there is no tax on money earned outside of the country. But the sales tax is a hefty 13 percent.

According to Christopher Howard, author of *The New Golden Door to Retirement and Living in Costa Rica*, a person could live on an income of $1,200 per month—and could live *well* on $2,000 per month. Of course, these numbers depend upon lifestyle choices.

The official currency is the Costa Rican colon, although a double economy with the dollar exists. One dollar equals approximately 390 colons; the currency devalues about 11 percent per year.

What about Property Ownership?

The short answer is "yes, but." Buying property in Costa Rica can be straightforward in some cases, but more complicated and convoluted in others.

There are three main categories of buying and owning property in Costa Rica. "Fee simple" ownership is the most comprehensive type of ownership, where foreigners enjoy the same rights and protections as Costa Rican nationals. Titles are registered in the *Registro Nacional*, along with any liens, judgments, or mortgages. Then there are the properties that are not titled (and have no recordings at the *Registro Nacional*). In some cases, legitimate ownership can be traced back through private documents; in other cases, ownership is basically through "squatter's rights." Most land in Costa Rica is this untitled land, and sifting through the process to establish legitimacy can be difficult. Some real estate professionals caution that these types of properties should be completely avoided.

The third property category is beachfront. Also called Maritime Zone lands or concession properties, they are handled quite differently. Some of this land (the first 50 meters from the "average high tide line") cannot be owned at all; it's public and anyone may use it. The next 150 meters may be "leased" or a concession for it granted, generally for 20-year, renewable periods. The owner may build on the property, assuming he or she obtains the proper permits. Rights may also be transferred.

Don't go to Costa Rica expecting pure white sand beaches; sand colors range from beige to almost black.

One important caveat: Unless you have been a resident for 5 years, you are not allowed to register beach property in your own name. You can, however, register it through a Costa Rican corporation with an agreement with the Costa Rican shareholder(s) that he/she/they will endorse the shares over to you at settlement so that you end up with all the shares; or, a legal trust may be set up by attorneys, accomplishing the same result.

Bottom line: Buying property or having "concessions" or "leases" on beachfront property is not uncommon. Be sure to hire an attorney who specializes in real estate issues to help you maneuver through the purchase of such a significant investment. A good commercial Web site with information on real estate is www.osapeninsula.com.

What's to Do?

Costa Rica is an ecological wonderland and a premiere ecotourism destination. The country has a dozen or so climate zones, and you can travel from rainforest to volcano to savannah to beach in the course of a day. The variety of plant and animal life is astounding, with more than 1,000 species of orchids and butterflies, almost as many bird species, and many different reptiles, amphibians, fish, and mammals. It's estimated that 6 percent of our planet's biodiversity is in Costa Rica! Surfing, whitewater rafting, fishing, kayaking, snorkeling, swimming, sunbathing—all things water related are high on the list of things to do. The bounty of national parks and preserves, volcano-watching, rainforest canopy tours, horseback riding, hiking, and golf help round out the outdoor activities.

You could also take advantage of the universities, colleges, or technological institutes in Costa Rica, including distance education through the Universidad Estatal a Distancia in San José. Classes, however, will almost certainly be taught in Spanish, so make sure your language skills are sharp!

Cultural opportunities exist, but not on a grand scale. There is some live theater, the symphony, several art galleries, and museums. Movie houses, fiestas, casinos, bars, and restaurants are also available. Soccer (called football) is the main sport. There are a number of clubs, including the Rotary, chess, Internet, and singles' clubs for expatri-

---

With a maximum width of 161 miles, you can enjoy a spectacular sunrise and sunset in the same day on different coasts; with more than 700 miles of coastline, a great water view isn't a problem!

ates in Costa Rica, and volunteer activities are plentiful. San José's downtown is compact enough to be pedestrian friendly.

What about Employment?

Unemployment in Costa Rica hovered around 6 percent in 2002. Tourism, agriculture, fishing, forestry, and commerce are the biggest industries. With the recent arrival of a number of multinational companies (MNCs) in Costa Rica, the employment picture has changed. Many MNCs are hiring bilingual or English-speaking employees to work in customer service or call centers that are being established at a rapid pace.

Can you work in Costa Rica? When you first apply for residency, you are usually granted conditional permanent residency; after a specified period of time, you may then apply for permanent resident status. Once you attain this level (it may take 5 years or so), you can live and work in Costa Rica without any restrictions. Many Americans, however, do not want to work at the low wages paid to Ticos (as Costa Ricans are also known), since salaries are much lower than in the States. Prior to obtaining permanent residency status, it is illegal for foreigners to work, unless a Tico can't fill the position. There are many opportunities for volunteer work, though.

What about Immigration Requirements?

If you want to check out Costa Rica for retirement, you can enter the country with a passport and stay for 90 days; if you want to say longer as a tourist, you need to apply for an extension through the Office of Temporary Permits in the Costa Rican Department of Immigration. Requests are evaluated on an individual basis.

If you're seeking residency (which doesn't affect your U.S. citizenship), you need to apply to the Costa Rican Consulate in Washington, D.C., which serves all states as well as the District of Columbia (202-328-6628). It normally takes about 4 months to process residency applications, but it may take as long as a year. Documentation needed as part of this process includes a police certificate of good conduct issued within the last 6 months from the area in which the applicant has lived for the past 2 years, birth certificate, marriage certificate (if applicable), and income certificate. If retired, you must demonstrate that you receive at least $600 per month income from a pension or qualified retirement plan outside of Costa Rica, or from interest and/or dividends from dollars deposited in a Costa Rican government bank. You must reside in Costa Rica at least 4 months a year. This is to meet eligibility requirements in the *pensionado* category. There are additional categories with requirements for residency, including annuitant income status, investor status, and entrepreneur status. For example, with the annuitant or *rentista* status, another common way for retirees to achieve residency in Costa Rica, the person applying for residency must demonstrate that he or she has outside investments that will guarantee a monthly income of $1,000 a month for 5 years. The *rentista* must also live in Costa Rica for at least 6 months a year.

There have been some laws proposed, however, that would remove the *rentista* status and increase the monthly income requirement from $600 to $1,000 for *pensionados* and from $1,000 to $3,000 for *rentistas*. Contact the Costa Rican Consulate for further information.

Where Are Some Notable Neighborhoods?

Certain areas of Costa Rica seem to attract more Americans than others. One popular area is around the capital, San José. The town of Escazu is fewer than 4 miles from downtown San José; Rohrmoser, La Sabana, and Pavas are also located near the city. Santa Ana and Ciudad Colon are a little farther away from San José; Ciudad Colon is an option if you'd like to live halfway between the beach and the city. San José and the surrounding Central Valley area is where you'll find the major services and infrastructure in Costa Rica.

Do you think life really is better at the beach? The Pacific coast is less humid and more populated than the Caribbean coast, so you may want to concentrate your search here. A lot of development is going on as the country gets ready for its share of the close to 80 million retiring American baby boomers. A town to consider on the northwest Pacific coast is Tamarindo, which is located on what is known as Costa Rica's "Gold Coast." In Tamarindo, you'll find a number of activities as well as a regional airport, and Liberia International airport is less than an hour away. There are a number of beaches (*playas*) with growing populations. Playa Hermosa, Playa Flamingo, and

---

A good source of information and help if you're considering Costa Rica is the Association of Residents of Costa Rica (ARCR). For $100 per year (nonresident rate), you receive *El Residente* magazine as well as assistance with legalities, insurance, work permits, real estate advice, social activities, and more. Contact them at www.casacanada.net or 506-233-8068. They also offer free seminars (locations vary) on relocating to Costa Rica.

Playa Grande are all to the north of Playa Tamarindo; Playa Nosaro and Playa Carrillo are to the south. Moving along to the more remote, but beautiful, Nicoya Peninsula, consider Tambor, which is more of a resort community, or perhaps Playa Montezuma. Natural beauty and better access to this area are positioning it to really take off.

The central Pacific coast has Playa Jaco, Playa Herradura, and Manuel Antonio. Playa Jaco is more of a tourist area; since it and Playa Herradura are easily accessible from San José, they are popular beaches, and a good number of Americans live here.

If you possess a pioneer spirit (not to mention a four-wheel-drive vehicle and the zest to live on the wild side), look at the Osa Peninsula, home to Corcovado National Park, which *National Geographic* has called "the most biologically intense place on earth." An 8-hour drive from San José, this area is a feast for the eyes, but it's not for those who need pampering. Puerto Jimenez is a little town in the Osa Peninsula that could do the trick.

As in any other place, housing costs and choices can vary tremendously from location to location. A few examples:

Apartment rentals in the San José suburbs run between $350 and $500 per month. To rent a home would be a few hundred more dollars per month. A spacious condo in Escazu, with a breathtaking view of San José, four bedrooms, four and a half baths, a maid's room, a pool and Jacuzzi, and 24-hour security, built in 2000, is listed for $750,000. A single-family home in Escazu, built in 1969 on .2 acres with four bedrooms, four and a half baths, and a pool has an asking price of $350,000. A new three-bedroom, three-bath home in Santa Ana with a two-car garage is listed for $189,000. Some Pacific coast prices: In Tamarindo, a two-bedroom, two-bathroom townhouse in a gated community lists for $120,000, whereas the asking price for a one-half-acre, five-bedroom, four-bath home with a spectacular view is $1.45 million. Playa Hermosa has a resort area called Los Suenos, which boasts a marina, golf course, beach club, and Marriott Hotel. Outside the resort, but only a short walk to the beach, a two-bedroom, two-bath home lists for $150,000. On the Osa Peninsula, 50 acres in the mountains with an ocean view would cost around $60,000, but beach property would be much more expensive.

From personal experience, we recommend Mike Martin of 77 Realty, a Realtor in Costa Rica who specializes in the area around San José (www.77realty.com or, when calling from the United States, 011-506-289-4802).

If considering a property purchase, be sure there is available water, adequate space for the location of a septic system, access to gravel roads year-round (flooding could be an issue), and that the site is away from lowlands, mangrove swamps, protected areas, and wetlands. You can (and should) haggle over prices. Again, be sure to enlist professional help prior to any real estate purchase and hire a good title company to ensure legitimate ownership rights—real estate fraud is not uncommon.

How Is Costa Rica's Health Care?

One of the many positive aspects of living in Costa Rica is the caliber and affordability of its medical care, including dental care. The health system can be accessed through several avenues. You can go the private, "pay as you go" route for doctors' visits and hospitalization at a much lower cost than you'd find in the States (in the capital of San José, a doctor's visit might cost $40, and a private hospital room averages about $100 per day). For about $50 per month, you can participate in the government-sponsored health plan, CCSS. Although the quality of care is good, the wait for appointments and the abbreviated office visits may not be as much to your liking. There is also government health insurance through Instituto Nacional de Seguro (INS), which is widely accepted by Costa Rica's health care industry. Or, choose a combination of private pay and public access (many doctors have their own private practice in addition to their public service); see doctors at a more leisurely pace for routine visits and pay them out of pocket, but use your coverage for expensive procedures.

The World Health Organization released a study in 2000 that compared health systems in 191 countries based on eight criteria, including cost, access, and level of care. In this list, Costa Rica ranked 36th (the United States ranked 37th).

How Safe Is Costa Rica?

The violent crime rate is low, but muggings and theft do occur. People should exercise the same caution they would in any big city or tourist area: Don't walk alone in deserted areas; don't leave valuables in your car; park in secured lots; patronize licensed taxis; and don't exchange money on the streets (where you are more likely to encounter credit card fraud and/or counterfeit money). Of course, no place is crime-free, so just keep your wits about you.

Costa Rica and the United States have similar infant mortality rates and life expectancies.

Strengths

People are friendly, and Costa Rica is receptive to foreign residents. The nice climate, good standard of living at a lower cost (if you avoid expensive areas and shop locally), stable government, fairly low crime rate, and good medical care all combine to make Costa Rica a real contender for retirement living. Your pets are allowed if you have a veterinary certificate. To drive, you need only your American (or international) driver's license while visiting on a tourist visa; when you obtain residency, you can use your American license to apply for your Costa Rican license. And you *can* drink the water! If you're a nature lover and a person of simple pleasures, Costa Rica could be for you.

Weaknesses

On the other hand, patience is not only a virtue in Costa Rica, it's a requirement. Red tape is a given, and things promised on a certain day may or may not materialize. Your day could be consumed renewing a driver's license, or it may take an hour in line for your turn at the bank. Roads are not very well-maintained—many are unpaved—so watch out for the potholes! It may be difficult to really get to know Costa Ricans, particularly if you don't learn the language and you choose to live in the areas heavily populated by other Americans.

MEXICO

Capital: Mexico City

Population (July 2003): 104,907,991

Natural Resources: Timber, natural gas, petroleum, copper, silver, gold, lead, zinc

Industries: Tourism, tobacco, mining, petroleum, iron, steel, food and beverages, clothing, durable consumer goods

Mexico

REPORT CARD

Overall Rating:	B
Climate:	A-
Cost of Living:	A
Health Care:	B
Transportation:	B
What's to Do:	B

If you're willing to venture outside of the United States for relocation after retirement, you have only to look to the north and south of our country's borders to find some attractive alternatives. We've addressed our northern neighbor, Canada, and a more southerly neighbor, Costa Rica. Now we'll turn our attention, as Frank Sinatra sang, "South of the Border, Down Mexico Way."

Imagine Texas, and then imagine Texas times three. That's about the size of Mexico—around 760,000 square miles. Mexico is bordered by the United States to the north, Belize and Guatemala to the south, the Gulf of Mexico and the Caribbean Sea to the east, and the Pacific Ocean to the west. The population is spread out among this country's rugged mountains, high plateaus, deserts, and lowlands. Depending on location, you can experience desert or tropical conditions. The country has 31 states and one federal district, governed by a president (Vincente Fox since 2000), a supreme court, federal and local courts, and a congress consisting of a senate and federal chamber of deputies.

It's estimated that about 600,000 Americans live in Mexico, which makes it the most popular foreign residence for U.S. citizens. Like Canada, it is reachable by car from the States, and when you add the ease of access to a lower cost of living, delightful weather, scenic beauty, democratic government, rich culture and history, friendly people, laid-back lifestyle, good medical care and infrastructure (DSL is available most places Americans live), and access to most of the goods and services you'd find in the United States, you may have found a winner!

Who Lives in Mexico?

The median age in Mexico is 24, and the population is growing at about 1.5 percent annually. The majority of

---

Mexico is ranked 8th in *International Living* magazine's 2003 Global Retirement Index and 41st in their 2003 Quality of Life Index.

the population (89 percent) is Roman Catholic, while 6 percent are Protestants, the next largest religious group. Ethnic groups include Amerindian-Spanish (60 percent), Amerindian or mostly Amerindian (30 percent), and Caucasian (9 percent). About 5 percent of the population is over 65 years of age, while more than 60 percent is between the ages of 15 and 64.

Culturally, a high value is placed on family life, but there are sharp class divisions, and it's estimated that more than half of Mexico's citizens live in poverty. Life expectancy averages about 72 years (compared to 77 for the United States), with men living an average of 69 years and women, 75 years. The literacy rate (defined as the percentage of the 15-and-older population who can read and write) is about 90 percent (compared to 97 percent in the United States).

What's It Like Outside?

Location (altitude and latitude) dictates climate in Mexico. The central plateau, which makes up about two-thirds of the country, enjoys cooler temperatures and lower humidity because of the elevation; annual average temperature is around 65 degrees, although the evenings can be chilly. Along the lowlands of the coast, it's hot and humid, with an average temperature ranging from 80 degrees on the Yucatan peninsula to 68 degrees on the northwest coast.

The rainy season runs from May to October, and rainfall varies with topography. In the central plateau region, annual rainfall varies from 20 inches in the north to 35 inches in the south, and some of the precipitation may actually be in the form of snow. (As a benchmark, think of New York City, with its annual rainfall of about 50 inches). The Sierra Madre Occidental snakes down the western side of Mexico, and the Sierra Madre Oriental is found on the eastern side—these mountain ranges block some of the rain in the central portion of Mexico.

On the Caribbean side of Mexico, the warm water and northeast trade winds result in larger rainfalls—20 to 60 inches, depending on the place (the northern

Keep in mind that your body may require some time to acclimate to the higher altitudes in the central plateau area. Mexico City, for example, has an elevation of over 7,500 feet—about a half-mile higher than Denver.

Yucatan tends to get the least rain). The Pacific and Gulf of Mexico coasts get from 10 inches to 60 inches; rainfall is more plentiful the farther south you go, and the presence of the Sierra Madre Occidental range behind sections of the western coast also contributes to higher rainfall. Hurricanes along the coastal areas, volcanoes and earthquakes toward the central and southern part of Mexico, and tsunamis (tidal waves) on the west coast are some of the natural disasters you could be exposed to while living in Mexico. But heck, we have the same stuff in the United States!

What's the Cost?

The cost of living is lower in Mexico than in the United States. Over the last several years, prices have increased in Mexico, but if your source of income is based on U.S. dollars, your money will go farther here. The peso is the basic unit of money in Mexico, and there are about 10 or 11 pesos to a U.S. dollar. One huge area of savings is property taxes. In Mexico, property taxes are .1 percent of the assessed value of the property, with the value determined at the time of purchase. So, if your home cost $150,000, your property tax would be only $150! Can't get much better than that! Property taxes have never been a source of money for Mexico's government, and that's what has kept them so low.

Food (especially fruits and vegetables), most utilities, pharmaceuticals and medical costs, alcohol and tobacco, clothing, home insurance, and repair services are also cheaper, and there's no need for heating or air conditioning in many regions of the country. Gas is high, though—in August 2003, it ran about $2.30 a gallon. As far as building costs are concerned, labor costs are lower, but material costs are higher, so it's pretty much a wash. In addition, homes in the areas with the most foreigners are more expensive.

According to Mike Nelson, author of *Live Better South of the Border*, multiplying your present expenses in the

To find a qualified Mexican real estate attorney (called a "notary"), contact the Embassy of Mexico in Washington, D.C., or one of the Mexican consulates located throughout the United States. Go to www.mexonline.com/consulate.htm for a listing. The phone number of the Embassy of Mexico in Washington, D.C., is 202-736-1000.

United States by 60 to 70 percent gives you an idea of what a comparable lifestyle in Mexico would cost. Nelson feels that $1,500 a month would be about the average amount a single person would need to live—$2,200 for a couple (2003 figures).

What about Property Ownership?

Yes, you can buy property in Mexico, and no, it's not always simple (sigh). When purchasing real estate in Mexico, you want to be sure to get title insurance and hire a competent attorney to review everything. That being said up front, we would also strongly advise against purchasing *ejido* land. What does this mean?

Ejido land is large parcels of land the Mexican government originally gave to farmers, Indians, and peasants, who could then farm or build on it but did not own the land or have title to it. It was communal property, with many sharing the same piece of land. Some foreigners have been evicted from their land or homes because they bought *ejido* property that turned out, of course, to not be theirs. Beginning in 1992, *ejido* land could become "regularized," meaning that those who used the land could convert it to private property so they could benefit from its sale. This process is complex and can easily take a year or more to complete properly (keep in mind that all the people who used the land have to come to a consensus). If the regularization process on the land you buy was not done properly, guess what—you won't really own it. How do you make sure the land you're buying is not *ejido* land? Be sure you're dealing with a reputable developer, have an attorney check the public records to see if the title is clear and there are no liens on the property, and get title insurance.

When buying property, you also need to know that foreigners cannot directly own land within about 31 miles of the coast (this land, of course, is wildly popular) or within about 62 miles of the country's borders. There is, however, a legal way to circumvent these restrictions (isn't there always?). It's called a trust deed, or *fideocomiso*. An authorized Mexican bank retains the deed to the re-

---

How to get title insurance? Two suggestions (both American companies): Stewart Title Company (www.stewart.com or 800-729-1900) or First American Title Insurance Company (www.firstam.com/title-intl/mexico.html or 214-979-0003).

stricted property, but the beneficiary of the trust has rights to the land (the beneficiary can use, rent, sell, or transfer the rights to another party) for up to 50 years. The trust deed can also be renewed by the beneficiary. It costs about $3,000 to set up the *fideocomiso*, then there is an annual fee of several hundred dollars.

Purchasing nonrestricted properties in Mexico results in simple-fee titles. If you're not paying cash, you can get mortgages through some Mexican as well as U.S. companies, but interest rates tend to be higher on loans for property outside of the United States. It's also worth knowing that real estate agents in Mexico are not licensed or regulated as they are in the States, and escrow is not as commonly used. At the risk of sounding like a broken record (or should we say CD!), the best advice is to get expert help from a Mexican notary (attorney), and again—don't forget the title insurance!

If you want to rent before you buy (it's always a good idea to do a test run if you're considering a place for re-location), you need to do your homework and nail down where you think you want to live. Once you've whittled down your search of possible rental areas, ask the locals, the people in the hotel where you are staying, and any friends/acquaintances in the area, and look at ads and at the classified sections of the newspapers. You may also go through a real estate agent; one source is the Mexican Association of Real Estate Professionals (www.icrea.org). You can also do Internet searches for property, but this is only a starting point.

What's to Do?

Mexico enjoys a diverse topography and rich history. Explore one of the many archaeological areas, including the Mayan sites of Tulum, Coba, and Chichen-Itzá, or examine the Aztec excavations at Cuexcomate and Capilco in Morelos, one of Mexico's 31 states.

Or, travel from jungle to desert to the warm aqua waters of the Caribbean. Spend a lazy day on the beach, go

---

The Mexican constitution guarantees a free university education to its citizens—available at the more than 30 public state universities, although fees are assessed for some services and students must purchase textbooks. In addition to the public universities, there are private colleges and universities as well as technical/vocational schools in the country.

golfing, celebrate at one of the many Mexican festivals, or visit the magnificent Copper Canyon. Attend the ballet or a concert, wander around a museum or an art show, and follow it up with a meal that emphasizes corn, beans, tomatoes, chilies, and fruit. In Mexico City, be sure to see the National Palace, President Vincente Fox's "office," which also displays murals by Mexican artist Diego Rivera.

What about Employment?

You can work in Mexico if you have the required permits and are sponsored by a company, are sponsored by people who require particular skills, or are an investor starting up your own company. According to Mexperience (www.mexperience.com), teaching English as a foreign language (with the proper certification), consulting, or setting up a restaurant or bar are common jobs for foreigners. If you desire to work in Mexico and establish permanent residency, you need to apply for an active immigrant permit and meet the requirements outlined above. Contact the National Immigration Institute of Mexico at 52-2-581-0164, or the Embassy of Mexico in Washington, D.C.

What about Immigration Requirements?

We've discussed the immigration requirements if you wish to work in Mexico. What if you don't want to work, but do want to become a permanent resident? In that case, you would apply for a retiree permit (a nonactive immigrant permit). In order to qualify, you must be at least 50 years of age and have at least $1,500 in income per month (if you're not yet 50, you can still apply this way—it just involves a little more paperwork). Contact the National Immigration Institute of Mexico or a Mexican consulate at the embassy in Washington, D.C.

Where Are Some Notable Neighborhoods?

We have identified a number of possible places to begin your search in Mexico, and they do tend to be where

---

Although it's been in Mexico only a little more than a dozen years, Wal-Mart is now the largest private employer in the country. The company is responsible for about 50 percent of new permanent jobs in Mexico.

most Americans relocate. As we mentioned earlier, these areas are more expensive because they are more popular among foreigners, so if your (admirable) goal is to completely integrate yourself into the culture, you may want to skip this section and do some additional research (refer to the references for this chapter). Otherwise, here are some places to consider.

La Paz. In 2003, *Money* magazine ranked eight cities, emphasizing "solid financial footing and good health care options." All but one were located in the United States, but the eighth was La Paz (which means "peace" in Spanish). The capital of the state of Baja California Sur, located about 100 miles north of the resort town of Cabo San Lucas, this city of about 200,000 (about 4,000 of whom are American) is located on the beautiful Sea of Cortez. This port city, with its vibrant town center, is also a college town, with the University of South Baja California located here. Sample listings: a three-bedroom/two-and-a-half-bath duplex with a carport, 5 minutes from downtown, listed at $89,500 (USD); a historic two-story home in a quiet neighborhood in the center of La Paz, with a view of the Bay of La Paz from the second floor, listed at $225,000 (USD). *Money* summed up the city this way: "La Paz is more a Mexican city than an expatriate's haven, but for those who love magnificent seaside sunsets, sugary beaches, sailing, diving—and the ability to stretch a retirement dollar—La Paz is a superb choice."

San Miguel de Allende. While La Paz was *Money* magazine's choice for 2003, San Miguel de Allende was their choice for 2002 (it was also the only non-U.S. city chosen that year). The town, with about 80,000 people (5,000 to 10,000 of whom are expatriates), is in the state of Guanajuanto, north of Mexico City. San Miguel de Allende has an altitude of over 6,000 feet, resulting in wonderful weather. There are many churches, and the town is also known as an arts community; it's home to a huge bilingual library, it has an English newspaper, and it offers many plays and other productions performed in English. San Miguel de Allende boasts more than 30 volunteer organizations as well.

According to *International Living* magazine, La Paz residents are said to earn the highest per capita income in Mexico.

There are even the conveniences of a Wal-Mart and Costco 45 minutes away in Queretaro for those who can't live without them.

As with real estate everywhere, factors such as location, amenities, views, eagerness of the sellers, competition, and condition of the home will affect the asking price. Some recent real estate prices (in U.S. dollars): a three-bedroom, three-bath house listed at $180,000; a three-bedroom, three and a half bath asking $425,000; a two-bedroom, two and a half bath listed at $200,000. (There were homes exceeding $1 million, as well.)

Nopalo. On the 800-mile Baja peninsula, the strip of land just south of San Diego, Nopalo is almost becoming a "Little America." The *New York Times* reported in October 2003 that in the towns of San Felipe and Rosarito, both on the peninsula, about 25 percent of the residents are American. In Nopalo, just south of Loreto, the paper states that "a totally American town is about to be built." Its American and Canadian developers expect that this planned community of 5,000 residences will become home for about 12,000 people. Given some major limiting factors—sparse rain, the need to pipe in water, and a lack of housing for workers—it will be interesting to see what develops (groundbreaking is slated for January 2004). So, what's the allure of the area? Affordable property close to the water, lower property taxes, greater freedom, and the laid-back style of Mexico are all obviously very appealing to many!

Other places. Additional places touted as potentially good retirement spots in Mexico include Lake Chapala (also called Lakeside), Mazatlan, Oaxaca, Guadalajara, Queretaro, and Manzanillo.

How Is Mexico's Health Care?

The U.S. State Department's consular information sheet on Mexico states: "Adequate medical care can be found in all major cities. Excellent health care facilities are available in Mexico City. Care in more remote areas is limited."

The World Health Organization released a study in 2000 that compared health care systems in 191 countries based on eight criteria, including cost, access, and level of care. In this list, Mexico ranked 61st (the

---

The winding cobblestone streets of San Miguel de Allende could be a challenge if you have bad knees.

United States ranked 37th). Mexico's ranking reflects the fact that half of its residents are uninsured, and much of the spending for health care is out of pocket. There is also difficulty in providing care to those in more rural areas.

If you look at the quality of health care for those at the top of the socioeconomic ladder, however, and put aside issues of equity, it's a different story. Those who can afford it avail themselves of private sector medicine, which provides excellent care. A doctor's visit may cost around $20 to $50; many retirees in good health pay for their health costs out of pocket; this is a gamble, however, if a catastrophic illness occurs. Some retirees purchase private health insurance, which runs about $1,000 per year. Dental and medical procedures often cost less than half of what they would in the States (for example, you can receive porcelain crowns for under $100, fillings for under $50, and cleanings for around $25).

Prescription drugs can often be purchased from 50 to 80 percent less than their cost in the United States.

According to David Eidell in *The People's Guide to Mexico*, one of the reasons for the lower cost is that "international patents expire in less than half the time as U.S. patents." Be aware that Medicare and Medicaid do not travel with Americans moving to Mexico (although Social Security does), and physicians often require cash up front. In addition, foreigners may be charged more than locals. It's best to get a written list of the charges prior to any procedure. Foreigners can benefit from Mexico's national health insurance program, the National Health Program, which is about $300 per year, but under this program, you don't have a choice of doctors.

Some U.S. companies do provide health insurance for those living in Mexico, including insurance covering evacuation to the States. Two to contact: International Medical Group (IMG) at 800-628-4664 and Blue Cross/Blue Shield of Delaware (International Division) at 800-342-0719. Many expatriates use Mexico's medical services for regular health issues but return to the United States for major surgery.

International Living magazine calls Mexico "one of the best places in the world for inexpensive, quality dental work."

How Safe Is Mexico?

Crime in the big cites, especially Mexico City, is certainly an issue. Even those who are paid to uphold the law have been implicated in criminal activities. Crime in Mexico, however, is similar to crime in the States: Big cities are generally associated with higher crime rates. Apprehension and conviction rates tend to be fairly low in Mexico, which exacerbates the crime problem.

General guidelines, such as being aware of your surroundings, locking up valuables, not traveling alone, using ATMs cautiously, and avoiding the use of "gypsy" cabs hold true no matter what country you're in.

The U.S. State Department, in its consular information sheet on Mexico, also suggests that you use toll roads rather than the free roads and travel on first-class buses. The areas featured in our "notable neighborhoods" are considered safe. To read the consular information sheet on Mexico and the warnings for specific areas by the U.S. State Department, go to www.travel.state.gov/mexico.html or call the Embassy of Mexico to request a copy (202-728-1600).

Strengths

Climate, cost of living, air transportation, urban roads, beauty, a variety of landforms, friendly people, a rich history, gorgeous beaches, and proximity to the United States are all plusses. If the words "serenity," "tranquility," "laid-back," and "peaceful" appeal to you, consider Mexico.

Weaknesses

Roads in rural areas are not always good, and in some cases are even dangerous. Pollution is an issue in some cities (particularly Mexico City, which restricts car traffic to help combat pollution); deforestation and the availability of clean water can also be problematic. Taking your American car into Mexico can be complex, as quite a few rules govern this. Choose your medical care wisely—all medicine is not created equal in Mexico. You may need an acclimation period to get used to the higher altitude of some of the central areas, as well as to the different microbes present in Mexico's ice, water, and fresh foods. *Mañana* doesn't always mean tomorrow when you're talking about

---

Speaking of insurance, if you drive your car into Mexico, you must purchase automobile insurance from a Mexican company. Mexico does not accept insurance issued outside of the country.

getting things done—patience is not only a virtue, it's a mandatory component of your expatriate personality.

Donna and Marshall R. live in Cabo San Lucas. Here is an e-mail describing their encounter with Hurricane Hugo in September 2003.

Hi all . . . just a quick note that we are okay! I'm at an Internet cafe, as my service is still down. Still no power at the house, so generator is getting a lot of use. Storm hit midnight Sunday/Monday. Storm was coming from the north/northeast—very hard with a lot of rain. We could not keep up with water coming in. Windows were literally bulging out, and I finally got real scared. Power went out at about 2:30 A.M. and generator started but failed. Told Marshall we need to go below and just be safe. Had all but a few rugs pulled up and left. About 4:30 A.M., a still came about, and it was the eye passing over. We went outside and got the generator started. Came back in then the storm started again. But this time coming from the south/southwest where shutters were. We finally felt safe and got a few hours sleep. When we got up, and walked out, Niagara Falls was coming down the stairs. Got everything mopped up pretty good. Lost tiles but not many from roof. Yard needs a lot of cleaning up. Pool isn't running, as it won't run from the generator, so until power is restored, we have a lot of toads arriving. All in all we are okay, but now have ordered shutters for all the upstairs windows.

I'll write when my Internet is up . . . don't worry . . . unless another damn storm comes.

Love from us,

Donna and Marshall and one scared cat! (tL)

Jody L., a retired U.S. federal worker living in Mexico, was traveling on a twin-engine train within the country. After they had traveled some distance, one of the engines broke down. "No problem," the engineer thought, and carried on at half power. Farther on down the line, the other engine broke down, and the train came to a standstill. The engineer decided he should inform the passengers about why the train had stopped and made the following announcement: "Ladies and gentlemen, I have some good news and some bad news. The bad news is that both engines have failed, and we will be stuck here for some time. The good news is that you decided to take the train and not fly."

PART III

HOW DO YOU ENJOY YOUR RETIREMENT FOR YEARS TO COME?

8

FOREVER YOUNG?

"I'm not afraid of dying, I just don't want to be there when it happens."
—*Woody Allen*

Average life expectancy has increased from 47 years at the turn of the last century to 77 years today. If you are 50 now, you can expect to live to be 80. What will you do with this gift of 30 years?

How can you stay healthy—physically as well as emotionally? Most of us want to live a long, long life. The Alliance for Aging Research reports that 63 percent of those surveyed want to reach the ripe old age of 100. Of course, we want these years to be better, not just longer. But how do we accomplish that? According to Dr. Walter Bortz, scientific expert on aging, genes account for about one-fifth of our longevity, and our lifestyle choices ac-

count for four-fifths. As Dr. Bortz states, "Living longer is a choice, not fate. Living longer is active, not passive. You create your own destiny."

The trick, therefore, is to capitalize on those things we can control. How can we be proactive and stave off disease? Does looking better help us feel better? And what are the financial repercussions of living longer? With nursing homes costing an average of $66,000 a year, according to Metropolitan Life Insurance Company, and medical experts bemoaning the shortage of geriatricians, it's in our best interest to remain as healthy as possible. Finally, since death is inevitable (along with taxes, of course!), how can we help our aging parents—and ourselves—prepare for this final act of our lives?

The phrase *carpe diem* translates to "seize the day" and includes the concept of "eat, drink, and be merry, for tomorrow we may die." So let's start with that thought. How should we eat, drink, and be merry?

"EAT, DRINK, . . ."

From Atkins to *The Zone*, the way you choose to eat really does run the gamut from A to Z! Notice we didn't use the word "diet." Strike that word from your vocabulary, since it conjures up images of deprivation, and it's often used as a short-term means to achieve a goal of losing weight, followed by a return to old habits. Instead, the idea is to foster a lifelong way of eating that is healthful and makes you feel good.

What *is* the best way to eat? Needless to say, judging from the millions of magazine articles, scientific studies, news reports, and books on the topic, nutrition is a field with many opinions and a lot of controversy. One reason is that, particularly in the area of losing weight, a certain approach may work for some people but not for others. There is, however, agreement in one area—obesity is a huge and growing (no pun intended) problem in the United States. About 25 percent of adults are obese, and obesity is associated with almost 30 medical conditions, including arthritis, some cancers, diabetes, coronary heart disease, and high blood pressure.

If we assess all the nutrition information that has been generated, several constants emerge.

Calories count. There is one ironclad rule that virtually no one disputes: To lose weight, the number of calories you burn has to exceed the number of calories you eat. To find out how many calories a certain food contains, go to www.caloriecontrol.org. This site also assesses your diet, offers recipes, and provides suggestions and tips for staying (or getting) healthy and fit.

High-quality carbohydrates are better for you. All carbs are not created equal. Think whole grains such as

---

Take it to the limit: The oldest person in the world (according to her baptismal record) was Elizabeth Israel, from Portsmouth, Dominica (she passed away on October 14, 2003). At 126 years old, she attributed her long life to eating foods without chemicals or pesticides, working hard, and going to church.

whole wheat bread, whole grain pasta, whole grain cereals, oatmeal, fruits, and vegetables.

Highly processed grains should be avoided. These include white bread, white rice, white pasta, cake, doughnuts, pancakes, waffles, and sugary cereals that aren't whole grain.

Protein is a requirement of a healthy diet. How many grams of protein do you need every day? The answer depends on how active you are. If you're sedentary, you need about .4 gram of protein per pound of body weight. If you are strength-training on a regular basis, you'll need .8 gram of protein per pound of body weight in order to rebuild those muscle fibers you break down during your workout. Lean meats, fish, poultry, dairy products, legumes, and peanut butter are all good sources of protein. One site that gives grams of protein for some common foods is www.nephron.com/proneed.html.

There are "good" fats and "bad" fats. Although the mantra has been to avoid all fats like the plague, more recent information has shown that, as with carbs, not all fats are created equal. Fats are necessary in the human body. There are two fatty acids our body can't even manufacture: omega-6 (linoleic acid) and omega-3 (alpha-linoleic acid). We call these two "essential fatty acids" because they are essential to our health and life. In addition, fat in food adds flavor and gives us a feeling of satiety, or fullness.

The trick in eating fats is to choose those that are heart healthy, which means those that include monounsaturated and polyunsaturated (omega-6 and omega-3) fats; these are generally plant-based fats that tend to be liquid at room temperature. You will find them in canola, olive, and safflower oils, as well as fish (we know, not a plant) and nuts. The fats to avoid are the saturated fats, which tend to be from land animals and are solid at room temperature (think lard, butter, the fat streaks in red meat), and the "tropical" oils (palm and coconut oil). In addition to saturated fats and tropical oils, trans fats are another type of fat to avoid. Trans fats are found in margarine, baked goods, and fried foods.

Fiber is essential. The American Dietetic Association recommends that we ingest 20 to 35 grams of fiber every day, but most Americans get only about half that. Good sources of fiber include whole grain

---

The American Institute for Cancer Research reports that from 30 to 40 percent of cancer could be prevented through better nutrition and other lifestyle choices.

cereals; legumes such as kidney beans, black beans, and lentils; apples with the peels; and popcorn.

The glycemic index is an important tool. It turns out that some carbohydrates cause a rapid rise, then a rapid drop, in blood sugar levels; these are called high-glycemic foods. Other carbohydrates cause a much slower, more even rise in blood sugar levels; these are the low-glycemic foods. Studies done at Tufts University and elsewhere indicate that eating high-glycemic carbohydrates can lead to overeating, while other researchers have found evidence linking diabetes and heart disease with high-glycemic patterns of eating. Foods are classified as having a high glycemic index (70 or above), medium glycemic index (56 to 69), or low glycemic index (under 55). For a list of the glycemic indexes of some common foods, go to http://www.mendosa.com/common_foods.htm or refer to *The New Glucose Revolution* by Jennie Brand-Miller.

Water is good for you. Water is vital to health, period.

Consume alcohol in moderation. There has been a lot of research on the relationship between alcohol consumption and heart disease, and studies demonstrate that moderate drinkers—women who have one drink a day and men who have one or two—have a lower risk of heart disease than nondrinkers. The American Heart Association does not recommend that you start drinking if you do not presently consume alcohol, since many more deaths, illnesses, accidents, and tragedies are associated with drinking than with not drinking.

How Much Should You Eat and in What Proportions?

Be proactive about your health, and help stave off disease, by keeping the aforementioned guidelines in mind. But knowing *what* you should eat is not enough; you need to know *how much* protein, fat, and carbohydrate you should consume each day. There are two ways to approach this problem: by understanding what percentage of your total intake each of these nutrients should represent, and by using "food pyramids" that graphically represent what you should eat.

You know your chronological age, but what is your biological age? Take the free "RealAge Test" (go to www.realage.com and click on "Take the RealAge Test"), which analyzes your lifestyle choices, and see how you can become younger!

The recommended percentages of various nutrients will differ depending on what "diet" you look at. Most, however, tend to emphasize nonprocessed foods, whole grains, and lean cuts of meat. The new bestselling entry into the weight-loss melee, *The South Beach Diet*, restricts processed carbohydrates but is more liberal with the complex carbs than is Atkins.

If you go the percentage route, you will first need to know how many calories your body requires each day. There are several ways to calculate this. You can use an online calorie calculator such as www.inch-aweigh.com/dcn.php, which takes into account gender, age, height, weight, and activity level, then calculates how many calories you need per day to maintain your present weight and how many calories you need if your goal is to lose weight. One pound is equal to 3,500 calories, so reducing your caloric intake (or increasing your activity level) to create a deficit of 500 calories a day will result in a loss of 1 pound per week. For healthy weight loss, don't attempt to lose any more than 1 or 2 pounds per week.

If math isn't your thing—or you have other things to do with your day than count calories—several food pyramids recommend the number of servings and kind of food to eat. The Food Guide Pyramid was designed by the United States Department of Agriculture (USDA). The current one, shown below, has been in existence since 1992; a revision will be completed in 2005.

THE FOOD GUIDE PYRAMID

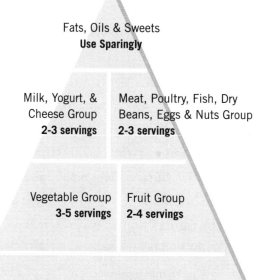

Fats, Oils & Sweets
Use Sparingly

Milk, Yogurt, & Cheese Group
2-3 servings

Meat, Poultry, Fish, Dry Beans, Eggs & Nuts Group
2-3 servings

Vegetable Group
3-5 servings

Fruit Group
2-4 servings

Breads, Cereal, Rice & Pasta Group
5-11 servings

You can download a listing of the nutritive values of food at www.nal.usda.gov/fnic/foodcomp (click on "Search" under "Search the Nutrient Database").

The Food Guide Pyramid is a condensed version of the U.S. Dietary Guidelines, which are revised every 5 years. The U.S. Dietary Guidelines are actually more specific recommendations, and many nutritionists and scientists fault the freestanding pyramid for not differentiating among healthy and nonhealthy fats, good and bad carbs, and so on.

Shown on this page is a second food pyramid. Created by Walter C. Willett, M.D., of the Harvard School of Public Health, it is called the Healthy Eating Pyramid.

Note that physical activity and weight control form the foundation of Dr. Willett's pyramid. On the second level, whole grains are encouraged, whereas on the USDA's Food Guide Pyramid, there is no differentiation between processed and whole grains. Another difference is that healthy unsaturated, monounsaturated, and polyunsaturated fats are given a prominent location on the Healthy Eating Pyramid, while there is no such distinction in the USDA's pyramid. As far as fruits and veggies go, both pyramids suggest eating lots of servings. But note that Dr. Willett excludes potatoes from the recom-

HEALTHY EATING PYRAMID

Use Sparingly

White Rice, White Bread, Potatoes, Pasta & Sweets

Butter
Red Meat

Dairy or Calcium Supplement, **1-2 times a day**

Fish, Poultry, Eggs, **0-2 times a day**

Nuts, Legumes, **1-3 times a day**

Vegetables **(in abundance)**   Fruits, **2-3 times a day**

Whole grain Foods **(at most meals)**   Plant oils, including olive, canola, soy, corn, sunflower, peanut and other vegetable oils

Daily Exercise & Weight Control

* Multiple Vitamins for Most   *** Alcohol in Moderation (unless contraindicated)**

From Eat, Drink, and Be Healthy *by Walter C. Willett M.D., © Simon and Schuster, 2001.*

For a more creative way of looking at serving sizes (for example, 2 tablespoons of peanut butter is equal to a golf ball), go to www.eatright.org and type "What is a serving?" into the search bar.

mended vegetables, placing them at the top along with sweets and unrefined grains, which are to be eaten sparingly. Dr. Willett views nuts and legumes as healthier forms of protein, so he gives them their own level, and he places fish, poultry, and eggs (he suggests that red meats should be eaten less) on a different level. He recommends fewer dairy products and suggests the use of a calcium supplement. The USDA's pyramid, in contrast, shows all nutrients coming from food. Lastly, both pyramids agree that sweets should be eaten frugally, but Dr. Willett also places foods that either have a high glycemic index or are high in saturated fat at the top of his pyramid. Moderate alcohol consumption is reflected in his pyramid, as is the taking of a daily multivitamin.

What's the moral of the story? You have to figure out what works for *you*. Keeping in mind the general guidelines discussed above, healthy eating that keeps you at a good weight and feeling energetic is what works.

How often should you eat? Again, there is no one correct answer. Since it's not so much the frequency as the quality and quantity of what's ingested that counts, the number of meals that prevents you from overeating at the next chow time is the frequency that is right for you.

Should You Take Vitamins and Minerals?

Finally, should you take supplements? Many of us do not get the RDA (recommended dietary allowance) or the DRI (Dietary Reference Intake) of certain nutrients. As a result, most experts suggest or see no harm in taking a good multivitamin/mineral supplement every day.

One mineral that most Americans don't get enough of is calcium. The most abundant mineral in the body, calcium is responsible for healthy bones and teeth as well as nerve transmission and muscle contraction. Although most calcium is stored in the bones, if there is not enough calcium in our bloodstream, the hormone parathormone takes it from our bones, increasing the risk

A number of other pyramids reflect healthy eating patterns; among these are Asian, vegetarian, Latin, and Mediterranean pyramids. These ethnic pyramids reflect actual, healthy, traditional ways of eating. To take a look at some of the alternative pyramids, go to www.oldwayspt.org, and click on "Traditional Diet Pyramids" under "Wise Eating."

of a brittle skeleton. Since absorption of calcium decreases with age, the RDA/DRI increases as we get older. The calcium RDA between the ages of 19 and 50 is 1,000 milligrams/day, but that number increases to 1,200 milligrams/day when you hit that magic age of 50. Vitamin D helps our bodies absorb calcium from our digestive tract; thus, you should choose a supplement that contains vitamin D.

Since adults may absorb only 30 to 50 percent of ingested calcium, it's a good idea to spread the intake of calcium-rich foods (as well as supplements) over the course of the day to ensure the maximum uptake of this important mineral.

Don't completely shun the sun. Our skin makes vitamin D when our bodies are exposed to ultraviolet B rays from the sun (or tanning booths). There has been such an emphasis on preventing skin cancer and wrinkles that cases of vitamin D insufficiency have been on the rise. The darker your skin, the longer you need to be in the sun to make vitamin D, since the pigment melanin (which gives color to the skin) prevents UV absorption.

How much time is enough? Several times a week, expose 25 percent of your body (such as your limbs or arms plus your face) for 25 percent of the time it would take for you to start turning pink in the sun.

Heart disease is the number one killer in the United States, and recent research has emphasized the importance of an amino acid called homocysteine in our blood. The American Heart Association states that too much of it is "related to a higher risk of coronary heart disease, stroke, and peripheral vascular disease (fatty deposits in peripheral arteries)." What does homocysteine actually do? The current thought is that an excess of this amino acid, which is necessary for healthy tissue, can damage blood vessel linings, leading to the accumulation of plaque, which can block the flow of blood. It has also been implicated in dementia.

Folic acid and vitamins B_6 and B_{12} may break down homocysteine in the bodies of some individuals. Good sources of folic acid include dark green leafy veggies, whole grains, walnuts, and lentils; cereals are often fortified with folic acid. B_6 can be found in bananas, nuts,

---

To find out the RDA of vitamins and minerals, check out www.nal.usda.gov; click on "Search our Web Site," and type "RDA for vitamins and minerals" in the search bar.

seeds, chicken, and potatoes. Good sources of B_{12} are eggs, poultry, milk, shellfish, and cottage cheese.

The bottom line is that we need to be informed consumers. New research continues to modify, verify, and vilify prior research. Common sense, knowing what works for you, and maintaining a healthy skepticism will probably serve you well in the nutrition arena.

"... AND BE MERRY"

Exercise can make us merrier, but, as with nutrition, you have to find out what works for *you*. Do you remember the original 1962 *Twilight Zone* episode, "Kick the Can," in which Charles Whitley, residing at the Sunnyvale Rest Home, believed that by thinking young and playing active games (like kick the can), he would truly *be* young? He was joined by most of Sunnyvale's residents, and indeed, by the end of the show, those who participated in the vigorous game had literally become children once again. (It *is* the *Twilight Zone*, remember.)

What a powerful statement about the effects of exercise!

Activities you enjoy, performed at a regular time, perhaps with another person who also commits to exercising, offer the best chance to make fitness a lifelong habit. Experts often advise that you exercise first thing in the morning, so that later in the day you don't get too tired or overwhelmed with other things to do and let exercise slide. In other words, insert this valuable activity into your schedule, just as you would grocery shopping, meeting a friend for lunch, or going to a movie; no one can easily *find* time to exercise. Before embarking on a new exercise regimen or plan, however, it's a good idea to ask your physician to check you out and give you the okay, especially if you have been relatively inactive.

The three pillars of physical fitness are strength-training, increasing flexibility, and cardiovascular workouts. Here's a list of some of the benefits of regular exercise.

* Increases feelings of self-worth.
* Reduces LDL ("bad") cholesterol and triglycerides.

Your dentist may be able to warn you of an impending stroke! X-rays taken with panoramic machines can detect calcifications in the neck arteries, indicating possible blockages. Alert your dentist to look for this "hardening of the arteries."

* Decreases body fat, including dangerous visceral fat (the fat surrounding organs) that is implicated in diabetes, high blood pressure, and cardiovascular disease.
* Makes your body more sensitive to the effects of insulin, decreasing the chances of developing diabetes.
* Lowers stress levels and relaxes you.
* Helps alleviate moderate levels of depression.
* Improves your appearance.
* Strengthens your heart so it pumps out more blood with each beat, resulting in a lower heart rate and lightened workload on the heart.
* Lowers blood pressure and decreases the risk of stroke and heart disease.
* Raises your levels of IgA (immunoglobulin A), which fights cold viruses.
* Increases muscular strength and endurance.
* Increases lean body mass, which in turn increases the number of calories your body burns at rest.
* Elevates mood.

* Improves joint flexibility, helping to ease joint pain and stiffness.
* Decreases your chances of getting gallstones.
* Adds or slows loss of bone mass (if it's a weight-bearing exercise), reducing chances of osteoporosis.
* Helps prevent fractures of the spine (back-strengthening exercises in particular).
* Results in the production of a natural antibiotic (dermicidin) by sweat glands.
* Improves blood circulation to the prostate gland.
* Lowers the risk of some cancers, including breast, kidney, endometrial, prostate, and colon cancers.
* Allows you to fall asleep more easily and sleep better.
* Improves the efficiency of the lungs, and delivers more oxygen to cells.
* Decreases risk of falling by improving balance and coordination (yoga is particularly effective).
* Suppresses appetite signals from the hypothalamus after vigorous workouts involving lots of heat production.

A fascinating study by the Mayo Clinic found the "fidget factor" could be one reason some people stay slender, even if they overeat. Hundreds of calories were burned each day by those who stretched, moved around, were restless, tapped their toes, or twiddled their thumbs.

* Hones planning, goal-setting, and decision-making skills.
* Increases energy (which may stimulate your sex life as well).

Whew! Although our list is not all-inclusive, you certainly get the idea that exercise is vital to good health!

When we hit our late twenties, we start losing muscle mass—about 1 percent each year. That doesn't seem like much, but by the time we're 50, we've lost approximately one-fifth of our muscle mass—and replaced a lot of that with fat! Since muscle is much more active metabolically (it burns more calories at rest than fat does), this loss, along with a more sedentary lifestyle, accounts for much of the creeping weight gain as we hit middle age. This weight gain is not inevitable—it can be reversed through lifting weights. In many cases, you can use your own body as the weight (think squats and pushups) or use fairly inexpensive free weights—you don't have to join a club and use their machines (although the social aspect of a club or organized class can be a great extrinsic motivator).

To make sure you're using correct form—not only to prevent injury, but also to get the most out of your workouts—it's a good idea to schedule a few lessons with a personal trainer to put you on the right path. Call your local health club for some recommendations. Costs vary, but they run somewhere around $50 an hour. Trainers can come to your home or your health club, or you can go to their place of business.

Dr. Miriam Nelson, director of the Center for Physical Fitness at Tufts University in Boston, recommends three 45-minute strength-training workouts a week and three 45-minute aerobic workouts a week. Alternate your strength-training days with aerobic days. Also, stretching while your muscles are warm will promote the best flexibility. If 6 days of working out seems daunting, start slowly, and see if you can work up to a higher, more intense level. Keep a list of the benefits of working out to help keep you motivated. If

---

Bill Phillips, author of the bestselling book *Body for Life*, advocates exercising first thing in the morning on an empty stomach. The idea is that if you exercise first thing, your stores of carbs will be low, and your body will be forced to draw on fats for energy. (One of the authors incorporated this single change into her workout routine and lost 10 pounds over the course of a year!)

you truly believe in the value of exercise, you'll set aside the time. Exercise is something you can't afford *not* to do!

Remember that a scale is not the only arbiter of change. Although it sounds like a cliché, muscle does weigh more than fat, so as you're becoming more fit, the numbers on the scale may not change that much even though you're losing inches. How you feel, how your clothes fit, and how you look naked standing in front of a full-length mirror are better judges of what's going on with your body! Will you be sore? Most likely. But take this as a good sign that you are producing stronger muscles. As your muscles get more powerful, the soreness will decrease. Of course, actual acute pain is a warning signal from your body that something is wrong. Don't overdo it!

Whether you walk, do yoga, bike, take step aerobics, play tennis or other sports, swim, dance, do core training (strengthening your "core" muscles—your abdominal,

back, chest, and shoulder muscles), lift free weights, or use machines, there are a host of rewards from regular exercise. The phrase "use it or lose it" truly applies to keeping your body, an incredible machine, in its best possible shape.

Okay, so you're eating right most of the time and you're exercising several days a week, but you still think the way you look on the outside doesn't reflect how young you feel on the inside. Or, you want to have your cake and eat it, too (then have it removed from your thighs). Should you consider a cosmetic procedure?

"If I Could Turn Back Time . . ." The title of Cher's song captures the essence of cosmetic surgery—turning back the clock to make our outward appearance more closely resemble the (hopefully!) energetic and vital people we feel we are inside. The American Society of Plastic Surgeons (ASPS) reports that in 2002 about 1.6 million people had surgical cosmetic procedures (such as a tummy tuck), and 4.9 million had nonsur-

---

Join the approximately three million mall walkers, and you won't worry about inclement weather, darkness, vehicles, or steep hills. About 2,500 malls open their doors as early as 6:30 A.M. just for walkers. Write to the National Organization of Mall Walkers to see whether there's a mall-walking club near you (P.O. Box 256, Hermann, MO, 65041).

gical cosmetic procedures (such as Botox injections).

ASPS statistics indicate that the top surgical procedures for patients aged 51 and over in 2002 were eyelid surgeries, facelifts, forehead lifts, liposuction, and nose reshapings. The most common nonsurgical procedures for the same age group were Botox injections, chemical peels, collagen injections, microdermabrasion, and sclerotherapy (a procedure that gets rid of distended veins).

Between 1992 and 2002, the number of cosmetic plastic surgeries performed by American Association of Plastic Surgeons members tripled. Almost 33 percent of these patients had more than one procedure during a single surgical session, and close to 40 percent of patients came back for more!

All this nipping and tucking doesn't come without a cost, however. Most cosmetic surgery is considered elective and will not be covered by insurance. In certain cases, such as drooping eyelids that interfere with vision, procedures may be covered. Check with your insurance company to be sure. Costs range from under $200 for microdermabrasion to almost $6,000 for a lower-body lift. Payment options may include paying all fees prior to the surgery, making a deposit when scheduling your procedure and paying a penalty for cancellation, using a credit card, or financing your procedure, sometimes through your doctor's office.

AARP, in conjunction with Roper Starch Worldwide, conducted a survey to find out who considers cosmetic procedures. It turns out only about one in five boomers is completely satisfied with his or her appearance, and about four in ten boomers are happy with how they look for how old they are. When boomers were asked if they

---

Remember that immunizations aren't just for kids! The Centers for Disease Control and Prevention (CDC) recommends a tetanus/diphtheria booster every 10 years, a onetime pneumococcal vaccine if you're over 65, and a flu shot every year if you're over 50 or fall into another risk group (adults with asthma or other chronic pulmonary or heart conditions; those with kidney disease, diabetes, or weakened immune systems; residents of long-term care facilities or nursing homes; and health workers who come in contact with those who are at high risk). Check with your doctor to see whether you need an MMR (measles/mumps/rubella), chicken pox, and/or hepatitis B vaccine.

would consider having cosmetic surgery, 14 percent of women and 5 percent of men said yes. If, however, the procedures were free, were guaranteed safe, and could remain secret, the numbers who said yes rose to 64 percent for women and 33 percent for men!

Choosing a physician for surgical cosmetic procedures shouldn't be taken lightly. The best advice is to pick a board-certified plastic surgeon. The rigorous credentialing process to become board certified ensures that the surgeon has the necessary training and expertise. Also, consider where the surgery will be performed. Your surgeon should have hospital privileges at the better medical centers. For more extensive surgeries, a medical center is your best bet. Asking friends for suggestions can also be helpful. Your internist or other physicians you see may be a good source for referrals as well. Whatever you do, don't let price be your only factor in choosing a physician for your cosmetic procedures!

The American Society of Plastic Surgeons provides a free referral service for board-certified surgeons by loca-

---

Men account for approximately 11 percent of those who've had cosmetic procedures.

tion as well as by procedure. Go to www.plastic-surgery.org and click on "Find a Plastic Surgeon" or call 888-475-2784. The site also provides a list of questions you should ask a prospective surgeon. (Type "What Questions Should I Ask?" into the search bar).

Of course, cosmetic procedures won't change who you are, but they may change how you feel about yourself. If you have realistic expectations about the results, are emotionally stable, recognize the inherent risks, can afford it, and know there will be some discomfort and healing time for some of the procedures, it may be something to consider.

Now, let's look at another way of staying "forever young"—nurturing your emotional health. Feeding our body nutritious food and keeping it in good working condition are very important, but we must nourish the brain and spirit as well.

The Importance of Giving

As we pointed out in chapter 1, social support is one ingredient in the recipe for a happier, healthier retirement and a happier, healthier, longer-living you. Research by Stephanie Brown in *Psychological Science* (July 2003), indicates that it may indeed be healthier to give than to receive. Dr. Brown's study found that "mortality was significantly reduced for individuals who reported providing instrumental support to friends, relatives, and neighbors, and individuals who reported providing emotional support to their spouse." In other words, during this 5-year study of older married adults, those who gave their time and support to others lived longer than those who didn't. Lending a helping hand not only helps others, it increases your longevity.

Marriage: For Better or Worse

Emotional health also benefits from marriage. A 2002 study from England reported that over a 7-year period, men were more likely to die from being single than from being smokers! Researchers Andrew Oswald and Jonathan Garner from the University of Warwick found that married men had a 6.1 percent lower risk of death than their single counterparts. For married women, the

---

To view the average 2003 cost of various procedures compiled by the American Society for Aesthetic Plastic Surgery, go to www.surgery.org/plasticsurgerycost.asp.

risk of mortality was 2.9 percent lower than for single women. Dr. Oswald summed up, "Forget cash. It is as clear as day from the data that marriage, rather than money, is what keeps people alive." It has been found, however, that unhappy marriages can have a negative effect on health. Depression, ulcers, elevation of stress hormones, increased blood pressure, and even a slower repair of wounds and more cavities have been associated with poor marital relationships. Although the research subjects in these studies were married, it's thought that the same results (good and bad) would also apply to any couple in a long-term, committed relationship.

Controlling Stress

Our ability to deal with the events life tosses our way can affect our sense of well-being. Consider these scenarios: buying a new house, caring for elderly parents, becoming a grandparent, beginning a new career, losing money in the stock market, learning a difficult piece on the piano,

preparing for the holidays, being involuntarily downsized, and retiring. How we react to each stimulus determines whether it is a "eustress" (good stress) or a "distress" (bad stress) for us. Eustress, a term coined by Canadian scientist Dr. Hans Selye, can be stimulating, challenging, and fun, while distress can lead to negative consequences such as anxiety, irritability, feelings of being overwhelmed, anger, and depression.

When we experience physical or psychological stress, our bodies churn out the stress hormones cortisol, epinephrine, and norepinephrine, which help regulate insulin; increase blood pressure, heart rate, blood sugar levels, and blood flow to the large muscles; and prepare us for the "fight-or-flight" response to the stressor. Under ideal circumstances, we experience the stress response, we resolve things, and our levels of stress hormones return to normal. The increase in energy we experience was a beneficial evolutionary response that helped our ancestors escape

According to the American Psychological Association, 43 percent of adults suffer "adverse health effects" from stress; 75 to 90 percent of all office visits to a physician are for stress-related ailments and complaints; and stress is linked to the six leading causes of death: heart disease, cancer, lung ailments, accidents, cirrhosis of the liver, and suicide.

predators. In modern society, however, the stress response is often initiated repeatedly (think of being stuck in traffic or dealing with an intractable illness), and the body is bathed in these stress chemicals often and for prolonged periods of time, perhaps resulting in fatigue, depression, anxiety, irritability, and pain in the muscles and joints. Older people with chronic stress also tend to have higher levels of a chemical called interleukin-6 that is associated with a decline in immune system function, as well as illnesses such as heart disease, arthritis, and diabetes.

Frequent negative stress, whether physical or psychological, exacts a toll on the body. One way to reduce stress is to try changing your response to the stressor. One person's distress could be another person's eustress. If you can change the way you perceive a stressor, you can deal with the stress more easily and return your body to its normal state more quickly. Let's say you're committed to doing a half-hour talk for the local Rotary, but you're feeling panicked. Using time management to prepare for your presentation, visualizing yourself making a successful presentation, and practicing your presentation until you feel comfortable could change what would be considered a distress, were you to wing it, to a eustress.

Additional techniques for stress reduction include biofeedback, meditation, slow and deep breathing, exercise (particularly yoga, Pilates, and t'ai chi), massage therapy, getting enough sleep, listening to soothing music or a relaxation tape, interacting with others, making a road map for your life and moving forward on it in measured steps, setting priorities, drinking chamomile or valerian tea, saying "no" to unwelcome requests, laughing, surrounding yourself with pink (it's calming) or yellow (energizing), connecting or reconnecting with your spiritual side, associating with positive-thinking people, stretching, practicing aromatherapy

---

More reasons to get unrelenting stress under control: The stress hormone cortisol is associated with deep abdominal fat, also called visceral fat, that surrounds organs. This fat, in turn, has been associated with heart disease and diabetes. Cortisol is also correlated with cravings for fats and carbs. Bruce McEwen of Rockefeller University conducted studies that determined that, over long periods of time, cortisol can damage or destroy neurons, or brain cells.

(especially with lavender), taking some time for yourself each day, avoiding stressful triggers (for example, keeping a book handy to read while you're on hold on the telephone), taking a walk, learning something new, playing with a pet, making a list of 10 things you are grateful for, and practicing mindfulness (a term coined by Dr. Jon Kabat-Zinn, founder and director of the Stress Reduction Clinic at the University of Massachusetts Medical Center, for giving your full attention to what you're involved in at that particular time).

Finally, remember that *you* are responsible for your own feelings—you are in charge of choosing your response to emotional stimuli. Replace flawed thinking (life "must" be fair; you "must" treat me like a king/queen; I "must" be perfect in all I do) with rational thought processes (I "prefer" that life is fair, but even though it isn't, I can still enjoy it; I "prefer" that you treat me like a queen, but I can't control your actions; I

"prefer" that I never make a mistake, but when I do, I know I'm still an okay person). Practicing this kind of thinking is called cognitive behavioral therapy or rational emotive behavior therapy. Try it—it works! But it takes time and practice to replace negative, ingrained thought patterns with newer, healthier ones. The payoff? A lot less stress in your life.

Let's face it—a life that is completely stress-free would be boring, but too much stress is unhealthy.

Avoiding Depression

Depression among older adults is frequently overlooked. In fact, it's estimated that millions of adults are living with depression. Although adults 65 and older make up 13 percent of the U.S. population, they accounted for almost 20 percent of all suicides in 2000. In spite of the dire statistics, the American Association of Geriatric Psychiatry found that only 50 percent of

Visualization or guided imagery can promote faster healing and reduce anxiety when it comes to surgery. Visualizing your operation in a positive way prior to surgery results in less pain, less blood loss, less medication, lower anxiety, and a quicker recovery time. Conditions such as asthma, obesity, and cancer can also be positively affected through visualization or guided imagery. One source of CDs or tapes on this method is Health Journeys (www.healthjourneys.com or 800-800-8661).

those who report their illness receive any type of treatment, and a number of those are undertreated or given medications that do not work for them. Sometimes there may be no obvious cause for the depression, or it may be the result of a change (decline in health, loss of spouse, retirement, etc.); certain medications may also mimic or cause depression. If you think you or someone you know is depressed, it's important to seek help from your physician or a mental health professional and to stick with treatment options until a successful one is found.

Keeping Your Brain Fit

When we discuss staying "forever young," we can't ignore the care of the 3-pound dynamo called the brain. Comprising about 2 percent of our weight but consuming close to 20 percent of our energy needs, this vital organ needs to be kept in the best shape possible. It had been, for about a century, a basic tenet in biology that brain cells don't regenerate—that once the brain matures, we have all the neurons we're ever going to have, and we can only lose them. Research done in the last decade, however, has upended this belief, and we now know that new cell growth has been observed in the most advanced parts of the brain involving learning

and memory. So, how do you keep your brain in fighting form?

Research by Dr. Marc Lochaum in the Department of Sport/Exercise Psychology at Texas Tech University found moderate physical exercise in adults prevented some effects of aging of the brain and helped maintain cognitive functioning. In addition to physical exercise, mental gymnastics can play a role in keeping our brains facile. One type of mental exercise is called "neurobics." A cute play on words, coined by Dr. Lawrence Katz and Manning Rubin by combining the word for brain cells, "neuron," with "aerobic" exercise, neurobics involves using your senses in ways you usually don't, doing something novel, and/or changing a routine. Switching hands to brush your teeth or to write, learning to play an instrument, studying a foreign language, taking a different route to a frequent destination, or getting dressed with your eyes closed are examples of neurobic exercises; these activities stimulate your neurons and rev up neglected nerve pathways.

More suggestions for maintaining your mental edge: Get sufficient sleep; don't smoke; be aware of side effects of medications; do crossword puzzles, brainteasers, acrostics, and riddles; avoid extreme stress; play bridge or chess; be socially engaged with others;

SYMPTOMS OF DEPRESSION

How can you tell if it's depression? Look for these common symptoms. If they last for more than 2 weeks, see a doctor.

* An "empty" feeling, ongoing sadness, and anxiety

* Tiredness, lack of energy

* Loss of interest or pleasure in everyday activities, including sex

* Sleep problems, including very early morning waking

* Problems with eating and weight (gain or loss)

* A lot of crying

* Aches and pains that just won't go away

* A hard time focusing, remembering, or making decisions

* Feeling that the future looks grim; feeling guilty, helpless, or worthless

* Being irritable

* Thoughts of death or suicide; a suicide attempt

Source: U.S. Administration on Aging

---

read; listen to music; play board games; garden; dance; and travel.

"Use it or lose it" applies as much to the brain as to the body.

". . . FOR TOMORROW WE MAY DIE."

"Nothing in life is certain except death and taxes." A wise man, that Mr. Benjamin Franklin. And we would be remiss, even though the chapter is named "Forever Young,"

to ignore the situation(s) that many of us find ourselves in—becoming less robust both physically and mentally as we grow older, caring for an aging parent or spouse, placing a spouse in a nursing home or other care facility, grieving over the death of a loved one, and/or making choices about death and dying for ourselves and others.

Elder Care

The "sandwich generation" refers to those caught between caring for their children and for aging parents.

Carol Abaya, columnist and sandwich generation expert, has added two new sandwich terms to the menu: a "club sandwich" refers to "those in their fifties or sixties, sandwiched between aging parents, adult children, and grandchildren;" and an "open-faced sandwich" is "anyone else involved in elder care." So, regardless of which type of sandwich you are or may become, it's helpful to know about some existing resources.

According to Abaya, more than one in four Americans is caring for an aging person in some capacity. Whether you're an in-home caregiver, regularly check in on an elderly person by phone or in the flesh, or coordinate care from a distance, here are a few suggestions for help.

The Eldercare Locator, sponsored by the Department of Health & Human Services Administration on Aging, provides information on state and area services for the elderly. Enter your state and zip code on their Web site (www.eldercare.gov), and up pops the list! You can also talk to an information specialist at 800-677-1116. The Web site includes such things as adult day care, facility options, and help with meals, and it is a great resource. You can also look under "Council on Aging" in the phone book for the agency closest to you. CareGuide (www.careguide.net or 888-389-8839) also provides information and articles on elder care.

You could hire a geriatric care manager. Whether you are providing care from up close and personal or from afar, these professionals can maneuver through the maze of services an elderly person may require. Although these managers are not federally or state regulated, they are usually licensed in nursing or social work. They can also be expensive, with hourly rates up to $150. In addition, although Medicare or long-term insurance may cover some of the services these managers recommend (such as a home health care worker), it usually doesn't cover the managers' services themselves. As with any person you hire, seek recommendations, check references and credentials, discuss fees, be sure the manager is compatible with the elderly person (and with you), and be sure there is a plan in place in case the manager has an emergency or

---

What's the most appropriate type of care for your elder or for you and/or your spouse when and if you get to that point: staying at home, assisted living, nursing home? Use the "Needs Assessment" tool that can be found online at www.carepathways.com. Click on "Needs Assessment" under Resources/Tools.

REGARDING ALZHEIMER'S DISEASE

Alzheimer's affects about 10 percent of people over 65 and close to 50 percent who reach the age of 85. The destruction and death of brain cells can continue for up to two decades and is ultimately fatal. Presently, Alzheimer's cannot be cured or stopped, although certain drugs (such as Aricept) have helped improve memory for some victims. Here is a checklist of common symptoms or potential signs of Alzheimer's.

1. Memory loss. One of the most common early signs of dementia is forgetting recently learned information. While it's normal to forget appointments, names, or telephone numbers, those with dementia will forget such things more often and not remember them later.

2. Difficulty performing familiar tasks. People with dementia often find it hard to complete everyday tasks that are so familiar we usually do not think about how to do them. A person with Alzheimer's may not know the steps for preparing a meal, using a household appliance, or participating in a lifelong hobby.

3. Problems with language. A person with Alzheimer's often forgets simple words or substitutes unusual words, making his or her speech or writing hard to understand. If a person with Alzheimer's is unable to find his or her toothbrush, for example, the individual may ask for "that thing for my mouth."

4. Disorientation to time and place. People with Alzheimer's can become lost on their own street, forget where they are and how they got there, and not know how to get back home.

5. Poor or decreased judgment. Those with

goes on vacation. To find a geriatric care manager, contact the National Association of Professional Geriatric Care Managers (www.caremanager.org or 520-881-8008), or contact the Eldercare Locator noted on page 355.

If the elderly person insists on staying in his or her home, but things aren't going well, it can often be difficult for a child to take over the role of parent and offer suggestions. Sometimes a trusted outsider, such as the elder's physician or religious leader, may be able to act as a go-between. By using the Eldercare Locator, you can get a recommendation for an assessment of the person's needs and what has to be done to keep him or her in the home. Otherwise, an agency involved in adult protection can get involved to take

Alzheimer's may dress without regard to the weather, wearing several shirts or blouses on a warm day or very little clothing in cold weather. Individuals with dementia often show poor judgment about money, giving away large amounts of money to telemarketers or paying for home repairs or products they don't need.

6. Problems with abstract thinking. Balancing a checkbook may be hard when the task is more complicated than usual. Someone with Alzheimer's could forget completely what the numbers are and what needs to be done with them.

7. Problems misplacing things. A person with Alzheimer's may not only forget where the house key is, but may also put things in unusual places: an iron in the freezer or a watch in the sugar bowl.

8. Changes in mood or behavior. Someone with Alzheimer's can show rapid mood swings—from calm to tears to anger—for no apparent reason.

9. Changes in personality. People's personalities ordinarily change somewhat with age, but a person with Alzheimer's can change a lot, becoming extremely confused, suspicious, fearful, or dependent on a family member.

10. Loss of initiative. The person with Alzheimer's may become very passive, sitting in front of the television for hours, sleeping more than usual, or not wanting to do usual activities.

If you recognize any warning signs in yourself or a loved one, the Alzheimer's Association recommends consulting a physician. Early diagnosis of Alzheimer's disease or other disorders causing dementia is an important step in getting appropriate treatment, care, and support.

Reprinted with permission from the Alzheimer's Association

the necessary steps to ensure the person's safety.

Assuming the person doesn't require lots of hands-on care, perhaps hiring a housekeeper, companion, or someone to run errands would work. Seek out recommendations for private hires from friends, colleagues, and professional health workers you may know, as well as from your church or other groups.

But what if the best alternative is moving the person out of the home? There are a few ways you can assess facilities. For example, contact Medicare (www.medicare.gov or 800-MEDICARE), and you'll be able to access all nursing homes that are Medicare or Medicaid certified, find out their staffing and inspection information, general information such as the number of beds and type of ownership, and quality measures (percent of residents physically restrained, percent of residents with pressure sores, percent of residents spending most of their time in a chair or in bed, etc.). Continuing care retirement communities (CCRCs) are accredited through the Continuing Care Accreditation Commission. You can see which CCRCs are accredited by logging on to www.ccaconline.org or calling the commission at 202-783-7286. CarePathways.com (www.carepathways. com) will match your elder with the appropriate facility for a fee ($300) and offers checklists that are helpful when considering the best environment for the elder. A checklist for independent living is located on page 446. Of course, none of these suggestions should be in lieu of personal visits to the facility and talking with the residents and their families, professional staff, and other employees.

To find the best physician for your elder, you can follow up on recommendations from friends, colleagues, relatives, and/or other health professionals. A local uni-versity medical center, nearby hospital, or the American Geriatrics Society (800-247-4779) are also good sources for referrals. A geriatrician or board-certified doctor with a certification in geriatrics could be an excellent fit.

End-of-Life Issues

Grief and loss are a normal part of life for virtually everyone, yet it's an area that still seems taboo in our society. It's often difficult to find the proper words when consoling someone, and talk of death and last wishes is often avoided, even as a loved one is dying.

If you're married, caring for a loved one, or want to make your own wishes known, a dialogue about the issues surrounding incapacity or death should take place. As difficult as it may seem, set up a meeting time, let the people involved know the topic of discussion, put on the coffee or tea, sit in some comfortable chairs, and start addressing these tough issues. A survey by the National Hospice Foundation found that three-fourths of Americans have not made their end-of-life wishes known

---

If you need an outstanding specialist for a particular medical issue, www.BestDoctors.com, a completely independent service that does not accept money from physicians to be listed, will do a search for a fee. You can also see their list of premier hospitals (for free).

through either oral or written communication. As a result, if a loved one is unable to make decisions, others are forced into second-guessing what his or her wishes are, sometimes resulting in anxiety, guilt, or conflict among family members. Assuming you're addressing these issues for yourself, here are some specific suggestions.

Health care proxy. If you become unable to make medical decisions on your own, you want someone who will be able to carry out your wishes. Your health care proxy should be someone you trust who has agreed to speak on your behalf and to advocate for you. Health care proxy forms can be state specific. Share these forms with your physicians and family members so they know who the health care proxy is. See a sample health care proxy form from www.SeniorSite.com; type "Proxy Form" in the search bar, then click on "Senior Site—Health Care Proxy Form."

Durable power of attorney. Just as you may need someone to speak for you medically, you may also need someone to speak for you financially and legally.

"Durable" power of attorney means that the person would represent you while you are incapacitated, or until the power is withdrawn or you pass away. If you are single/divorced/widowed, you may want an adult child to act as your durable power of attorney. Some documents combine the durable power of attorney with health care forms. Durable power of attorney forms can vary by state; they are legal documents and should be carefully worded, perhaps with input from an attorney. You can purchase copies online (by state) through www.MedLawPlus.com or www.FindLegalForms.com. Again, family members as well as your attorney need to be made aware of your durable power of attorney.

Living will/advance directive. Under what conditions do you want to be resuscitated or attached to a respirator? What are your feelings about pain management and palliative care? Do you want to be kept alive no matter what the prognosis? How do you feel about donating your organs? Do you want to die at home or have hospice care, as opposed to dying in a hospital? A living will/advance

---

For help in starting difficult discussions about end-of-life issues, you can download the booklet "Conversations Before the Crisis" by the Last Acts Partnership. The full text is on the Web (www.lastacts.org, click on "Publications," then the title), or contact Last Acts at 202-296-8071.

directive reflects your medical wishes if you are incapacitated. Having your preferences in writing (again, you need to share these with the relevant people) will help your doctor(s), health care proxy, and family members carry out your desires. Surveys have found that only about one-fourth of people have a living will/advance directive. See a sample of one on page 456.

Funeral arrangements. Consider leaving written instructions about your final arrangements. What do you want your obituary to say? Do you want an open or closed casket? Or, do you want to be cremated or to donate your body to science? Which funeral home should handle your remains? Who should conduct the funeral or memorial service? Who would you like as your pallbearers? Any thoughts on readings, flowers, etc.? Do you already own a cemetery plot? One of the author's fathers had placed his wishes in writing about the things that were very important to him. He had written his own obituary, stressing his love for his wife and children, service to

his country, professional accomplishments, and minor league pitching career; this is what was published. He preferred a certain funeral home (which was used) and stated his desire to die at home (which he did with the help of hospice care). Again, let someone (or preferably two people) know about your wishes, or at least where to find them in writing in the event of your passing.

In addition to the forms that deal with end-of-life issues, you need to communicate information about your other records of importance (mortgages, deeds, financial records, will, etc.). We provide a sample form (the Estate Planning Register) on page 465 that helps you compile, organize, and specify where your documents are located. And don't forget to talk about items that may be meaningful to children or relatives. Asking family members if there are any things (jewelry, furniture, or clothing, for example) they would like after you're gone (and then documenting this in your will) can prevent dissent among relatives later.

Purchase a casket over the Internet? In 1996, the Federal Trade Commission mandated that funeral homes must accept caskets purchased from other suppliers. This has resulted in real savings (averaging 50 percent or so over funeral home prices), and delivery is usually guaranteed in 1 or 2 days. In addition, monuments, flowers, urns, vaults, and markers can be ordered online at significant savings.

Grief and Loss

"Death is a punishment to some, to others a gift, and to many a favor." This quote from Seneca may apply to those who die, but often the living are bereft, with tremendous feelings of sorrow, bewilderment, and loneliness. How to cope? Consider a support group: Churches, hospitals, hospice programs, health providers, and neighbors and friends may be able to suggest a forum in your community. Support groups can help both emotionally and practically. Meeting others who are going through what you're experiencing and getting advice on practical matters can be quite therapeutic. The Internet can be a source of comfort as well; there are many groups you can join online to share your concerns and grief (www.growthhouse.org/chat is an example).

AARP is well-known for its grief and loss outreach. They offer a grief support line (866-797-2277), a one-to-one peer program that pairs a volunteer who has experienced a similar loss with the bereaved, and a number of grief programs and publications. Contact AARP (www.aarp.org, and enter "Grief and Loss" in the search bar, or 800-424-3410).

A number of excellent books have been written about grief and loss. We've provided several suggestions in the resources for this chapter.

Boomers will delay the inevitable through better nutrition, exercise, medication, supplements, and behavioral changes. Being a proactive cohort, they will aim for a "good death" for themselves and their loved ones. To paraphrase Dylan Thomas, baby boomers will not go gentle into that good night.

true LIFE **Vera K. is 80 years old.**
She relocated from England over 20 years ago, lives in Cincinnati, and is married to a man 20 years younger. She plays competitive tennis (doubles) four to five times a week with women in their thirties and forties. Her zest for life, belief that age is just a number, and willingness to try new things is an inspiration to her friends and family. (tL)

Inside every older person is a younger person—wondering what the hell happened!

HOW DO YOU MAKE YOUR MONEY LAST AS LONG AS YOU DO?

"A rich man is nothing but a poor man with money."
—W. C. Fields

According to *Advisor Today*, retirees' number one fear is "running out of money before they run out of life." The percentage of people saying they have saved for retirement decreased from 75 percent to 71 percent between 2000 and 2001. The 2001 Annual Retirement Confidence Survey, conducted by the Employee Benefit Research Institute, also shows that today's workers feel less secure about having enough money to retire comfortably: Sixty-three percent felt secure in 2001, compared to 72 percent in 2000.

No doubt, the steady stock market drop that began in early 2000 is taking its toll. According to an AARP survey conducted in November and December of 2002, about 20 percent of Americans have postponed their retirement; 10 percent of retirees have returned to work because of financial considerations; and almost 10 percent said their investments had decreased by more than half. Of those working, 80 percent feel they won't be able to retire completely.

In the United States, retirees have traditionally relied on three sources of income: pension benefits, Social Security, and personal savings. Many companies have moved from traditional "defined benefit plans" to "defined contribution" plans such as 401(k)s that place the onus on the employee for investment decisions. (There's a detailed discussion of these plans on page 376.) And even though Social Security is often viewed as a safety net, almost half of retirees rely on Social Security as their chief source of income. As for personal savings, about a third of Americans have said they haven't saved anything for retirement!

So, how do you ensure a comfortable retirement? The uncertainty of the stock and bond markets has made this question more critical than ever for today's retirees.

HOW MUCH MONEY DO YOU NEED TO RETIRE?

In a way, this is a trick question. One rule of thumb says you need only 60 to 80 percent of your current income to retire, since it costs money to make money—workers pay for transportation, a work wardrobe, and meals, plus they pay Social Security taxes and invest in retirement funds. In addition, many retirees have already put their kids through college and plan to downsize their homes. Some experts, however, suggest you may need 100 percent or more of your current income (especially when you first retire) if you still have kids in school, have parents who rely on you for some financial support, have to pay a larger share of your health insurance, plan on traveling extensively or pursuing new interests, would like to eat every meal out, or want to relocate to a more expensive resort-type setting. The real answer to "How much do you need?" is that you can't rely on anyone's rule of thumb—you need to make your own judgments after considering your own retirement plans.

Each of us is different. Some of us are eternally optimistic, while others have a dim view of the world. Some people save money to a fault, while others seem never to have a spare dime. Here's another catch-22: The earlier you start planning for retirement, the better. The earlier you start, however, the less you will know what your specific needs will be down the line. Will you need long-term care insurance? Will you have to move to a home with your bedroom on the main level for mobility purposes? As you grow older, you will have a much better idea of how you want to live in your retirement years, but if you wait until you are older to start planning for retirement, you will have less time to prepare for it.

The best way to start thinking about retirement is to think about the choices you'll be making. If you are within 5 years of retirement, you probably have a fairly good idea of the lifestyle you desire. You may know you want to work part time, volunteer, and develop some new skills. You might be trying to decide whether you should relocate to a warmer climate, buy a second home, or downsize your housing in order to travel and spend less time on chores. Each of these decisions comes with some type of cost—financial, emotional, or both.

Many people don't really have a handle on what life is costing them now. We get a paycheck, pay our bills, and if there is anything left over, we spend it or add it to our savings or investments; if we're short, money comes out of savings. Here are some specific things to consider as you think about your financial retirement plan.

Reexamine your 401(k) plan. First and foremost, once you retire, you won't be saving money from your paycheck to your 401(k) plan anymore. So money may start to come out of it rather than go into it every month.

Reslice the pie. Medical care and medications will likely become a much larger part of your overall expenditures, and the cost of leisure travel, which has held fairly steady in recent years, may spiral upward as the 78 million boomers start marching toward postponed vacations. There are many variables to consider—how long you'll live, the return on your investments, future inflation rates, and unexpected retirement expenses, to mention a few.

Reexamine homeownership. Even if your mortgage will be paid before you retire, you will still have real estate taxes and insurance to pay. If these amounts are cur-

---

A savings rule of thumb: Put at least 10 percent of your annual gross income aside for retirement. If you've hit 50 and haven't started saving, increase this to at least 20 percent.

rently escrowed and paid for you by the lender, remember to account for them separately when planning for the future. Also, remember that without a mortgage, you will have no mortgage interest tax deduction, so you may see your income tax payments go up. (See the pros and cons of having a mortgage on page 383.)

Separate the necessities from discretionary expenses. Heat, electricity, telephone, health insurance, food, and car expenses are among the things you might have a hard time foregoing. Vacations, club expenses, hobbies, subscriptions, dining out, entertainment, and charitable contributions are discretionary items and may vary quite a bit from year to year. And don't forget the support you may give to your kids, your grandkids, and maybe even an elderly relative.

Don't forget the important capital items. Do you have several cars now that you will continue to have in retirement? How often will you replace those cars, and what will you spend to do so? Will you lease, borrow, or pay cash? Will your home need improvements (a new roof, landscaping, painting, emergency repairs), and what will they cost? Will you be maintaining two homes? If so, what will be the added cost?

Plan for inflation. It can be your biggest enemy (although making bad investments and spending too much on frivolous things can be just as bad). An unfortunate reality is that many people ignore inflation when calculating what they'll need down the road. This is a huge mistake. While working, your raises generally help you keep up with inflation. When you retire, you need to plan for income increases just to pay for price increases. While inflation has been very low in recent years (prices for the goods we buy have increased about 2.5 percent per year for the past decade), this may not always be so. For example, in 1980 the inflation rate was 13.5 percent—in just that 1 year! And many of the things you will be buying in retirement may increase at

---

What about the new Medicare drug benefit (Part D) that is scheduled to take effect in 2006? According to Steve Kerch, personal finance editor at CBS.Marketwatch.com, "the Economic Policy Institute says only 50 percent of Medicare users will wind up saving money under the plan; the rest will pay more or pay the same and be forced into a system that may not be to their liking." This conclusion applies to those who will be 65 and older in 2006.

much higher rates than the average rate of inflation.

Decide on a reasonable inflation rate for the sake of projection—say, somewhere between 3 and 4 percent for most of your ordinary expenses, 5 to 7 percent for health care. The chart below, which assumes a 4 percent rate of inflation on purchasing today's equivalent of $25,000 in goods and services, illustrates inflation's tremendous impact.

EFFECTS OF INFLATION

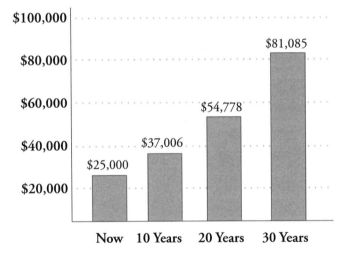

Assuming a 4% inflation rate, 30 years from now it will take more than $80,000 to purchase what $25,000 does today!

Anticipate health insurance costs. They are becoming a huge concern. Currently, Medicare is available at age 65. Whether you retire before or after age 65, you still must anticipate your health insurance costs. Since many businesses subsidize the cost of health insurance, expect that paying the full amount will cost you much more than the amount currently deducted from your paycheck; if you retire prior to age 65, this may amount to an additional $8,000 to $12,000 per year. You may find that your employer provides some coverage upon retirement, but you need to know which family members are covered and how long that coverage lasts. An online study conducted between July and September 2002 by the Kaiser Family Foundation and Hewitt Associates involving 435 companies found that, within several years, more than 20 percent were probably going to discontinue health coverage for future retirees.

If you need health insurance for someone who has a serious health condition, your insurance premiums may be considerably higher. Even when you qualify for Medicare, you may still pay for supplemental coverage and wrestle with the cost of prescriptions. If your health

---

If you're looking to compare health plans, try www.eHealthInsurance.com or 800-977-8860.

plan now subsidizes your drug costs, that coverage may stop in retirement. In that case, expect your prescriptions to cost up to four times more—out of your pocket.

Consider long-term care insurance. More than 40 percent of Americans aged 65 or older will enter a nursing home at least once, with an average stay of 3 to 5 years—and since women live an average of 7 years longer than men, it's more likely they'll end up in a nursing home. A 2003 Metropolitan Life Insurance survey estimated that it costs about $66,000 a year, or about $180 a day, for a private room in a nursing home. Keeping inflation in mind, those numbers will boggle the mind 15 to 30 years from now, when boomers may need long-term care.

Among the largest companies selling long-term care insurance are Transamerica, Occidental, GE Capital, John Hancock, Unum Provident, MetLife, CAN, and Penn Treaty. There are a lot of questions to ask if you're considering this type of insurance: How long has the company been around, and how long has it been selling this type of insurance? How healthy are its finances? (Check www.ambest.com or www.insure.com/ratings for financial strength ratings.) What conditions are necessary to qualify for benefits? Is the policy guaranteed to be renewable? Exactly what services are covered (does it cover home care and Alzheimer's, for example)? How long after you need services do the benefits kick in? Is being admitted to a hospital a necessary prerequisite to receiving benefits? What is the benefit period of the policy? Do the benefits keep pace with inflation? Do you need to keep paying the premiums once you start collecting benefits?

Invest less aggressively. Add an element of conservatism to your investment decisions. You will need to make investments, and investments always have risks. The risks could be just temporary declines in the market value of a good company's stock, or they could be more severe—bonds defaulting, elimination of a dividend you were counting on for your income, or even bankruptcy. If you place too many large bets, you increase the possibility of a failed retirement plan. Because of this, practice diversification, and plan your investment strategy with prudence; don't put all your dollars into one or two companies; place most of your faith in companies that have successfully weathered the past (especially after the three

---

You can further investigate insurance companies by calling your state's insurance department.

years of investment trauma between 2000 and 2003); and use a mix of investments, such as a combination of bonds, CDs, money market funds, real estate, and stock. Mutual funds are great tools that offer instant diversification within almost all investment asset classes. Don't bet on long shots, or if you must, keep those bets to sizes that you can afford to lose. (For more help with diversification, see pages 389 to 391.)

Be careful when selling a business. If you plan to sell your business and use the proceeds from your years of sweat and toil to provide a nest egg for retirement, be sure to plan for contingencies. If you're getting all the cash up front, that's great, but many business sales are structured with payouts lasting 5 years, 10 years, or more. If you have one of these structures, what are you going to do if the new owner fails? Will you be in a position to take back control (and will you even know before it's too late)? How will you replace this cash flow? Are you on the hook for the liabilities of the business because you had to cosign notes pledging some or all of your personal assets? Be very careful here, and be sure your accountant and legal advisor explain all the contingencies and risks of the sale agreement.

Reexamine your life insurance. You may be close to dropping that old term life insurance policy because the premium is going up. If you find that your assets and income are comfortable and your investments are positioned conservatively, your spouse might not need it. But if you still have debts or your plan looks tight, or if your 401(k) and company stock took a beating in the market, you may want to keep that policy in place to ensure that your spouse's future is secure. (For more on life insurance, see pages 385 to 389.)

Think about how you think about money. It's an odd statement, but a fairly new area called "behavioral economics," which combines psychology with finances, has found that people don't necessarily follow the "rules" economic theory predicts. For example, people often view a tax refund as "found money" and treat it differently than they would a paycheck. Another example con-

---

How long will it take your invested money to double? Using the "Rule of 72," start with the number 72 and divide it by the expected rate of return. For example, if your money is invested at 4 percent, divide 72 by 4 = 18. Thus, it would take 18 years for your money to double.

cerns an experiment involving an auction for tickets to a Boston Celtics basketball game. Researchers from MIT found that those in the experimental group who were told they could pay with a credit card were willing to bid twice as much for the tickets as those who were told they would have to pay by cash or check. The moral: Think about how you think about money—and how it affects your decision-making process.

Adopt a different way of looking at things. Instead of asking how much money you need to retire, you could ask how much you should *withdraw* from your savings to ensure your money will last as long as you do. Although 5 percent is often used as a rule of thumb, there is considerable debate about the answer to this question, and it depends somewhat on your age when you retire and your life expectancy. One common recommendation is to spend 3 to 5 percent or less of your accumulated savings in the initial retirement year. Obviously, the more you keep invested, the more you will earn for the future. Compounding produces a bigger effect the longer funds stay invested. Then, to keep pace with inflation, increase your withdrawal by the inflation rate for that year. This works out fine if you're earning a good return; but if the market has a bad year, you may have to deny yourself an inflation raise that year to en-

sure that your money lasts. Or, make intermittent adjustments to increase your withdrawals based on inflation—doing so every year could cause the money to run out more quickly. Also, as a hedge against a big market dive, consider putting some funds in a short-term bond fund as a cash reserve, and then replenish it by selling longer-term investments, if necessary.

Finally, if you don't mind potentially wild fluctuations in your living expenses, you could take out a fixed percent, say 3 to 4 percent, of your savings every year. You probably won't run out of money, but the amount you can spend will vary with the value of your investments. A variation on this is to subtract the annual inflation rate from your annual investment return to determine the percentage of your savings you can spend for the upcoming year. According to Jonathan Pond, president of Financial Planning Information, if you retire at age 65 or thereabouts, withdraw between 6 and 7 percent of your money in the first year of retirement; if you retire in your early sixties or late fifties, withdraw 5 to 6 percent your first year. Then, use inflation to calculate how much to withdraw each subsequent year. For example, if you spent $50,000 in your first year and inflation was 3 percent that year, you would plan to spend $51,500 in 2004 (3% of 50,000 = 1,500). (These guidelines assume an average annual return of 7.5 percent.) Or, to be very safe, Pond suggests you withdraw only 4 percent of your savings the first year no matter how old you are when you retire. The bottom line is, if you remove too much of your asset base and inflation is higher than you expect, or your returns are lower, you could easily run out of money before you run out of time to spend it!

Contemplate end-of-life issues. Are you trying to preserve your family's wealth for your children, or do you plan to give it away to charity? Or are you hoping to have very little left at the time of your death? Do you have real estate or family heirlooms? Have you developed the tools for your plans to be implemented?

About 60 percent of American adults lack a very important document: a will. If you die intestate (without a will), state law, not your personal wishes, will determine what happens to some or all of your assets. You might be surprised how your state thinks your assets should be divided! A will can also prevent unnecessary expenses for your loved ones. Attorney fees can range from a few hundred dollars for a simple will to thousands of dollars for more complex documents. If you want to attempt to do it yourself, you can purchase books or software from a place such as Nolo (www.nolo.com or 800-728-3555) that helps you create or customize a will. Prices range

from $14 to $50. If nothing else, trying it yourself first will give you a better understanding of the issues that will arise and the information you will need when sitting down with an attorney, and it may save you some of the cost of a professional's time. Keep in mind that whenever you move to a different state, your will should be reviewed and possibly updated.

Many of the standard estate planning measures are geared towards heterosexual, married U.S. citizens. Others for whom these categories do not apply need to take special care in their end-of-life planning. Special rules also apply to those who live in one of the community property states (Arizona, California, Idaho, Louisiana, Nevada, New Mexico, Texas, Washington, and Wisconsin).

Will your spouse, partner, or some third party make financial or medical decisions for you if you are unable to do so yourself? When life-altering events overtake us, it's often too late to go back and put a plan into action. Refer back to chapter 8 for some practical suggestions and examples regarding a durable power of attorney for finances, choosing a health care proxy (also called a health care power of attorney), completing an advance directive (also called a living will), and talking about these difficult topics with loved ones. To help you organize and list your important documents, refer to page 465 for an "Estate-Planning Register."

WHAT ARE YOUR SOURCES OF RETIREMENT INCOME?

Now that you've thought about some general issues that will affect your retirement planning, you need to think about where the money will come from.

Work

Perhaps you'll be among the majority of boomers who plan to continue working after their primary career ends. This would certainly be a source of income, and it could also help with your health insurance costs.

Social Security

Available as early as age 62, this government pension fund provides a base level security net for most people who worked in the private sector and their nonworking spouses (even former spouses). The benefit varies with the number of quarters worked (for which taxes were paid into the Social Security system) and the level of income earned. Be aware that some individuals are not qualified to receive a benefit or will receive only a reduced benefit. This is true of some people who were employed by state and local governments or school districts and who receive pension income from state pension programs. There is an offset to the Social Security benefit for a portion of the retirement benefit received from these state plans. Information regarding these offsets is available from the state pension agencies and from the Social Security Administration Web site (www.ssa.gov). Two relevant publications about these offsets are the "Windfall Elimination Provision," SSA publication number 05-10045, and the "Government Pension Offset," publication number 05-10007. Or, you can call the Social Security Administration at 800-772-1213.

Rather than prepay funeral costs, preplan with your family and set up a separate account for funeral purposes. If you or a loved one have a prepaid plan already or feel you would like to purchase one, know what protections a reputable funeral home guarantees through the Consumer Preneed Bill of Rights. Contact the National Funeral Director's Association at www.nfda.org or 800-228-6332.

For those born before 1937, a full retirement benefit is paid if the benefits start at age 65; for the rest of us, the age when full benefits will be paid gradually increases to 67 for those born in 1960 or later. For example, individuals born in 1942 will get full benefits only if they begin taking them at age 65 and 10 months or later. How can you determine your full retirement age? Use the Social Security chart at www.ssa.gov (click on "Plan your retirement," then "Find my retirement age") or call 800-772-1213.

Although retirees can start collecting benefits at age 62, the benefits will be reduced, thus requiring them to determine whether a reduced benefit starting earlier is better than a regular benefit starting later. If an early benefit is elected, however, the retiree will receive the reduced amount for the rest of his or her life. Sixty percent of people take their benefits early.

To make things more confusing, if you continue to work after the benefits start, your earnings may increase the amount of your Social Security benefits subject to regular income taxes (see a discussion of this in chapter 10). In addition, if you're receiving Social Security benefits *and* working prior to the month in which you reach full retirement age, your Social Security benefits may be reduced to reflect your employment earnings. The reduction is $1 in benefits for each $2 you earn above a limit ($11,640 in 2004) during the years prior to the year in which you reach full retirement age. During the year in which you reach full retirement age, the formula is more generous, using a reduction of $1 in benefits for each $3 you earn above a limit ($31,080 in 2004). Also, in the year you reach full retirement age, benefits are reduced only for your earnings prior to the month in which you reach full retirement age. During and after the month in which you reach full retirement age, you are no longer subject to a reduction of your Social Security benefits resulting from your employment earnings.

The Social Security Administration mails an annual statement of projected benefits to those who are 25 and older and not yet receiving benefits. You may also contact them at www.ssa.gov/mystatement or call 800-772-1213 to request a copy. Keep in mind that the benefits projected in the statement are based on assumptions as to your future earnings, so be sure to read the fine print in order to understand those assumptions.

For example, let's say that Paul S. started collecting benefits of $600 per month ($7,200 for the year) at age 64, even though his full retirement age was 66, and he also worked and earned $20,000 for 2004. Since his earnings were over the $11,640 limit by $8,360, his benefits are reduced by $4,180 because Paul loses $1 in benefits for each $2 he makes over the limit.

Here's another example of how this reduction works in the year during which you reach full retirement age. Assume Karen H. was age 64 at the beginning of 2004 and reached full retirement age in August. She worked from January through July, earning $33,000 while receiving $600 per month in benefits. Since her earnings were $1,920 more than the $31,080 limit, her benefits are reduced by $640 because, in Karen's case, the reduction is $1 for each $3 of earnings over the limit. How does Social Security know what you are making? Well, in an ideal world you'd call them and tell them your estimated income for the year, rather than waiting for them to gather the information from income tax records. They will then adjust your payments accordingly. If you overestimate or underestimate what you make, they will adjust future benefit payment checks or pay you a lump sum, if the situation warrants it, so you're "even."

Company or Government Defined Benefit Plans

Some companies and many governmental agencies, schools, hospitals, and colleges continue to offer traditional pension plans, also called defined benefit plans. Most of these plans pay a monthly stipend for life (they may also offer the option of taking a reduced pension payment so that your surviving spouse will still receive a benefit). Usually, this benefit is fixed and does not have inflation protection. Although these plans rarely allow a lump sum distribution, some are now being converted to cash balance plans, which may, in fact, provide for a lump sum distribution option at retirement.

Other than choosing among the various distribution options and timing when the pension begins, there is

---

For more information about working and Social Security, see SSA publication number 05-10069, "How Work Affects Your Benefits" at www.ssa.gov. Click on "Publications," then on "Recently Published or Revised Publications," then on "How Work Affects Your Benefits."

little one can do to change the value of a traditional pension benefit. Most benefits are calculated based upon a formula which uses the number of years employed and the average salary level (commonly the last 3 or 5 years of salary prior to retirement). The result is a benefit that could be as much as 50 percent of pay for someone employed for 20 years or even 70 percent of pay for someone who worked 30 years or more. Early retirement provisions may permit a reduced income starting at age 62 (usually 80 percent of the age 65 benefit). It's best to check with your employer to determine the various provisions of your plan.

While there may be few risks associated with pension plans (the primary risk falls on the plan's sponsor to fund the plan enough to provide the guaranteed benefit), two should be considered. First, because the benefit is usually fixed, inflation will erode its value over time. Second, there may be some risk of benefit reduction should the employer become insolvent. Although a federal pension guarantee program, the Pension Benefit Guaranty Corporation (PBGC), protects worker benefits from such insolvencies, it has an annual maximum limit of approximately $40,000 for workers who retire at their normal retirement age, so some expected pension benefits could be lost in the event of a company's demise.

It is also important to understand that you are usually locked into your distribution choices. For example, you may choose to take a pension benefit that is reduced by 20 percent so that it will continue, in the event of your death, for the life of your spouse. If your spouse predeceases you, the reduction will probably not be restored (although some plans do offer restoration options).

Some businesses offer supplemental pension benefits for executive, professional, and/or managerial employees. These come in many forms and are called many different things—top hat plans, nonqualified deferred compensation, supplemental pensions, executive pension plans—but, essentially, they are promises to pay a pension or lump sum benefit when the employee attains certain goals, such as a specific length of service or retirement.

These programs are customized to the company or to a particular subset of employees and are not required to provide uniform benefits. Of some concern is that these benefits do not have to be prefunded by the business.

You can apply for Social Security retirement/disability/spouse's benefits online. Go to www.ssa.gov.

Even if prefunded, these plans are vulnerable if the company experiences a financial decline, and company insolvency may eliminate them, as creditors will have a higher claim on the assets of the employer. For example, when accounting firm Arthur Andersen became insolvent following the Enron debacle, retired partners of the firm lost their pension benefits because the firm's retirement plan was unfunded. (Even if it had been fully funded, the claims of other creditors most probably would have decimated the retired partners' funding.) Another example occurred when a large agribusiness company went into Chapter 11, and executives who had been encouraged to retire years earlier with the promise of extra financial support from an executive pension plan found that their monthly checks stopped coming in the mail.

Keep in mind that employer pension benefits are fully taxable and do not survive the death of the employee, unless the retiree has elected a "contingent annuitant" option at the time of retirement. This means the pension is a fixed amount for the retiree and when the retiree dies, the contingent annuitant—normally, the spouse—continues to receive a monthly benefit payment. This payment may be the same as or less than the retiree was receiving, based on the election made by the retiree at the time of retirement. Although this provides desired security in many cases, there is a cost in the form of a reduced benefit from what the retiree would receive if there were no contingent annuitant. For those lucky enough to have both a retirement benefit and a partner, the contingent annuitant decision is one of the most important retirement planning decisions.

A second distribution option that may be available to a retiree is the election of guaranteed payments to himself or herself or to a beneficiary for a specified time period, such as a "10-year certain" benefit. In this case, if the retiree (or the retiree and the spouse) dies, a designated beneficiary would receive up to 120 monthly payments—the 10-year certain benefit—minus the ones received by the primary annuitant(s) prior to death. On the other hand, if the retiree (or the retiree and the spouse) lives beyond the period of the guaranteed benefit, the pension will continue for the balance of the re-

---

For questions about pension guarantees, contact the Pension Benefit Guaranty Corporation at www.pbgc.gov or 202-326-4000.

tiree's life—the 10-year certain option just ensures that there will be a minimum of 120 monthly payments to the retiree or the beneficiary.

Defined Contribution Plans

Another type of retirement plan is an employer defined contribution plan (also known as profit-sharing, 401(k), 401(3)(b), and money purchase pension plans). Profit-sharing and money purchase pension plans represent dollars that your employer has placed into a retirement trust for you on a pretax basis. Section 401(k) plans often include both employee contributions (called salary deferrals) and employer matches, both generally on a pretax basis. When you retire, these funds are available to you to supplement your other retirement income. The funds that your employer put into the plans may be subject to a vesting schedule determined by how long you have

been employed (the longest vesting schedules are now 6 years from date of hire). If you have been employed for a shorter period than is required for full vesting, the employer contributions to your account will be reduced or eliminated if you leave the company; however, the dollars you put in the plan through 401(k) deferrals are not subject to vesting—they are yours from day one.

All dollars distributed from retirement plans are usually subject to taxes, but, like everything else in life, there are exceptions. Some plans permit after-tax salary deferrals to be invested, allowing only the earnings to be tax deferred. In this case, distributions of the after-tax contributions are not subject to taxation, but distributions of the earnings on all contributions are. For example, assume Jennifer, age 65, had contributed $31,000 in after-tax contributions to her qualified retirement plan and will receive a joint and survivor annuity of $1,000 per

If you own a business, look into making enhancements to your retirement plan in order to increase your retirement savings. This can be especially useful for those business owners who do not have any employees, since pension nondiscrimination rules will generally require that the employees be covered along with the owner. Under the current rules for 2004, businesses like these can defer and shelter from income taxes up to $44,000 per year in a defined contribution plan and up to the annual amount necessary to fund a pension of $165,000 per year in a defined benefit plan for the owner.

month over both her life and the life of her husband, David, who is also 65. Using IRS-prescribed mortality tables, which show that an estimated 310 monthly payments will be made while either Jennifer or David is alive, $100 of each payment will be tax free. After 310 monthly payments have been received, each future payment will be 100 percent taxable.

Most people avoid taking a taxable lump sum payment upon retirement and elect to either take income out of the plan as needed (and be taxed on it as withdrawals are made) or transfer the lump sum payment (tax free) from the retirement plan to an Individual Retirement Account (IRA) via either a tax-free rollover or a tax-free direct transfer, thus allowing the earnings and growth of the plan's assets to go untaxed until withdrawals are made at a later date. A tax-free rollover must be completed within 60 days of the date of the distribution, whereas a tax-free direct transfer of a lump sum distribution goes directly from the trustee of the original plan to the trustee of the new plan. For more information on lump sum distributions, see pages 393 to 395.

Individual Retirement Accounts

Think of traditional IRAs—we'll get to Roth IRAs in a bit—as a tax-deferral wrapper around a pool of investments. The funding may have come from funds transferred from a retirement plan (called a rollover) or from annual contributions, which are often deductible. The annual funding and rollovers can be mixed together in the same account. Once in this pool, the investments enjoy protection from annual income taxes (they are taxed only when funds are distributed). IRAs can also hold some after-tax contributions. These deposits enjoy tax-deferred growth, even though the principal was previously taxed. The IRS has special rules for taking distributions from IRAs containing after-tax contributions. It's

---

Although Susan E., in her grief, failed to roll over a distribution from her deceased husband's qualified pension plan within the required 60 days, her alert CPA realized it was possible to obtain a waiver of the 60-day requirement in those cases where a failure to waive the requirement would be unduly harsh and unfair. Ten months after filing a request with the IRS for another chance to accomplish the tax-free rollover, a new 60-day period was granted.

the responsibility of the taxpayer to keep good records of such contributions so that no income taxes are paid on the distribution of the after-tax amounts.

Congress has capped the amount of total contributions that can be made in any tax year to both IRAs and 401(k) plans. In 2001 the limitations on contributions to IRAs and 401(k) plans were increased from $2,000 and $10,000, respectively, to $5,000 for IRAs in 2008 and $15,000 for 401(k) plans in 2006, with the increases being phased in over the intervening years and with additional adjustments for inflation thereafter. The limitation for 2004 is $3,000 for IRAs and $13,000 for 401(k)s. Additional "catch-up" contributions are also allowed for those who are 50 or older. For IRAs, the catch-up contribution is $500 for 2004 and increases to $1,000 in 2006. For 401(k) plans, the catch-up contribution is $3,000 for 2004 and increases to $5,000 in 2006.

Roth IRAs

A new IRA was established several years ago that permits after-tax funding combined with tax-free earnings and tax-free distributions at retirement. Those who have more than 10 years until retirement (or until the funds will be distributed) and who qualify to use the Roth IRA will generally find it to be a very effective investment tool offering the ability to achieve tax-free returns.

For example, assume $3,000 is invested in a Roth and a traditional IRA at the beginning of each year for 20 years. Earning an average return of 8 percent each year, the principal would grow to approximately $148,000. For someone in the 25 percent marginal tax bracket, the traditional IRA would provide $10,500 per year of after-tax income over the following 20 years, while the Roth would provide about $14,000 of after-tax income per year. The $3,500 lower amount from the traditional IRA is caused by the 25 percent tax on the $14,000 annual distributions, which the Roth IRA does not have.

Disability Income

Most disability income plans terminate at age 65; there may be exceptions, however, such as military disability plans or privately funded disability insurance plans.

For a good overview of IRAs and the rules that govern them, go to www.bankrate.com (go to "IRA Center," then click on "Breaking down the IRAs").

Payments may or may not be tied into a future pension plan benefit. If they are, the disability payment may end at age 65, but the pension benefit should continue.

Other Investments

Rental real estate, common and preferred stocks, government and corporate bonds, certificates of deposit (CDs), municipal bonds, money market funds, and bank savings accounts represent the usual final frontier in a retiree's support base, although you may also receive alimony, get an inheritance, or have income from a partnership or other sources.

Each of these can provide income or an income supplement in varying degrees. Some have income tax advantages. Rental real estate offers tax deductions for depreciation, interest (if there are borrowings), and property taxes. Most common stocks and some preferred stocks currently enjoy a maximum tax of 15 percent on dividends received, and that rate also currently applies to long-term capital gains on the sale of stock (both preferential rates are scheduled to expire on December 31, 2008). Most municipal bonds are free of federal taxation and may be free of state taxation if you are filing a state tax return in the state issuing the bond.

Think of your investments as the engine that will power your retirement income. The larger the engine, the more financial horsepower you will generate to propel your retirement lifestyle.

SO, NOW WHAT?

You've thought about your expenses and reflected on your sources of retirement income. As part of your recipe for a financially successful retirement, you've decided when you plan to retire, determined how much you've

---

There has been much discussion about the huge, $10 trillion transfer of inherited wealth from their parents to the baby boomers. As a result, some analysts feel that boomers won't have to worry that much about saving. It turns out that over one-fourth of the largest bequests (those more than $100,000) will end up going to the already wealthiest one-fifth of boomers, and more than two-thirds of us won't get any inheritance, according to the AARP Public Policy Institute. Lesson: Start saving!

saved and plan to save (and *how*) before you retire, estimated how much your desired lifestyle will cost, guesstimated how long you'll live, factored in the effects of inflation and taxes, and thought about what (if anything!) you want to leave to others when you're gone. Remember that you and your spouse's assets and income may need to last into your late eighties or even nineties. For many, that's a planning horizon of 25 or 30 years or more, maybe equal to your entire working career.

Retirement Calculators

One way to get an estimate of how much money you need to retire is to use a retirement "calculator." Although not a perfect tool, it can help you determine a reasonable approximation of what you'll need to satisfy your goals. A few caveats, however: Most calculators assume an average annual return and ignore the fact that investment returns fluctuate (don't we know it!). Thus, even if you achieve your assumed average annual rate of return on your investments, you could achieve a lower return in the early years of retirement and a higher return in the later years, causing you to not meet your goals.

Be conservative when inputting the numbers on a retirement calculator—err on the low side for rate of return and on the high side for inflation rates, presume you'll live to a ripe old age, and assume you'll need more than the oft-quoted 70 percent of your current income. Play it safe, and plug in 100 percent. Several free calculators to try: Quicken.com Retirement Planner at www.quicken.com (type "Retirement Planner" in the search bar, then click on "Plan for Retirement with the Quicken Retirement Planning Financial Calculator"); the American Savings Education Council's "Ballpark Estimate" worksheet at www.sec.gov (type "Ballpark Estimate" into the search bar, then follow the clicks from there); or the ING Retirement Calculator at www.ing-usa.com (click on "Tools and Calculators," then "Retirement Calculator"). The "Income from Savings Calculator" at www.bankrate.com (click on "Calculators," then on "How long will your savings last?" under "CDs/Savings") allows you to predict your savings and how long you'll live, then calculates how long your money would last under those conditions or how much you should withdraw if you want it to last as long as you predict you will.

Monte Carlo Simulations

Another approach to determining how much money you'll need to retire is to use a Monte Carlo simulation. This type of calculation addresses the inherent wide swings of the stock market and doesn't presuppose a fixed annual return. It incorporates more of a bell curve, which the market does not always follow, either. The more complex Monte Carlo simulations, however, generally will allow you to project the success rate of your retirement assumptions.

Try out a retirement calculator using this type of simulation at http://www3.troweprice.com/ric/RIC/. You can also purchase software for Monte Carlo calculations; for example, Efficient Solutions sells MCRetire for about $30 (www.effisols.com or 203-744-4023). Or, if you have an account at Vanguard (Vanguard allows free trial software), Financial Engines, Morningstar, T. Rowe Price, or Fidelity Investments, you can pay to access their more complex Monte Carlo simulations. Keep in mind, though, that whatever type of forecasting you do, the original assumptions need to be sound in order to increase your probability of success. Remember the axiom: "Garbage in—garbage out."

Maybe You Should Start with Pencil and Paper

You need to be able to estimate how much you are going to spend in retirement as a starting point, even if you use a retirement calculator to project into the future. So before you start, why not complete the worksheet "How Much Do You Need for Retirement?" in Appendix 2. It's a helpful method of determining what you need when you retire and will help you quantify what you're spending now and compare it to what you predict you'll spend in retirement. Then, you'll calculate your best estimate of your retirement income. Finally, you'll subtract your retirement expenses from your retirement income and see what you get!

It's good to try at least two of the three methods to calculate what you need for retirement (online calculator, Monte Carlo simulation, and/or worksheet). Hopefully, the results are nice, big, positive numbers (meaning an excess of income over expenses). But what if they're not? You'll have to go back to the basics and decide what to do. Maybe your assumptions are faulty: Is your estimated in-

---

The statistics and probability involved in these calculations date back to the days of the Manhattan Project, when mathematician Stanislaw Ulam coined the phrase "Monte Carlo simulations" while working on problems associated with the development of the atomic bomb.

flation rate too high or the estimated return on your investments too low? If that's not the case, can you work longer before retiring or maybe part time after you retire? Cut spending before you retire, and save more? Reassess what you need to spend in retirement? What about those discretionary items we mentioned earlier? Can you trim your subscriptions, eliminate some travel, move to an area with a lower cost of living or lower taxes, stay in the same area but downsize your home, consider homesharing, rent out space in your home (if it's legal), cut back on charitable contributions, ask your grandchildren to pay their own way through college, consider a reverse mortgage, or forgo the inheritance you planned for your children? A professional may help you fine-tune your retirement planning. Also, take a look at some of the general suggestions we've made for Growing Your Own Personal Money Tree on page 399.

Finances Not Your Thing?

You may want to bounce your ideas about your retirement goals and ways to reach them off a professional. A certified public accountant (CPA), certified financial planner (CFP), insurance agent, or investment broker might meet your needs. A professional should be able to help you organize your thoughts, give investment and saving advice, and provide insight into the various rates of return and expected inflation factors or other costs you are trying to forecast. If you haven't been actively involved in number-crunching most of your life, the guidance of a professional can be well worth the cost of his or her advice. This cost can vary, of course, depending on the time involved; the scope of the planning project; the size and complexity of your asset base; whether it's a onetime meeting or an ongoing relationship of planning, monitoring, and recommending future adjustments; and how the professional bills his or her time.

Our recommendation would be start out with either a CPA or a CFP. After working with you to get your planning done, they may refer you to an investment broker and possibly also to an insurance agent to help you implement your plan. These professionals should be able to provide a comprehensive plan that details which investments you should make and what type of insurance, if any, you need, as well as provide estate planning, tax-saving tips, etc. For help in locating a CPA, contact the American Institute of Certified Public Accountants (AICPA) at 888-777-7077.

If you go with a CFP, recognize that there are several kinds of fee arrangements. A CFP may be compensated by commission, by fee, or through a combination of fees and commissions. Fees could involve charging you an hourly rate, charging by the "job" (for example, setting up your financial plan), or charging a percentage of the value of your investments (usually about 1.5 percent). Compensation is probably not the best way to choose a CFP. Their reputations and references are usually the best measure. Be aware that some clients—and even some financial professionals—feel there is a conflict of interest when commissions are involved because the planner might be tempted to steer clients toward purchases that involve larger commissions. All planners should be willing to divulge exactly how they are compensated. To locate a financial planner who works primarily on commission, contact the Society of Financial Service Professionals at www.financialpro.org or 888-243-2258. Planners can be located by name, location, or specialty. For fee-based planners, get in touch with the National Association of Personal Financial Advisors (NAPFA), which locates planners by zip code, at www.feeonly.org or 800-366-2732.

Of course, as you probably do when searching for doctors, dentists, or other professionals, ask for suggestions from your attorney, friends, neighbors, and colleagues.

NOT QUITE 20 QUESTIONS

Let's take a look at some answers to common questions, which may help shed more light on the thrill of retirement planning!

1. Should You Have a Mortgage?

This is a big question to address in your retirement planning, since you will probably have limited or no earned income from which to pay your mortgage. Having a mortgage is both a financial security issue and an investment issue. Although many think that no one truly benefits by having debt, it really depends on how much the debt costs and what return you get on the funds you borrow. Many people who are used to making real estate investments look at borrowing funds against the real estate as an acceptable risk. In fact, most investors in investment real estate probably feel that holding debt on that real estate is essential, but keep in mind that a personal residence is not investment real estate and does not generate income to help pay the debt.

You can justify having mortgage debt in retirement if, by borrowing, you invest the dollars not spent on the house, generating after-tax returns that exceed the after-tax cost of the mortgage (interest only). Note that your mortgage payment is only part interest, with the remainder being a paydown of debt. So, if you borrow (or continue to have a mortgage of) $100,000 with an interest rate of 5 percent, your cost of borrowing is $5,000 per year. Since the $5,000 is tax deductible, it may be costing you only $4,000 per year after considering the value of the tax deduction (assuming a 20 percent tax rate), for a 4 percent net of tax borrowing rate. Assume you put that money in a common stock or a stock mutual fund with the expectation of receiving a 2 percent annual dividend and of the stock's appreciating at 6 percent per year. Since dividends and long-term capital gains (gains from investments held longer than 12 months) are currently taxed at the maximum rate of 15 percent, there is a net after-tax return of $6,800, or 6.8 percent. So, by having that $100,000 mortgage and taking the risk of the stock mutual fund, you could have $2,800 per year of additional cash. Of course, some of this cash may have to be used to pay the principal on the debt, but that is essentially savings for you. Alternatively, if that money were invested in a bank CD with a 3 percent taxable return, you would be paying more in interest than you are receiving in return.

So, is having a mortgage worth it? Ultimately, you have to be the judge. Probably a small mortgage in proportion to total resources is worth the risk, but certainly heavy amounts of debt would be unwise for a retiree's household.

2. Should You Purchase Long-Term Care Insurance?

The answer is pretty much a catch-22. If you need to buy it, you probably can't afford it, and if you *can* afford it, you probably don't need it because you can self-pay if the need arises! There are a few things to keep in mind: The United Seniors Health Cooperative recommends that no more than 7 percent of your yearly income should go toward long-term care insurance. *Consumer Reports* recommended in November 2003 that you skip this type of insurance if your net worth is under $200,000 (Medicaid will kick in), if your net worth is more than $1.5 million (you can pay for it yourself), or if you can't pay for what you think you need or won't be able to pay rising premiums that may be imposed. Sue Stevens at Morningstar.com suggests that if your net worth is either $150,000 or less or $10 million or more, you should forgo long-term care insurance; otherwise, consider it.

You should also be aware that since Medicaid is designed for those with little money, a married couple must possess very few assets before it will kick in—that is, spouses are financially responsible for one another. Medicare, on the other hand, doesn't usually cover the type of custodial care that a nursing home provides. Private insurance doesn't cover nursing home care, other than perhaps some short-term recovery periods. Note, too, that there is often a waiting period (say, 90 days) before your policy covers certain benefits (hospice care and respite services may not have a waiting time).

So, what does it cost? Using the calculator at the Federal Long-Term Care Insurance Program (www.ltcfeds.com, click on "Premium Calculator" under "Resources"), a 35-year-old requesting very basic coverage and a lifetime limit of $110,000 (keep in mind the average yearly cost in a nursing home is now over $65,000) would pay $25.20 a month for coverage; a 51-year-old with more inclusive coverage and an unlimited benefit coverage would pay $163 per month; and a 65-year-old with the same coverage as the 51-year-old would pay $292 per month. Obviously, the type of coverage and your age play a huge role in the size of your premiums.

There is no doubt that long-term care insurance is a facet of retirement planning that needs to be addressed. You may find some consolation in the facts that the average stay in a nursing home is only about 3 years, that only about 5 percent of people over the age of 65 lives in a nursing home, and about 25 percent of those over 85 do. Of course, if you have family or children who are willing to take care of you, perhaps this discussion is moot!

3. What Are Some Life Insurance Guidelines?

The first piece of advice about life insurance is that it should generally not be purchased as an investment, nor, if you purchase permanent life insurance, should it be considered forced savings. After all, the life insurance agent is often paid large commissions when selling you permanent life insurance, and you're also paying for death benefits. These costs come out of your premiums and are not invested. Also, the ability to dip into the cash value of a policy actually equates to borrowing, not tapping into a savings account.

When you think about your retirement lifestyle, it's also time to think about your insurance needs. You may have purchased life insurance in order to replace your income if you died, pay off a mortgage or major outstanding loans, or provide for your children's education. Do you have a big estate or dependent relatives? Do you own a business? Are you married? If you answered "yes" to any of these questions, you may want to consider whether insurance is for you. Depending on your answers, you may no longer need insurance, you may need less insurance, or you may need more.

There are two basic categories of life insurance. The first, term insurance, is for a specific period of time, after which you need to decide whether to drop or continue the coverage. Term insurance offers death benefits only; if you die during the term you are insured, your beneficiary gets paid (this money is exempt from federal income tax, but not necessarily from estate tax); if you don't die, your beneficiary doesn't get paid. For example, say you are married, you and your spouse are retired, and you have a $100,000 mortgage left on your home which you plan to have paid off in 10 years. Consider buying a $100,000 term insurance policy and paying annual premiums for 10 years, then dropping the coverage once the mortgage is paid off. Or, you might be able to save money by using decreasing term insurance, a policy that provides for a smaller death benefit each year, rather than a constant death benefit. Either could give you the protection you need. Or, say you still have debts or your retirement plan looks tight, or your 401(k) and other investments took a beating in the market—you may want to keep a term policy you have purchased in place to ensure that your spouse's future is secure should you die first.

Term life insurance tends to be fairly inexpensive since it's very competitive. Keep in mind, though, that the cost of term insurance is based on your age and health, in addition to the amount of the death benefit, so the older you are, the more expensive the premiums are. You can choose to have the premiums increase each year, or you can choose for them to stay the same for a certain number of years before they increase; neither of these options is necessarily better than the other since a premium that stays level for a number of years will likely be initially higher than one that increases each year. In some cases, companies will pass on their increased costs to you by increasing your premiums, and some require you to prove you're in good health to continue your lower premiums. You may be able to convert your term insurance to permanent insurance.

Compare insurance policies at sites such as www.reliaquote.com/termlife/, or www.insure.com (click on "Life"). These sites will also help you calculate how much life insurance you need, based upon your circumstances. Another life insurance needs calculator can be found at http://moneycentral.msn.com (type "Life Insurance Needs Estimator" into the search bar).

The other category of insurance, permanent insurance, differs from term insurance in that there is a savings component to it, in addition to a death benefit. You can cash in your policy, you can borrow against it, or you can use it to supplement your retirement income (which is why it's also called cash-value life insurance). Permanent life insurance costs more than term (and will be more expensive the older you are when you purchase it), and don't forget that you're still paying those commissions (permanent insurance is more lucrative than term for those selling insurance). The beneficiary or beneficiaries will receive the death benefit exempt from federal income tax (but not necessarily from estate taxes), the premiums you pay usually do not vary from year to year, and the insurer can't cancel your coverage if you suddenly become a poor risk. The longer your permanent policy is in force, the greater the cash value, since much of the early premiums may go toward sales commissions and other administrative costs. In addition, assuming the dividends are high enough to keep the policy in force, you may ultimately be able to choose for your dividends to pay your premiums.

There are three types of permanent insurance: traditional whole life, universal life, and variable life. In general, whole life is best for the conservative investor—you get a fixed amount of accumulation of cash value over the term of the policy. Universal life is more flexible and allows the insured to adjust the premiums (you may even skip premiums at times, depending on the contract) but is tied to the insurer's success in the markets. And variable life is the riskiest type of permanent insurance—performance of the policy is tied to the investments you choose for your policy.

If you feel you need life insurance, the general rule of thumb is to purchase term insurance if you need it for a period of up to 10 years, but to purchase permanent life insurance if your need is for 20 years or more. The murkier part falls between the 10- to 20-year period. For most people, once you hit about 50, the reasons for purchasing term insurance have dwindled, and you're looking more at permanent life insurance. If you are comfortable with your assets and income, and your investments are positioned conservatively, you may not need any life insurance.

Actually, one of the biggest reasons to consider life insurance is to protect your heirs from estate taxes, which can gobble up 48 percent of your net worth (in 2004), stepping down to 45 percent (between 2007 and 2009). To avoid the taxman, consider setting up an irrevocable life insurance trust, which is not in your name, to protect your heirs. Since you do not own the policy yourself, the death proceeds are not taxable to your estate.

There are other permutations of life insurance, such as increasing and decreasing term insurance, but the bottom line is to determine if you need life insurance, and if so, how much and for how long. The calculators mentioned earlier will help you, but your best bet is getting advice from a professional who doesn't have a vested interest in pushing insurance. Don't be talked into purchasing life insurance just to cover your funeral expenses—except, possibly, in the event that your estate will not have any assets available for these costs.

4. How Can You Use Insurance as an Alternative to Electing a Joint and Survivor Payout from a Defined Pension Plan?

If you have a defined benefit pension, near the time you start receiving your pension, you must elect to have either the full pension paid over your life or a reduced pension paid over both your life and that of your spouse. This is not a simple decision because it comes at a cost, usually a permanent 10 to 20 percent reduction in the amount of the pension benefit. Once this election is made, it usually cannot be changed or altered. Therefore, if a life benefit is elected for a spouse but that spouse dies first (or you get a divorce), the pension has been reduced

in anticipation of a benefit that never materialized.

One solution to this dilemma is to elect the full pension and buy a life insurance policy on your life, to replace the lost income of the pension in the event that you predecease your spouse. Alternatively, should the spouse die first, or if you end up divorced, the insurance policy can be cancelled since there would no longer be a need to replace the pension upon your death. Or, you could keep the insurance policy as a source of a legacy for your heirs. Keep in mind when evaluating this option that the life insurance death benefit payable to your spouse is not subject to either federal estate tax or income tax.

As an example of this strategy, consider George T., age 55, and his wife, Sally. George's company has a defined benefit plan that will pay him $36,000 per year ($3,000 per month) for the rest of his life when he retires at age 65. He has several choices for providing a continuing benefit for Sally if he predeceases her and is considering the one that will pay her $24,000 ($2,000 per month) for the rest of her life. Under this election George's pension benefit will be reduced to $28,800 ($2,400 per month). In the event that Sally predeceases George, even very early in his retirement, the retirement benefit would not be reinstated back to the $36,000. Alternatively, assuming he is healthy, George could use the $7,200 difference ($36,000 minus $28,800) to buy a life insurance policy that would pay $600,000 to Sally in the event of his death. If Sally invested this amount in tax-free municipal bonds yielding 4 percent, she would receive $2,000 per month in income—just what the pension benefit would have been. Should Sally predecease George, however, George could drop the life insurance policy and have the full $36,000 available, not just the reduced pension benefit of $28,800.

5. How Do You Determine Your Asset Allocations?

We've all heard the mantra "Diversify." How do you decide *where* to put your money and *how much* to put there? If there were a magic, definitive answer to this question, this entire discussion would be unnecessary.

The way you divide up your investment portfolio among different asset groups (stocks, bonds, real estate, money markets, cash, etc.) is called asset allocation. Studies of large pension funds over the past 30 years have determined that about 92 percent of the success of your portfolio is due to asset allocation, 5 percent is due to the specific stocks and bonds you choose, and about 2 percent is due to market timing. The other roughly 1 percent? Who knows?

Before deciding on your own asset allocation, however, you need to be able to answer a few questions:

When do you need the money? Are you 15, 10, 5 or just a couple of years away from retirement? Some experts believe that as you get closer to retirement you need to allocate your assets differently; historically, stocks can be volatile, so if you're close to retirement, more money should be put into lower-risk asset classes, such as bonds. Others argue that you continue to invest your entire life, so your asset allocation can remain basically the same. Usually, however, the closer you are to needing the principal, the less risk you will want to undertake.

What type of a risk taker are you? Are you willing to go for aggressive growth? Are you looking to limit your

---

Harry Markowitz and Bill Sharpe shared the Nobel Prize for Economics for their work in asset allocation. Trying to minimize risk while maximizing returns is called modern portfolio theory. Volatility (risk) can be reduced and returns enhanced by adding different asset classes in different proportions rather than just having one asset class (such as large-company stocks).

risk? Are you concerned only about security? Or are you somewhere in the middle? Figuring out your personality traits in this area—and deciding whether you want to be risky, conservative, or moderate—will also determine how you invest. On the one hand, some people think they are risk takers, but when they see their stocks plummet, quickly become conservative. People who think they are conservative, on the other hand, may become bigger risk takers when they see they aren't achieving the growth they had envisioned.

What is your financial situation? How much give do you have in your projections? If you have more "wiggle room" for downturns, you will, of course, be better off than if you have to meet your estimates exactly.

You often hear the word "diversification" mentioned with asset allocation. Even if you were a very aggressive investor, it would still be wise to put some of your money into lower-risk asset classes. Does the phrase "putting all your eggs in one basket" ring a bell?

Conversely, if you're very conservative, you still should not shun all stocks. Following the principles of asset allocation provides the opportunity to maximize returns while minimizing risk, but will almost always involve investing in stocks, as well as in bonds. Placing some money in a more volatile asset group will help you achieve growth, even as you try to minimize risk. Playing it too safe can also allow inflation to erode your nest egg, compromising your retirement lifestyle.

Diversification also means diversity *within* an asset class. For example, placing all your stock funds into just one company would not be advisable.

So, what are some examples of asset allocation? Here are several from Fidelity.com that combine investment styles with time horizons.

1. Eighty-five percent stocks; 15 percent bonds. Consider if you don't need the money for at least 7 to 10 years, and you're a risk taker.

2. Seventy percent stocks; 25 percent bonds; 5 percent money markets. Consider if you don't need the money for at least 7 years, are still fairly aggressive, yet want to balance your risk taking with more conservative asset allocations.

3. Fifty percent stocks; 40 percent bonds; 10 percent money markets. Consider if you don't need to dip into the principal for at least 4 years but are looking for both growth and income.

4. Twenty percent stocks; 50 percent bonds; 30 percent money markets. Consider if you need some income now, will tap into your principal within the next 2 to 4 years, and are willing to trade greater returns for lower risk.

Of course, none of these examples guarantees any specific return or even success—they're just examples of asset allocations.

What about diversifying within an asset allocation? If you don't have the financial savvy, time, or desire to do this, it's time for professional help. Consider a CFP or a registered investment advisor. If you're the do-it-yourself type, you can get help from various sources. Today, virtually every financial institution offers free basic literature on how your assets should be allocated among investments. With a phone call, you can get most of it in print, or, on the Internet, try Smart Money.com's Allocation System at www.smartmoney.com (type "One Asset Allocation" into the search bar, then click on "One Asset Allocation"; click on "SmartMoney One for Retirees" if you're already retired). Another one to try: CNNMoney.com's asset allocation calculator at www.money.com (type "Get the Right Asset Allocation" into the search bar, then click on "Calculators").

6. Should You Take Your Social Security Benefits Early?

It is often better to start taking a reduced Social Security benefit early (at age 62 or later), rather than waiting until full retirement age to start collecting the full benefit. Although several factors enter into this decision, the most important one is often life expectancy. The longer you live, the better it is to be collecting the larger, full retirement benefit; at some point, the full retirement benefits will exceed the smaller early retirement benefits, even though the early benefits would have been paid over more years. If, however, you fail to live long enough to reach the point where the cumulative full retirement benefits exceed the cumulative early benefits, it would have been better to elect the early benefits. (Now, if only we had a crystal ball. . . .)

For example, let's say you were born between 1943 and 1954 and are entitled to receive a Social Security benefit of $22,000 per year at your full retirement age of 66. You retire at age 62 and decide to start collecting Social Security immediately, which means (according to the law) your annual benefit would be reduced by 25 percent to only $16,500 per year; however, you would be collecting it for 4 more years than if you had waited for your full retirement age of 66. If you end up living to age 70 (ignoring cost of living adjustments), you would have received a total of $132,000 by electing the reduced benefit at 62. If, instead, you had waited to take the full benefit at 66, you would have received only $88,000. So, you would have made a good choice (of course, you're dead, but that's a separate issue!). At age 78, the two amounts would be equal—in other words, you would have received a total of $264,000 under either option, but keep in mind that the amounts are not really equal at age 78 since it is always better to receive something good sooner, rather than later. So, assuming you had selected the early benefit, you still would have made a good choice, since, using present value principles, it would be preferable to have started receiving benefits early because you would have had the use of the money. On the other hand, if you lived to age 85, you would have received a total of $418,000 by waiting to receive benefits at the full retirement age of 66, as compared to only $379,500 if you had elected the age 62 reduced benefit. The better choice in this case would depend on a present value determination, and the answer would depend on what interest rate you select for the calculation.

In addition to life expectancy, several other factors enter into the decision of whether to start collecting Social Security before full retirement age. These other factors include whether your Social Security benefits will be reduced

SPOUSAL BENEFITS

A spouse is entitled to a Social Security benefit that is, at full retirement age, generally the greater of one-half of the other spouse's benefit at full retirement age or the benefit computed on his or her own working record. If payment of your spousal benefit starts before you reach full retirement age, the amount payable to you will be permanently reduced by a percentage based on the number of months prior to your full retirement age. For example, Mary, who was born in 1947, plans on starting her spousal Social Security benefit at age 62. Since her full retirement age is 66, her monthly benefit will be only 35 percent of her spouse's full retirement age benefit because she will be getting the benefits for an additional 48 months. For a chart showing the reduction in benefits that start prior to full retirement age (both for benefits based on your own earnings history and for a spousal benefit), go to www.ssa.gov (click on "Plan Your Retirement" and then click on "Find My Retirement Age").

due to a decision to continue working in the years between age 62 and your full retirement age (see the discussion of this earlier in the chapter), the impact of income taxes on your decision (see the discussion in chapter 10 on taxation of Social Security benefits), the interest rates at which you can invest funds, and whether you are planning for Social Security benefits of two partners where the second partner's benefit is derived from the first.

Although we doubt that delaying the start of Social Security benefits makes sense to very many individuals (except perhaps to those who plan to continue to work between age 62 and their full retirement age), we do want to point out that delaying the start of the benefits beyond your full retirement age can increase your annual Social Security benefit. For those born in 1943 or later, the annual benefit will be increased by 8 percent for each year beyond full retirement age that you delay the starting date (if born in 1941 or 1942, the annual increase is 7.5 percent, and if born in 1939 or 1940, it is 7 percent). Hopefully, it's apparent from the above discussion on electing to receive benefits early that making up for the loss of one year's benefit will take a number of years (more than

12) of collecting the higher benefit just to break even.

So it seems that taking the "bird in the hand" approach of starting the benefit as soon as possible will often result in the greatest benefit for many of us, but a number of factors (health, other employment, income tax considerations, interest rates, and partner benefits) may also need to be considered before making a choice.

7. If a Lump Sum Distribution Is Available, Should You Take the Money and Run?

There are really two questions here; the first is whether you should take a lump sum distribution from a qualified employer plan, and the second is what you should do with the funds if you do take such a distribution.

If the plan in question is a *defined contribution plan*—say, a 401(k) plan—that is 100 percent funded, the most likely reason to consider a lump sum distribution is if you are unhappy with the investment alternatives within the plan. Taking a lump sum distribution and rolling it over into an IRA will provide you with the many opportunities available for qualified plans. If

For additional questions about Social Security, an excellent Web site is the National Committee to Preserve Social Security and Medicare, www.ncpssm.org/ask/index.html, where you can "Ask Mary Jane."

the plan is a *defined benefit plan*, we believe you should give serious consideration to taking a lump sum distribution whenever it is available, and then roll it over to an IRA. We suggest this because most defined benefit plans are not fully funded (meaning that the funds necessary to pay out the benefit obligations are not all there). If the employer falls on hard times and cannot continue funding the plan (remember Enron), your full benefit will likely not be paid. Even though defined benefits from a qualified plan are insured by the Pension Benefit Guaranty Corporation, the amount of the insurance is limited and may not cover your entire benefit. Taking a lump sum distribution and rolling it over into an IRA ensures that your benefits will be there, no matter what happens to the employer.

In the event you do take a lump sum distribution from a qualified plan, the next question is what you should do with the money. We believe that you should almost always roll the distribution over to a traditional IRA, and then give careful consideration to how the IRA should invest the funds. If you expect to be in the lowest tax bracket of your life, you should consider making an election to convert the traditional IRA to a Roth IRA, if you are eligible. Under this election you will be taxed on the lump sum distribution, but future distributions

from the Roth IRA (generally after age 59½) will be tax-free. You should consider seeking the advice of a qualified professional, particularly if the amount of the distribution is large.

Whenever you are going to receive a lump sum distribution that you intend to roll over into an IRA, be sure to have your employer do a direct transfer to your IRA, rather than distributing the funds to you. Whenever you receive such a distribution, your employer is required to withhold 20 percent for federal taxes. Even though you can still roll over the entire amount of the distribution (you have 60 days to do it), you will have to compensate for the taxes that were withheld. For example, when Kim T. received a $400,000 lump sum distribution from her employer, $80,000 (20 percent) in taxes was withheld, leaving a net amount of only $320,000. Since Kim wanted to do a 100 percent rollover into her IRA but did not have any funds of her own, she ended up having to take out a personal loan from her bank for $80,000 so she could complete the rollover. After she filed her income tax return and received a refund of the $80,000 withheld, she was able to repay the bank loan—but she ended up incurring significant interest costs that could have been avoided if her employer had transferred the $400,000 distribution directly to her IRA. You can get specific answers to questions on IRAs answered at www.irahelp.com (click on "Forum").

Although the thrill of having all that money at once may be enticing, and it may be tempting to keep it available to meet current expenses or as a safety net rather than rolling it over to an IRA, keep in mind that the distribution represents retirement savings and you may need it to last the rest of your life. If you're not extremely well-disciplined, you might chew it up on shopping, traveling, or meeting current expenses (many people do). In addition, and significantly, if you do not roll over the distribution into an IRA, it will be fully taxable at your current tax rates, leaving less to be invested for your retirement years. Resist the temptation to take a lump sum distribution without rolling it over to an IRA, even if the dollar amount seems small.

8. What Rules Govern Early Withdrawal from IRAs, 401(k)s, etc.?

Distributions from pension plans (or IRAs) before the account holder reaches age 59½ are generally subject to a 10 percent tax penalty unless the distribution is structured to conform to certain "safe-harbor" rules. Possibly more important is that minimum distributions must

start no later than the calendar year following the year you turn age 70½ and then be continued over your life expectancy in order to avoid significant tax penalties for failure to make distributions of the funds.

9. Should I Use a Traditional IRA or a Roth IRA for Retirement Savings?

The single biggest difference between a traditional IRA and a Roth IRA is that a tax deduction is available for contributions to a traditional IRA, assuming you meet the requirements, but the distributions are fully taxable. On the other hand, although contributions to a Roth IRA are not deductible, the distributions are generally not taxable.

In deciding which IRA is better for you, some general guidelines should help. The ability to compound earnings over a number of years and then distribute those earnings tax-free using a Roth IRA is a powerful device for accumulating retirement savings. If you're in a low tax bracket now but think you'll be in a higher tax bracket when distributions will be received, a Roth IRA is likely the better choice. The loss of the tax deduction available when using a traditional IRA is more than outweighed by the tax-free income from a Roth IRA, which you can receive in future years when you expect to be in a higher tax bracket. Even if you will be in the same tax bracket in future years when

A TECHNICAL TIP

A provision related to retirement plan distributions offers special onetime tax treatment for a lump sum distribution that includes shares of your employer's stock. Called Net Unrealized Appreciation (NUA), it allows you to receive a distribution of some or all of the shares of your company's stock that you have accumulated in the plan, instead of having the plan sell the stock and distribute the cash, and to pay taxes only on the cost basis of those shares to the plan, instead of on the fair market value of the shares at the time of the distribution. Taxes on the balance of the value of the stock are not paid until it is sold. Assuming the stock is sold at a gain, that portion of the gain realized up to the time of the distribution will automatically be treated as long-term capital gain. Any additional gain will be either short term or long term, depending on how long the stock is held after the distribution before it is sold. With maximum federal long-term capital gains rates now at 15 percent, it may be advantageous to use this provision if the employer's stock has appreciated significantly within the plan. Of course, this is an alternative to selling the stock and rolling the cash proceeds completely tax deferred into an IRA. Which of these two options is better requires some detailed calculations.

you receive distributions, a Roth IRA is still likely the better choice, due to the ability to generate compounded tax-free earnings and then distribute them tax-free. The most likely situation in which a traditional IRA could be a better choice is when you are in a higher tax bracket in the year you make a tax-deductible contribution to the traditional IRA than you will be when you receive the taxable distributions. Even in this situation, it is possible that the Roth IRA may still be the better choice, depending on how many years you will be leaving the funds in the IRA generating tax-free compounded earnings and how much higher your tax rate is expected to be in the year in which distributions are expected to be received.

Another consideration with respect to using a traditional IRA is that your ability to make a tax-deductible contribution when you are also an active participant in an employer's qualified plan is severely limited. In fact, if you are married and your joint modified adjusted gross income (MAGI)—essentially, your total income with certain adjustments—is in excess of $150,000, your ability to make a tax-deductible contribution to a traditional IRA is affected even if your spouse participates in an employer's qualified plan and you do not. So, what are these thresholds that you need to be under in order to obtain a full deduction for a traditional IRA?

a. If you are single, your MAGI needs to be $45,000 or less in 2004 or $50,000 or less in 2005 and later years.

b. If you are married filing jointly, your MAGI needs to be $65,000 or less in 2004. This amount increases to $70,000 in 2005, $75,000 in 2006, and $80,000 in 2007 and beyond.

Enough said about traditional IRAs! They will work for some, but the Roth IRA is often the better choice.

But remember, some people are not eligible for a Roth IRA. If you're single with MAGI greater than $110,000, married with MAGI greater than $160,000, or married but filing separately with MAGI greater than $10,000, you can't put any money into a Roth IRA.

As noted above, contributions to a Roth IRA are not deductible and distributions from them after age 59½ are nontaxable. In order to receive nontaxable distributions from a Roth IRA after age 59½, the IRA must have been in existence for at least 5 years after the first year for which a contribution was made. There are also limited circumstances (such as for first-time homebuyers) in which nontaxable distributions can be received prior to age 59½.

In 2004, up to $3,000 a year can be contributed by each taxpayer to a Roth IRA, and this amount increases to $4,000 for 2005 through 2007, and then to $5,000 for 2008 and beyond. Additionally, if you are over 50 years old, you can also make a "catch-up" contribution of $500 in 2004 and 2005 and $1,000 in 2006 and later years. In addition to the above limitations on contributions to a Roth IRA, the contribution cannot exceed your compensation for the year.

Here is how eligibility for the contribution amounts to a Roth IRA is determined.

a. If you are single and make $95,000 or less, you are eligible for the maximum contribution amount. If your MAGI is between $95,000 and $110,000, your maximum contribution is reduced under an IRS-prescribed formula. If your MAGI is over $110,000, no contribution is allowed.

b. If you are married with MAGI of less than $150,000, you are eligible for the maximum contribution amount. If your MAGI is between $150,000 and

$160,000, your maximum contribution is reduced under an IRS-prescribed formula. If your MAGI is over $160,000, no contribution is allowed.

c. If you are married and file separately, you are allowed only a limited contribution, and only if your MAGI is less than $10,000.

Although distributions of your contributions made prior to age 59½ would not be taxable, early distributions of the earnings on your contributions generally would be taxed, and, with certain exceptions, there would also be a 10 percent penalty on a distribution of earnings prior to age 59½. You may make contributions at any age with a Roth IRA, but you cannot make a contribution in any tax year in which your MAGI exceeds the allowable limits. Unlike a traditional IRA for which you have to start making withdrawals at 70½, there is no time at which you are required to make distributions from a Roth IRA.

A final point: If you conclude that a Roth IRA is better for you than a traditional IRA, you are allowed to convert an existing traditional IRA to a Roth IRA as long as your MAGI is under $100,000 (either joint or single, but not married filing separately) in the year of the conversion. Such a conversion, however, means you will be taxed on the entire balance in the traditional IRA as of the date of the conversion, although no penalty will be imposed for early withdrawal. This decision should be based on your tax rate in the year of the conversion, your expected tax rate in future years when you will be making distributions from the Roth IRA, and the number of years you will be able to keep the funds in the Roth IRA earning tax-free compounded earnings.

10. In What Order Should You Fund Benefit Plans?

When deciding whether to fund 401(k)s, traditional IRAs, or Roth IRAs, understanding the differences in tax treatment is important. Most 401(k) funding and traditional IRA funding offers current tax deductions; Roth IRAs do not. Some 401(k) funding may be supplemented by employer matching dollars, another enhancement. Usually, when all the factors are considered, it is beneficial to fund 401(k) plans first, at least to the extent needed to receive the full amount of an employer match. Then, the next amount of funding is often best put into a Roth IRA (if eligible). If you are not eligible for a Roth, the choice likely reverts to funding a 401(k) to the maximum limit before considering after-tax funding of a traditional IRA.

11. What Is a Reverse Mortgage?

A reverse mortgage is a loan against the equity you have built up in your home. It allows you to receive extra income, and when you die, vacate, or sell your house, the loan is repaid. You must be 62 years of age or older to obtain a reverse mortgage, and the loan applies only to your primary residence. There are several possibilities—you can receive a lump sum, monthly payments, a line of credit, or some combination of these options. The homeowner retains ownership of the home during the reverse mortgage period. Since these types of mortgages can be complex and involve fees, you need to be comfortable with how the costs stack up against how much you will receive in loan advances and how much equity will remain at the end of the reverse mortgage period.

There are several types of reverse mortgages, but the only kind insured by the federal government are the home equity conversion mortgages (HECMs). According to AARP's Web site, "HECM loans are the lowest-cost multipurpose reverse mortgages available, and in most cases they provide the largest total cash benefits as well." Other types of reverse mortgages are offered by state or local governments, banks, mortgage companies, or other private lenders.

If you are pursuing an HECM, then by law you must meet with a U.S. Department of Housing and Urban Development (HUD)-approved mortgage counselor ahead of time. For general info, go to www.aarp.org/revmort or call AARP at 800-209-8085; for a list of lenders, contact www.reversemortgage.org or 202-439-1760; for a list of approved counselors, contact HUD at www.hud.gov (this site is a little tricky—click on "Consumer Info," under "Homes," then click on the link with information about reverse mortgages). Or you can call them at 202-708-1112.

GROWING YOUR OWN PERSONAL MONEY TREE

Let's face it—if financial planning for retirement were simple, there would be no need to have hundreds of books about the topic or an entire industry built up around it. There are many variables to consider, and a small change—such as a 2 percent difference in the return on your investments, or a 1 percent change in the estimated rate of inflation—can make a huge difference when you're talking time spans of 10, 20, or even 30 years. We've compiled a list of savvy strategies that, whether you're retired or not, can help increase the amount of money available to you. Although each one is relatively simple, instituting just a few can make a powerful difference.

Check your credit report. Your credit score is often used to determine the interest rate for a mortgage or terms of credit for other purchases, such as a car. Three-fourths of Americans don't know this score, or whether it's correct. To order a copy of your credit report, contact Equifax (www.equifax.com or 800-685-1111), Experian (www.experian.com or 714-830-7000), or TransUnion (www.TransUnion.com or 800-888-4213). Scores may vary from one credit bureau to another, so to be safe, order a copy from all three companies, which will cost around $45 total. You can also purchase your credit report from www.myFICO.com. If you feel there is an error, you can then ask the company to correct it. Or, if you are denied credit, you can ask the company that denied you to divulge the source of the negative credit report. You are then given 30 days to request a free copy of your report from that credit bureau.

Time your car buying. Consider buying a car at the end of the model year, particularly if you're flexible about the model and accessories. Because dealers have lots of inventory, this is a good time for great deals. Also, dealers will often be more willing to deal at the end of a quarter and at the end of the year, when they are trying to meet sales quotas.

Be a shrewd home buyer. Purchase the least expensive home in a good neighborhood in the best school district. These homes tend to appreciate more quickly, so you get the best return on your investment.

Consider a home equity loan. Think about getting a home equity loan (without closing costs) to pay off your mortgage. This might work if your first mortgage balance is fairly low, especially if you can get a fixed rate on the equity loan. You can also use a no-cost, lower-rate equity loan to pay off higher-interest debts, such as credit card or auto loan debt. Also, interest on a home equity loan is often tax deductible, while interest on the credit card and

---

When paying off loans early, particularly auto loans, watch out for "precomputed" loans, which provide for interest refunds or rebates when the loan is paid off early. Usually the payoff amounts are determined using a calculation like the so-called "Rule of 78s," which accelerates much of the interest into the early months of the loan (as much as three-fourths of the interest may be in the first half of the loan term) and leaves you stuck paying much more interest than if you were paying off a loan with simple interest. The use of the Rule of 78s has dwindled in recent years due to legislation that restricts its use.

auto loans is not. But don't fall into the trap of financing credit card or car loan debt over longer periods just because you are using home equity loans.

Pay off debts. Which debts should you pay off first? Start with the ones that have the highest interest rates, particularly if they're not deductible, such as credit cards and auto loans (assuming you have a simple interest car loan). Then, tackle student loans, home equity loans, and mortgages.

Be careful with those credit cards. If you have an introductory low-interest-rate credit card, be wary. Rates often dramatically increase after the initial time frame is over.

Remember: Little changes add up. In Allyson Lewis's book, *The Million Dollar Car and $250,000 Pizza*, she illustrates how your spending today affects your future financial health. For example, instead of having your favorite Italian carryout once a week, take the $30, invest it—say, at 7 percent—and at the end of 25 years, you'll have $105,800!

Lower your insurance premiums. Elect high deductibles for car and homeowner's insurance. Use your monthly savings from the lowered insurance cost to save for the deductibles in case of a claim—after the deductibles are set aside, enjoy the savings. If you're over 55, ask for a discount.

Reduce your life insurance premiums. Check life insurance policy rates from time to time. Rates may decrease, and you may be able to cancel your policy and purchase another one at a better rate, especially for term insurance.

Compare homeowners' insurance quotes and companies. Insurance companies are dropping or turning away customers who have made (in their opinion) too many claims, live in areas susceptible to bad weather (such as Texas and Florida), or have poor credit histories. If you're looking around for other options, check out www.Quotesmith.com. If you're interested in how an insurance company ranks in terms of payment (and nonpayment) of claims, look at www.badfaithinsurance.org.

Carry homeowner's and auto insurance with the same company. You will often get a discount if you purchase your homeowner's and auto insurance from the same company.

Bite the bullet on car insurance premiums. Pay your auto insurance premiums on time and in total. Some states allow your insurance to be cancelled if your payment is even 1 day late, and most companies charge a fee for installment payments.

Buy insurance before you need it. If you are planning on purchasing life or disability insurance, get it when you don't need it. It will cost less, and you may not be able to purchase it later on if a problem develops with your health.

Consider this health insurance option. COBRA (Consolidated Omnibus Budget Reconciliation Act of 1985) is a law mandating the availability of health insurance for up to 18 months after you leave your job—paid for by you, of course. The law applies to most employers with 20 or more workers. Under COBRA, you will pay no more than 102 percent of the employer's cost for your insurance. It's pricey, but this may be a better option than purchasing an individual policy. You can use it as a stopgap policy after you retire, if you don't qualify for Medicare and are looking to purchase a health insurance policy. Another option is the AARP Health Plan: In 21 states, a program called Medical Advantage covers those 50 to 64 and includes physician visits, medical tests, and surgery. If you don't qualify for Medicare yet and don't have your own insurance, it may be something to consider. Contact AARP at 800-424-3410. And don't forget to check out www.eHealthInsurance.com to compare plans.

Choose the best Medicare health plan for you. Call the Medicare hotline (800-MEDICARE), or go to www.medicare.gov and click on "Medicare Personal Plan Finder" in the first column, lower left. You'll be able to narrow down your health plan choices and choose the plan that's right for you.

Save money by using Internet phone calls. If you make lots of international or long-distance calls, consider calling over the Internet. Though presently a fledgling industry, it's one that is growing, and the previous problems of voice quality and delays are being addressed. Two companies to investigate are Vonage (www.vonage.com), where you pay a monthly fee as well as add-on charges for international calls, and Free World Dialup (www.pulver.com/fwd). For Free World Dialup you must purchase a special phone to use with the Internet that costs around $175, but there are no additional charges. You can purchase a router for around $40 if you want to use the computer and make a call at the same time. One caveat: The person you're calling must also be a Free World Dialup subscriber. For both Vonage and Free World Dialup, a broadband connection is necessary.

Compare calling plans. If you're not comfortable with

According to *The Motley Fool*, a financial education company,
Americans carry an average credit card debt of almost $8,600.

Internet calling, try these Web sites that compare calling plans and recommend what's best for you based on your particular circumstances: www.TollChaser.com, www.ReallyCheapLD.com, or www.SaveOnPhone.com.

Get free Internet service. If you use the Internet 10 hours a month or less, try www.netzero.net or www.access-4-free.com. They're free!

Spend less than you make. Enough said!

Clip coupons. Use the Internet to obtain codes to receive discounts/rewards at brick-and-mortar stores, as well as for online shopping. Try www.coolsavings.com or www.pricebandit.com. Individual retailers often have newsletters that contain promotions as well.

Get rid of your PMI. Drop your private mortgage insurance if the amount borrowed is less than 80 percent of the appraised value of your home. Have an appraisal done if home prices have risen, or make additional payments on your mortgage to lower the balance.

Find a deal. Use these Web sites to compare prices and products in many categories: www.MySimon.com and www.PriceGrabber.com. Or, go to www.SeniorDiscounts.com, which lists "over 120,000 deals for folks over 50!"

Maximize your interest on savings bonds. Cash in savings bonds on the day that they mature (or as soon thereafter as possible). This will ensure you get the maximum interest. A bank can supply this date, or you can get it online at www.publicdebt.treas.gov (click on "Stopped Earning Interest" under "Savings Bonds").

Take advantage of veterans' benefits. If you are a veteran, you may qualify for lower prescription prices if you were honorably discharged, are enrolled in the VA Health Care System, and have the prescription filled at a VA pharmacy. You may also save on health care, receive a free burial plot and marker, and get a break on loans by VA-approved lenders. Go to www.va.gov/health_benefits, www.cem.va.gov, or www.Homeloans.va.gov, or call the VA at 877-222-8387.

Switch annuities. Some annuities perform better than others. If you find a better one than what you have, see if you can change.

Donate money to charity. When making charitable donations, a good rule of thumb is that the organization should allot at least 65 percent of contributions directly to its programs and 35 percent or less to overhead. Looking for some guidance? The American Institute of Philanthropy is a watchdog organization that provides a list of its top charities: www.charitywatch.org. (Although this isn't a money-saving tip, it helps ensure that your money does the most good.)

Get more for your money. For a variety of other

money-saving tips, check out www.cheapskatemonthly. com or www.stretcher.com.

 Marjorie and Daniel K. managed to save enough money over the years to fund the college education of their three children. When it came time for the first child to start college, however, Marjorie and Daniel realized that the sale of their invested funds would entail a significant income tax on the capital gains. After getting advice from their tax advisor, they realized that they could minimize the income tax by giving the investments to their children in the amounts and at the times necessary so that the children could sell the investments and pay their own college expenses. Since the children were in a much lower income tax bracket, the tax cost was reduced significantly. ⓣⓛ

WHAT CAN YOU DO NOW?

Time is your friend if you start planning early, but if you wait too long to start, it will turn on you and become your enemy.

The longer time horizon you have, the more you can do to increase the likelihood of meeting your retirement goals.

Reaching retirement doesn't mean you stop planning. Continue to monitor your financial health throughout your retirement years, and use the help of a professional if necessary. Let's look at a case study of a couple planning for retirement to see that it's not as overwhelmingly complicated as it sounds.

CASE STUDY

As we've already noted, the combined impact of your estimated annual expenses, inflation, and the return on your investments is very significant in your retirement planning. In order to demonstrate this, we went to a certified financial planner and asked him to complete a retirement financial plan for a hypothetical couple, Joe and Jane Retiree.

Scenario One

Joe and Jane Retiree are both 55 years old. They currently earn $100,000 per year, and they have $225,000 of savings that will remain in a combination of tax-de-

---

For some specific tax issues affecting retirement that were not addressed in this chapter, see chapter 10.

ferred and taxable investment accounts until they retire in 10 years. Joe expects to be able to add $5,000 to his 401(k) account next year and increase that amount by 10 percent in each succeeding year, and to also add an additional $5,000 each year to their joint taxable investment account. Jane plans to add $5,000 each year to her 401(k) account until they retire. Joe expects to earn 8 percent per year on his 401(k) account, while Jane is expecting a return of 8.5 percent on her 401(k) account. On the joint taxable investment account, they expect to earn 5 percent interest income on their bonds and a combined 10 percent on appreciable securities (2 percent in dividends and 8 percent in appreciation). Their goal is to retire at age 65 on Social Security, supplemented by their investments; they plan to spend $60,000 in their first year of retirement (plus the amount they need for income taxes) and to increase this amount for inflation at 3 percent per year.

As you can see from the table below, unless they alter their planning, they will run out of money at age 85. Since most financial planners advise that you plan as if you will live to age 90, they need to either start saving more for retirement now, reduce their annual expenses once they retire, or work at least part time in retirement. If not, they may last longer than their money does.

Scenario Two

After reviewing these figures, Joe and Jane Retiree realized that they could not meet their retirement goals. So, after considering their options, they determined that since they couldn't increase their annual savings, they needed to reduce the amount of their spending in retirement. Also, they determined that it was not likely that they would earn more than 8 percent per year on their 401(k) accounts or on their taxable joint investment account, so they reduced their previous assumptions on investment returns to 8 percent, comprised of a 2 percent dividend and a 6 percent annual appreciation. As you can see from the table below, this retirement plan does work—the big question, however, is can they live on $50,000 per year? If not, they may need to consider part-time jobs in retirement.

"What's the quickest way to double your money? Fold it in half."
—Will Rogers

Joe and Jane Retiree: Scenario One

Age	After-Tax Income	Annual Expenses	Excess (Shortfall)	Asset Value
66	79,838	80,635	(797)	659,343
67	80,035	83,054	(3,019)	656,324
68	80,065	85,546	(5,481)	650,843
69	79,898	88,112	(8,214)	642,629
70	79,504	90,755	(11,251)	631,378
71	79,860	93,478	(14,618)	616,760
72	77,928	96,282	(18,354)	598,406
73	76,682	99,171	(22,489)	575,917
74	75,083	102,146	(27,063)	548,854
75	77,478	105,210	(27,732)	521,122
76	81,044	108,367	(27,323)	493,799
77	79,619	111,618	(31,999)	461,800
78	77,830	114,966	(37,136)	424,664
79	75,642	118,415	(42,773)	381,891
80	73,013	121,968	(48,955)	332,936
81	69,901	125,627	(55,726)	277,210
82	66,254	129,395	(63,141)	214,069
83	61,800	133,277	(71,477)	142,592
84	57,109	137,276	(80,167)	62,425
85	58,047	141,394	(83,347)	Uh-oh!!!

Joe and Jane Retiree: Scenario Two

Age	After-Tax Income	Annual Expenses	Excess (Shortfall)	Asset Value
66	76,418	67,196	9,222	637,085
67	77,473	69,212	8,261	645,346
68	78,462	71,288	7,174	652,520
69	79,373	73,427	5,946	658,466
70	80,188	75,629	4,559	663,025
71	80,894	77,898	2,996	666,021
72	81,475	80,235	1,240	667,261
73	81,915	82,642	(727)	666,534
74	82,197	85,122	(2,925)	663,609
75	82,298	87,675	(5,377)	658,232
76	82,202	90,306	(8,104)	650,128
77	81,884	93,015	(11,131)	638,997
78	81,318	95,805	(14,487)	624,510
79	80,481	98,679	(18,198)	606,312
80	79,341	101,640	(22,299)	584,013
81	77,868	104,689	(26,821)	557,192
82	81,291	107,830	(26,539)	530,653
83	84,314	111,064	(26,750)	503,903
84	83,618	114,396	(30,778)	473,125
85	82,683	117,828	(35,145)	437,980
86	81,488	121,363	(39,875)	398,105
87	80,009	125,004	(44,995)	353,110
88	77,897	128,754	(50,857)	302,253
89	75,370	132,617	(57,247)	245,006
90	72,418	136,595	(64,177)	180,829

WHAT ARE THE TAX ISSUES AFFECTING RETIREMENT?

"The art of taxation consists in so plucking the goose as to get the most feathers with the least hissing."
—*Jean Baptiste Colbert*

Although retirees face most of the same tax issues as everybody else, certain issues are more likely to come up. Some of these issues include the state tax considerations involved in relocating, the possibility of obtaining a moving expense deduction if and when we move, the rules for determining the taxability of Social Security payments and retirement distributions, and, even though none of us want to think about this, estate taxes. But not to worry! In this chapter we provide answers to your questions and, since no taxation discussion would be complete without some savvy tax-saving ideas, we'll add some end-of-year tax tips, as well.

WHERE YOU LIVE AFFECTS YOUR TAXES

Question: What do the following nine states have in common? Alaska, Florida, Nevada, New Hampshire, South Dakota, Tennessee, Texas, Washington, and Wyoming. Answer: They do not have a broad-based income tax. Is this important to know? Perhaps. Although you'd probably rather not think about them, taxes are a crucial part of your retirement planning. Many federal and state taxes, including income tax, property tax, sales tax, and estate tax, can be particularly relevant to retirees.

In fact, taxes can be your largest expense—add them up to prove it to yourself!

For example, if you are planning to relocate and are considering only the absence of a state income tax without taking into account other taxes (such as sales, property, and intangible taxes), you are making a mistake. Keep in mind that if a state does not have an income tax, it must be getting its revenue somewhere else. That is why the answer to the question above is "perhaps"—there are other taxes to consider.

Look at Alaska, for instance. It has neither an income tax nor a sales tax. Sounds like a retirement haven from a tax standpoint, right? But when you consider that Alaska has one of the highest costs of living in the United States, and that more than 50 percent of municipalities in this state assess their own sales tax (which can reach 7 percent), it may not be the best choice for a person on a limited income. You may also find unanticipated taxes in the form of refuse collection fees, mental health levies, fees for cleaning up the environment, "occupational privilege taxes," etc. Of course, before examining tax issues, you should look at lifestyle issues. If the climate, medical facilities, cultural/social/recreational opportunities, overall cost of living, and other qualities you are looking for seem a good fit, *then* look at the tax implications. Let tax considerations help you choose among locations, but don't allow taxes to be the most important consideration in your decision.

So, how to make sense of the tax issues? Obviously, when deciding where to live from a tax perspective, the entire tax package in the area you are contemplating must be considered. (We provide a state-by-state summary of individual income taxes and sales taxes at the end of this chapter.) Property taxes, including the availability of homestead exemptions, can also be a significant factor in your total tax package, but they vary so much from location to location that it is almost impossible to provide a meaningful table to help you. Although the property tax rate is important, it is equally important to understand *how* properties are valued and assessed. For example, one jurisdiction may typically value real estate much lower than its fair market value, while another may

---

"Death and taxes and childbirth. There's never a convenient time for any of them!"
—Margaret Mitchell, *Gone with the Wind*

be right at market. Comparing just the two tax rates will not necessarily lead you to a good conclusion as to which has the lower property tax because it ignores the valuation issue. Call the county assessor's office and find out what the current tax rate is per thousand dollars of assessed valuation, and at what percent of real fair market value you can expect a residence to be assessed for property tax purposes. If that is too cumbersome for you, ask the real estate agents you speak with how property taxes are determined in areas of interest to you, and talk to people who have recently relocated to or purchased homes in the area.

Beyond these taxes, though, other state tax issues need to be addressed. States vary in what income they tax. Although the typical state does tax most forms of income, there are significant differences. For example, New Hampshire and Tennessee tax only interest and dividends. This can be the equivalent of no tax at all if your income is coming from pensions, withdrawals from your IRA, and Social Security. In other words, when choosing a place to live and factoring in the tax cost, you have to consider your individual circumstances to see how a particular location's taxes will affect you. In spite of the many articles and books ranking retirement locations based on cost, it's difficult to give a definitive list of the best places (taxwise) for retirement.

Of course, federal tax issues may also play a significant role in planning for your retirement. Many people don't need to explore the tax consequences of moving because they know they are staying put! But what about such tax issues as withdrawing from your retirement accounts too soon or withdrawing too little, or too late? How can the taxation of Social Security benefits affect your retirement? Will you have an income tax on the profit from selling your residence, even if you're just moving down the street to a smaller (or larger) home? What are some general tax tips to ensure you're retaining as much income as possible? For the many people who retire from a primary job but work at a second career, there could be tax implications as well. For example, if you do decide to work in your new location, can you deduct your moving expenses even if the job is only temporary? Let's explore some of these tax issues.

STATE INCOME TAXES

Most states have an income tax. It's rare, however, for it to be as simple as a flat tax rate applied to all of your income. Generally, a state will start with the income on your federal tax return and then make adjustments to it in arriving at your state taxable income. In fact, of the 41 states that impose a broad-based income tax, 35 base it on your federal tax return to some extent. Common adjustments in going from federal to state taxable income are subtraction of your Social Security income that was taxed for federal purposes (the table at the end of this chapter shows the 26 states that do not tax Social Security), of interest income from U.S. government bonds and notes (state income taxation on this type of interest is prohibited by the U.S. Constitution), and of certain pension income, and an add-back for any state income taxes deducted on your federal tax return.

Some states base their taxable income on a modified federal adjusted gross income (income less certain adjustments, such as those for IRA deductions), while others are based on a modified federal taxable income (adjusted gross income less deductions for contributions, interest expense, state property taxes, etc.).

After determining taxable income, most states apply some type of a graduated tax rate to calculate the total tax. The table at the end of this chapter shows the income tax rates in each of the states with an income tax. It is important to note that most states have a range of income tax rates, rather than just one. Thus, rather than taxing all income at, say, 7 percent, a state may tax the first $3,000 at 2 percent, the next $10,000 at 3 percent, the next $30,000 at 4 percent and so on until it eventually gets to the tax rate of 7 percent on the amount of taxable income in excess of, say, $100,000. So, in addition to looking at the maximum tax rate used, one must also consider the structure of the tax brackets used by a state in actually calculating the tax. Clearly, then, in order to arrive at any sound conclusions on a state's income tax burden, it is not enough to look only at the tax rate. Rather, you need to estimate the sources of your income in retirement and then put pen to paper and estimate a particular state's income tax with reference to its definition of taxable income, its tax rates, and its tax brackets. The conclusions you reach based on an actual calculation may be significantly different than the conclusions you reach just by looking at the tax rates.

For summary information on state individual income tax rules applicable to retirees, go to www.retirementliving.com and click on "Taxes by State."

Tax Freedom Day

One way to try to figure out which state is least expensive in terms of taxes is by looking at "Tax Freedom Day," which is determined each year by the Tax Foundation (www.taxfoundation.org), a nonprofit, nonpartisan research and public education organization. Tax Freedom Day, which was on April 19 in 2003, is the day on which the average American's federal, state, and local tax bill is fully paid from his or her year-to-date earnings. As the Frasier Institute, a think tank, puts it, Tax Freedom Day is "the day you stopped working for the government and started working for yourself." In other words, this is the day (on average) that an individual has made enough to pay Uncle Sam, plus state and local taxes, and is now beginning to make the money that he or she will actually be able to spend on other things. As taxes get higher, Tax Freedom Day falls later in the year, while a decrease in taxes causes Tax Freedom Day to come earlier. So, the earlier Tax Freedom Day occurs, the sooner your tax obligation has been met! What is interesting, and less publicized, is that the Tax Foundation calculates Tax Freedom Day by state, taking into account the incomes of residents of the state as well as their total tax burden, and also performs separate calculations for federal, state, and total taxes. On this basis, and looking only at the state tax burden, the states faring the worst (having a later Tax Freedom Day) are Maine, New York, Minnesota, Rhode Island, and Connecticut. Those with the lowest state tax burden (having an earlier Tax Freedom Day) are Alaska, New Hampshire, Delaware, Tennessee, and Texas.

Another Way of Looking at the "Tax Bite"

The calculation of Tax Freedom Day does not take into consideration any special incentives given to retirees, such as for retirement income or for real estate taxes. Kiplinger, a leading provider of financial advice, recently looked at the state income tax, property tax, and sales tax burden of a hypothetical retired couple living on a combination of Social Security, pension income, and IRA distributions, as well as on interest and dividends.

For the full 2003 report on Tax Freedom Day, go to www.taxfoundation.org and type "Tax Freedom Day" into the search bar.

Assumptions were also made as to the value of their residence, which varied by state, and expenditures. On this basis, the highest-cost states from just an income tax standpoint were Montana, West Virginia, Minnesota, Wisconsin, and Hawaii, while the lowest-cost states were seven of the nine states mentioned at the beginning of this chapter as having no broad-based income tax, plus seven others—Delaware, Illinois, Kentucky, Michigan, New York, Pennsylvania, and South Carolina. (Even though they have no broad-based income tax, Tennessee and Florida were relatively high in the rankings at numbers 19 and 20, respectively, due to Tennessee's tax on interest and dividends and Florida's tax on intangibles. We should note here that in 2004, Florida will increase its exemption from $20,000 to $500,000 of the value of intangibles for a couple filing a joint intangible tax return, after which it imposes a tax of $1 per $1,000 in value—thus making this tax less of a consideration for most retirees after 2003.) To see Kiplinger's full report, go to www.kiplinger.com (type "State Taxes Vary Greatly for Retirees" into the search bar, then click on "The Retirement Tax Bite, State by State" at the end of the article).

Comparing the Tax Freedom Day study with the Kiplinger study, we see that Minnesota comes out as an expensive state in both analyses, and Alaska, Delaware, New Hampshire, and Texas come out again as being states with good tax deals. Is this the final answer? Of course not. As you'll see with some other studies trying to determine the tax-friendliest states, results are always predicated on the assumptions used in the study.

Property and Sales Taxes

As noted earlier, income taxes are not the sole criteria by which the total state tax burden needs to be judged. Property and sales taxes can also be significant; in fact, since retirees can spend a disproportionate amount of their retirement incomes in purchasing a residence, a state's property tax may be far more significant in determining the total tax burden than its income tax. In the Kiplinger study described above, the states were also ranked by their total tax burden on the same hypothetical retired couple. In this ranking, the states with the highest total state tax burden were Pennsylvania, New Jersey, Wisconsin, Vermont, and Maryland, while those with the lowest state tax burden were Delaware, Alaska, Kentucky, South Carolina, and New York. Now, incorporating this third study, only Alaska and Delaware are still considered the best tax-deal states.

In a final study that we want to cover (sorry for all the

discussion of studies, but hopefully the point is being made that the results depend on the assumptions!), Bloomberg (www.wealth.bloomberg.com) looked at the total state taxes paid by four hypothetical families, each with a different mix of income and income type (capital gains, salary, interest, dividends, etc.), different value of real estate and other assets, different spending, and so on. Bloomberg then ranked the states for each of the four families, then averaged the results together and ranked them. What makes this study different from the ones discussed earlier is that these families were at the higher end of the financial spectrum. For example, family number one had $500,000 in adjusted gross income and a home worth $500,000, while family number two had income of $100,000 and two homes worth a total of $1.25 million, and so on. The results showed that, on average, Wyoming had the lowest total state tax, followed by Alabama and Nevada (tied), Tennessee, and Louisiana. States faring the worst were Rhode Island, Vermont, Wisconsin, New York, and Maine.

So, What Does All This Mean?

Looking at these four studies—Tax Freedom Day, the two Kiplinger studies, and the Bloomberg study—there is no consensus. There isn't one state that is found on all four lists as being either tax friendly or tax unfriendly. The results of the studies all depend on the assumptions made when doing the analyses.

Let's face it. In the end, it should be clear that each state needs to raise revenue in order to meet its obligations. Some get revenue from unique sources such as oil reserves (Alaska) or gambling revenues (Nevada), but most states get the bulk of their revenues from the local taxpayers. The tax rates and the various exemptions, such as for retirement income, vary by state and by type of tax. So don't just assume you should move to a state without a broad-based income tax; you might find that the real estate tax, sales tax, or some other tax is significantly higher there than in some other state which does have an income tax. Or maybe one of the states with an income tax does not tax the type of income you will be relying on in retirement—such as Social Security income, interest and dividend income, or distributions from a qualified profit-sharing or pension plan.

Taxes are important to consider when planning your retirement. The amount of tax you pay is significant in determining what you have left for all of your other expenses. It is, however, probably a mistake to pick a retirement location based solely on tax considerations; yet it is also a mistake to conclude anything with respect to the total tax burden in any state without actually looking at your own facts and the tax laws of the states you are considering and estimating what your tax burden will be. As with many things in life, it may be wise to seek help in this exercise. We suggest that you ask the advice of a certified public accountant, particularly a CPA specializing in individual taxation.

CHANGING YOUR STATE OF TAXATION

Assuming you have decided to move to a new location, one question will come up: How does a state determine *who* is subject to its taxes? Since sales and property taxes follow from the location of the sales transaction or the property being taxed, there's rarely an issue as to who is subject to them. Determining whether an individual is subject to a state's income tax can be more complex, however. Often a state will subject an individual to its income tax if that individual either resides in the state or is a domiciliary of the state. Most people are domiciled in the same state in which they reside, but this is not always the case. The term "resident" generally refers to someone living within a state more than a minimum amount of time during a tax year (for example, someone working on

a long-term project in Ohio could be a resident of Ohio, even if it's not her domicile), while the term "domiciliary" generally refers to an individual who is domiciled within a state (that is, "where the heart and home are," regardless of where his current place of abode may be). A domicile is generally the place to which an individual intends to return after a temporary absence.

Each state has its own rules as to whose income it will tax—it is possible to be taxed in a state where you are domiciled, even though your actual place of abode is outside the state. Likewise, it is possible to be taxed in a state where your actual place of abode is, even though you are domiciled elsewhere. It is even possible to be taxed in two different states at the same time; when this happens, the taxpayer is generally able to claim a credit in one of the states for the income taxes paid in the other. The result is that taxes will be paid at the higher rate of the two states.

This becomes especially important when you have two (or more) places of abode, as do the Florida sunbirds who escape to the north for the less humid summers. Do they pay income tax to the northern state in which their summer residence is located, or, as winter residents of Florida, do they escape state income taxes altogether (except for the Florida .1 percent tax on intangibles in excess of the exempt amount noted earlier)? They could end up being taxed in their summer location, either because they are domiciled there, or possibly because they were physically present there for more than a specified number of days during the tax year.

Not surprisingly, since all 50 states have their own tax laws, there is no standard test for income taxability, although there are some broad concepts most states use. States generally impose an income tax on an individual who maintains a place of abode within the state and actually occupies it for more than a specified number of days during the year (commonly 183 days), regardless of whether that individual is also domiciled in that state.

When a state is determining taxability based on residence, it is often necessary to keep track of every day an individual is in that state in order to determine if the threshold of taxability has been met. For example, Lewis and Julie S. lived most of their married lives in Virginia. When they retired, they moved to a new residence in Palm Beach, Florida, which they viewed as their permanent home and domicile. They also kept their old home in Virginia, however, so that they could return to it during the spring and summer months to be with their families. In 2003 they were in their Palm Beach home from January 1 through April 30, their Virginia home from May 1 through November 1, and then back in their Palm Beach home for the rest of the year. Unfortunately, even though they thought of themselves as tax-free residents of Florida, Virginia treats anyone who lives within the state for more than 183 days during the year as a resident, and it required Lewis and Julie to pay Virginia income tax on all of their income for the year. Had they reduced their 185 days in Virginia by just 2 days, they could have completely avoided the Virginia income tax.

States will often also tax an individual who is domiciled within the state, regardless of whether he or she actually has a residence within the state, and often regardless of whether the individual has even been in the state during the tax year. For example, many states will tax the income of a domiciliary who has converted her residence to rental property and moved to a foreign country for a 3-year assignment after which she intends to return to the state. To add to the confusion, some states will only tax the income of a domiciliary who has also actually been within the state for more than a minimum number of days during the year, thus not taxing the income of the expatriate described above.

It is generally relatively easy to determine if someone is subject to income taxes in a state due to physical residence in the state—it's often a matter of counting the number of days of physical residence in the state and comparing that to the state's definition of resident. Determining whether someone is taxable in a state as a domiciliary is not always so easy, however, particularly when the individual has more than one home. As you might expect, a common tactic of taxpayers is to claim domicile in a state that has no income tax, or one with a very low income tax, while residing for much of the year in a state that does impose an income tax. Over the years a number of criteria have been used by the courts in resolving the issue of domicile. Some of the more significant criteria are as follows.

* Voting registration
* Driver's license
* Automobile registration
* Bank/brokerage accounts
* Country club memberships
* Church memberships
* Location of safe deposit boxes
* Address used on federal tax return
* Ownership of real estate

So, again, what does all this mean?

It will often be clear in which state taxes must be paid. Property taxes follow the location of the property, and sales taxes follow the state where the sale is completed.

Income taxes are usually paid in the state of residence, which is usually also the state of domicile. Income taxes, however, can get muddy, especially when more than one residence is involved. There is no simple answer that covers all 50 states. Taxpayers are well-advised to seek professional advice whenever they intend to own and occupy residences in multiple states in order to gain a complete understanding of each state's rules on who is subject to the requirement to file an income tax return. Forewarned is forearmed—these rules can often be used to your advantage, but to do so you need to understand them (or find someone who does!).

true LIFE

George W. devoted his career to building a landscaping business into a very successful enterprise in his home state of Kentucky.

As he neared retirement age, he decided to sell all of the stock in his business and move to Florida to devote his efforts to golf, travel, and other forms of relaxation. While meeting with his tax advisor, however, he learned that by moving to Florida first, establishing domicile and residency there, and *then* selling the stock, he would avoid having to pay Kentucky income tax on the sales profit. Clearly, he was now able to afford a much larger retirement home. This strategy should work when moving to any of the states that do not have an income tax. ⓛ

HOME SWEET HOME AND THE TAX CONSEQUENCES OF SELLING

For many of us, our homes are one of our most valuable assets—and have also been one of our most profitable investments. The housing market over the past 30 years has generally been spectacular. Under the old tax law in effect through mid-1997, the gain from the sale of a principal residence could escape current taxation as long as the sellers reinvested the net proceeds (sale price less selling expenses, but not minus the mortgage) into a new principal residence. The gain not taxed was deferred and used to reduce the tax cost of the replacement residence. This would have the effect of increasing the gain when the replacement residence was eventually sold, but once again, this gain could be deferred into the next replacement residence, and so on for residence after residence. This rule worked fine for most home sellers; after all, the goal was usually to sell an existing residence and move into a larger or nicer, and usually more expensive, residence. But for retirees selling their principal residence and planning to downsize for their retirement years, this tax break usually left them with some tax to pay whenever the net proceeds from the sale of their old residence were not all reinvested in the new residence. In fact, since the gain from the sale of many earlier residences could have continued to be deferred and used to reduce the tax cost of replacement residences, a failure to reinvest some or all of the proceeds from the sale of the last residence at the time of retirement could have caused some or all of the deferred gains over a multitude of residences to finally become taxable.

Fortunately, in 1997 Congress changed this rule and replaced it with a kinder, gentler tax break, especially for retirees who wanted to downsize. Under the new rule now applicable to the sale of a principal residence, some or all of the gain on the sale is not taxable as long as the taxpayers owned and lived in the residence as their principal residence for at least 2 years during the 5-year period ending with the date of the sale. The amount of gain that is not taxable is limited to $250,000 for a single taxpayer (or a married taxpayer filing separately) and $500,000 for a married couple filing a joint tax return. Significantly, unlike under the old law, this gain is eliminated from taxable income and is not deferred to reduce the tax basis of any replacement residence. In fact, there is no requirement to even purchase a replacement principal residence, which is one of the reasons this change is so beneficial to retirees and others looking to downsize. This tax break is available to taxpayers without regard to age and can be claimed multiple times, but generally only once every 2 years.

It is important to remember that when calculating the amount of gain on the sale of a principal residence, any gain deferred due to the purchase of a new principal residence under the old law, as discussed above, must be used to reduce the cost of a replacement residence.

What Is Meant by "Principal Residence"?

For those taxpayers owning and using more than one residence, it is important to be able to determine which constitutes the principal residence. For this purpose, the principal residence is generally located in the state in which the taxpayers are domiciled, and it's the home in which the taxpayers live most of the time. A principal residence can be a house, townhouse, duplex, condominium, cooperative apartment, or mobile home, but it cannot be just a lot. In fact, although it is not all that common, a principal residence can even be a houseboat.

For example, Stephanie and Mike B. own a residence in which they reside in Washington, D.C. They also own and occupy a house in Long Beach Island, New Jersey, and spend most of every summer at the shore and make occasional trips there during the off-season (for example, for Thanksgiving and New Year's Eve). Their Washington, D.C., residence is their principal residence. In the event that Stephanie and Mike sold their Long Beach Island house and realized a profit on the sale, they would not be able to escape taxation on the profit since it is not their principal residence.

As outlined above, it is generally necessary to have both owned and occupied the residence as your principal residence for at least 2 full years out of the 5-year period ending on the date of the sale to avoid taxation of a gain. Thus, it is possible to move out of a principal residence and rent it out for almost 3 years prior to a sale and still eliminate the gain from taxable income, since the 2-year test looks at the entire prior 5-year period.

It is important to ensure that the requirement for 2 years of use as a principal residence in the 5-year period preceding the date of sale is met. Imagine the pain if the sellers could not get to settlement in time to qualify. For example, Francesca and Saul A. owned and occupied a home as their principal residence for 10 years prior to moving out and renting it on January 1, 2001, due to a bad housing market. They then managed to sell it, with settlement scheduled for December 31, 2003, just barely meeting the 2- (out of 5-) year requirement that would have entitled them to eliminate all of the gain on the sale, except for an amount equal to the depreciation deductions claimed against rental income. Francesca and Saul would, however, lose the entire tax break if settlement were delayed until January 2004. Why? Because not settling on the house until 2004 would mean that they hadn't used it as a principal residence for 2 full years out of the 5 years preceding the date of sale. As they say, timing is everything!

Although the applicable rule requires 2 years of both ownership and use, there are exceptions—isn't that always the case in taxation! In this case, however, the exceptions are intended to help (surprise, surprise). If the taxpayers need to sell their principal residence prior to qualifying under the 2-year test, they can still qualify for a reduced exclusion if the primary reason for not qualifying for both the ownership and use test is due to (1) a change in the place of employment, (2) health reasons, or (3) unforeseen circumstances. In each of these cases, the maximum amount of the exclusion is reduced by a formula that compares the number of qualifying days (or months, at the taxpayer's election) of ownership and use prior to the date of sale to 730 days (or 24 months).

For example, if Joan and her spouse needed to sell their principal residence in Cincinnati after owning and living in it for only 1 year and move to Cleveland due to a change of jobs, the amount of the maximum exclusion would be reduced from $500,000 to $250,000 (or 50 percent of the maximum exclusion, since they lived in the residence for only 50 percent of the time required for the full amount)—still a pretty good deal, since few of us

---

Since this tax rule requires only 2 years of ownership and use as a principal residence in order to qualify for a $500,000 tax break, some people use it to qualify for what is almost a tax-free business. They are known as serial home buyers. They purchase another principal residence every few years, always trying to find a residence that will appreciate, either due to a rising housing market in the area or their own efforts in sprucing it up. After the 2-year ownership and use test has been met, they sell the residence, pocket the tax-free profit, and move to another principal residence and start the process over.

are fortunate enough to own a house for only 1 year and sell it for a profit of $250,000.

The health exception applies to your illness or injury or that of a close relative (such as a spouse, parent, grandparent, child, brother, or mother-in-law). The third exception, unforeseen circumstances, covers a number of contingencies that could force a sale of a principal residence: divorce or legal separation, multiple births resulting from the same pregnancy (not likely to apply to most retirees!), unemployment, and death, including the death of a close relative. For example, in 2003, Janine sold her principal residence in New York City, which she had purchased in late 2002, in order to move to Virginia to live with her mother, who was unable to care for herself. Since the sale of Janine's residence was primarily so that she could move to Virginia to care for her mother, Janine was eligible to claim a partial exclusion of the gain on the sale of her New York residence.

Another special rule provides that taxpayers can exclude the gain from the sale of a principal residence only one time in each 2-year period. Once again, however, the exceptions that apply when the 2-year ownership and use tests are not met apply here as well. To read more about the tax rules applicable to the taxation of the gain from the sale of your home, go to www.irs.gov and type "Publication 523" into the search bar or call the IRS at 800-Tax-Form.

What Are Some Other Home-Selling Issues?

In addition to the rule allowing taxpayers to avoid tax on some or all of the profit on the sale of their principal residence, there are several other tax considerations to take into account when selling your home.

✳ The deduction for property taxes in the year of sale is prorated between the buyer and seller based on the number of days in the real property tax year that each owned the residence. Don't forget to check your settlement sheet for the tax charge (or credit) proration and include it on your income tax return for the year of the sale.

✳ Any points you may have paid on a prior refinancing of your home that were not deductible previously (points on a refinancing are generally not deductible when paid) are deductible when the mortgage is paid off at closing.

✳ Taxes such as transfer taxes, stamp taxes, and other miscellaneous charges and taxes paid at settlement are not deductible, nor is the commission paid to the real estate agent. All of these costs, however, are taken into account in determining your gain on the sale.

✳ Any gain that was not taxable to you on the sale of a previous residence under the old rules that allowed you to defer the gain and use it as a reduction of the tax cost of a replacement residence must be taken into account in determining the gain on the sale of your current residence. Thus, if you deferred a $200,000 gain in 1990 on the sale of your last principal residence and have an additional $250,000 gain on the sale of your current principal residence, your taxable gain on the current sale would be $450,000—still not a problem if you qualify for the entire $500,000 exclusion.

✳ When you are selling your residence and moving, it is usually a great time to consider contributing unneeded items to charity. Examples would be furniture you no longer need and household items that you no longer have room to store. If you contribute more than $5,000 in goods, you'll generally need a qualified appraiser and Form 8283, Section B, attached to your tax return. To obtain a copy of this form, go to www.irs.gov and type "Form 8283" into the search bar or call the IRS at 800-Tax-Form.

Can You Deduct the Costs of Moving to a New Location?

As a general rule, the expenses of moving to a new location will not be deductible unless the move is in connection with the start of a job in the new location. Thus, for those moving for the sake of their new job called "retirement," the moving expenses will rarely be deductible. Since the tax rules do not require that the job in the new location be forever, however, it is possible to gain a deduction for these expenses—if you are willing to meet the requirement that you work full time for at least a specified period of time after the move. Regardless of age, a retiree who works in the desired retirement location for the required 39 weeks or more prior to actual retirement (78 weeks if you are self-employed) can gain a deduction for the moving expenses while also having a great opportunity to settle into the new community prior to actual

A recent reprint by CCH Incorporated of the U.S. Income Tax Law enacted on October 3, 1913, was 26 pages long. In its first year, CCH's Income Tax Service publication, which explained the new tax law, grew to around 400 pages. Today, the CCH Standard Federal Tax Reporter includes over 55,000 pages!

retirement. For example, shortly after Brian and Jill S. moved to Palm Coast, Florida, following his retirement from a 30-year teaching career in Saint Paul, Minnesota, Brian was able to obtain a full-time job working in the Palm Coast public library, where he put his love of books to good use and met many of his new neighbors. After he had completed 39 weeks of full-time employment, Brian and Jill's moving expenses were deductible, even though Bill then retired completely so he and Jill could begin their retirement dream of traveling to each of the seven continents.

So, what are the requirements to be able to deduct moving expenses? Essentially, two major tests must be met. First, you must work full time in the new location for at least 39 weeks during the first 12 months after the move (and it doesn't have to be in the *same* job), or, if self-employed, you must work full time for at least 78 weeks during the first 24 months. The second test, likely the easier of the two tests to meet, is that your new principal job location must be at least 50 miles farther from your old residence than your old principal job location. So, if your commute to work each day used to be 10 miles each way, your new job would have to be at least 60 miles from your old residence to meet this test.

A special rule allows for the deduction of moving expenses for individuals who have been working abroad and who move in connection with their permanent retirement. Among other requirements, the expatriate must have both lived and worked outside the United States—so those of you living in Detroit and working in Windsor, Canada, will not qualify. For example, Mark and Rita Z. lived for 5 years in Costa Rica, where Mark worked for a large U.S. multinational corporation. Following this assignment, they moved to Sarasota, Florida, and retired. Since Mark both lived and worked outside the United States and moved in connection with his permanent retirement, their moving expenses were deductible, and they didn't need to satisfy the usual requirement to work for at least 39 weeks in the first year after a move.

Deductible moving expenses include the costs of packing, crating, and transporting your furniture and other household goods plus the costs of your travel to the new location (airfare, several nights in hotels, etc.). Also included are the costs of connecting and disconnecting utilities and the costs of shipping your cars and pets.

If you are interested in reading more about the rules for deducting moving expenses, get a copy of IRS Publication 521 by going to www.irs.gov and typing "Publication 521" into the search bar or calling the IRS at 800-Tax-Form.

WILL UNCLE SAM REALLY TAX YOUR SOCIAL SECURITY BENEFITS?

As unbelievable as it might sound, your Social Security checks are very likely to be taxable, at least in part. IRS Publication 915 (go to www.irs.gov and type "Publication 915" into the search bar) explains the rules for determining whether your benefits are taxable and, if so, for determining the taxable portion. Worksheets to help you with the calculations and examples are also provided, perhaps explaining why it takes the IRS 28 pages to explain all of this. Our goal here is to give you a general idea of the rule for the taxation of Social Security benefits without making your head swim with all the complexities of the actual calculation.

In general, a comparison is made between a "base amount" (see opposite) and the total of one-half of your Social Security benefits plus 100 percent of the rest of your income, including your nontaxable income. For simplicity, let's call this second amount your benchmark income. If your base amount is equal to or more than your benchmark income, none of your Social Security benefits are taxable. If your benchmark income exceeds your base amount, however, some or all of your benefits will be taxed. So, what are the base amounts that your benchmark income must not exceed in order to avoid being taxed on your Social Security benefits?

- ✳ $25,000 if you are single, a head of household, or a qualifying widow(er);
- ✳ $25,000 if you are married filing separately and lived apart from your spouse for the entire calendar year;
- ✳ $32,000 if you are married filing jointly;
- ✳ $0 if you are married filing separately and lived with your spouse at any time during the year.

Once your benchmark amount exceeds the base amount, a portion of your Social Security benefits is taxable. Initially, up to 50 percent of your benefits will be taxed. If, however, your benchmark amount exceeds $44,000 on a joint return or $34,000 on a single return, you will be taxed on up to 85 percent of your benefits. As we are sure you realize, having a benchmark amount of $44,000 is not a very high litmus test. For example, assume John and Tess C. (both over 65 and filing a joint income tax return) received $9,000 in Social Security benefits and also had a taxable pension of $20,000 and nontaxable interest income from their State of Delaware bonds of $4,000. Their benchmark income amounts to $28,500 (half of the $9,000 Social Security + all of the pension + all of the nontaxable interest income). Since their base amount (see page 224) of $32,000 is greater than their benchmark amount, none of their Social Security benefits are taxable.

Including nontaxable income in the determination of your benchmark income can create a situation where income such as municipal bond income (which is generally not subject to federal income taxes) can cause your Social Security benefits to be partially taxable—effectively making your municipal bond interest taxable! Retirees who are close to having a benchmark income in excess of the base amount should think carefully about the impact that buying municipal bonds might have on the taxability of their Social Security benefits.

Taxing Social Security benefits may seem outrageous, and in many cases it is. After all, you paid for these benefits by paying Social Security taxes for many years, and you paid these taxes using your after-tax earnings. Although it is true that many retirees will receive Social Security benefits greater than the total of the Social Security taxes they paid during their working years (thus, taxing these benefits is not all that unfair after all), it is also true that many of us will receive benefits far less than the taxes we paid and really have a loss, not income!

By using a base amount of $0 for those who are married but file separately, the IRS has prevented retirees from escaping some or all of the tax on the benefits of the spouse with the lower earnings by using married-filing-separately status.

There is a special lump sum election available to those who may have received benefits in the current year that relate to a prior year—for example, those who disputed a ruling that they were not eligible for Social Security benefits and won, receiving a lump sum payment covering both the current and prior years. Under this election, you may be able to figure the taxable portion of some of the benefits under a benchmark amount calculation using the prior year's/years' income.

WHEN SHOULD YOU TAKE DISTRIBUTIONS?

The question of when you should start taking distributions from your tax-deferred IRA, 401(k), or other qualified retirement plan (defined as a qualified employee plan, a qualified employee annuity plan, and a tax-sheltered annuity plan under Section 403[b]) involves several issues. The whole idea of a retirement plan is to have funds put away to cover living expenses in retirement. To prevent these funds from being dissipated before retirement there is, in general, a 10 percent penalty if you withdraw them before you are at least 59½ years old, in addition to the regular income tax on the withdrawal. As with most rules in taxation, there are a few exceptions to this penalty, such as those for early retirement, disability, and distributions made after the death of the plan participant.

Since retirement benefits are intended to be paid out during your lifetime, instead of held for distribution to your beneficiaries after your death, another penalty is imposed if you do not withdraw at least a minimum amount (prescribed under IRS tables) each year, starting in the year after the year in which you turn 70½. The penalty for failure to withdraw the minimum amount from a traditional IRA could be as much as 50 percent on the amount that should have been, but was not, distributed. For this purpose, the minimum required distributions are determined under IRS prescribed tables, which are based on your life expectancy. IRA trustees, custodians, and issuers must provide information re-

lating to required minimum distributions to IRA owners by January 31 each year. If you want to compute these figures yourself, IRS Publication 590 (Individual Retirement Arrangements) explains how, and it includes these tables in its Appendix C. Go to www.irs.gov and type "590" into the search bar for forms and publications.

Since your assets within these retirement accounts are generating earnings (such as interest, dividends, and appreciation) on a tax-deferred basis, it is frequently best to hold off as long as possible before you start taking distributions. Of course, this assumes you have other sources of funds on which you can live. Examples of these other sources would be tax-free municipal bond interest income, previously taxed savings, lower-taxed dividend income, and long-term capital gain income. You must also take into account our system of progressive tax rates, under which your earnings start off being tax-free and are then taxed at ever-increasing tax rates. You would gener-

---

Other than distributions (withdrawals) from a Roth IRA, the portion of distributions from a retirement account into which you made after-tax contributions and lump sum distributions (all of which were discussed in chapter 9), amounts that you receive from your tax-deferred retirement plans will generally be fully taxable as ordinary income, regardless of what you do with the amounts distributed.

ally not want to defer a distribution from a retirement account from a year in which it would have been taxed at 15 percent to a year in which it will be taxed at 25 percent—although it is possible that you could be ahead even in this case if the future year of taxation is far enough into the future. The benefit of continued compounded earnings on the untaxed assets still within your retirement accounts could eventually offset even this 10 percent difference.

So, a quick and easy answer would be to defer these distributions as long as possible, but only if your tax rate is not expected to go up. If it is expected to increase, then you need to do your homework to determine whether to take distributions sooner, rather than later. It is important to keep in mind when making this decision that you will be required to start making the required minimum distributions no later than the year following the year in which you turn 70½ years old.

WHAT ABOUT ESTATE TAXES?

Graduated federal estate taxes are imposed on the taxable estate of a decedent (which is determined by subtracting deductible liabilities and expenses from taxable assets at the time of death, less an exemption amount). In 2001, major changes were made in the federal estate tax rules. These changes also have the effect of altering the taxation of estates in many of the states, since they often base their state death taxes on the federal rules. Under the federal changes, the maximum exemption amount for purposes of determining the taxable estate was set at $1.5 million, and the maximum estate tax rate was reduced to 48 percent for 2004, as compared to a $675,000 exemption and a maximum tax rate of 55 percent in calendar 2001, before the changes were enacted. Between 2005 and 2009, the exemption amount will increase to $3.5 million, while the maximum tax rate will be reduced to 45 percent. In the year 2010, the federal estate tax will be completely repealed, but only for 1 year (how weird can our lawmakers get?). Starting in 2011, the federal estate tax law in effect in 2001 will become the law again, assuming that Congress does not take any action to extend or permanently enact these changes for future years.

Since none of us can be assured of dying in 2010, we will still need to give consideration to the impact of federal estate taxes when doing our retirement planning. Due to the unlimited marital deduction available for bequests to a surviving spouse (who is a U.S. citizen)—in other words, you can leave everything to your husband/wife with no federal estate tax being imposed on your estate—

and the ever-increasing estate tax exemption, it should be possible for most married individuals to avoid having a federal estate tax imposed on their estates when they die. Surviving spouses, however, will be in a more difficult position when they die (but, of course, that might not be the worst of their problems!) if the estate is larger than the exemption amount, unless they remarry and leave assets to their new spouse. This presents an opportunity to plan for taking maximum advantage of the exemption amount in the estate of the first spouse to die, often through the use of a trust, in order to reduce the estate tax on the second spouse's death. It would be wise to consult a qualified estate planner (generally a CPA, CFP, or attorney) to undertake an analysis of the federal estate tax rules, to be able to determine whether any tax planning is needed, and to reach valid conclusions on the effect of this tax on your estate plan. It goes without saying that it is critical you have a current and valid will executed, and that you should have your estate planning and will reviewed any time you move to a different state.

Each state has its own rules on estate and inheritance taxes. These state "death taxes" are imposed on either the estate itself or the amount of property transferring to a beneficiary, or both. Some have a tax equal to the maximum credit on the federal estate tax return for state death taxes paid, thus effectively negating the impact of the state's death taxes. Other states have a tax that could be greater than the federal credit. Some states impose a tax on the transfer of property after death—often with exemptions for certain transfers—and others do not have such a tax. Due to the diversity of these rules in the various states and the impact of the changes in the federal rules noted above on many of these state death taxes, it is impossible to generalize the impact of state taxes on an estate. These taxes should be part of the analysis that ought to be undertaken with the assistance of a qualified professional.

YEAR-END TAX PLANNING

Although tax planning should be an ongoing process throughout the year, it is often relegated to year-end, when many of us start giving some thought to what can be done to reduce the tax bill. It is also the time of year when we are all running out of time to accomplish whatever can be done for tax reduction. Since tax and financial planning for retirement involves making the best use of the assets you have, it seems that closing this chapter with some tax planning tips is appropriate.

Consider paying your mortgage payment that's due

on January 1 before the end of the year. This will accelerate your deduction for mortgage interest.

Think about taking out a home equity loan to pay off credit card and other personal debt, such as auto loans. The interest on a home equity loan of up to $100,000 is generally deductible, while the interest on a credit card or other personal debt is not. Additionally, you can often get a better interest rate on a home equity loan. The biggest risk in doing this is that you might end up paying off this debt over a longer period, which would be a terrible thing to do. Who wants to finance an automobile over 10 or 15 years? You need to be disciplined here, and be sure to continue to pay these loans off at the same pace (or faster) than when they were credit card or personal debt.

Use appreciated securities that have been held for at least 1 year to make charitable contributions. Obviously, this would work best for larger contributions, and it allows you to forever avoid paying income tax on the appreciation while getting a tax deduction for the full value of the asset contributed. The charity can sell the security tax-free, so everybody ends up a winner. If you're planning on giving a donation, check out the charity through these Web sites and phone numbers: Better Business Bureau (www.give.org or 703-276-0100) and the American Institute of Philanthropy (www.charitywatch.org or 301-913-5200).

Never contribute a depreciated security to charity. If you do, you will get a tax deduction for the value of the security, but you will never get a deduction for the decline in value from when the security was purchased. Instead, sell the security, deduct the loss on the sale, and contribute the net proceeds of the sale to the charity.

See if you qualify for job-related deductions. In order to take a deduction for work-related expenses, you need expenditures that equal more than 2 percent of your adjusted gross income, since they fall into the category of miscellaneous deductions. Here are some examples of allowable deductions: mileage (37.5 cents per mile for 2004) for that portion of your non-commute drive that is work related; union dues and professional organization

---

Of course, accelerating deductions such as charitable contributions, interest, and taxes into the current tax year or deferring current-year income such as a bonus to a future year might not make sense if you expect your tax rate to be higher next year.

fees (generally, work-related organizations that you are required to join and professional organizations that you are required or choose to join); work-related magazines/journals/books; purchase of uniforms that are required for the job; the cost of training and continuing education related to your job. You can also deduct job-hunting costs under certain circumstances, even if you are currently employed. Your search must be for a job in your present occupation, it cannot be a search for a first job, and there can't be a significant time break between the end of your last job and your looking for a new one. So, if you meet these criteria, you can deduct postage, stationery, résumé services, phone calls, transportation related to your job search, outplacement agency fees, etc.

Check whether you can take other miscellaneous deductions; these are deductible if they (in the aggregate) exceed 2 percent of your adjusted gross income. They include fees and other expenses paid for tax preparation, investment advice, and estate planning. So if H&R Block prepares your 2004 tax returns, you can include their fee as a miscellaneous deduction in the year that you pay it.

Schedule your medical expenses for maximum tax benefit. Medical expenses are only deductible if they exceed 7.5 percent of your adjusted gross income, so, if you are getting close to that 7.5 percent threshold, consider

bunching your expenses. For example, can you accelerate that next dentist appointment or time elective surgery to produce the best tax result? Or maybe you should put them both off until next year, when other medical expenses will help get you over the 7.5 percent amount.

If you are paying for college tuition for your children but don't qualify for the Hope Scholarship or the Lifetime Learning tax credits, consider having the student claim the credit instead. This will require that you forego claiming your child as an exemption, but it's possible doing so did not save you much anyway due to the phaseout of the deduction for dependents of high-income taxpayers. If the child does not have a tax against which to claim the credit, consider gifts of appreciated securities that can then be sold, generating a tax against which the credit can be claimed and creating proceeds that can be used to pay the tuition, room, board, etc., you would otherwise have paid.

Accelerate charitable contributions by contributing assets to one of the mutual funds qualified as a charitable organization. You will be able to direct those funds to charities of your choice in future years. One such fund is the Fidelity Charitable Gift Fund. For more information, go to www.charitablegift.org.

Deduct the cost of using your automobile for charitable purposes, such as when you participate in fund-raising activities on behalf of the United Way. The IRS allows this deduction to be computed using a standard rate of 14 cents per mile for 2004. It could increase in future years.

Consider a charitable remainder trust. Using this estate-planning tool, you make a donation in trust of appreciated property to a charitable organization. You receive an annuity for life, get to take a tax deduction for the value of your gift that is going to charity (after factoring in the value of your annuity), and also avoid capital gains taxes on your contribution. With the right strategy, you end up with more cash in your pocket because of the contribution—but, of course, your heirs will not inherit the property you donated.

Defer income. If you think your income will decrease the following year, placing you in a lower marginal tax bracket, ask employers to hold off year-end bonuses until the new year. If you are self-employed, bill your customers in the next year as well. But be careful when deferring earnings into a future year in which you will be retired. You may end up with a higher total Social Security tax cost if you are over the limit on compensation subject to this tax in the year of deferral since it will likely be fully subject to the tax in the next year, due to your retirement.

Give away all your unwanted clothing and household articles. Many charities out there (Salvation Army, AMVETS, St. Vincent de Paul, etc.) can make good use of such items, and you will get a tax deduction for their fair market value.

See if you can claim a credit for Federal Insurance Contribution Act (FICA) overpayments. For 2004, FICA is collected on 6.2 percent of your income, up to a maximum of $5,450 (it's collected on income up to $87,900). This amount is indexed each year to a higher amount to reflect inflation. If you switched jobs and your total earnings during the year were in excess of the $87,900, you will

---

Not sure what that nice business suit you longer need is worth? You can purchase It'sDeductible software or access it online through a company called Income Dynamics. It'sDeductible lists suggest values for thousands of typically donated items. The software costs $29.95, with an upgrade for $24.95, or you can purchase an online subscription for $29.95. Contact Income Dynamics at www.incomedynamics.com or 402-330-9599.

likely have overpaid your FICA. If so, you can claim a credit for the overpayment on your income tax return.

If your itemized deductions are barely more than the standard deduction, consider bunching them together every other year, so that you claim the standard deduction one year and itemize the next. The same idea works when your itemized deductions don't exceed the standard deduction, but would if you bunched them together every other year. This is only workable for deductions for which you have some control over the time of payment, such as charitable contributions, state estimated tax payments, and possibly property taxes, since the deductions would all have to be paid during the year in which you claim them.

Estimate your state tax liability and prepay it at the end of the tax year rather than when you file your state tax return in April. This gets the payment as a deduction on the federal return in the current year.

Don't include your prior year's state tax refund in your federal income if you did not itemize deductions on your federal tax return last year, even if you receive a form from your state government showing the amount of this refund to report on your federal tax return. Under the tax benefit rule, such refunds are not taxable since you received no tax benefit from the payment of the taxes in the prior year. The tax benefit rule could also apply if you were subject to the alternative minimum tax in the prior year, since state taxes are not deductible for this tax calculation.

If you have securities in your taxable investment accounts that have declined in value below their cost, but which you want to hold onto because you expect them to increase in value in the future, and you also have an IRA account in which you hold securities, consider selling the loss securities in your taxable account and re-purchasing them in your IRA. Obtain the necessary funds in your IRA by selling securities that you can re-purchase in your taxable investment accounts. If you execute the trades on the Internet, the commissions for the two purchases and two sales should not be much more

---

Be sure to save the required acknowledgement from the charity for any gift of $250 or more and receipts and cancelled checks for gifts under $250. If you contribute over $500 in property, attach Form 8283 to your tax return; if you donate over $5,000 in property, you'll need a qualified appraiser and Form 8283, Section B, attached to your tax return.

ALTERNATIVE MINIMUM TAX

This tax was originally designed to ensure that wealthy taxpayers don't avoid income taxes by taking advantage of such tax preferences as the deferral of income from the exercise of incentive stock options and accelerated depreciation. It is expected to apply to millions of Americans due to the combination of the impact of inflation on taxable income and the narrowing of the difference between the 35 percent maximum tax rate for regular income tax purposes and the 28 percent maximum tax rate for alternative minimum tax calculations. Since state income and property taxes are not deductible in determining your alternative minimum tax, taxpayers in high-tax states such as New York and California are particularly vulnerable to this tax. If the alternative minimum tax applies to you, your tax planning takes on an entirely different focus, whereby you could very well end up trying to defer tax deductions into future tax years and to accelerate income into the current tax year.

than $80, while the deductible capital loss could be in the thousands of dollars.

Time your capital gains and losses on your tax return. If you have a net long-term capital gain, it is subject to a maximum tax rate of 15 percent. If you have a net capital loss, it is deductible (subject to a $3,000 limit per year) against your ordinary income and could save you up to 35 percent. Therefore, consider selling enough of your securities that have declined in value so that you end up with a net capital loss of at least $3,000. Or, sell securities that have declined in value this year in order to get the $3,000 capital loss deduction and wait until next year to sell the securities that have increased in value to generate a net long-term capital gain and get the benefit of the 15 percent tax rate.

true
LIFE **Marie L. had a grave site worth $6,000 that she did not intend to use and wanted to donate to a charity.**

Since she did not itemize her deductions and would have gotten only minimal tax savings from the contribution, however, she gave the grave site to her daughter Kate, who did itemize her tax deductions. Kate then contributed the grave site to a charitable organization operating a children's hospital for its use for the burial of a child of an indigent family and claimed a substantial tax deduction for its value. There was no gift tax on the transfer of the gravesite to Kate since it was worth less than the $11,000 annual exemption that applies to gifts. (L)

Consider setting up a Roth IRA for your kids. If you have children who have part-time jobs, think about establishing a Roth IRA for them. They are permitted to contribute to a Roth IRA the lesser of the amount of their earnings or $3,000 in 2004. This amount increases to $4,000 in 2005 and again to $5,000 in 2008. By the time they are ready to move out, they may have a nice little down payment on their first home! A Roth IRA is preferable to a traditional IRA for this purpose since your children with part-time jobs should pay very low taxes or no taxes, so an IRA deduction will be of no benefit to them. On the other hand, the tax-free compounding within a Roth IRA for many, many future years will be invaluable to them.

Be careful when buying mutual funds in your taxable accounts close to year-end. Many funds declare dividends at the end of their tax years and, if they do, you will have taxable income on the distribution even though you just bought the fund and probably have no real income. You do get to increase your tax cost for the amount of the reinvested dividends, but that will only reduce your future capital gain when you dispose of the shares. Why pay taxes sooner than you need to? Call the fund before you invest and find out the date on which the dividends will be payable.

Choose a tax professional wisely. If you need help doing your taxes, what are the options? More than half of Americans seek help during tax time. Of course, your needs determine the level of expertise you'll require. Starting at the basic level, you could purchase computer software and do it yourself. Two popular programs in-

---

The rules governing eligibility of home office deductions are almost a book unto themselves! Although these deductions can sometimes be claimed, important exclusions and exceptions apply, and you should definitely avail yourself of professional advice if you work at home. That being said, these deductions can be taken. For information, go to www.irs.gov (type "Publication 587" in the search bar).

clude Intuit's TurboTax and H&R Block's TaxCut with purchase prices of $30 to $80, depending upon the sophistication of the software. Next, there are tax preparers such as H&R Block or Jackson Hewitt. These companies could be a cost-effective option if your return is not complex, as they often charge per form they fill out for you. An enrolled agent is the next step up the ladder. Enrolled agents specialize in taxes, are licensed by the federal government, and can represent you before the Internal Revenue Service. You can find enrolled agents listed under "Tax Preparation" in the Yellow Pages or call 800-424-4339 for a list of agents in your area. CPAs and tax lawyers top the list and would be the most expensive. If you're dealing with complex or major issues such as divorce, retirement, death, or buying or selling investment property, you may want to access this level of expertise. To locate a tax professional, contact the National Association of Tax Professionals (www.TaxProfessionals.com or 800-558-3402) or the CPA Directory (www.CPAdirectory.com or 516-409-8357). Online searches can be by zip code.

If you're a married couple, weigh whether to file jointly or separately. Benefits of filing jointly include a lower tax rate schedule and the option to claim certain deductions and credits that will be either eliminated or reduced if you file separately, such as tax credits for education or dependent care costs. The benefit of filing separately is being able to use a lower adjusted gross income for purposes of determining the required reduction of certain itemized deductions. For example, if one of you has high health care costs and a low income, the required reduction of medical expenses by 7.5 percent of adjusted gross income will have less impact. The same holds true for the miscellaneous deductions subject to a reduction of 2 percent of your adjusted gross income. What if you think your spouse is up to something sneaky in the tax returns? By insisting on filing separately, you may be on safer ground. Signing a joint return makes both you and your spouse liable for unpaid taxes. If your marriage is heading toward divorce, it may be wise to start disentangling yourself by filing separately. Finally, filing separately reduces the total tax in a number of states, but some of these states, such as Ohio, allow separate filing only if the federal return was filed separately.

"In spit of the cost of living, it's still popular."
—Kathleen Norris, American writer

2003 Tax Rates by State

State	Personal Income Tax Rate (%)	State and Local Sales Tax Range (%)	State Does NOT Tax Social Security Benefits	State	Personal Income Tax Rate (%)	State and Local Sales Tax Range (%)	State Does NOT Tax Social Security Benefits
Alabama	2–5	4–9.5	X	Nebraska	2.6–6.8	5.5–6.5	
Alaska	None	0–7	X	Nevada	None	6.5–7.25	X
Arizona	2.9–5	5.6–10.1	X	New Hampshire	5 (on dividends and interest only)	None	X
Arkansas	1–7	5.125	X				
California	1–9.3	7.25–8.5	X	New Jersey	1.4–6.4	6	X
Colorado	4.6	2.9		New Mexico	1.7–8.2	5–7.2	
Connecticut	3–5	6		New York	4–7.7	4–8.5	X
Delaware	2.2–6	None	X	North Carolina	6–8.25	4.5–7.5	X
Florida	None	6–9.5	X	North Dakota	2.1–5.5	5+	
Georgia	1–6	4	X	Ohio	.74–7.5	6–7.5	X
Hawaii	1.4–8.3	4	X	Oklahoma	.5–6.5	4.5+	X
Idaho	1.6–7.8	5	X	Oregon	5–9	None	X
Illinois	3	6.25-8.5	X	Pennsylvania	3.07	6–7	X
Indiana	3.4	6	X	Rhode Island	25% of federal tax liability	7	
Iowa	.4–9	5–7					
Kansas	3.5–6.5	5.3–8.3		South Carolina	2.5–7	5–7	X
Kentucky	2–6	6	X	South Dakota	None	4+	X
Louisiana	2–6	4	X	Tennessee	6 (on dividends and interest only)	7–9.5	X
Maine	2–8.5	5	X				
Maryland	2–4.75	5	X	Texas	None	6.25–8.25	X
Massachusetts	5.3–12	5	X	Utah	2.3–7	4.75+	
Michigan	3.9	6	X	Vermont	3.6–9.5	5	
Minnesota	5.4–7.9	6.5–7.5		Virginia	2–5.75	4.5	X
Mississippi	3–5	7	X	Washington	None	6.5–8.5	X
Missouri	1.5–6	4.2		West Virginia	3–6.5	6	
Montana	2–11	None		Wisconsin	4.6–6.75	5	
				Wyoming	None	4	X

APPENDIX 1: CHECKLISTS

SMART IDEAS CHECKLISTS

Exterior

❑ Low-maintenance exterior (vinyl, brick)

❑ Low-maintenance shrubs and plants

❑ Deck, patio, or balcony surfaces are no more than ½" below interior floor level if made of wood

Overall Floor Plan

❑ Main living on a single story, including full bath

❑ No steps between rooms/areas on the same level

❑ 5' × 5' clear/turn space in living area, kitchen, a bedroom, and a bathroom

Hallways

❑ Minimum of 36" wide, wider preferred

❑ Well lit

Entry

❑ Accessible path of travel to the home

❑ At least one no-step entry with a cover

❑ Sensor light at exterior no-step entry focusing on the front-door lock

❑ 32"-wide door

❑ Nonslip flooring in foyer

❑ Entry door sidelight or high/low peephole viewer; sidelight should provide both privacy and safety

❑ Doorbell in accessible location

❑ Surface to place packages on when opening door

Thresholds

❑ Flush preferable

❑ Exterior maximum of ½" beveled

❑ Interior maximum of ¼"

Interior Doors

❑ Minimum 32"-wide interior doorways

❑ Levered door hardware

Windows

❑ Plenty of windows for natural light

❑ Lowered windows or taller windows with lower sill height

❑ Low-maintenance exterior and interior finishes

❑ Easy-to-operate hardware

Garage or Carport

❑ Covered carports and boarding spaces

❑ Wider-than-average carports to accommodate lifts on vans

❑ Door heights may need to be 9' to accommodate some raised-roof vans

❑ 5' minimum access aisle between accessible van and car in garage

❑ If code requires floor to be several inches below entrance to house for fume protection, can slope entire floor from front to back to eliminate need for ramp or step

❑ Ramp to doorway if needed

❑ Handrail if steps

Faucets

❑ Lever or pedal-controlled handles

❑ Thermostatic or anti-scald controls

❑ Pressure-balanced faucets

Kitchen and Laundry

Counters

❑ Wall support and provision for adjustable and/or varied-height counters and removable-base cabinets

❑ Upper wall cabinetry—3" lower than conventional height

❑ Accented stripes on edge of countertops to provide visual orientation to the workspace

❑ Counter space for dish landing adjacent to or opposite all appliances

❑ Base cabinet with roll-out trays and lazy Susans

❑ Pull-down shelving

❑ Glass-front cabinet doors

❑ Open shelving for easy access to frequently used items

Appliances

❑ Easy-to-read controls

❑ Washing machine and dryer raised 12"–15" above floor

❑ Front-loading laundry machines

❑ Microwave oven at counter height or in wall

❑ Side-by-side refrigerator/freezer

❑ Side-swing or wall oven

❑ Raised dishwasher with push-button controls

- ❑ Electric cooktop with level burners for safety in transferring between the burners; front controls and downdraft feature to pull heat away from user; light to indicate when surface is hot

Miscellaneous

- ❑ 30" × 48" clear space at appliances or 60"-diameter clear space for turns
- ❑ Multilevel work areas to accommodate cooks of different heights
- ❑ Open under-counter seated work areas
- ❑ Placement of task lighting in appropriate work areas
- ❑ Loop handles for easy grip and pull
- ❑ Pull-out spray faucet; levered handles
- ❑ In multistory homes, laundry chute or laundry facilities in master bedroom

Bathroom

- ❑ Wall support and provision for adjustable and/or varied-height counters and removable base cabinets
- ❑ Contrasting color edge border at countertops
- ❑ At least one wheelchair-maneuverable bath on main level with 60" turning radius or acceptable T-turn space and 36" × 36" or 30" × 48" clear space
- ❑ Bracing in walls around tub, shower, shower seat, and toilet for installation of grab bars to support 250–300 pounds

- ❑ If stand-up shower is used in main bath, it is curbless and minimum of 36" wide
- ❑ Bathtub—lower for easier access
- ❑ Fold-down seat in the shower
- ❑ Adjustable/handheld showerheads, 6' hose
- ❑ Tub/Shower controls offset from center
- ❑ Shower stall with built-in antibacterial protection
- ❑ Light in shower stall
- ❑ Toilet 2½" higher than standard toilet (17" to 19") or height-adjustable
- ❑ Design of the toilet paper holder allows rolls to be changed with one hand
- ❑ Wall-hung sink with knee space and panel to protect user from pipes
- ❑ Slip-resistant flooring in bathroom and shower

Stairways, Lifts, and Elevators

- ❑ Adequate handrails on both sides of stairway, 1¼" diameter
- ❑ Increased visibility of stairs through contrast strip on top and bottom stairs, color contrast between treads and risers on stairs, and use of lighting
- ❑ Multistory homes may provide either preframed shaft (i.e., stacked closets) for future elevator, or stairway width must be minimum of 4' to allow space for lift
- ❑ Residential elevator or lift

Ramps

- ❏ Slope no greater than 1" rise for each 12" in length, adequate handrails
- ❏ 5' landing provided at entrance
- ❏ 2" curbs for safety

Storage

- ❏ Adjustable closet rods and shelves
- ❏ Lighting in closets
- ❏ Easy-open doors that do not obstruct access

Electrical, Lighting, Safety, and Security

- ❏ Light switches by each entrance to halls and rooms
- ❏ Light receptacles with at least two bulbs in vital places (exits, bathroom)
- ❏ Light switches, thermostats, and other environmental controls placed in accessible locations no higher than 48" from floor
- ❏ Electrical outlets 15" o.c. from floor; may need to be closer than 12' apart
- ❏ Clear access space of 30" × 48" in front of switches and controls
- ❏ Rocker or touch light switches
- ❏ Audible and visual strobe light system to indicate when the doorbell, telephone, or smoke or carbon monoxide detectors have been activated

- ❏ High-tech security/intercom system that can be monitored, with the heating, air conditioning, and lighting, from any TV in the house
- ❏ Easy-to-see and -read thermostats
- ❏ Preprogrammed thermostats
- ❏ Flashing porch light or 911 switch
- ❏ Home direct wired to police, fire, and EMS (as option)
- ❏ Home wired for security
- ❏ Home wired for computers

Flooring

- ❏ Smooth, nonglare, slip-resistant surfaces, interior and exterior
- ❏ If carpeted, use low (<.50"-high pile) density, with firm pad
- ❏ Color/texture contrast to indicate change in surface levels

Heating, Ventilation, and Air Conditioning

- ❏ HVAC should be designed so filters are easily accessible
- ❏ Energy-efficient units
- ❏ Windows that can be opened for cross ventilation, fresh air

Energy-Efficient Features

- ❏ In-line framing with 2" × 6" studs spaced 24" on center

- Air-barrier installation and sealing of ductwork with mastic
- Reduced-size air conditioning units with gas furnaces
- Mechanical fresh air ventilation, installation of air returns in all bedrooms, and carbon monoxide detectors
- Installation of energy-efficient windows with low-E glass

Reduced-Maintenance/Convenience Features

- Easy-to-clean surfaces
- Central vacuum
- Built-in pet-feeding system
- Built-in recycling system
- Video phones
- Intercom system

Other Ideas

- Separate apartment for rental income or future caregiver
- Flex room that can used as a nursery or playroom when the children are young and as a home office later; if combined with a full bath, room could also be used for an aging parent/aging in place

Source: ToolBase, a service of the National Association of Home Builders (NAHB) Research Center

MOVING PLANNER CHECKLIST

8 to 10 Weeks before Your Move

- Select an agent to perform your move and make arrangements for moving day. (Avoid peak periods for moving, if possible. The first few days and the last few days of the month are times when everyone wants to move.)
- Contact the chamber of commerce or visitor's bureau in your new community for information on your new city.
- Contact the IRS and/or your accountant for information on what moving expenses may be tax deductible.
- Remove unused items from your attic, basement, storage shed, etc.
- Start to use up things you can't move, such as frozen foods and cleaning supplies.

4 to 6 Weeks before Your Move

- Conduct an inventory. Decide what to move and what not to move.
- Make arrangements for your trip (hotel/airline reservations, driving route, etc.).
- Schedule a moving sale for items you won't move. Donate other items to charitable organizations (ask for a receipt for tax records).

- ❏ Arrange for packing. Your moving agent can make these arrangements and provide special packing cartons.
- ❏ Gather your personal records: medical, dental, school, birth, baptism, marriage, etc. Send transcripts of school records in advance to the new school.
- ❏ Close local department store and other local charge accounts.
- ❏ Arrange with employer to forward tax withholding forms.
- ❏ Locate all motor vehicle registration and licensing documents and check the auto licensing requirements for your destination.
- ❏ Make arrangements to discontinue (current location) and commence (future location) the following services:
  - ❏ Newspaper delivery
  - ❏ Water softener service
  - ❏ Electricity (check for refund)
  - ❏ Water service
  - ❏ Gas service (check for refund)
  - ❏ Fuel or oil delivery
  - ❏ Garbage collection
  - ❏ Lawn/pool service
  - ❏ Other household services
- ❏ Mail change of address cards to:
  - ❏ Post office
  - ❏ Social Security office
  - ❏ Insurance companies
  - ❏ Credit card companies
  - ❏ Magazine publishers
  - ❏ Friends and relatives
  - ❏ Mail-order accounts

2 to 3 Weeks before Your Move

- ❏ Fill, transfer, and pack prescriptions for family and pets.
- ❏ Arrange for shipments of plants and pets. Get immunization records for pets.
- ❏ Safely dispose of or give away all flammables (paints, paint removers, etc.), as they will be impossible to move.

The Week before Your Move

- ❏ Defrost refrigerator and freezer, plus allow air-drying to prevent mildew. Arrange for disposal of frozen foods (sell, give away, or eat).
- ❏ Clean oven.
- ❏ Transfer/close checking and savings accounts.
- ❏ Drain fuel and oil from lawn mowers and other power equipment.
- ❏ Drain garden hoses.
- ❏ Pack items to be carried in car. Label "Do Not Move."
- ❏ Gather valuables from safe deposit box, drawers, jewelry cases, personal records. Pack safely to take with you.

- Send clothing, draperies, curtains, rugs out for cleaning and leave in wrapping. Take down curtain rods, shelves, TV antenna or satellite dish.
- Have car serviced for trip and have proof of insurance in car.

Moving Day

- Remember to pack a box of the basics you'll need on move-in day (tools, paper products, all-purpose household cleaners, etc.). Be sure to have it loaded last so that it will be first off at your new home.
- Pack suitcases for trip.
- Remove all bed linens.
- Be available to check items on inventory sheet.
- Conduct a last-minute walk-through with your van operator. Make sure windows are closed and locked, closets empty, lights out and doors locked.

Delivery Day

- Be available to check off items on the inventory as they are removed from the van.
- Be present during unloading so that you may direct the placement of your furniture in your new home.
- Check the condition of your belongings. If any items are damaged or missing, note this on the inventory list and report it to your destination agent so they can assist with the handling of details.

Source: North American Van Lines

RELOCATION CHECKLIST

If you're considering relocating to a foreign country, think about these issues first!

1. What is required to obtain legal residency? Can I meet these requirements? What's the cost? How often does residency have to be renewed? What are the conditions of renewal, and what is the cost?
2. What is required to visit, or while you are waiting for residency? (visas, length of stay permitted, restrictions on residents on visa, or in tourist or temporary resident categories)
3. What is the political situation? (dictatorship, democracy, monarchy, etc.)
4. How stable is the country? (history of coups, potential for future unrest)
5. Weather (Do you like four seasons? Hot weather? Temperate all year? Snow?)
6. Income taxes (Are you taxed on income brought into the country? Are you allowed to earn income in the country? If so, how is it taxed?)
7. Other taxes (sales taxes, import duties, exit taxes, vehicle taxes, property taxes, etc.)
8. How much will it cost you in fees, duties, and taxes to bring into the country your personal possessions? (cars, boats, appliances, electronic equipment, personal effects, artwork, etc.)

9. Rental property (rental rates, laws protecting tenants, lease laws, rental taxes)

10. Purchase of property (property values, taxes, restrictions on foreign ownership, purchase taxes, legal and registration fees, laws about foreign property owners, history of government respect for these laws, expropriation laws, squatter's rights; if you're going to build, building regulations, quality of local construction companies, construction guarantees once finished, construction costs)

11. Communications (Are there reliable phone and fax lines, cellular phones, connections to Internet and other computer communication services? Are there local newspapers, radio, TV in a language you understand? Is there cable television or satellite TV available?)

12. Transportation (How are the roads? Are flights available to places you wish to go? How are the bus, train, ferry services? How costly is it to travel to and from your chosen country to frequent destinations, to bring in or visit family, business interests, etc.?)

13. What time zone is your proposed country of residence in compared to areas with which you may want to be in frequent telephone communication, such as where there are family or business interests?

14. Shopping (Would you have a choice of items that you wished to purchase to compare prices? In case of malfunction, are parts and service available locally for appliances, electronics, photographic equipment, computers, vehicles, furniture and fixtures, etc.? Is computer software support and repair service available?)

15. Are the types of food to which you are accustomed readily available, both in restaurants and markets?

16. If you have hobbies, are clubs, supplies, and assistance available?

17. What cultural activities are available?

18. What entertainment is available?

19. What recreational facilities are available? (golf courses, tennis, swimming pools, health clubs, recreation centers, other participatory sports)

20. Will your appliances, electronics, and electrical equipment work on the available power supply?

21. If you like the beach, are good beaches available? Are they nude or topless? What is the water temperature?

22. What is the situation with poisonous plants, insects, snakes, and dangerous animals?

23. What is the violent crime rate? Sneaky crime (theft, car and house break-ins)? What support can be expected from the police department? How helpful

are the police to local residents and foreign residents?

24. How do the local residents treat foreign visitors and residents?

25. What are the local investment opportunities? Is there any consumer or investment protection legislation for investors? What return can you expect on investments?

26. Is the banking system safe and reliable? Can the banks transfer funds and convert foreign currency checks, drafts, and transfers? Are checking, savings, and other accounts you may need available to foreigners? Is there banking confidentiality? Are there exchange controls? Can money brought into the country be taken back out again?

27. Are good lawyers, accountants, investment advisors, and other professionals available?

28. How is the health care system? Are there diseases that are dangerous to foreigners, and if so, does the local health care system address the problem? What is the quality of hospitals, doctors, dentists? What is the availability of specialists? How is the ambulance service? Is dentistry up to standards you are used to?

29. How is sanitation? Can you drink the water? Do restaurants have good sanitation standards? Are pasteurized milk and dairy products available? Do meat, fish, and vegetable markets have satisfactory sanitary standards?

30. How is the education system? If you have children, are good private schools available in the language in which you would like them educated? What is the school year?

31. If you are interested in having domestic staff, what is the cost of cooks, housekeepers, gardeners, etc.?

32. What legislation is there to protect foreign residents? What rights do foreign residents have in comparison to citizens? What is the government's past record in respecting the rights of foreign citizens?

33. What natural dangers are there? (hurricanes, tornadoes, typhoons, volcanoes, earthquakes, droughts, floods)

34. Where does the country stand environmentally? What are the environmental issues? What is the history in dealing with environmental concerns?

35. Is there controlled growth and well-managed development?

36. Can pets be brought to the country?

Reprinted with permission by the Association of Residents of Costa Rica

INDEPENDENT LIVING CHECKLIST

First Impression

❑ Do you like the facility's location and outward appearance?

❑ Is the facility convenient for frequent visits by family and friends?

❑ Is the facility near a shopping and entertainment complex?

❑ Can the resident access a medical complex easily?

❑ Is public transportation available/accessible?

❑ Are you welcomed with a warm greeting from the staff?

❑ Does the staff address residents by their names and interact with them during your tour?

❑ Do you notice the residents socializing with each other, and do they appear content?

❑ Can you talk with residents about how they like living there and about the staff?

❑ Is the staff appropriately dressed, friendly, and outgoing?

❑ Do the staff members treat each other in a professional manner?

❑ Are visits with the residents encouraged and welcome at any time?

❑ What percentage of the apartments has been rented and is occupied?

❑ Is there a waiting list? If so, how long do they estimate it will be for a unit to become available?

Living Area and Accommodations

❑ Have the common areas and apartments been designed to allow you to live as easily and independently as you would like? Is the floor plan well-designed and easy to follow?

❑ Are doorways, hallways, and rooms accommodating to wheelchairs and walkers?

❑ Are elevators available for those unable to use stairways and handrails available to aid in walking?

❑ Are floors of a nonskid material and carpets conducive for safe walking?

❑ Does the residence have good lighting, sprinklers, and clearly marked exits?

❑ Is the residence clean, free of odors, and appropriately heated/cooled?

❑ Are the common areas in general attractive, comfortable, and clean?

❑ Is there an outside courtyard or patio for residents and visitors, and can they garden?

❑ Does the residence provide ample security, and is there an emergency evacuation plan?

❑ Are there different sizes and types of units available with optional floor plans?

- Are single units and/or double-occupancy units for sharing with another person available?
- Does the residence have furnished/unfurnished rooms? What is provided or what can residents bring?
- May they decorate their own rooms? Is there adequate storage space?
- Is a 24-hour emergency response system accessible from the unit with own lockable door?
- Are bathrooms private, with handicapped accommodations for wheelchairs and walkers?
- Do all units have a telephone and cable TV, and how is billing handled?
- Does kitchen unit have refrigerator/sink/cooking element, and can food be kept in the units?
- May residents smoke in their units, or are there designated public areas?

Moving In, Contracts, and Finances

- What's involved with the moving in/out process?
- Is there a written statement available of the resident's rights and responsibilities?
- Is a contractual agreement available that clearly discloses health care, accommodations, personal care, supportive services, all fees, as well as admission and discharge provisions?
- Find out what the payment schedule is and if residents own or rent their unit.

- How much is the monthly fee? How often can it be increased and for what reasons? Is there a limit on the amount of increase per year? What is the history on monthly fee increases?
- Are residents required to purchase renters' insurance for personal property in their units?
- Do billing, payment, and credit policies seem fair and reasonable? If able, may a resident handle his/her own finances with staff assistance? Must a family member/outside party be designated?
- When may a contract be terminated, and what are the policies for refunds and transfers? Is there an appeals process for dissatisfied residents?
- What happens if funds are depleted and full payments can no longer be made?
- Are there any government, private, or corporate programs available to help cover the costs?
- What additional services are available if the resident's needs change? Is staff available to coordinate these services?
- Is there a procedure to pay for additional services such as skilled nursing care or physical therapy when the services are needed on a temporary basis?

Health/Personal Care/Services

- Can the facility provide a list of available services, and are residents and families involved in developing the service agreement? Who provides these services? What are their qualifications?

❏ How are medical emergencies handled? Does the residence have a clearly stated procedure for responding to medical emergencies? Is there an arrangement with a nearby hospital?

❏ Is there a staff person to coordinate home care visits from a nurse, physical or occupational therapist, etc. when needed on a temporary basis?

❏ To what extent if any are medical services available, and how are these services provided?

❏ Are housekeeping, linen service, and personal laundry included in the fees, or are they available at an additional charge? Are on-site laundry facilities available and convenient?

❏ Does the residence provide transportation to doctors' offices, the hairdresser, shopping, and other activities desired by residents, and can it be arranged on short notice?

❏ Are pharmacy, barber/beautician, and/or physical therapy services offered on-site or nearby?

Social and Recreational

❏ What kinds of group/individual recreational activities, if any, are offered? Who schedules them?

❏ Is there an organized activities program with a posted daily schedule of events?

❏ Do volunteers and family members come into the residence to participate/conduct programs?

❏ Does the facility schedule trips or go to other events off-premises?

❏ Do residents participate in activities outside of the residence in the neighboring community?

❏ Are the resident activity (social) areas appropriate and desirable to the prospective resident?

❏ Are there supplies for social activities/hobbies (games, cards, crafts, computers, gardening)?

❏ Are religious services held on the premises or arrangements made for nearby services?

❏ Are there fitness facilities, as well as regularly scheduled exercise classes?

❏ Does the residence create a sense of community by allowing residents to participate in certain activities or perform simple chores for the group as a whole?

❏ Are residents' pets allowed in the residence? Does the facility have pets, and who cares for them?

Staff

❏ Ask about the residence's practices and philosophy regarding staffing.

❏ What are the hiring procedures and requirements for eligibility? Are criminal background checks, references, and certifications required?

❏ Is there a staff-training program in place, and what does it entail?

❏ Is staff courteous to residents and to each other? Do they respond to calls for assistance in a timely manner?

❏ Is the administrator or appropriate staff person generally available to answer questions or discuss problems, and would you be comfortable dealing with them on a daily basis?

Food

❏ Does the residence provide any meals? If so, how many times a day, how many days a week, and how does the menu vary from meal to meal?

❏ What about special diets; does a qualified dietitian plan or approve menus?

❏ Are residents involved in menu planning, and may they request special foods?

❏ Does the dining room environment encourage residents to relax, socialize, and enjoy their food?

❏ Are common dining areas available, and when may residents eat meals in their units?

❏ Are meals provided only at set times, or is there some flexibility? Are snacks available?

❏ How many meals are included in the fee? If a resident becomes ill, is tray service available?

❏ Can residents have guests dine with them for an additional fee? Is there a private dining room for special events and occasions, if desired?

Licensure and Certification

❏ If the state requires the residence to be licensed, does it have a current license displayed?

❏ If the state requires the administrator to be licensed/certified, does she/he have a current license/certification?

❏ Is the facility a member of a trade or professional association?

❏ What reputation does the facility have in the community? How long has it been in business? Is it in good financial health? Does the facility follow generally accepted accounting procedures?

❏ If the facility is sponsored by a nonprofit organization and managed under contract with a commercial firm, what are the conditions of that contract?

❏ Is there a resident council or organization through which residents have a means of voicing their views on the management of the community?

Source: www.CarePathways.com (To view additional checklists, including those for home care, assisted living, CCRCs, and nursing homes, go to this Web site, then click on "Resources/Tools," then on "Facility Checklists.")

APPENDIX 2: FORMS AND WORKSHEETS

SHOULD YOU STOP WORKING?

Examining the nonfinancial benefits of working can help you decide if you should continue to work at your present job, cut down on the hours you work, change jobs, or perhaps fulfill a passion—volunteer, start your own business, learn a new skill, etc.

Check yes or no for each of the following:

1. Working gives me a sense of accomplishment.
   Yes ❑   No ❑

2. I frequently socialize with my colleagues.
   Yes ❑   No ❑

3. I like my days to have structure.
   Yes ❑   No ❑

4. My feelings about myself are at least partly defined by my work.   Yes ❑   No ❑

5. I get more satisfaction from work than leisure.
   Yes ❑   No ❑

6. I look forward to going to work.
   Yes ❑   No ❑

7. The pros of my job outweigh the cons.
   Yes ❑   No ❑

8. I can't think of many other things I'd rather be doing than going to work.
   Yes ❑   No ❑

9. There is a dream job I've always wanted to pursue.
   Yes ❑   No ❑

10. It's easier to continue working than to organize each day myself.
    Yes ❑   No ❑

How many times did you answer "Yes"? If at least half of your answers are in the affirmative, work provides significant psychological benefits that will need to be replaced by other activities if you stop working.

BED AND BREAKFAST: DO YOU HAVE THE RIGHT SKILLS?

Many skills are needed to run a successful bed and breakfast. Do you have what it takes?

Before spending a lot of time and money, use this personal assessment survey to help determine if you and your partner (if you have one) have the skills needed.

Answer each question honestly by placing a check mark in the appropriate box. Complete the survey for yourself and for your partner. Have your partner do the same.

Compare your answers. What are your strengths and weaknesses? Did you find any of your answers surprising? Consider ways to compensate for your weaknesses. You should now be better prepared to make some realistic decisions about starting a bed and breakfast.

Personal Assessment Survey

Topics	You		Partner	
	Yes	No	Yes	No
1. I enjoy getting up early in the morning and preparing meals.	❏	❏	❏	❏
2. I am a highly organized person and manage my time well.	❏	❏	❏	❏
3. I am self-motivated and a self-starter.	❏	❏	❏	❏
4. I can do several different tasks at one time.	❏	❏	❏	❏
5. I enjoy entertaining.	❏	❏	❏	❏
6. I find it easy to get along with most people.	❏	❏	❏	❏
7. I am a tolerant/patient person.	❏	❏	❏	❏
8. I can handle conflict without alienation.	❏	❏	❏	❏
9. I work well under pressure.	❏	❏	❏	❏
10. I can work long hours and face a variety of interruptions.	❏	❏	❏	❏
11. I learn from my mistakes and make changes as needed.	❏	❏	❏	❏
12. I enjoy cooking for others.	❏	❏	❏	❏
13. I keep my home neat and clean at all times.	❏	❏	❏	❏
14. I enjoy performing daily and routine home maintenance.	❏	❏	❏	❏
15. I am a cheerful person.	❏	❏	❏	❏

Topics	You		Partner	
	Yes	No	Yes	No
16. I enjoy interior decorating and remodeling.	❏	❏	❏	❏
17. I enjoy gardening and landscaping.	❏	❏	❏	❏
18. I have a regular income.	❏	❏	❏	❏
19. I communicate well on the phone (Ex: taking reservations).	❏	❏	❏	❏
20. I write well and regularly (Ex: confirming reservations).	❏	❏	❏	❏
21. I am a persistent person.	❏	❏	❏	❏
22. I consider myself a risk-taker.	❏	❏	❏	❏
23. I have a high energy level.	❏	❏	❏	❏
24. I enjoy providing service to others.	❏	❏	❏	❏
25. I consider myself a flexible person.	❏	❏	❏	❏
26. I have a good sense of business.	❏	❏	❏	❏
27. I can handle the business end of a bed and breakfast.	❏	❏	❏	❏
28. I handle emergency situations well.	❏	❏	❏	❏

Now, identify your strengths and weaknesses. If you plan to proceed, your strengths should outweigh your weaknesses or you need to determine ways to compensate for the weak areas.

Strengths   **Weaknesses**

What are some ways you can compensate for your weak areas?

1.

2.

3.

4.

By Eleanor Ames (reprinted with permission)

TO RELOCATE OR NOT TO RELOCATE: THAT IS THE QUESTION

Complete the following questionnaire to find out whether you could be a candidate for relocating. If you have a significant other, he or she should also complete this quiz.

1. Do you have a significant other?
   a. Yes
   b. No

2. How is your physical health?
   a. Never felt better
   b. More good days than bad
   c. Physician on speed-dial

3. How is your financial health?
   a. Rolling in dough
   b. Enough (even though I would like more)
   c. Thank heaven for Social Security!

4. Is the climate in your current location:
   a. Something you'd love to flee
   b. Tolerable
   c. Ideal

5. To what extent does your children's location influence where you live?
   a. Not an issue
   b. Could play a role
   c. Would be a priority in choosing a location

6. What is the level of social support in your current location?
   a. Low/None
   b. Medium
   c. High

7. What is your level of involvement in your current community?
   a. Low/None
   b. Medium
   c. High

8. When making a decision, you usually:
   a. Carefully weigh alternatives
   b. Do your homework, but also trust your instincts
   c. Rely on your "gut" or intuition

9. What is your history of moving to new areas?
   a. Story of my life
   b. A few times
   c. Born and raised in current area

10. Which of these most closely describes your attitude?
   a. New relationships are the spice of life.
   b. "Make new friends, but keep the old."
   c. Old friends are the best friends.

11. Which of the following phrases most closely describes you?

    a. Extroverted

    b. Combination extroverted/introverted

    c. Introverted

12. I am:

    a. Not responsible for aging parents

    b. Not fully responsible for aging parents

    c. Responsible for aging parents

13. I am:

    a. Not into babysitting or have no grandkids

    b. Someone who loves every minute with my grandkids, but . . .

    c. Crazy about my grandchildren—they are a high priority

14. I tend to:

    a. Enjoy travel to new locations

    b. Return to favorite spots

    c. Be a homebody

15. How do you feel about change?

    a. Ready and willing

    b. Generally accepting

    c. Dread it

16. Outside interests:

    a. Many and varied

    b. Some

    c. Hardly any

Scoring

Count your answers for each letter:

(a) _____

(b) _____

(c) _____

Give yourself 1 point for each (a), 2 points for each (b), and 3 points for each (c).

16–29 points: Start packing. You have the characteristics that make you a good candidate for relocation.

30–38 points: Think carefully about moving. You're on the bubble.

39–47 points: Probably best to stay put! Your characteristics and feelings about your relationships and community could make relocating difficult.

COMPARE YOUR HOUSING COSTS

	Your Home/Year	New Home/Year
MORTGAGE/RENT PAYMENTS	_____	_____
HOMEOWNER DUES	_____	_____
PROPERTY TAXES	_____	_____
UTILITIES		
Sewer/Water	_____	_____
Gas/Electric	_____	_____
Phone	_____	_____
Cable TV/Internet	_____	_____
Trash Service	_____	_____
INSURANCE		
Home	_____	_____
Car(s)	_____	_____
MEMBERSHIPS		
(Golf, swim, etc.)	_____	_____
TOTAL	_____	_____

ADVANCE DIRECTIVE

Part A: Appointment of Health Care Agent

(Optional Form)

(Cross through this whole part of the form if you do not want to appoint a health care agent to make health care decisions for you. If you do want to appoint an agent, cross through any items in the form that you do not want to apply.)

1. I, _____ , residing at _____

_____ , appoint the following individual as my agent to make health

care decisions for me: _____

(Full Name, Address, and Telephone Number of Agent)

Optional: If this agent is unavailable or is unable or unwilling to act as my agent, then I appoint the following

person to act in this capacity:_____

(Full Name, Address, and Telephone Number of Backup Agent)

2. My agent has full power and authority to make health care decisions for me, including the power to:

A. Request, receive, and review any information, oral or written, regarding my physical or mental health, including, but not limited to, medical and hospital records, and consent to disclosure of this information;

B. Employ and discharge my health care providers;

C. Authorize my admission to or discharge from (including transfer to another facility) any hospital, hospice, nursing home, adult home, or other medical care facility; and

D. Consent to the provision, withholding, or withdrawal of health care, including, in appropriate circumstances, life-sustaining procedures.

3. The authority of my agent is subject to the following provisions and limitations:

_____

4. If I am pregnant, my agent shall follow these specific instructions:

_____

5. My agent's authority becomes operative *(initial only the one option that applies)*:

_____ When my attending physician and a second physician determine that I am incapable of making an informed decision regarding my health care; or

_____ When this document is signed.

6. My agent is to make health care decisions for me based on the health care instructions I give in this document and on my wishes as otherwise known to my agent. If my wishes are unknown or unclear, my agent is to make health care decisions for me in accordance with my best interest, to be determined by my agent after considering the benefits, burdens, and risks that might result from a given treatment or course of treatment, or from the withholding or withdrawal of a treatment or course of treatment.

7. My agent shall not be liable for the costs of care based solely on this authorization.

By signing below, I indicate that I am emotionally and mentally competent to make this appointment of a health care agent and that I understand its purpose and effect.

_____   _____

(Date)   (Signature of Declarant)

The declarant signed or acknowledged signing this appointment of a health care agent in my presence and, based upon my personal observation, appears to be a competent individual.

(Witness) _____ (Witness) _____

_____ _____

_____ _____

(Signatures and Addresses of Two Witnesses)

ADVANCE DIRECTIVE

Part B: Health Care Instructions

(Optional Form)

(Cross through this whole part of the form if you do not want to use it to give health care instructions. If you do want to complete this portion of the form, initial those statements you want to be included in the document and cross through those statements that do not apply.)

If I am incapable of making an informed decision regarding my health care, I direct my health care providers to follow my instructions as set forth below.

(Initial all those that apply.)

1. If my death from a terminal condition is imminent and even if life-sustaining procedures are used there is no reasonable expectation of my recovery:

_____ I direct that my life not be extended by life-sustaining procedures, including the administration of nutrition and hydration artificially.

_____ I direct that my life not be extended by life-sustaining procedures, except that if I am unable to take food by mouth, I wish to receive nutrition and hydration artificially.

2. If I am in a persistent vegetative state, that is, if I am not conscious and am not aware of my environment nor able to interact with others, and there is no reasonable expectation of my recovery:

_____ I direct that my life not be extended by life-sustaining procedures, including the administration of nutrition and hydration artificially.

_____ I direct that my life not be extended by life-sustaining procedures, except that if I am unable to take food by mouth, I wish to receive nutrition and hydration artificially.

3. If I have an end-stage condition, that is, a condition caused by injury, disease, or illness, as a result of which I have suffered severe and permanent deterioration indicated by incompetency and complete physical dependency and for

which, to a reasonable degree of medical certainty, treatment of the irreversible condition would be medically ineffective:

_____ I direct that my life not be extended by life-sustaining procedures, including the administration of nutrition and hydration artificially.

_____ I direct that my life not be extended by life-sustaining procedures, except that if I am unable to take food and water by mouth, I wish to receive nutrition and hydration artificially.

4. _____ I direct that, no matter what my condition, medication to relieve pain and suffering not be given to me if the medication would shorten my remaining life.

5. _____ I direct that, no matter what my condition, I be given all available medical treatment in accordance with accepted health care standards.

6. If I am pregnant, my decision concerning life-sustaining procedures shall be modified as follows:

_____

7. I direct *(in the following space, indicate any other instructions regarding receipt or nonreceipt of any health care)*:

_____

By signing below, I indicate that I am emotionally and mentally competent to make this Advance Directive and that I understand the purpose and effect of this document.

_____   _____
(Date)   (Signature of Declarant)

The declarant signed or acknowledged signing these health care instructions in my presence and, based upon my personal observation, appears to be a competent individual.

(Witness) _____   (Witness) _____

_____   _____

_____   _____

(Signatures and Addresses of Two Witnesses)

Living Will

(Optional Form)

If I am not able to make an informed decision regarding my health care, I direct my health care providers to follow my instructions as set forth below. (*Initial* those statements you wish to be included in the document and *cross through* those statements which do not apply.)

A. If my death from a terminal condition is imminent and even if life-sustaining procedures are used there is no reasonable expectation of my recovery:

_____ I direct that my life not be extended by life-sustaining procedures, including the administration of nutrition and hydration artificially.

_____ I direct that my life not be extended by life-sustaining procedures, except that if I am unable to take food by mouth, I wish to receive nutrition and hydration artificially.

_____ I direct that, even in a terminal condition, I be given all available medical treatment in accordance with acceptable health care standards.

B. If I am in a persistent vegetative state, that is, if I am not conscious and am not aware of my environment nor able to interact with others, and there is no reasonable expectation of my recovery:

_____ I direct that my life not be extended by life-sustaining procedures, including the administration of nutrition and hydration artificially.

_____ I direct that my life not be extended by life-sustaining procedures, except that if I am unable to take food by mouth, I wish to receive nutrition and hydration artificially.

_____ I direct that, even in a terminal condition, I be given all available medical treatment in accordance with acceptable health care standards.

C. If I am pregnant, my decision concerning life-sustaining procedures shall be modified as follows:

_____

By signing below, I indicate that I am emotionally and mentally competent to make this Living Will and that I understand its purpose and effect.

_____   _____
(Date)   (Signature of Declarant)

The declarant signed or acknowledged signing this Living Will in my presence and, based upon my personal observation, the declarant appears to be a competent individual.

(Witness) _____   (Witness) _____

_____   _____

(Signatures and Addresses of Two Witnesses)

Organic Donation Addendum

(If you want to be an organ donor, you can attach this page to your living will or advance directive. Sign it and have it witnessed.)

Upon my death, I wish to donate:

_____ Any needed organs, tissues, or eyes.

_____ Only the following organs, tissues, or eyes: _____ _____

_____ _____ _____ _____

I authorize the use of my organs, tissues, or eyes:

_____ for transplantation; _____ for therapy; _____ for research;

_____ for medical education; _____ for any purpose authorized by law.

I understand that before any vital organ, tissue, or eye may be removed for transplantation, I must be pronounced dead. After death, I direct that all support measures be continued to maintain the viability for transplantation of my organs, tissues, and eyes until organ, tissue, and eye recovery has been completed.

I understand that my estate will not be charged for any costs associated with my decision to donate my organs, tissues, or eyes or the actual disposition of my organs, tissues, or eyes.

By signing below, I indicate that I am emotionally and mentally competent to make this organ donation addendum and that I understand the purpose and effect of this document.

_____ _____

(Date) (Signature of Declarant)

The declarant signed or acknowledged signing this organ donation addendum in my presence and based upon my personal observation appears to be a competent individual.

(Witness) _____ (Witness) _____

_____ _____

(Signatures and Addresses of Two Witnesses)
Source: Office of the Attorney General, State of Maryland

HOW MUCH DO YOU NEED FOR RETIREMENT?

Current Monthly Expenses (Prior to Retirement):

Ongoing

Mortgage/Rent	$_____
Car payments	$_____
Credit card bills	$_____
Other loan repayments	$_____
Taxes (income, property, etc.)	$_____
Home insurance	$_____
Medical/Dental insurance	$_____
Auto insurance	$_____
Other insurance (life, etc.)	$_____
Utilities	$_____
Cable	$_____
Telephone	$_____
Groceries	$_____
Clothing/Laundry	$_____
Entertainment	$_____
Gas for autos	$_____
Subscriptions	$_____
Memberships	$_____
Saving for retirement	$_____
TOTAL	$_____
Multiply by 12 for annual expenses	$_____

Irregular Expenses (calculate annual total):

Gifts	$_____
Education	$_____
Household maintenance	$_____
Auto maintenance	$_____
Medical/Dental expenses	$_____
Travel/Vacation	$_____
Donations	$_____
Other	$_____
TOTAL	$_____
TOTAL ANNUAL EXPENSES	$_____

(Keep in mind that sometimes there are large, onetime expenditures such as replacing a roof, renovating a kitchen, replacing a deck, buying a car, etc.)

Now, let's repeat this calculation, assuming you are retired (the "Saving for Retirement" line from above has been deleted). Predict what your expenses will be.

Retirement Monthly Expenses:

Ongoing

Mortgage/Rent	$_____
Car payments	$_____
Credit card bills	$_____
Other loan repayments	$_____
Taxes (income, property, etc.)	$_____

Home insurance	$_____
Medical/Dental insurance	$_____
Auto insurance	$_____
Other insurance (life, etc.)	$_____
Utilities	$_____
Telephone	$_____
Groceries	$_____
Clothing/Laundry	$_____
Entertainment	$_____
Gas for autos	$_____
Subscriptions	$_____
Memberships	$_____
TOTAL	$_____

Multiply by 12 for
annual expenses $_____

Irregular Expenses (calculate annual total):

Gifts	$_____
Education	$_____
Household maintenance	$_____
Auto maintenance	$_____
Medical/Dental expenses	$_____
Travel/Vacation	$_____
Donations	$_____
Other	$_____
TOTAL	$_____
TOTAL ANNUAL EXPENSES	$_____

Now, take a look at possible sources of income when you are retired.

Salary/wages/tips	$_____
Social Security*	$_____
Pensions**	$_____
IRA distributions	$_____
Investment income	$_____
Rental income	$_____
Partnership income	$_____
Alimony	$_____
Inheritance	$_____
Other	$_____
TOTAL INCOME	$_____

Multiply by 12 for
annual income $_____

*As mentioned in chapter 9, the Social Security Administration mails a statement of projected benefits to those 25 and older not yet receiving benefits. You may also contact them at www.ssa.gov/mystatement or 800-772-1213 to request a copy. Be sure to read the fine print in order to understand the assumptions that have been made.

**Contact employer(s) for a description of the plan and the estimated benefits.

Subtract your total annual retirement expenses from your total annual retirement income. If there is nothing left over, or the answer is negative, you must increase your income or cut your expenses. How will you go about bridging this gap?

ESTATE-PLANNING REGISTER

(Or, your heirs are gonna love you for this!)

Copies given to: _____

_____

General Information

Name: _____

Social Security Number: _____

Safe Deposit Box Number: _____

Location of Key and Box: _____

Safe Location and Combination: _____

Computer Program or File and Password: _____

Backed-up Computer Files: _____

Accountant Name/Phone Number/Address: _____

_____

Attorney Name/Phone Number/Address: _____

_____

Financial Planner Name/Phone Number/Address: _____

_____

Insurance Agent Name/Address/Phone Number: _____

_____

Stockbroker Name/Address/Phone Number: _____

_____

Employer Address/Phone Number: _____

_____

Employer Address/Phone Number: _____

_____

Other: _____

Personal Documents (Location)

Birth Certificate: _____

Baptismal Certificate: _____

Burial/Cemetery Information: _____

Marriage Certificate: _____

Medical Records: _____

Military Records: _____

Social Security Card: _____

Letters of Last Instructions: _____

Other: _____

Legal Documents (Location)

Original Will: _____

Copies of Will: _____

Trust Agreements: _____

Living Will: _____

Health Care Proxy: _____

Durable Power of Attorney for Finances: _____

Tax Records: _____

Titles and Deeds (Location)

Car(s): _____

Home: _____

Other Real Estate: _____

Cemetery Plot (or Other Arrangement): _____

_____

Other: _____

Insurance Policies (Companies, Numbers, and Location)

Life: _____

Health: _____

Disability: _____

Long-Term Care: _____

MediGap: _____

Homeowner's: _____

Auto: _____

Other: _____

Financial Accounts

Annuities: _____

Savings Account: _____

  Account Number: _____

Savings Account: _____

  Account Number: _____

Checking Account: _____

  Account Number: _____

Checking Account: _____

  Account Number: _____

Checkbook: _____

IRA Plans: _____

  Account Number: _____

Keogh Plans: _____

  Account Number: _____

Brokerage Firm: _____

  Account Number: _____

  Contact/Phone Number: _____

Brokerage Firm: _____

  Account Number: _____

  Contact/Phone Number: _____

Mutual Funds: _____

  Account Number: _____

Employee Benefit Information: _____

Business Agreements: _____

Cash: _____

Credit Cards

Company: _____

  Account Number: _____

Company: _____

  Account Number: _____

Company: _____

  Account Number: _____

Loans

Car: _____

Real Estate: _____

Additional Obligations: _____

_____

Other: _____

RESOURCES

CHAPTER 1

Sources

Moen, Phyllis, William A. Erickson, Madhurima Agarwal, Vivian Fields, and Laurie Todd. *The Cornell Retirement and Well-Being Study: Final Report.* Ithaca, New York: Bronfenbrenner Life Course Center, Cornell University, 2000.

Dorfman, Lorraine. 2002. Stayers and leavers: professors in an era of no mandatory retirement. *Educational Gerontology* 28(1):15–33.

Moen, Phyllis, et.al. 2001. Couples' work/retirement transitions, gender, and marital quality. *Social Psychology Quarterly* 64(1):55–71.

Carter, Mary Anne, and Kelli Cook. 1995. Adaptation to retirement: role changes and psychological resources. *The Career Development Quarterly* 44:67–82.

Holtzman, Elizabeth. University of Massachusetts. "Retirement: The Emotional Aspects." 4 April 2002. www.umass.edu/fsap/articles/retire.html.

AIG SunAmerica. Re-Visioning Retirement Survey. 2002.

Glass, Thomas, et. al. 1999. Population-based study of social and productive activities as predictors of survival among elderly Americans. *British Medical Journal.* 319(8):478–83.

Michael, Yvonne, et. al. 2001. Living arrangements, social integration, and change in functional health status. *American Journal of Epidemiology.* 153(1):123–31.

Lykken, David, and Auke Tellegen. 1996. Happiness is a stochastic phenomenon. *Psychological Science.* 7(3):188–89.

Kunkel, Suzanne, et. al. 2002. Longevity increased by positive self-perception of aging. *Journal of Personality and Social Psychology.* 83(2): 261–70.

Joens-Matre, R. R., and Ekkekakis, P. 2002. Can short walks enhance affect in older adults? *Journal of Sport & Exercise Psychology.* 24: S75–76.

Wilson, Sven E. 2002. The health capital of families: an investigation of the inter-spousal correlation in health status. *Social Science and Medicine* 55: 1157–1172.

Web Sites

www.aarp.com (formerly known as the American Association of Retired Persons)

www.familycareamerica.com (emotional issues of aging)

www.QueenDom.com (locus of control, optimism/pessimism, goal setting, personality, intelligence, and health-related assessments)

www.authentichappiness.org (Dr. Martin Seligman's site with 15 questionnaires)

Recommended Reading

Authentic Happiness by Martin Seligman, Ph.D. Free Press, 2004

The Complete Guide to a Creative Retirement by Rob Kelly. TurnKey Press, 2003

Couple Skills by Matthew McKay, Ph.D., Patrick Fanning, Kim Paleg, Ph.D. New Harbinger, 1994

The Creative Age by Gene Cohen, M.D., Ph.D. Quill, 2001

Feeling Good by David D. Burns, M.D. Avon, 1999

The Feeling Good Handbook by David D. Burns, M.D. Plume, 1999

The Healing Journey Through Retirement by Phil Rich, Ed.D., MSW, et al. John Wiley and Sons, 1999

How to Talk to Your Senior Parents About Really Important Things by Theresa Foy DiGeronimo, M.Ed. Jossey-Bass, 2001

Learned Optimism by Martin Seligman, Ph.D. Free Press, 1998

Life Strategies and *Life Strategies Workbook* by Phillip C. McGraw, Ph.D. Hyperion, 2000

New Passages: Mapping Your Life Across Time by Gail Sheehy. Ballantine Books, 1996

Nothing is Impossible by Christopher Reeve. Random House, 2002

Self Matters by Phillip C. McGraw, Ph.D. Simon and Schuster, 2001

10 Essentials of Highly Healthy People by Walt Larimore, M.D. Zondervan, 2003

The One Hundred Simple Secrets of Great Relationships by David Niven, Ph.D. Harper San Francisco, 2003

The Virtues of Aging by Jimmy Carter. Ballantine Books, 1998

What Do You Want to Do When You Grow Up? Starting the Next Chapter of Your Life by Dorothy Cantor and Andrea Thompson. Little, Brown & Company, 2002

What Happy People Know by Dan Baker, Ph.D. and Cameron Stauth. Rodale, 2003

What Should I Do with My Life? by Po Bronson. Random House, 2002

CHAPTER 2

Web Sites

www.archives.gov/aad (explore over 50 million records online at the National Archives databases)

www.cyndislist.com (has almost 200,000 links)

www.ancestry.com (provides access to census information, birth, death, and marriage records)

www.familytreemagazine.com (lists *Family Tree Magazine*'s 101 best Web sites, including ethnic resources)

www.adultstudentcenter.com (advice on returning to college)

www.2young2retire.com (suggestions on reinventing retirement)

www.serviceleader.org (global volunteerism)

www.career-planning.com (its name describes it)

Recommended Reading

Bears' Guide to Earning Degrees by Distance Learning by John B. Bear, Ph.D. and Mariah P. Bear, M.A. Ten Speed Press, 2003 (also publishes guides in specific areas such as education, computer, law, etc.)

The Complete Idiot's Guide to Genealogy by Christine Rose, CG, CGL, FASG, and Kay Germain Ingalls, CGRS. Alpha Books, 1997

101 Secrets for a Great Retirement: Practical, Inspirational, and Fun Ideas for the Best Years of Your Life by Mary Helen Smith and Shuford Smith. McGraw-Hill/Contemporary Books, 2000

Second Acts: Creating the Life You Really Want, Building the Career You Truly Desire by Stephen M. Pollan and Mark Levine. Harper Resource, 2002

Too Young to Retire: An Off-the-Road Map to the Rest of Your Life by Marika and Howard Stone. Writers' Collective, 2003

Unpuzzling Your Past: A Basic Guide to Genealogy by Emily Anne Croom. Betterway Publications, 2003

Volunteering: The Selfish Benefits: Achieve Deep-Down Satisfaction and Create That Desire in Others by Charles Bennett. Committee Communications, 2001

CHAPTER 3

Web Sites

General

www.cdc.gov/travel (Center for Disease Control)

www.fodors.com (big name in travel)

www.frommers.com (another big name in travel)

www.generousadventures.com (on-line auction of trips; profits go to charity)

www.nudeplaces.com (if your birthday suit is your favorite outfit)

www.oanda.com (currency converter for 164 currencies)

www.roughguides.com (can read entire text online)

www.spafinder.com (almost 30 categories of spas to choose from)

www.who.int/ith (World Health Organization)

Budget Travel

www.budgettravel.msnbc.com (Arthur Frommer's Budget Travel online)

Solo Travel

www.travelaloneandloveit.com (free newsletter; monthly solo travel tips)

Recommended Reading

Magazines

Condé Nast Traveler

National Geographic Traveler

Outside

Travel and Leisure

Travel 50 & Beyond

Transitions Abroad

Arthur Frommer's Budget Travel

General

1,000 Places to See Before You Die by Patricia Schultz. Workman Publishing Company, Inc., 2003

European Vacation Rentals by Steenie Harvey. Avon Travel Publications, 2002

Haunted Places: The National Directory by Dennis William Hauck. Penguin USA, 2002

The Travel Doctor by Mark Wise, M.D. Firefly Books, 2002

Watch It Made in the U.S.A by Avalon Travel. Avalon Travel Publishing, 2002

Budget Travel

Rick Steves' Europe Through the Back Door 2003 by Rick Steves. Avalon Travel Publishing, 2003 (also has other books in his travel series)

Unbelievably Good Deals and Great Adventures That You Absolutely Can't Get Unless You're Over 50, 2003–2004 by Joan Rattner Heilman. McGraw-Hill/Contemporary Books, 2003

Travel by Auto

2003 Trailer Life Directory: Campgrounds, RV Parks, and Services by TI Enterprises. Trailer Life Books, 2004

Bed & Breakfasts and Country Inns, 14th edition, by Deborah Edwards Sakach. American Historic Inns, 2003

Crossing America: You Can Ride Across the U.S. on Your Motorcycle by Dick Peck. Q3 Press, 2002

Great American Motorcycle Tours by Gary McKechnie. Avalon Travel Publishing, 2002

The Official Guide to American Historic Inns, 8th edition, by Deborah Edwards Sakach. American Historic Inns, 2003

Woodall's North American Campground Directory, 2003 by Woodall Publications. Woodall Publications, 2003

Solo Travel

Gutsy Women: More Travel Tips and Wisdom for the Road by Marybeth Bond. Travelers' Tales Inc., 2001

The Single Woman's Travel Guide by Jacqueline Simenauer and Doris Walfield. Citadel Trade, 2001

Travel Alone & Love It: A Flight Attendant's Guide to Solo Travel by Sharon Wingler. Chicago Spectrum Press, 1996

Traveling Solo: Advice and Ideas for More than 250 Great Vacations by Eleanor Berman. Globe Pequot Press, 2003

Traveling with Grandchildren

Have Grandchildren, Will Travel: The Hows and Wheres of a Glorious Vacation with Your Children's Children by Virginia Spurlock. Pilot Books, 1997

AAA Traveling with Your Grandkids by Virginia Spurlock. American Automobile Association, 2001

Volunteer Vacations

Get Outside: A Guide to Volunteer Opportunities and Working Vacations in America's Great Outdoors by American Hiking Society. Falcon, 2002

How to Live Your Dream of Volunteering Overseas by Joseph Collins. Penguin USA, 2002

Volunteer Vacations: Short-Term Adventures That Will Benefit You and Others by Bill McMillon, et al. Chicago Review Press, 2003

CHAPTER 4
Web Sites

www.designlinc.com (universal design)

www.homeexchange.com (swapping homes)

www.realtor.com (investigate real estate; link up with realtors)

www.retirementliving.com (retirement communities and senior housing by state)

Recommended Reading

America's 100 Best Places to Retire by Elizabeth Armstrong (editor). Vacation Publications, 2002

The Brand-New House Book: Everything You Need to Know About Planning, Designing, and Building a Custom, Semi-Custom, or Production-Built House by Katherine Salant. Three Rivers Press, 2001

Choose the Southwest for Retirement by John Howells. Globe Pequot Press, 2000

The 50 Best Small Southern Towns by Gerald Sweitzer. Peachtree Publishers, 2001

50 Fabulous Planned Retirement Communities for Active Adults by Robert Greenwald. Career Press, 1998

Home Buying for Dummies by Eric Tyson and Ray Brown. For Dummies, 2001

House Selling for Dummies by Ray Brown and Eric Tyson. For Dummies, 2002

Places Rated Almanac by David Savageau. John Wiley & Sons, 1999

The Roaring 2000s: Building the Wealth and Lifestyle You Desire in the Greatest Boom in History by Harry S. Dent, Jr. Simon and Schuster, 1998

Sex and Real Estate by Marjorie Garber. Anchor, 2001

Smart Homes for Dummies, Second Edition, by Danny Briere. For Dummies, 2002

Where to Retire (magazine)

Where to Retire: America's Best and Most Affordable Places by John Howells. Globe Pequot Press, 2003

Where to Retire in Florida by Richard and Betty Fox. Vacation Publications, 1999

CHAPTER 5

Web Sites

www.bestplaces.net (uses data about climate, cost of living, etc. to help determine your best place to relocate or work)

www.bestretirementspots.com (thirteen states and four international locations; lots of links and ads)

www.livesouth.com (information on living in Florida, Georgia, Nevada, North Carolina, South Carolina, Tennessee, and Virginia)

www.privatecommunities.com (investigate communities in 18 states and the Dominican Republic and Jamaica)

www.seniorhousing.about.com (information on retirement communities and nursing homes, with links to hundreds of other sites)

www.seniors-place.com (places to retire, shopping, and services)

Recommended Reading

Isle of Palms: A Lowcountry Tale by Dorothea Benton Frank. Berkley Publishing Group, 2003

Sullivan's Island: A Lowcountry Tale by Dorothea Benton Frank. Jove Publications, 2000

Also refer to the reading list for chapter 4.

CHAPTER 6

Web Sites

www.gayretirement.org (info on gay/lesbian retirement communities)

www.privateislandsonline.com (buy your own private island)

www.rvclub.com, www.rv.net, and www.rvamerica.com (general RV sites)

www.demko.com (gerontologist David J. Demko's Age Venture News Service)

www.ashevillechamber.org or 828-258-6101 (Asheville Chamber of Commerce)

www.lvchamber.com or 702-735-1616 (Las Vegas Chamber of Commerce)

www.naples-florida.com or 239-262-6141 (Naples Chamber of Commerce)

www.sarasotafl.org or 800-522-9799 (Sarasota information center)

www.newrver.com/women.html

Recommended Reading

Choose a College Town for Retirement by Joseph M. Lubow. Globe Pequot Press, 1999

Complete Idiot's Guide to RVing by Brent Peterson. Alpha Books; 2001

Full-Time RVing: How to Make it Happen by Sharlene Minshall. Gypsy Press, 2000

Golf Travel by Design: How You can Play the World's Best Courses by the Sport's Top Architects by the editors of *The Golf Insider*. Globe Pequot Press, 2002

Suburban Nation: The Rise of Sprawl and the Decline of the American Dream by Andres Duany, Elizabeth Plater-Zyberk, and Jeff Speck. North Point Press, 2001

2003 Trailer Life Directory: Campgrounds, RV Parks, and Services by TL Enterprises Inc. Trailer Life Books, 2004

All in the Same Boat: Family Living Aboard and Cruising by Tom Neale. International Marine/Ragged Mountain Press, 1996

The Liveaboard Report: A Boat Dweller's Guide to What Works and What Doesn't by Charlie Wing. International Marine/Ragged Mountain Press, 1993 (emphasis on sailboats)

CHAPTER 7
Web Sites
General
www.escapeartist.com ("restart your life overseas," real estate)

www.internationalliving.com ("reinvent yourself overseas")

www.transitionsabroad.com (recommended books and general information on travel, living, and working abroad)

www.demko.com (gerontologist David J. Demko's Age Venture News Service)

Canada
www.canada.gc.ca (Government of Canada)

www.cic.gc.ca (Citizenship and Immigration)

www.hc-sc.gc.ca/ (Health Canada's official Web site)

Costa Rica
www.american-european.net (real estate in Costa Rica)

www.casacanada.net (living, vacationing, or traveling to Costa Rica)

Mexico
www.peoplesguide.com (information on traveling and living in Mexico)

www.mexperience.com (good source for travel, living, and business information)

Recommended Reading
General
International Living magazine

The Grown-Up's Guide to Retiring Abroad by Rosanne Knorr. Ten Speed Press, 2001

Canada
Immigrating to Canada and Finding Employment: A Do-It-Yourself Kit for Skilled Workers Under the Latest Immigration Policy. A Step-by-Step Settlement and Job Search Guide (revised) by Tariq Nadeem. Self-Help Publisher, 2003

Costa Rica
Choose Costa Rica, 6th edition, by John Howells. Globe Pequot Press, 2002

The New Golden Door to Retirement and Living in Costa Rica, 12th edition, by Christopher Howard. Costa Rica Books, 2002

Potholes to Paradise by Tess Borner. Silvio Mattachionne, 2001

Tico Times (English-language newspaper: 506-258-1558 or www.ticotimes.net)

Mexico
Live Better South of the Border in Mexico: Practical Advice for Living and Working by Mike Nelson. Fulcrum Publishers, 2000

The People's Guide to Mexico, 12th edition, by Carl Franz. Avalon Travel Publishing, 2002

CHAPTER 8
Resources

Roberts, Susan B. 2000. High-glycemic index foods, hunger, and obesity: Is there a connection? *Nutrition Review*. 58(6): 163–69.

Brand-Miller J.C., S.H. Holt, D.B. Pawlak, and J. McMillan. 2002. Glycemic index and obesity. *American Journal of Clinical Nutrition*. 76(1):281S–5S.

Web Sites
General
www.aarp.org (click on "Health and Wellness")

www.cdc.gov (tons of information from the Centers for Disease Control and Prevention)

www.clinicaltrials.gov (contacts for joining clinical trials)

www.healthfinder.gov (links to federal government health information)

www.healthscout.com (check out media coverage of health-related topics)

www.mayoclinic.com (have information from this famous clinic at your fingertips)

www.medlineplus.gov (from NIH; updated daily)

Elder Care
www.ElderRage.com (caring for elderly parents)

End-of-Life Issues
www.partnershipforcaring.org (working "to improve how people die in our society")

Exercise and Health
www.backroads.com or 800-GO-ACTIVE (trips designed for all fitness levels)

www.discoverfitness.com (begin/maintain an exercise program/ tips to stay motivated)

www.firstpath.com (fitness and fat calculators, guide to equipment, nutrition information)

www.4woman.gov (about women's health by the Department of Health and Human Services)

www.justwalk.com (track your exercise and weight-loss goals)

www.traillink.com (locate old rail lines that have been converted to public trails)

www.walkingvacations.com or 800-828-8768 (variety of international walking vacations)

www.zapfitness.com or 828-295-6198 (offers running camps and exercise physiology testing)

Recommended Reading
Brain Fitness
The Memory Bible: An Innovative Strategy for Keeping Your Brain Young by Gary Small, M.D. Hyperion, 2003

Cosmetic Procedures
The Non-Surgical Facelift by Michael Byun, M.D., et al. Addicus Books, 2003

Secrets of a Beverly Hills Cosmetic Surgeon: The Expert's Guide to Safe, Successful Surgery by Robert Kotler, M.D. Ernest Mitchell Publishers, 2003

Elder Care
How to Care for Your Parents' Money While Caring for Your Parents by Sharon Burns, Ph.D., CPA, and Raymond Forgue, Ph.D. McGraw-Hill Trade, 2003

Caring for Yourself While Caring for Your Aging Parents: How to Help, How to Survive by Claire Berman. Owl Books; 2001

Elder Rage, or Take My Father . . . Please!: How to Survive Caring for Aging Parents by Jacqueline Marcell. Impressive Press, 2001

How to Care for Aging Parents by Virginia Morris and Robert Butler. Workman Publishing Company, 1996

Emotional Health
The Joy Diet by Martha Beck. Crown, 2003

End-of-Life Issues
Chicken Soup for the Grieving Soul: Stories About Life, Death and Overcoming the Loss of a Loved One by Jack Canfield and Mark Hansen, editors. Health Communications, 2003

Conquering the Mysteries and Lies of Grief by Sherry Russell. Publish America, 2002

Final Gifts: Understanding the Special Awareness, Needs, and Communications of the Dying by Maggie Callanan and Patricia Kelley. Bantam, 1997

What Dying People Want by Dr. David Kuhl, M.D. Public Affairs, 2002

Exercise and Health

Health (magazine)

Men's Health (magazine)

Prevention (magazine)

Runner's World (magazine)

Body for Life by Bill Phillips. HarperCollins, 1999

The Complete Mall Walkers Handbook by John Bland, M.D., with Jenna Colby, R.D., L.D, Fairview Press, 1999

Dr. Ian Smith's Guide to Medical Websites by Ian K. Smith, M.D. At Random, 2001

The Essential Medication Guidebook to Healthy Aging Merck-Medco, edited by Les Paul, M.D., M.S., and Becky Nagle, Pharm.D., BCPS. Ballantine Books, 2002

Fight Fat After Forty by Pamela Peeke, M.D., M.P.H. Penguin USA, 2001

Fitter after Fifty by Ed Mayhew, 1st Books Library, 2002

Healthcare Online for Dummies by Howard and Judi Wolinsky. For Dummies, 2001

Improve Your Golf with Yoga Techniques by Ashok Wahi, et al. Princeton Design Group, 2001

The South Beach Diet by Arthur Agatston, M.D. Rodale, 2003

CHAPTER 9

Web sites

General Retirement Advice

www.ihatefinancialplanning.com (breezy style but good advice)

www.fidelity.com

www.money.cnn.com

www.motleyfool.com

www.quicken.com

www.schwab.com

www.wiser.heinz.org/managesavings.html (saving and investing for women)

Recommended Reading

Beyond the Grave: The Right Way and the Wrong Way of Leaving Money to Your Children (and Others) by Gerald M. Condon, Esq. and Jeffrey L. Condon, Esq. HarperBusiness, 2001

The Complete Idiot's Guide to Retiring Early by Dee Lee, CFP, and Jim Flewelling. Alpha Books, 2001

Everyone's Money Book by Jordan E. Goodman. Dearborn Trade Publishing, 2001

50 Simple Things You Can Do to Improve Your Personal Finances by Ilyce R. Glink. Three Rivers Press, 2001

The Investing Bible by Lynn O'Shaughnessy. John Wiley & Sons, 2001

The Finish Rich Workbook by David Bach. Broadway, 2003

J.K. Lasser's Choosing the Right Long-Term Care Insurance by Benjamin Lipson. John Wiley & Sons, 2002

J.K. Lasser's Your Winning Retirement Plan by Henry K. Hebeler. John Wiley & Sons, 2001

Long-Term Care: Your Financial Planning Guide by Phyllis Shelton. Kensington Publishing Corporation, 2003

Personal Finance for Dummies by Eric Tyson. For Dummies, 2003

The Retirement Bible by Lynn O'Shaughnessy. John Wiley & Sons, 2001

The Retirement Savings Time Bomb . . . and How to Defuse It by Ed Slott. Viking Press, 2003

The Wall Street Journal Guide to Planning Your Financial Future by Kenneth M. Morris and Virginia B. Morris. Fireside, 2002

Why Smart People Make Big Money Mistakes and How to Correct Them: Lessons from the New Science of Behavioral Economics by Gary Belsky and Thomas Gilovich. Simon and Schuster, 2000

CHAPTER 10

Web Sites

www.bankrate.com (click on "state taxes" for a state by state summary)

www.bestplaces.net (cost of living feature allows you to compare taxes between two cities)

www.irs.gov (source for Internal Revenue Service information)

www.moneycentral.msn.com (click on "taxes" to prepare and file taxes electronically)

www.retirementliving.com (Retirement Living Information Center has information on taxes for every state, as well as other resources concerning retirement)

Recommended Reading

J.K. Lasser's Your Income Tax by J.K. Lasser Institute. John Wiley & Sons, 2004

Plan Your Estate: Absolutely Everything You Need to Know to Protect Your Loved Ones, 6th edition, by Denis Clifford and Cora Jordan. Nolo Press, 2002

Protect Your Estate: Definitive Strategies for Estate and Wealth Planning from the Leading Experts by Robert A. Esperti and Renno L. Peterson. McGraw-Hill Trade, 1999

Taxes for Dummies 2004 by Eric Tyson and David J. Silverman. Hungry Minds, Inc., 2003

Helpful IRS Publications (Find these at www.irs.ustreas.gov)

17 Your Federal Income Tax

502 Medical and Dental Expenses

521 Moving Expenses

523 Selling Your Home

524 Credit for the Elderly or the Disabled

526 Charitable Contributions

550 Investment Income and Expenses

554 Older Americans' Tax Guide

561 Determining the Value of Donated Property

564 Mutual Fund Distributions

590 Individual Retirement Arrangements (IRAs)

915 Social Security and Equivalent Railroad Retirement Benefits

939 General Rule for Pensions and Annuities

INDEX

Boldface page references indicate maps, illustrations, and graphs.

Underscored page references indicate boxed text.

(see above)